AS/400 Client/Server Programming with Visual Basic 4.0

Chris Peters

Second Edition, January 1996

DISCLAIMER

Every attempt has been made to provide correct information. However, the publisher does not guarantee the accuracy of the book and does not assume responsibility for information included or omitted from it. The tools and their related information have not been submitted to any formal IBM test and are provided on an as is basis without any warranty either expressed or implied. The implied warranties of merchantability and fitness for a particular purpose are expressly disclaimed. The use of this information or the implementation of any of these techniques is a customer responsibility. The packages are supplied as examples of how Visual Basic can be used.

ISBN: 1-883884-27-6

Midrange Computing
5650 El Camino Real, Suite 225
Carlsbad, CA 92008

Second Edition, Rev. 0 (V3R1)

Acknowledgments

Many thanks for your technical skills and willingness to share them with me:

- Mark McCall—Murphey Favre Securities Services, Washington Mutual Bank
- Ann Johnson—Murphey Favre Securities Services, Washington Mutual Bank
- Randy Mangham—Auto Parts Club, San Diego, CA

For personal and creative support:

- Joey-Noel Peters
- Mark McCall—Murphey Favre Securities Services, Washington Mutual Bank
- Cliff Pryor—Murphey Favre Securities Services, Washington Mutual Bank
- Terry Monahan—Murphey Favre Securities Services, Washington Mutual Bank

- Jeff Messersmith—Murphey Favre Securities Services, Washington Mutual Bank
- Bill Haight—Murphey Favre Securities Services. Washington Mutual Bank
- Sandi Lorenzi, Paul Mutton, Jodie Sargent, Cindy Threlkeld, Debbie Windishar—Murphey Favre Securities Services, Washington Mutual Bank

For material support or essential participation:

- Mark Fleming—Midrange Computing Technical Books, Carlsbad, CA
- Anita Craig—Midrange Computing Technical Books, Carlsbad, CA
- Terry Spencer—ConAm Property Management, San Diego
- Amy Englehart—Murphey Favre Securities Services, Washington Mutual Bank
- Ron Dale—Murphey Favre Securities Services, Washington Mutual Bank
- Carol Kinzebach—Murphey Favre Securities Services, Washington Mutual Bank
- Gary Patterson—Bulter and Curless Assoc., Raleigh, NC
- Matt Fulton, Highland Heights, OH

Special Acknowledgment

- To Todd and Roxanne Peters, who might enjoy seeing their name in print, and Ellen, who, for the period of time that I was writing this book, did nearly everything else... Thank you.

Table of Contents

Microsoft Visual Basic Version 4.0
For 32-bit Windows Development

Copyright © 1987-1995 Microsoft Corp.

1

Introduction

Dear Editor:

I've just returned from the VBITS (Visual Basic Insider Technical Summit)—a four-day soirée of Microsoft Visual Basic training sessions. During the four days, I happened on a few amusing observations (at least I'm amused) regarding the Microsoft community of client/server developers and how the AS/400 is regarded.

I went into the camp of the Microsoft programmers expecting to witness a tsunami of PC- and LAN-based solutions as it prepared to roll over the medium and large IS shops. And yes, there's a mighty big wave out there, gathering size and speed, but it seems I, as an AS/400 professional, might be standing on higher ground than I thought (more on that in a minute).

Visual Basic is clearly on top of the MS development hill. Even the Visual C++ guys say so. There were 1,350 attendees at this VBITS conference (one of three around the country)—up from 450 last year. Next year's attendance is expected to reach 3,000.

The first three days went as you might expect. There was a presentation on Windows 95 (along with crowd hostility over its tardiness), inspiring speakers, success stories, and breakout sessions. The fourth day was devoted to client/server—my favorite.

I began the "Client/Server Boot Camp" sessions, feeling humbled in the presence of 350 c/s programmers. But as I sat there, things got interesting.

Apparently, the LAN boys are growing up. They're becoming aware of some of the problems of running a multiuser, mission-critical business system. They started talking about things like security and backup. Hmmm... My ears perk. I didn't expect to hear this stuff. They went on. They discussed sector locking for record updates, multiuser updates, program-level checking, and file normalization. I start to grin. Then came more. New stuff to many of them, like commitment control, disk mirroring, and journaling (called transaction logging). I'm squirming now. I crane to poke my head above the others. I want to see if anyone else is so amused as I, and is also looking around. Jeez, we in the mid- and large-scale environments have been living this stuff for years! I want to jump up and yell at these people, "Ooo! Ooo! AS/400! AS/400!"

There were also the expected c/s concepts and terms—SQL, RI, ODBC, DB/2... More letters than a mailman. However, attendant to these was the latest c/s methodology—"Keep as much processing on the server as possible. Use the client for data presentation and editing only." This tack, they say, facilitates efficient performance, security, data access, and system management. No kidding.

Imagine the irony of it—the PC guys coming full circle, feeling the need for such banal IS services as security and centralized data management. The strictly-PC-LAN people seem to be playing right into our hands. They just don't know it yet, that's all.

I was feeling pretty self-important as we broke for lunch. I was soon shaken from this state of mind, though, when the young programmer sitting next to me asked idly between bites, "What kinda server you on?"

"AS/400," I said proudly.

"Too bad," he said flatly.

I nearly choked. Did I hear right? Did this micro-snob say, 'Too bad?' I thought I could feel blood running from my ears.

"What's going on here?" I thought. "The 400 has everything you want and more! Can't you see that? Why are you trying to reinvent all these things?"

I kept my mouth shut. There was nothing to be gained by badgering this guy. Besides, he had already spotted a fresh tray of pizza and was making his move.

I brooded through the rest of the day's sessions, puzzled. I felt like my fellow AS/400 professionals and I were being awkwardly ignored—like the girl in high school that was so good looking that no one ever asked her to dance. Perhaps it just goes to show you—maybe requisite knowledge is not as important as the path to its discovery.

Chris Peters
Nine Mile Falls, WA

The Purpose of This Book

This book has two main purposes:

- To introduce the PC programming language Visual Basic (VB) to AS/400 programmers.
- To present a detailed, basic AS/400 client/server (c/s) arrangement as a means for getting started with client/server computing.

Visual Basic for AS/400 Programmers

This book presents Visual Basic to AS/400 programmers and AS/400 IS management professionals using familiar AS/400 comparisons. The benefit of such an approach is that it allows you to take advantage of already learned concepts, and to expedite the process of learning Visual Basic and AS/400 client/server concepts.

> **Note:** *In order to understand the programming information presented in this book, you should have a knowledge of the AS/400, RPG/400, and AS/400 Control Language (see "Prerequisite Knowledge" on page 9).*

A Practical AS/400 Client/Server Approach

Client/server is new to AS/400 shops, and Visual Basic is even newer. Little has been accomplished in implementing these new tools for a variety of reasons.

- Too many choices.
- Difficulty in deciding where to dive in and how deep.
- Uncertainty in determining the effect of client/server on overall IS direction.

- Overwhelming volume of unfamiliar information.
- Hard to find appropriate applications.
- Once a good candidate application is found, how do you proceed?
- How will programmers learn a PC language and client/server when they're so busy already?

Further, if you plunge into a client/server commitment, what happens to all the great things that AS/400 shops have been able to do for their companies for so long? Have they been jeopardized? If you do the opposite and cling to old ways, what happens to the perceived worth of your system as time goes on? It just gets older and less respected. And, if no progress is made for a long time, isn't it difficult to catch up?

These are all points well taken, and they contribute to anxiety over client/server implementation. Regardless of the uncertainty about client/server, its popularity continues to grow. Indeed, it's all you hear about! But why? Where is all the clamor coming from? Certainly not from AS/400 IS directors—they're not eager to add another platform to those already supported. Certainly not from AS/400 programmers—they've learned all the languages they care to. It's coming from above and below. From the executives and the users— both compelling forces. It seems every nontechnical executive who has read an in-flight magazine is asking, "Are we client/server yet?" A more justified comment comes from the users: "Gee, on my PC at home I can use a mouse and just click what I want..."

There is, however, a middle ground where an AS/400 shop can remain pretty much the same, while taking advantage of the best parts of the client/server tools. The AS/400 is still the main player, where most of the processing takes place in more or less the usual way, and client/server tools are just that—tools to be used to enhance current processes and enable new ones.

This book, then, represents a starting point into AS/400 client/server applications where the established nature of an AS/400 installation is retained. An AS/400 shop is pretty hard to beat, whether contrasted to mainframes or LANs, and an AS/400 shop it should stay.

Why Visual Basic?

Why choose Visual Basic? Why not C++ or Visual C? Because VB is easier. It's easier to learn, it's easier to think about, and it's easier to use. The people in the AS/400 programming community are not, for the most part, micro-minded digit heads. They care little about low-level PC processes, and find VB's capabilities to be quite satisfactory. Visual Basic can perform quite well as a standalone PC language and, when linked to external routines written in C (Dynamic Link Libraries or DLLs) can do practically anything C can.

With version 4.0, Microsoft has shown a strong commitment to Visual Basic. In response to criticisms of the capabilities of the language, Microsoft has made great strides to give VB an extensive, object-oriented platform built around Microsoft's Object Linking and Embedding (OLE) automation. That is not to say that VB has lost it's charm as a simple development system—it hasn't—but now there is less room for criticism and more room to grow.

In addition, VB has developed significant momentum and acceptance as a partner to AS/400 languages because it's much less disruptive to learn. Taking on the task of learning C or Small Talk is much more ambitious than learning VB. For the most part, VB may be self-taught; the same can not readily be said of C. Another possible cause of VB's apparent spontaneous acceptance may be that many AS/400 programmers have had some exposure to BASIC in the past. (You remember—find the average of the test scores...)

One last reason to choose VB: Microsoft has established VB as the macro language in MS Office products. That means that those spreadsheet macros up in accounting that nobody knows how to maintain since what's-his-name left can someday be supported by IS.

The Client/Server Approach Used in This Book

One of the most difficult things about getting into c/s computing is deciding which strategy to follow. The options are many and diverse—PC Support, Client Access/400, full server duty through a File Server I/O Processor (FSIOP) card, distributed processing, distributed data bases, etc. In most cases within this book, the strategy adopted is the most simple, yet adequate, solution available. The relative roles of AS/400 and PC are to remain the same as they are in a non-client/server environment—that is, the data and primary processes reside on the AS/400 and PCs are used for presentation, user interface, and manipulation of data delivered up by the 400. There is no viable reason to move complicated business processes and files from the 400 to PCs.

That is not to say that other PC languages and client/server strategies don't have merit—they do—but, within most AS/400 shops, there just isn't justification for a more complicated approach.

So, like water flowing downhill, Visual Basic has garnered considerable acceptance and momentum as the PC language of choice for developing in-house client/server applications.

Making VB RPG-like

As AS/400 programmers, we are used to certain ways of doing things. In this book the position taken is that the more RPG-like Visual Basic can be made during presentation, the better.

VB is capable of operating in ways that are more familiar to RPG programmers. Variables can be declared, and code can be designed to behave in an accustomed AS/400 manner. More familiarity means more control. It also means the VB language is less of an invader into the AS/400 environment and less threatening.

It is believed that, if you can think about your VB programs in the same way that you think about your RPG programs—if they're more similar than different—that you'll be much more likely to actually use VB and make it a part of your tools. Once in use, if a purely PC-like way of coding VB needs to be developed, it can be done more easily with an established start. Once you're familiar with the language, the benefit of some PC-style techniques is easier to appreciate.

Overview

Things in This Book

- Visual Basic programming concepts presented in AS/400 programmer terms.
- An AS/400 client/server strategy and implementation.
- Visual Basic tutorials.
- Client/server tutorials.
- Example Visual Basic source code.
- Example AS/400 source code.
- Introductions to contemporary PC programming concepts and terms.

- The AS/400 Spool File Download Utility.

Things NOT in This Book

- Discussions of advanced, standalone Visual Basic features.
- Radical notions of discarding existing AS/400 systems, programming, and support mechanisms.
- Departures from traditional AS/400 methodologies.

Who This Book is For

This book is primarily intended for AS/400 programmers who want to acquire VB programming and client/server skills. This is not a book about programming, per se. Indeed, the position taken is that you already know how to program, just in different languages. This is analogous to learning Spanish when you already know English. Spanish words can be explained using English, while the formation of logical thoughts is the same in either language.

Additionally, the client/server strategies presented may interest nonprogrammer AS/400 professionals.

Who This Book is NOT For

This book is not meant to be a comprehensive presentation of all that is the Visual Basic programming language. Some advanced features of the language are only identified, not explained. Although many important VB features are covered, this book is limited to aspects of VB pertinent to c/s applications with an AS/400. It is recommended that one of many good VB texts be consulted for a full explanation of advanced features not covered.

What You Need

For Visual Basic:

- A PC—386 or better.
- Windows 3.1 or Windows 95 (Windows 95 is required for 32-bit program development).

- Visual Basic Professional Edition or Enterprise Edition (version. 4.0). VB Standard Edition works but limits your potential. The professional edition is recommended for all but the casual programmer.

For Client/Server:

- A PC—386 or better, attached to an AS/400.
- Windows 3.1 or Windows 95.
- Visual Basic Professional Edition or Enterprise Edition (version 4.0). VB Standard Edition works but limits your potential. The professional edition is recommended for all but the casual programmer.
- Client Access/400 (V3R1 or better) or PC Support for the AS/400 (V2R1 or better).

> **Note**: *Microsoft Word 6.0A (or another word processor capable of creating ".RTF" files) is required to create help systems.*

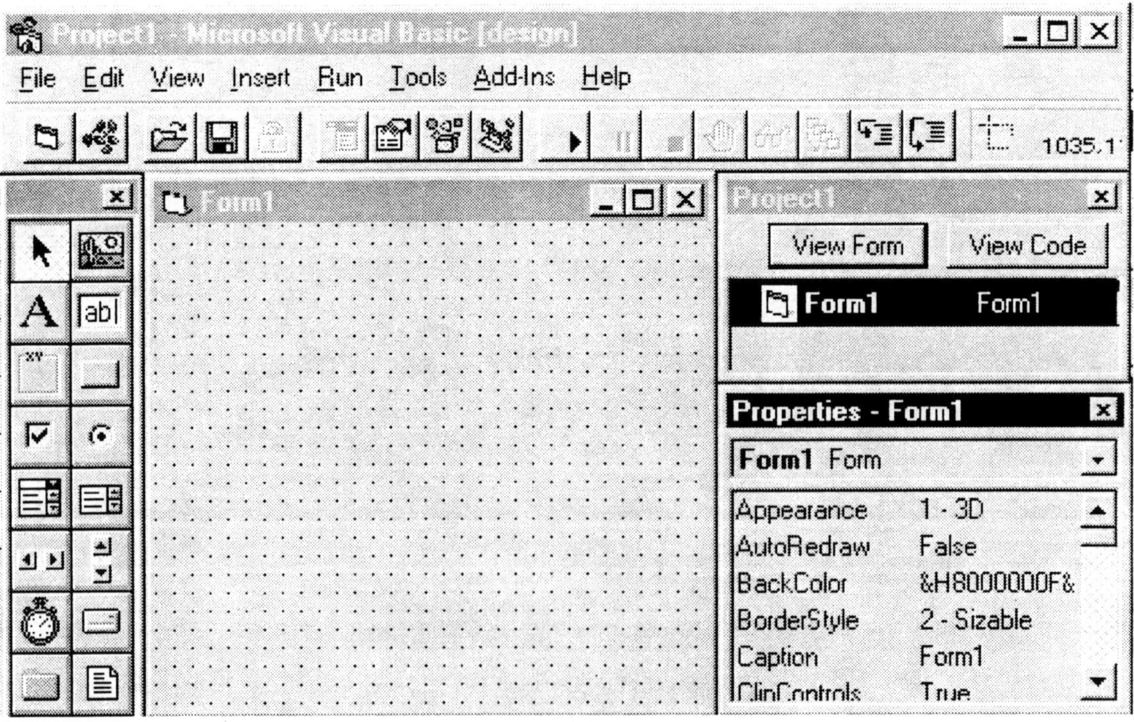

Prerequisite Knowledge

Obviously, if concepts in this book are presented in AS/400 terms, those terms must be familiar to you. The AS/400 terms used are, by far, the most frequently used in real installations.

The prerequisite knowledge required has been split into two levels:

- At a user's level:
    - PCs
    - Windows and Windows-based applications
    - Client Access or PC Support running under Windows
- At a programmer's level:
    - RPG/400
    - DDS
    - Control Language
    - OS/400
    - Program calls and parameter passing
    - Screen handling

and, to a lesser degree:

- SDA
- PDM

The principles inherent in Visual Basic are very similar to those present in other languages, including RPG and CL. It's true that the PC-based languages have different ways of doing things, but the similarities far outnumber the differences. When boiled down, two languages very often can do practically the same things in practically the same way.

Simplicity of Presentation

A problem with many programming guides (Visual Basic's included) is that they must present all details of language statements and usage for completeness. While this approach is understandable and desirable for a reference book, it makes it hard to learn programming. All code statements in this book are presented in their most practical formats—the one you would use the most—and extraneous details are not discussed. You are urged to consult the *Visual Basic Programmer's Guide*, the *Visual Basic Language Reference*, and online VB help for complete information regarding VB language details.

> **Note**: *Throughout this book, you'll see the symbol 💻. This signifies an action that you perform on the PC, usually in Visual Basic, step by step. There are many step-by-step exercises in this book. You are strongly urged to go through the exercises and create the Visual Basic and client/server projects as they are presented.*

Microsoft Visual Basic Version 4.0
For 32-bit Windows Development

Copyright © 1987-1995 Microsoft Corp.

2

Visual Basic Program Development

This chapter explains how a Visual Basic programming project is organized—the elements of a VB project. Also discussed is how to develop a VB program using the VB development environment. It is assumed that you have successfully installed Visual Basic on your PC. If you have not, install it now. Refer to your *Visual Basic User's Manual* for instructions.

Step by Step: Visual Basic Help System

1. Bring up VB by double clicking on the " Visual Basic 4.0" icon in the VB program group.
2. Click on the Help menu. Click on the item "Learning Microsoft Visual Basic."

This brings up the following screen:

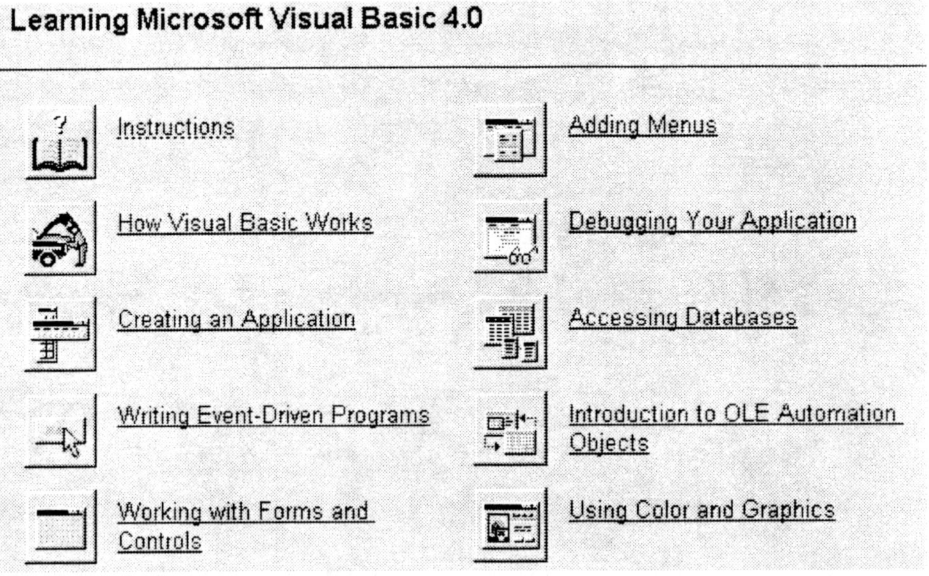

Select the tutorial "How Visual Basic Works." Be sure to browse through this tutorial as it is a good first exposure to the terms used in VB, and a good example of what VB screens can look like.

16- and 32-bit Environments

VB 4.0 is really two separate packages—one for 32-bit environments and one for 16-bit environments. If you're developing applications for Windows NT or Windows 95, use the 32-bit version. Otherwise, use the 16-bit version.

Elements of a Visual Basic Project

New VB programmers are often unsure about the elements of a VB project and how they fit together. In this chapter, the organization of a VB programming effort (called a *project*) is presented.

VB File Types and Uses

The Project File

An interactive project that you might develop on the AS/400 has components that make up the participants in the project. Commonly, those components are:

- A display file as defined in DDS, (perhaps with the help of SDA). The display file may contain multiple screen formats.
- An RPG program to control the screen formats, accept input, and interact with other AS/400 files.
- A CL program to set the program environment (overrides, etc.), or to interact with the AS/400 in a way that RPG can't.

Visual Basic projects are organized in much the same way as an AS/400 project. There are several files that contain source code for screens and processes, but in VB there are some improvements over the AS/400 way. Imagine that, on the AS/400, you have a little file that contains the names of all the source code members needed for a particular project. The file might contain entries like these:

```
SRCLIB / QDDSSRC ( ( PGM01D )  SCREEN01 )   - screen format 1
SRCLIB / QDDSSRC ( ( PGM01D )  SCREEN02 )   - screen format 2
SRCLIB / QDDSSRC ( ( PGM01D )  SCREEN03 )   - screen format 3
SRCLIB / QRPGSRC ( ( PGM01R ) )             - RPG program
SRCLIB / QCLSRC  ( ( PGM01C ) )             - CL program
```

Imagine further that AS/400 programmers have a sophisticated program editor that combines the features of SEU and SDA. This program editor can read this little file, load all the source members into a work space and allow you to work on them all at the same time.

This is how the VB Development Environment works. The file that contains the names of the source files is called a *project file*. In VB versions prior to 4.0, the project file was called a *make file* because its extension name was ".MAK." Now the project file gets an extension name of ".VBP" for Visual Basic Project.

An example of a project file name is:

```
PROJ01.VBP
```

An example of project file contents is:

```
Form=PROJ1.FRM
Module=PROJ1; PROJ1.BAS
ProjWinSize=136,448,184,200
ProjWinShow=2
Name="Project1"
HelpContextID="0"
StartMode=0
VersionCompatible32="0"
MajorVer=1
MinorVer=0
RevisionVer=0
AutoIncrementVer=0
ServerSupportFiles=0
VersionCompanyName="Evergreen Interactive"
```

These entries define the elements of a VB project—that is, the source files that contain the specs. There are also entries to tell the VB Development Environment how to present those elements, how to compile the code, etc.

VB Source Files

In the preceding example, PROJ01.FRM is a file containing source code for a screen format. In VB, each screen format has its own source file and is called a *form*, hence the file extension name ".FRM."

PROJ01.BAS is a file containing source code for processes in the project. This is analogous to RPG calculation specifications. This file contains BASIC language statements, hence the extension name ".BAS." Within VB, this type of file is called a *standard module*. (Form source files can contain code, too, so they're also listed among the modules.)

The other lines in the project file are inserted by VB to keep track of environment settings and version control levels. For the most part, you needn't worry about them. You don't have to create the ".VBP" file; it gets built by the VB Development Environment as you add source files to your project.

Aside from convenience, the obvious advantage of this type of setup is that components may be shared by multiple projects. For example, Project A uses source files:

```
PROJA.FRM          a screen format,
```

and

```
CALC.BAS           calculation specifications,
```

Project B uses source files:

```
PROJB.FRM          a screen format,
```

and

```
CALC.BAS           calculation specifications.
```

Both projects share the code in CALC.BAS. A word of warning, though. Sharing source files among projects can be a problem. If a developer working on Project A doesn't realize that the file CALC.BAS is also a component to Project B and makes changes, unpredictable results may occur in Project B. Of course, the same potential for problems exists on the AS/400 when sharing source members.

There is a good time and place for sharing source files in VB, as will be presented.

You've already seen the three main types of source files that go into a VB project:

- VBP Project files (contains the names of other files used in the project).
- FRM Form files (contains specs for a screen format or form).
- BAS Module files (contains calculation specs in the BASIC language).

File extension names are not limited to ".VBP" for project files or ".FRM" for form files, etc., but VB uses these names as defaults. It's just as well to let VB use these names and get accustomed to the conventions. In AS/400 terms, most programmers would know what to find in a file named QRPGSRC or QDDSSRC; they wouldn't immediately know what kind of code is contained in a file named SRCMBRS or DAVESRC. There are, of course, exceptions to these naming conventions. One such exception is a *constants file*.

A constants file is a file that is dedicated to containing only definitions of named constants and is used by all ".FRM" (forms) and ".BAS" (modules) in a project. On the AS/400, this would be like having a special set of RPG specs that define constants and can be copied into RPG program source. It is generally understood that a constants file is shared among separate projects and the contents of the file are not altered.

A common extension name for constants files is ".GBL," which is derived from the word GLOBAL. Microsoft-supplied constants files usually have a ".TXT" extension.

Another type of source file (which won't receive much attention in this book) is the *class module* file. This file normally has an extension name of ".Cls." A *class* is a description of an *object*. The concepts of *classes* and *objects* are more advanced PC programming characteristics and needn't concern you yet. (See Chapter 15, "Introduction to Classes, Objects, and Collections.")

There is one last type of file—the *custom control* file. These files have extension names of ".VBX" and ".OCX." Custom controls are add-ins to the VB environment providing features not included with the base product. For example, suppose you are creating an application and you want to be able to play a multimedia sound effect. That functionality is not built in to Visual Basic. It must be added in the form of a custom control. There are all kinds of custom controls—one for almost any feature you need. But why, you may ask, do you have to add features? Why aren't all the capabilities of VB built in? Because of baggage for distributed applications, that's why. When you distribute a VB program, you must include a run-time support library like VB40032.DLL (32-bit) or VBRUN300.DLL (16-bit), which includes support for the built-in VB features. If your application uses an add-in custom control, the corresponding DLL must then also be included. Controls that are included with the VB base product are called *intrinsic controls.*

The Project Box

Although a discussion of the VB Development Environment is yet to come, you should know about one element of the manager now. The *project box,* normally located on the right side of your screen, contains the names of all of the files used in your project and, in the title bar at the top, displays the name of the project itself.

The project box looks like this:

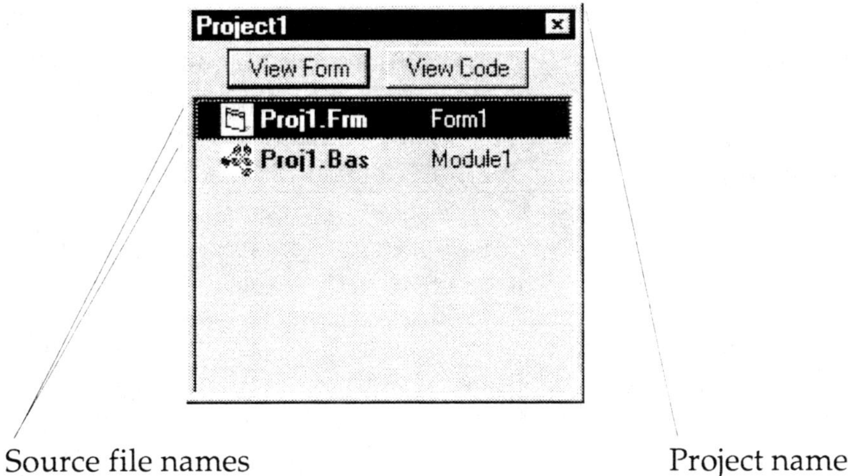

Managing VB Project and Source Files

Managing (opening, copying, renaming, and saving) VB project files is much like saving other files in Microsoft Windows. The task is made a bit more complicated, however, by the multifile nature of VB projects.

Where to Keep Your Files

It is a good idea to create separate folders for your projects. You don't want your projects mixed in with each other or with VB files. VB tries to use the folder where you installed the VB program files ("C:\VB" in Windows 3.1 or "C:\Program Files\Microsoft Visual Basic" in Windows 95 by default), so that's not a good choice. Create a folder off the "C:\Program Files\Microsoft Visual Basic" folder called "PROJECTS." When you start a new project, create a folder off the "PROJECTS" folder to contain the files. You'll see later, when the Setup Wizard and distribution diskettes are discussed, that this is a pretty good arrangement.

Opening VB Project and Source Files

When you start the VB Development Environment (by double clicking on the Visual Basic icon in the VB program group), you start a project called Project1 by default. This is just like starting other Microsoft Windows applications. In Microsoft Word, you automatically open Document1; in Excel, you automatically open Book1 or Sheet1 (depending on the version of Excel.) Visual Basic works the same way by opening default project Project1. Additionally, VB automatically opens the first display screen (called a *form*), and names it Form1. You recall that each form used in a VB project has its own source file. The source file for Form1 is given the name FORM1.FRM.

Because of VB's default naming during startup, you must rename the project and source files as you save them. Even though each project has its own folder, you don't want them all using the names Project1, Form1, etc. Certainly you will have more than one project, so you can't let VB use the default names.

Notice the default names Form1, Project1, and FORM1 in the following screen:

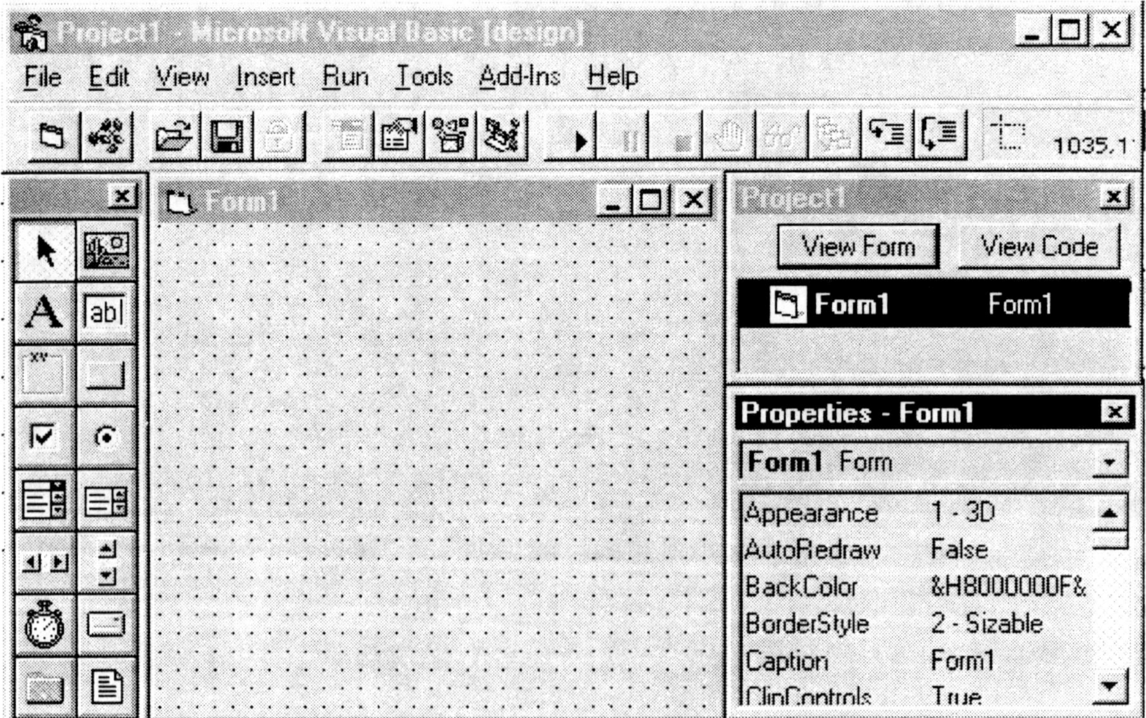

Also notice that "Form1 Form1" is highlighted in the project box. When you save a source file in VB, the highlighted file is the one being saved.

Step by Step: Opening VB Project and Source Files

1. For illustration purposes, bring up Visual Basic (double click on the " Visual Basic 4.0" icon on the Visual Basic program group).
2. Click on the File menu.

   Note the commands:

```
Save File

Save File As...

        .

        .

Save Project

Save Project As...
```

You use these commands to save, rename, and copy your VB project and source files. Selecting the commands "Save Project As..." or "Save File As..." brings up a dialog box for you to specify a different project or file name. Take a second and note the "..." at the end of these command options. This is the Windows standard for indicating that further information is required, usually through a dialog box. The VB applications that you develop should conform to standards like this for credibility and ease of use. More will be said about Windows standards later. For now, just be observant of the ways that Windows applications operate.

Saving, Renaming, and Cloning VB Project and Source Files

When you click on "Save Project" or "Save File," the project file or the highlighted source file is saved using its current name. When you click on "Save Project As..." or "Save File As..." you are prompted through a dialog box for a new name for the file. That's how you assign new names to your project and source files. Note that the former file still exists under its original name. VB does not remove it.

Step by Step: Saving a File Under a New Name

A project named Project1 with one form file, Form1.frm, always comes up automatically each time VB is started.

1. Highlight "Form1.frm" in the project box.
2. Select command "Save File As..." from the File menu.
3. Specify a new name for the form source file, like "VB01SCR1.FRM," to show that this form is screen format 1 of program VB01. Keep the extension name of ".FRM." VB automatically revises the project file with the new name for the form file.
4. Select command "Save Project As..." from the File menu.
5. Specify a new name for the project file like "Vb01.Vbp" to show that this is the project file for VB program VB01. Keep the extension name of ".VBP."
6. The result of this exercise is just clutter on your disk, so click on "Cancel."

Notice that, as you rename your files, the VB Development Environment automatically starts editing the new files. This means that you can't save a file under a different name and continue editing under the original name (like you can with source members in AS/400 SEU).

You can't change the names of all the files by merely changing the name of the project file. The renamed project file contains the unchanged source file names. You have to change the names of the source files, too.

Use the renaming technique to copy or clone files. Bring up a project that contains a source file that you want to clone. Highlight the file in the VB project box and save it to a new file name by keying the name into the space provided in the "Save File As..." dialog box. Cloning a project file can be accomplished the same way, but be aware that the cloned project file will still contain the original source file names. You can edit the project file with any text editor and specify the new files names, or you can get the VB Development Environment to rebuild it for you, as will be seen next.

Adding and Removing Source Files

Recall that the project file (".VBP") is a list of the source files (".FRM," ".BAS," ".GBL") that are used in the project. The VB Development Environment adds or removes entries in the project file automatically when you select the File menu commands "Add File..." or "Remove File." With "Add File..." you are asked for a file name; with "Remove File," the selected file within the project box is removed.

> *Note: Custom control files are added and removed using the Custom Controls dialog box found on the Tools menu.*

In real life on the AS/400, a programmer seldom creates a set of specs for a display file or an RPG program out of thin air. Instead, he/she clones a similar source member and starts from there. In VB, that process is accomplished using "Add File..." If you clone a project file, and that project file contains file names that you don't want, you use "Remove File" to get rid of them.

The Visual Basic Development Environment

When you click on the VB icon, you bring up the VB Development Environment. VB's Development Environment is your singular interface for development of a project. It's like SDA and SEU rolled into one.

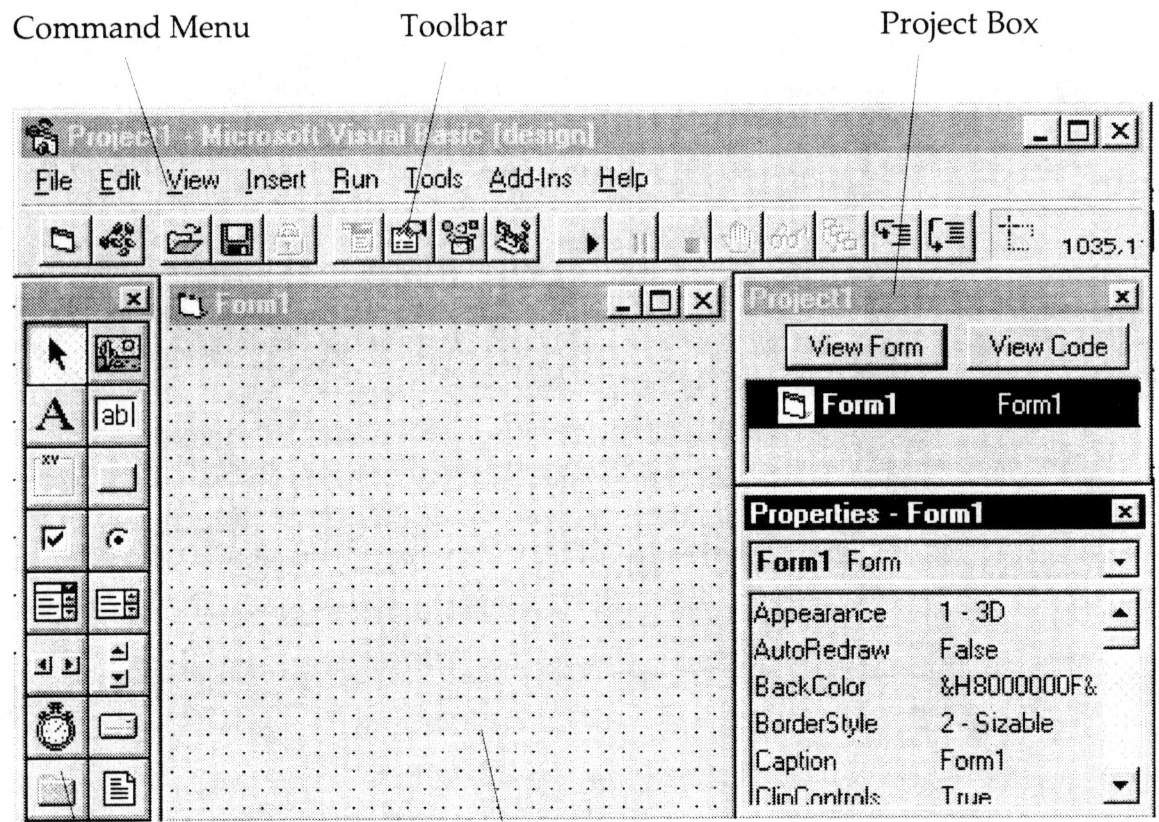

***Note**: The windows on the above illustration have been resized from their original dimensions for clarity.*

Command Menus

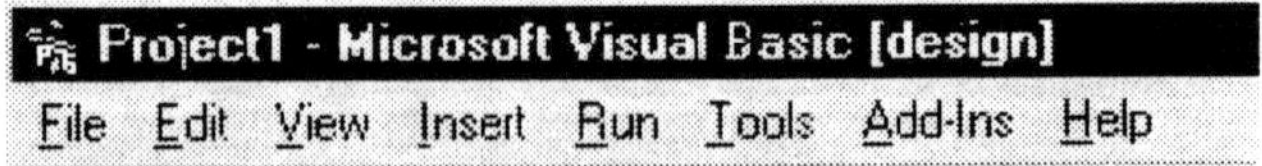

The command menus operate the same as other Windows applications. Four of the menus are common (File, Edit, View, and Help) and are not discussed; four others (Insert, Run, Tools, and Add-Ins) are more unique to VB.

The Insert Menu

You use the Insert menu to add elements to a VB project like a form or a module.

The Run Menu

VB is like AS/400 CL in that it can be run either as a compiled program or one statement at a time as an interpreted program. The Run menu commands allow you to run, end, restart, or resume execution of the program you're editing without ever leaving the VB Development Environment.

As will be presented later, Visual Basic has extensive debug capabilities. Unlike the AS/400, you don't have to compile a VB program to run it in debug. Source statements can be interpreted and run in VB, so you can run your program, uncompiled, from the VB Development Environment. The Run menu gives you commands to set breakpoints or to step through the program line by line.

The Tools Menu

The Tools menu contains methods to view the contents of a field as your program runs, access to a menu editor, and options for specifying preferences for the VB Development Environment.

As in SEU, you may set up your editor in various ways. In SEU, you can set options for full- or half-screen rolling of source code, lowercase allowed, etc. You set similar editor options in VB using the "Options" command on the Tools menu. The VB Development Environment, being a visual development tool, is naturally very colorful. Different parts of source code are represented in separate colors. For example, comments are normally shown in green. From the "Options" command in the Tools menu you may specify the look of your editor.

Also available from the "Options" command is "Project" options. This is loosely analogous to the parameters on the AS/400 CRTRPGPGM command, and is used to specify which screen form is displayed at program startup and where to find any associated help files.

The Add-Ins Menu

The VB Development Environment is capable of accepting additional features in the form of *add-ins*. These are not features of the application you're developing, but rather features of the VB Development Environment itself. An example of an add-in is the source code control system that comes with the VB Enterprise

Edition. The Add-Ins Manager, as the name suggests, controls the products that you may add into the VB Development Environment. Access to two VB advanced features—Data Manager and Report Designer—is also available from the Add-Ins menu, but does not fall within the scope of this text.

The Toolbar

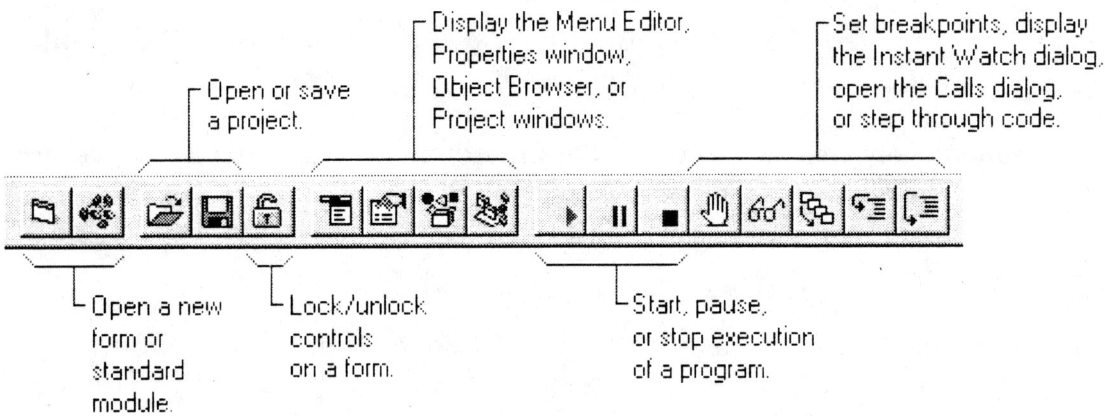

Some of the buttons on the toolbar are shortcuts to commands on menus. It's faster and easier to click on a button than it is to select a command, so VB developers assigned some of the frequently used commands to buttons on the toolbar. Two of the buttons on the toolbar are much like those in other Microsoft products—"Open" and "Save." The others are peculiar to VB (and VBA—Visual Basic for Applications).

The toolbar buttons are:

Creates a new form.

Creates a new standard module.

Opens an existing project.

Saves the current project.

Locks and unlocks the controls

Displays the Menu Editor.

Displays the Properties window.

Displays the Object Browser.

Displays the Project window.

Starts an application from design time.

Pauses execution of a program while it's running.

Stops execution of an application and returns to design time.

Toggles the breakpoint on the current line.

Displays the value of the current selection in the Code window.

Displays the structure of active calls.

Traces through each line of code and steps into procedures.

Executes code one procedure or statement at a time in the Code window.

The Project Box

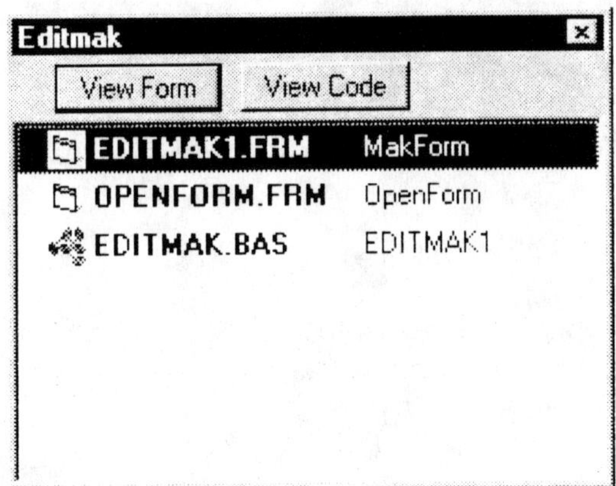

The project box is a list of the source files that make up the project. This is your main tool for switching between various forms and modules used in your program. Highlight the file you want to work on and then click on either "View Form" or "View Code."

> ***Note***: *Forms can contain code just as modules can.*

The Toolbox

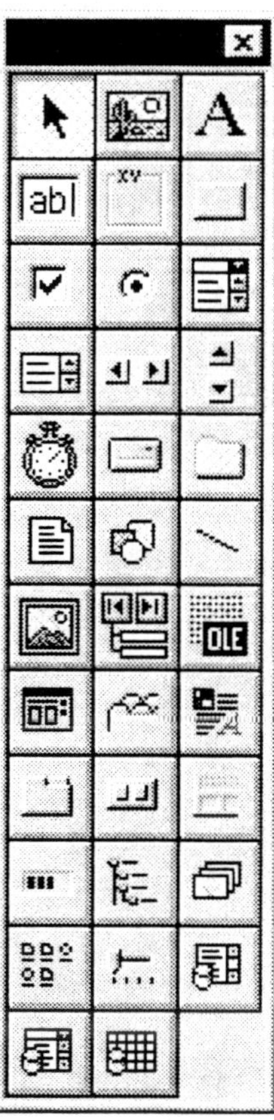

The toolbox is a collection of buttons that represent *controls*. Controls are the things that you put on a form to create a functional screen. They're things like titles, descriptions, fields, and command keys that are placed on an otherwise blank screen. Of course in VB, these things, called *objects,* have different names.

In AS/400 terms, a control is like a command key that you enable on an AS/400 screen format. In VB, you can just click on a control type in the toolbox to select it and then draw it on a form with the mouse. Controls are covered in detail in the next chapter.

The Form Design Window

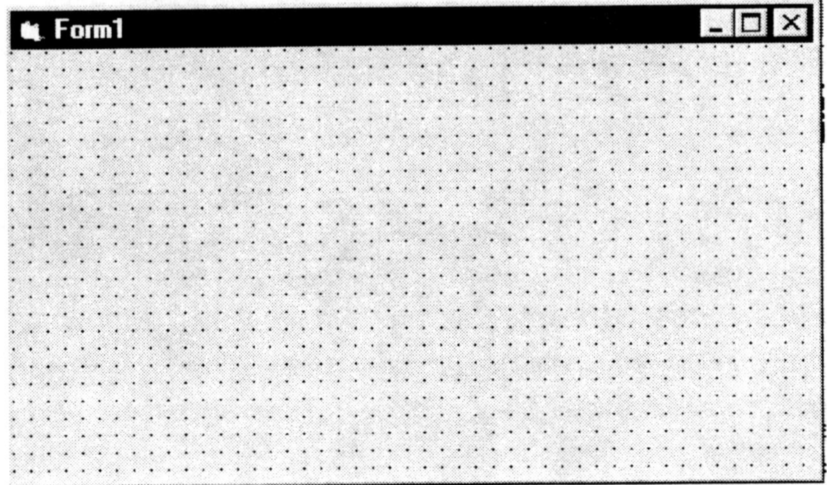

The form design window is like the SDA part of the VB Development Environment. It's where the screens used in a VB application are laid out. Each form used in a project gets its own form design window. You select a form design window by clicking the form in the project box. You are allowed to have multiple form design windows open at the same time.

To close a window, double click on the little "X" in the upper right corner.

The Code Window

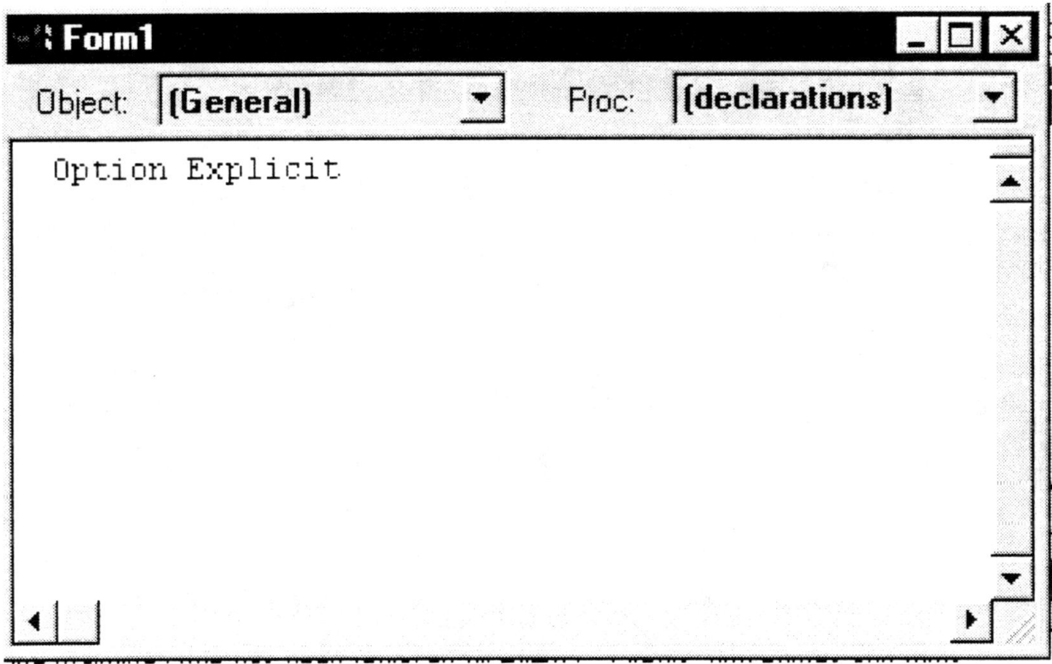

The VB Development Environment has one more window. This is the *code window*, and represents the SEU part of the VB Development Environment. The code window is where Visual Basic language statements are edited. Think of it as an access to the project calculation specifications. Navigating through the different sections of code takes some getting used to, though. It's done by selecting a section of code, like a subroutine, from a list.

In an AS/400 RPG program, code is separated into logical or reusable sections by using subroutines, and then those subroutines are executed by the mainline code. The same is true in VB, except the subroutines are called *procedures* and *functions*, and the mainline code has been replaced by *events*. Events, procedures, and functions are discussed in detail later, so for now just be aware that the code window is how you get at them.

Notice the two boxes at the top of the code window:

Object: (general) Proc: (declarations)

When clicked, these boxes display lists of code sections that may be edited. It's like having a list of subroutines used in an RPG program that you can click to edit.

Development Environment Startup—The Auto32ld.Vbp and Auto16ld.Vbp Files

When the VB Development Environment is started, it reads a default startup project file called Auto32ld.Vbp (for 32 bit) VB or Auto16ld.Vbp (for 16 bit) VB. This type of file is called an *auto load* file. Auto32ld.Vbp comes with VB and is installed into the "C:\Program Files\Microsoft Visual Basic" folder. Auto16ld.Vbp is installed into "C:\VB."

As shipped, the contents of the Auto32ld.Vbp file are (Auto16ld is similar):

```
Object={F9043C88-F6F2-101A-A3C9-08002B2F49FB}#1.0#0; comdlg32.ocx

Object={BDC217C8-ED16-11CD-956C-0000C04E4C0A}#1.0# 0; tabctl32.ocx

Object={3B7C8863-D78F-101B-B9B5-04021C009402}#1.0#0; richtx32.ocx

Object={6B7E6392-850A-101B-AFC0-4210102A8DA7}#1.0#0; comctl32.ocx

Object={FAEEE763-117E-101B-8933-08002B2F4F5A}#1.0#0; dblist32.ocx

Object={00028C01-0000-0000-0000-000000000046}#1.0#0; DBGRID32.OCX

Reference=*\G{BEF6E001-A874-101A-8BBA-00AA00300CAB}#2.0#0#C:\WINNT\SYS-
TEM32\OLEPRO32.DLL#Standard OLE Types

Reference=*\G{00025E01-0000-0000-C000-000000000046}#3.0#0#C:\vb4\de-
bug.32\dao3032.dll#Microsoft DAO 3.0 Object Library

Name="Project1"
```

These are specs that control how the VB Development Environment looks when it's started and which custom controls are added to the toolbox. Notice the lines ending in ocx. Those are the custom control lines.

Unless you have a need for a custom control, it's just extra baggage. Also, load time for your projects is greatly increased because of these entries. For most development environments, and for the purposes of this book, it is recommended that the custom controls be removed from the auto load files.

Step by Step: Remove the ".OCX" Entries from the Auto32ld.Vbp File

1. Make a copy of Auto32ld.Vbp under another name (one you can remember, or at least find, later).

2. Start the VB Development Environment. Open the Tools menu and select "Custom Controls." You should see:

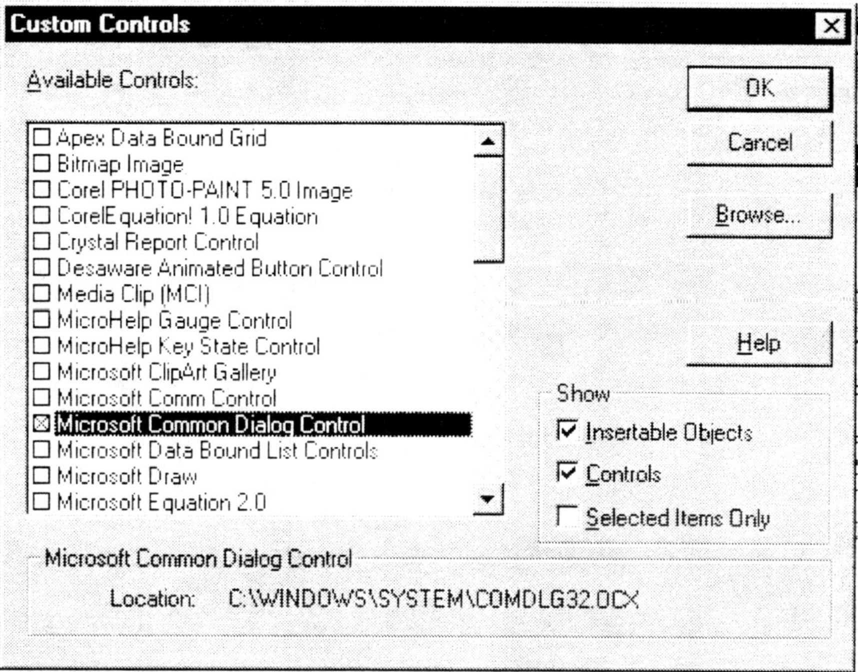

This dialog box is your means of specifying which custom controls you want to include with your project.

3. Remove all the check marks except the one next to "Microsoft Common Dialog Control." Retain this control, as it is very useful. Click "OK."

The next time you load VB, you should get a work space that looks more like this:

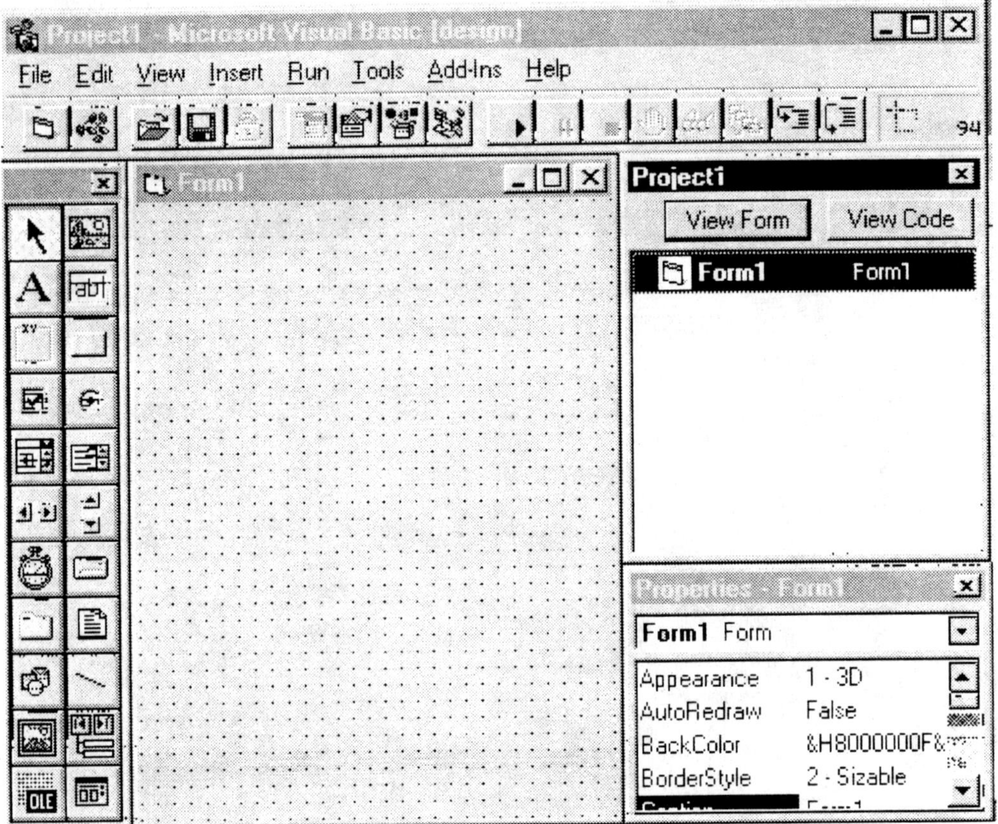

Notice that the toolbox is much smaller, with fewer buttons. The buttons that remain are the basic ones that come with the VB Development Environment. For the purposes of most of this book, these will do.

Environment and Project Settings

In AS/400 SEU, you can change the way the editor behaves by pressing F13 and keying "Y" or "N" to items like "Full screen roll" or "Lowercase allowed." The VB Development Environment has an equivalent in the "Environment..." tab on the "Options" command (Tools menu).

Most of the settings are a matter of personal choice, but there are a few recommendations:

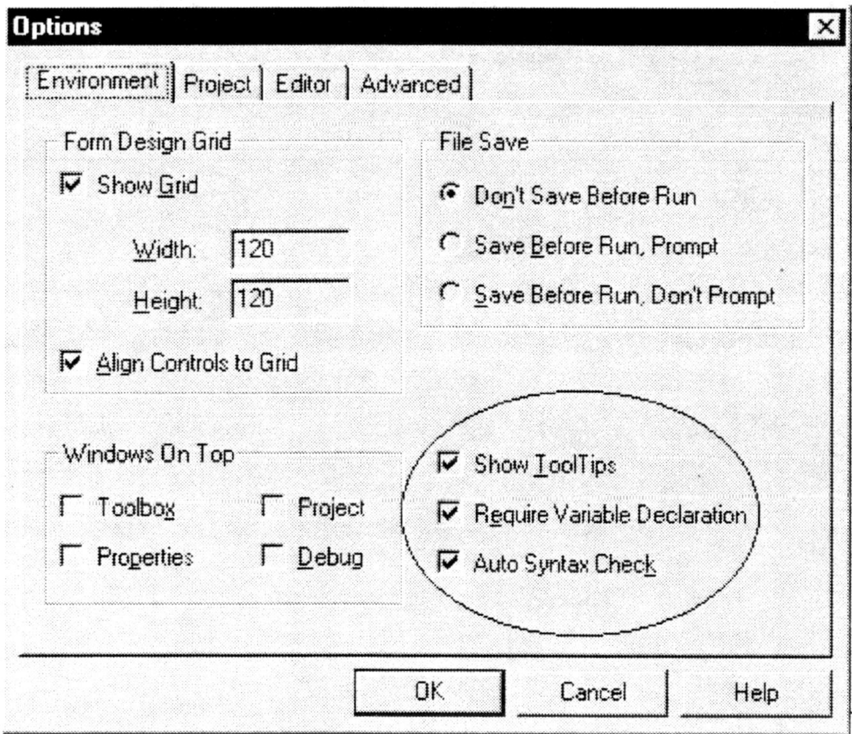

It is highly recommended that you specify "Show ToolTips," "Require Variable Declaration," and "Auto Syntax Check"—especially the last two.

Visual Basic allows you to implicitly declare a variable merely by using it in code, as you'll see. This feature should be turned off by checking "Require Variable Declaration."

The last option—"Auto Syntax Check"—is handy during coding to immediately identify errors.

The Project Option Settings

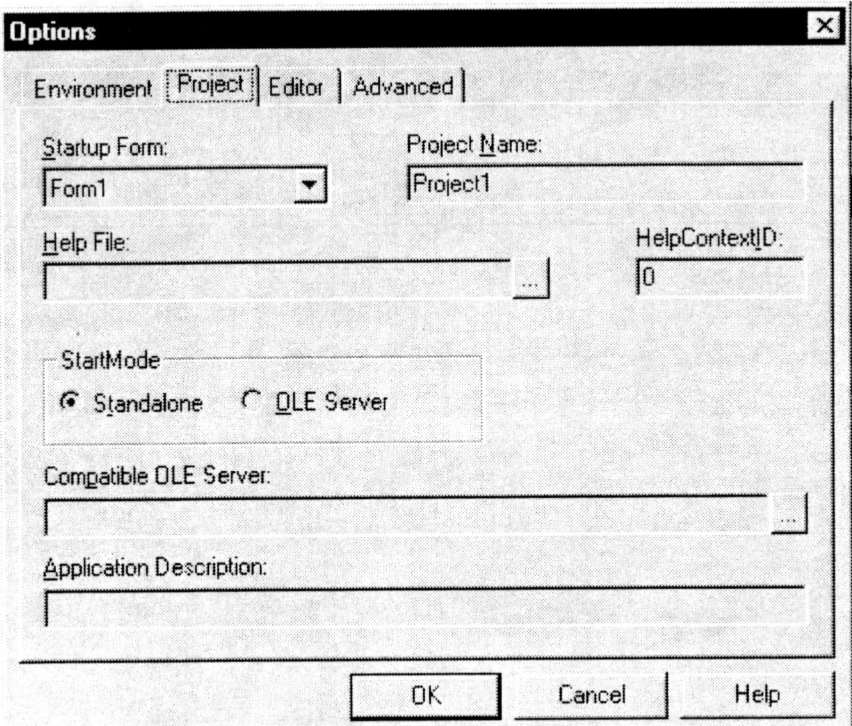

Visual Basic requires you to specify which of your project's forms is to be displayed when your application is started. VB automatically fills the setting for "Startup Form" with the first form you define (initially named Form1), but if you want your application to show some other form when started, you must specify it yourself. If you change Form1's name to something else, you don't have to change this setting. VB changes it for you.

If, for some reason, you want to create an application with no forms, you can specify a setting of "Sub Main" and create a procedure called "Main" that is called when the application is run.

The other options need no modification at this time.

Editor Options

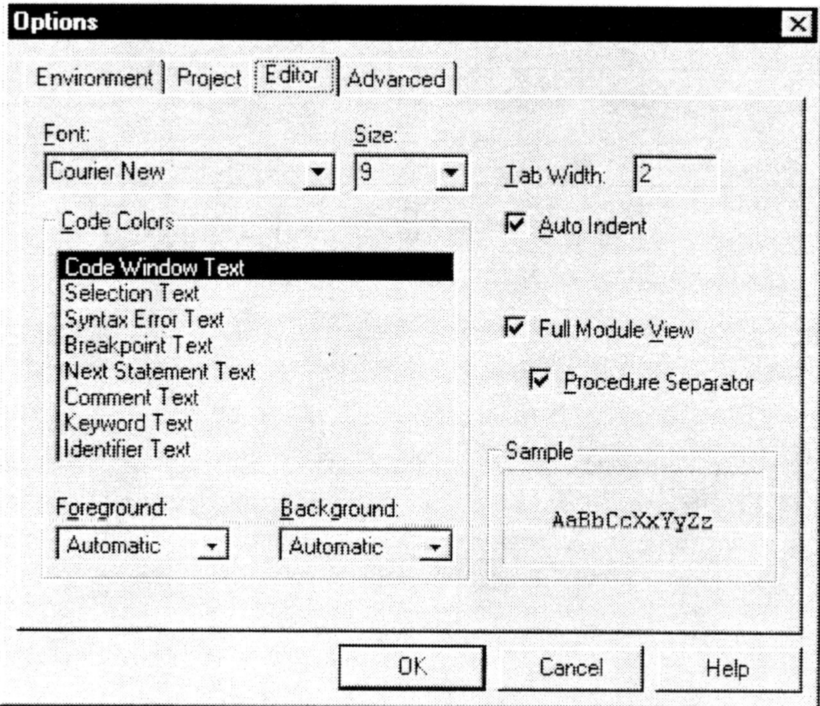

This is where you can change the colors and font of the editor itself. Notice that the default font for VB code is Courier New. This is because Courier is a nonproportional font and aligns well vertically to show indentation. Again a couple of recommendations—"Full Module View" with "Procedure Separators" displays the most code at one time with nice little lines offsetting the procedures (procedures are VB's subroutines).

Design Time vs. Run Time

You're already familiar with the concepts of *time* in a development project. In RPG, you can define a compile-time, a pre-execution time, or an execution-time array. Never mind the arrays, it's the concept of time that's important. In VB, you have only design time and run time. *Design time* refers to the period when you're using the VB Development Environment. *Run time* refers to the period when the program is running. Don't be confused. You can run your program, without compiling it, directly from the VB Development Environment, so you might think that's design time. It's not. It's run time. Run time is run time, even if you start the program from the VB Development Environment.

Development Environment Help

One of the things you loaded on your PC when you installed Visual Basic was a great deal of online help. It's like having an entire RPG or CL manual sitting behind SEU, with usage descriptions, syntax, and examples. You can even paste the example code into your program.

Focused Help

Aside from great help available from the menu, VB has other means of getting focused help on the subject you want. You can select various areas of the VB Development Environment with the mouse and then press F1. While coding, you can also place the cursor under a BASIC op code and press F1 to get a full explanation of the op code, the syntax, and an example of how it might be used.

Step by Step: Getting Focused Help in VB

1. Bring up VB.
2. Double click on "Form1" in the form design window. You should see:

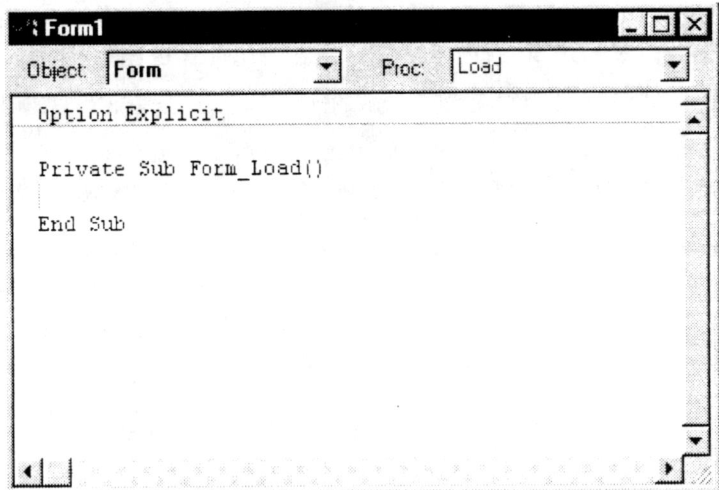

3. Key "beep" and press F1.

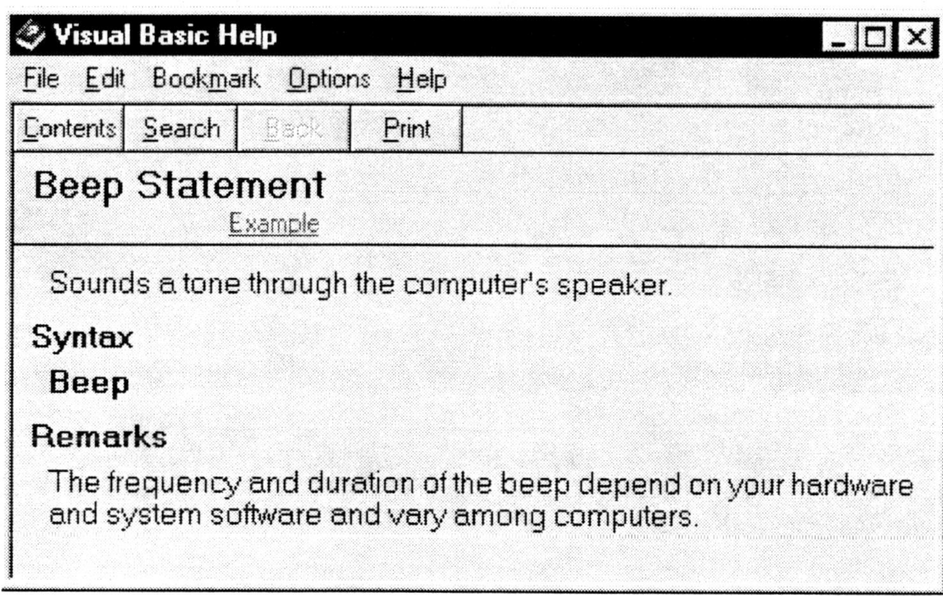

4. Click on "Example."

This is an example of how to use "Beep" in code. But wait. There's more.

5. Highlight the code with the cursor:

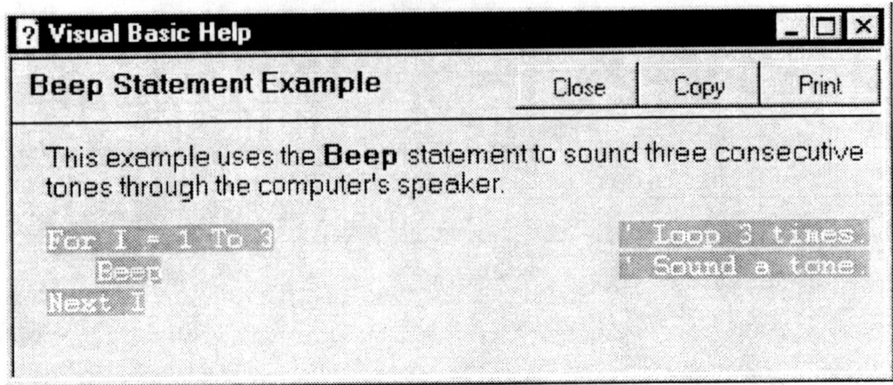

6. Click on "Copy." If all has gone well, you have loaded the code in the example into the clipboard, which is a temporary storage area available to all Windows applications.

7. Get out of Help.

8. Press the Backspace key until the op code "Beep" is removed.

9. From the Edit menu select "Paste."

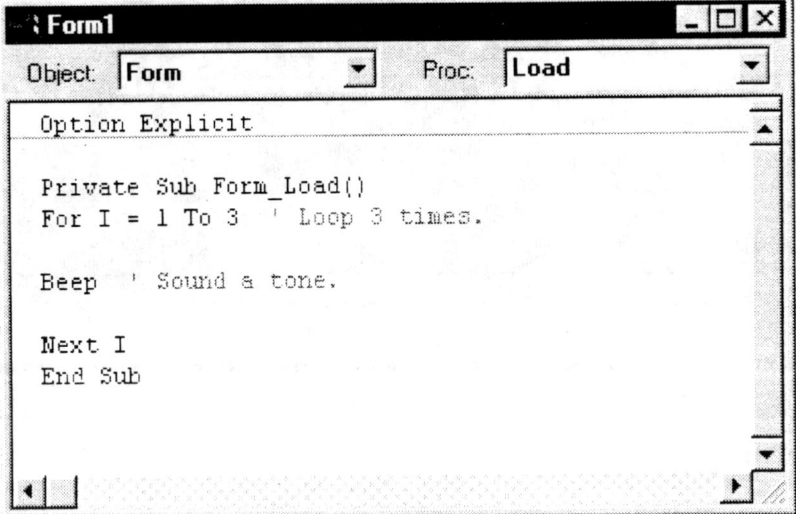

You have pasted in code from an example. In fact, this is enough code to be a program.

10. From the toolbar, click on the "Run" button: .

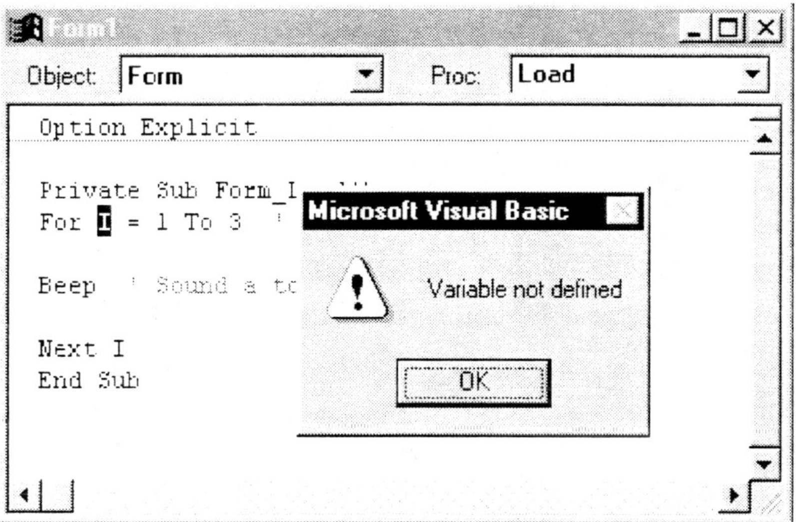

The program won't run because the variable named "I" has not been declared. Notice the the variable name has been highlighted in code.

Recall that you've changed your environment setting "Require Variable Declaration." That's how the top line of code—"Option Explicit"—got there.

11. Click "OK." As an illustration of implicit variable declaration, place a single quote in front of "Option Explicit," turning that line into a comment. This overrides explicit declaration of variables. Click the "Run" button again. This time you should hear a little chirp as the beep statements are processed. The variable "I" was defined on the fly. (This sounds great, but there's a problem, which is discussed in Chapter 5.)

12. Click on the "End" button, , to end the little program and return to the VB Development Environment.

13. Discard the specs by either exiting VB without saving the files, or by clicking on "New Project" from the Files menu and not saving the file.

Well, the stage is set. Your patience during this initial setup process is appreciated. The next chapter gets you going with VB programming.

Summary

Elements of a VB Project

You see how a Visual Basic project is much like an AS/400 project. There are source files that contain the specifications for forms and modules.

A list of the source files is kept in the project file. The project file has an extension of ".VBP."

The VB source file types are:

- .FRM A form or screen form file.
- .BAS A module or calculation specifications file.
- .GBL A module containing only constants—not to be altered.
- .CLS A module containing specifications describing a class.

The file names used in a project are displayed in the project window, as is the name of the project itself. The File menu commands are used to manage the files (open, add, remove, copy/clone). The VB Development Environment maintains the entries in your project file as you add/remove/rename your source files, or you can edit the project file with any text editor.

VB assigns default names to your project and files when you start the VB Development Environment. You should change the default names when the project and source files are saved.

The VB Development Environment

The VB Development Environment is a combination of a screen design aid (like SDA), and a source editor (like SEU). It brings all the source files together at the same time for editing.

The components of the VB Development Environment are the:

- Command menu
- Toolbar
- Project box

- Toolbox
- Form design window
- Code window

When started, the project manager reads a startup project file:

```
C:\VB\Auto16ld.Vbp
```

or

```
C:\Program Files\Microsoft Visual Basic\Auto32ld.Vbp
```

You can edit the ".Vbp" file with any text editor to remove the ".OCX" entries so that the VB Development Environment loads faster and only contains the necessary controls.

The VB Development Environment settings tailor the way the editor behaves. Most settings are personal choice, but you should specify that you want to "Require Variable Declaration."

The VB Development Environment comes with extensive online help.

To get help you can:

- Click on the Help menu and look in the table of contents.
- Click on the Help menu and search for help by topic.

To get more focused help you can:

- Position the cursor on a button, window, toolbar, etc., and press F1.
- Key a BASIC language function or procedure name and press F1.

VB help comes with examples of syntax and code usage that can be pasted into your program.

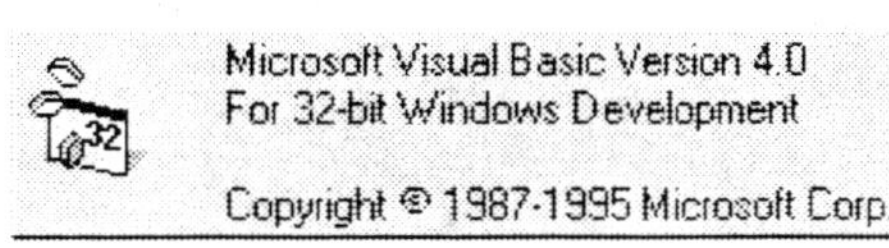

3

Starter VB Concepts

Now that you are familiar with the elements of a VB project and the functions of the VB Development Environment, you are ready to learn actual VB programming concepts. This chapter covers Visual Basic coding and the BASIC language, presented, whenever possible, in AS/400 terms.

Event-oriented Processing

You're already familiar with *event-oriented processing*. When a screen is displayed to the user and the user presses Enter, that's an event. You might call it the *Enter Event*. You've seen it many times on Windows screens, but instead of pressing Enter, you click on a button labeled "OK." When a user presses F3 on an AS/400 screen, that's the *end event*. F12 is analogous to the *cancel event*, and so on.

Windows applications have many more events available, however. For instance, the presence of the mouse requires events like click, double click, and mouse move.

The VB program is aware of everything that happens, as it happens. It's not like the 400, which doesn't react to events like keystrokes until you press Enter and send the contents of the display file back to the CPU. VB works more like display file attributes described in DDS and present in the intelligence of an AS/400 workstation. That is, if you specify a display file attribute of "numeric only" for an AS/400 display field and the user tries to key a letter into the field, the workstation is aware of the keystroke as it happens, and reacts. That's how VB works. In VB, the events are associated not only with the screen but also with things *on* the screen.

Of course, you know that the things that are placed on an otherwise blank form are called *controls,* and they're placed there by clicking a button in the Toolbox and drawing the control on the form like you draw any Windows object (click, drag, and release). (You may also double click a button in the Toolbox and get a default size and shape for the control.)

Procedures

Procedures are sections of code that are like RPG subroutines. The code inside a procedure represents a logical unit of work. There are two kinds of procedures:

- Event procedures
- General procedures

Event procedures come with VB. General procedures must be written by the programmer. Once a general procedure is defined, it must be explicitly invoked in code. By contrast, an event procedure remains idle until called upon to respond to events caused by the user or triggered by the system. You can place a general procedure in either a form module, standard module, or class module.

Within general procedures there are three types:

- Sub procedures
- Function procedures
- Property procedures

> **Note:** *As if things aren't complex enough, most VB programmers refer to function procedures as* functions *and sub procedures as* procedures.

Event Procedures

It was previously stated that event procedures 'come with VB.' That is, these procedures are built in to the controls that come with VB. They are the chunks of code that are to be executed when the user or the program triggers an event. You can't write your own event procedures.

Event procedures may be best understood by illustration.

The object here is to place a control (a *label* that is like a constant on an AS/400 display screen) on a form, and then see the event procedures associated with the label.

Step by Step: Seeing Control Events

1. Start a new project. Click on the form "Form1" to select it. Double click on the *label control* button in the toolbox. It looks like this: A .

   You should see:

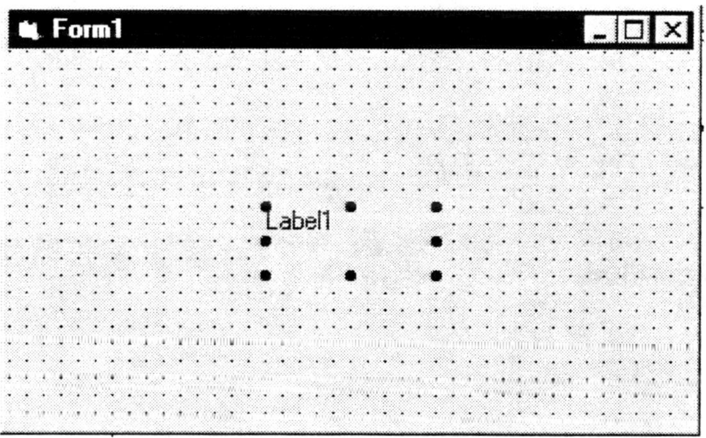

   Notice that VB is trying to name things again. This time it gives the first label placed on the form the name "Label1."

2. Double click inside the label. You should see:

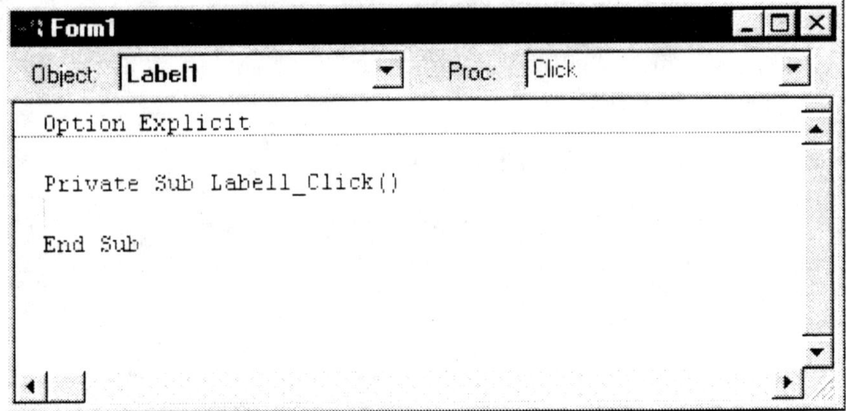

This is the code window for the event "Label1_Click" and shows the code that is executed when the click event occurs. Notice the name of the control "Label1" showing in the object box and the event "Click" showing in the procedure box. The code that you want to execute when the user clicks inside the box "Label1" should go between the lines "Private Sub" and "End Sub."

3. Click on the arrow to the right of the procedures list box. You should see:

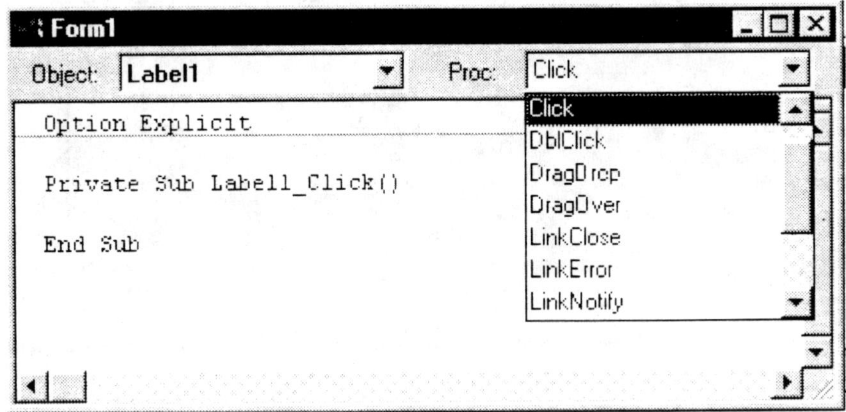

This is a list of all the events that can happen to a label. You can click on a label, double click on it, drag a mouse pointer over it, etc.

4. Click on the list box arrow for objects. You should see:

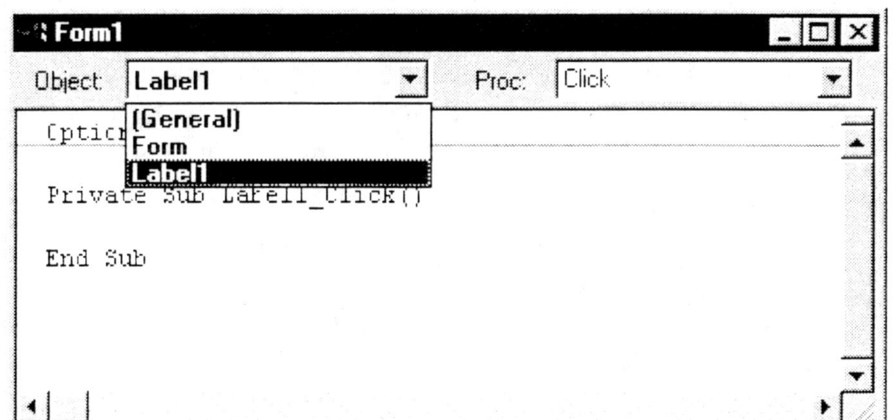

Note: The list containing the two things you've defined—the form "Form1" (actually defined by VB) and the label "Label1." Visual Basic calls these things objects. In VB, objects are just about anything you define—forms are objects, controls are objects, etc.

To restate, VB keeps your code in subroutine-like sections called procedures and functions (actually sub procedures, function procedures, and property procedures). Each event gets a procedure assigned by VB. You bring the code for a procedure into the code window by selecting the object in the object list and then the event. (VB automatically brings up the most common event for that object when you select it—in this case, "Click.")

General Procedures

You've seen how each object that you create has events associated with it, and that each event gets a code area called a procedure or a function. This type of procedure is known as an *event procedure*. You may also define a *general procedure* that has no associated event and, therefore, must be called explicitly.

Think of general procedures as subroutines. They are called like RPG subroutines, and defined similarly with "Sub *subroutine-name*" and "End Sub." The RPG equivalent would be "*subroutine name* BEGSR" and "ENDSR."

You can pass parms to a VB procedure, and the procedure can change the value of the parms and return them to the calling routine. A procedure can also change values contained in variables, and the calling routine may have access to them.

> ***Note:** VB variables and procedures have an attribute called* scope, *which determines how much of the VB program gets access to them. Scope is presented in Chapter 5.*

The logic about when to use procedures is pretty much the same as in RPG, too. Suppose you have an RPG program with several screens that allow the user to press F3 to exit anytime she/he wants. The section of code to exit:

```
C                 *INKC       IFEQ  *ON
C                             MOVE  *ON         *INLR
C                             RETRN
C                             ENDIF
```

is short, and really doesn't warrant its own subroutine. If the exiting code was longer, involving more processing, like:

```
C                 *INKC       IFEQ  *ON
   *  Display confirmation screen . . .
C                             EXFMT RUSURE
   *  F12 pressed to cancel exit . . ?
C                 *INKL       IFEQ  *OFF
   *  Perform exiting processing . . .
C                             EXSR  TOTALS
C                             .
C                             .
C                             .
C                             MOVE  *ON         *INLR
C                             RETRN
```

```
C                                   ENDIF

C                                   ENDIF
```

you would be inclined to put this code in a subroutine and call it whenever the user presses F3. The same goes for VB. When the need for the same code exists in several places in your program, use a general procedure.

The General and Declarations Area of a Form or Module

The remaining entry in the objects list is *general*. This is a free-form coding area where you can start a new procedure or declare variables. If you define a general procedure, it goes into the procedures list.

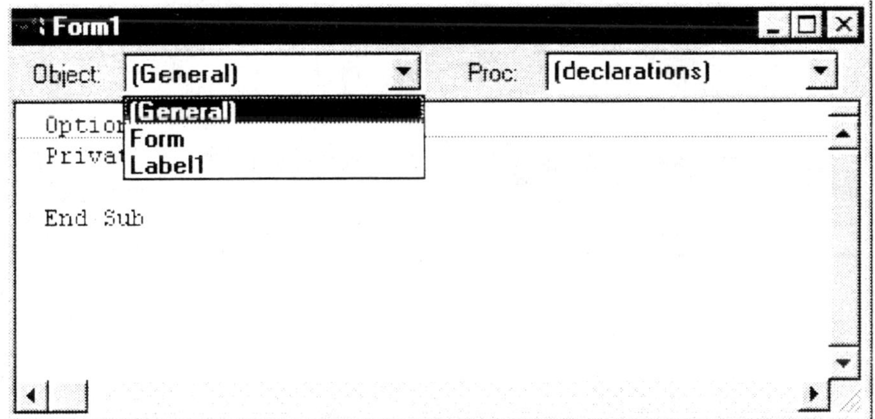

Step by Step: Code Areas and Procedures

1. Bring up VB and highlight "Form1" in the project box:

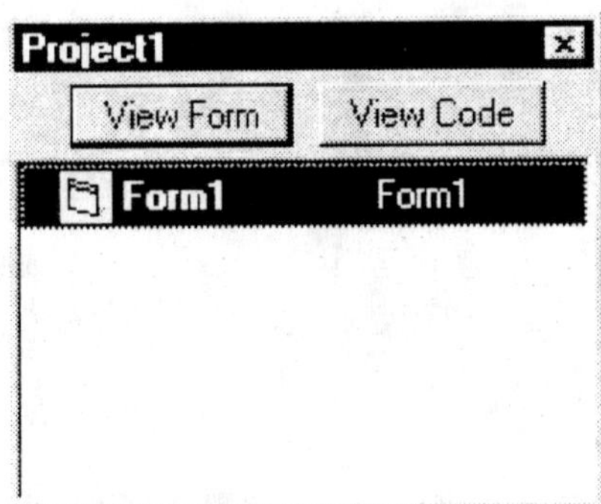

2. Click on "View Code." You should see:

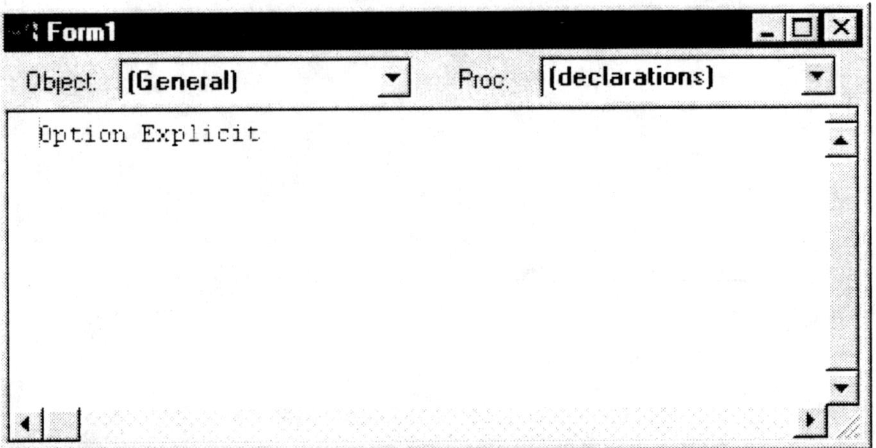

This is the declarations section of the *form*. Each form has a declarations area. Each module also has a declarations area. The declarations area of modules is where you create your own procedures.

> ***Note:*** *The automatic insertion of "Option Explicit" establishes that variables be explicitly declared. If you remove this statement, implicit declaration of variables is allowed for this module only.*

3. Move the cursor to a new line, type "sub test" and press Enter. You should see:

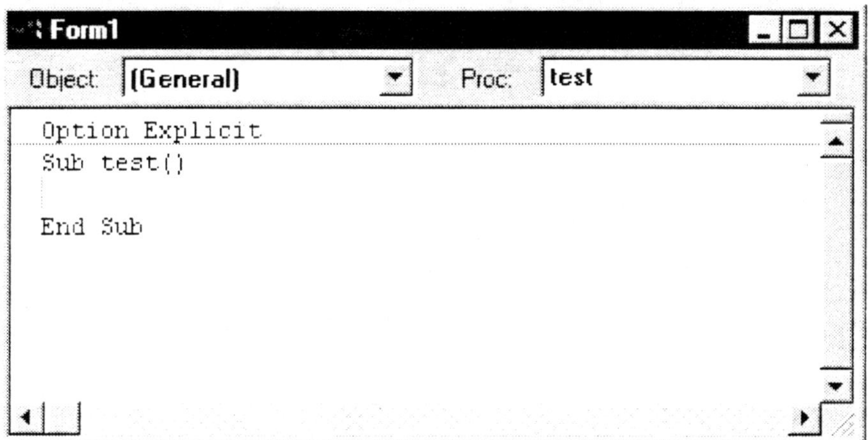

Do you see what happened? The VB Development Environment saw the word "sub" and created a procedure. Notice that the word "test" now appears in the procedure box as the active procedure; if you open the procedures list you see "test." VB even provides the end bound of the procedure—the "End Sub" statement.

4. Highlight the code in the procedure. You should see:

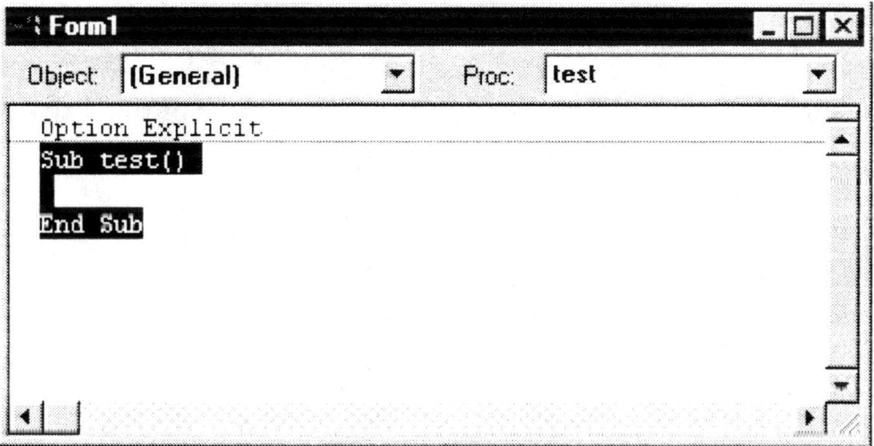

5. From the Edit menu, click on "Cut" to remove the code. Notice that the procedure is no longer present in the procedures list box.

6. Now type "function test" and press Enter. You should get a similar result:

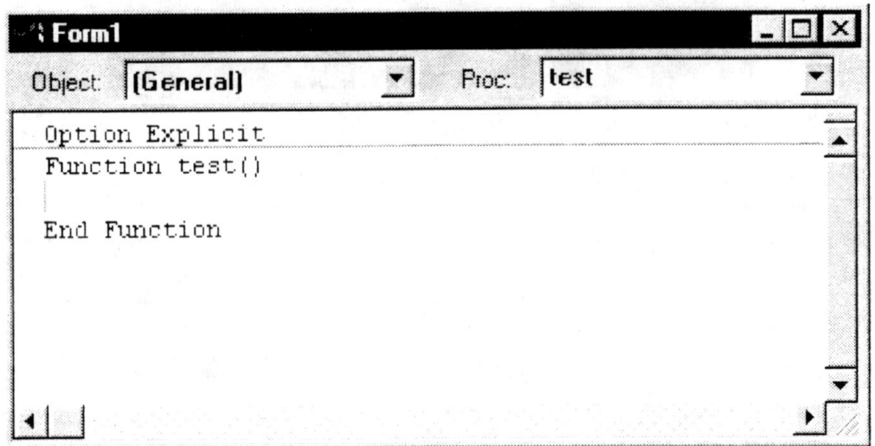

The VB editor starts a new function, as it did for general procedures. Functions can only be started in the declarations area (the free-form coding area) of a form or module.

You can also start a new procedure or function by clicking the "New Procedure..." command on the Edit menu.

Functions

A function is a particular kind of procedure. There's no convenient AS/400 comparison. The concept of functions is familiar to PC programmers, but not to AS/400 programmers, and has been kind of an indicator of the threshold between the two. It's not very difficult to learn, though.

Consider this AS/400 code used to call a program to retrieve the contents of a data area and pass it back to the calling program:

```
C                        CALL   'GETARA'          99    Call failed
C                        PARM DTAARA
C              *IN99     IFEQ   *OFF
C                        etc...
```

In a VB-functions way of thinking, the syntax for the same task looks like this:

```
*IN99 = GETARA(DTAARA)
```

Indicator 99 gets a value of "0" or "1" depending on the results of the call effort. Assuming it's successful, the variable DTAARA gets filled with a value.

The difficult thing to understand about functions is the equal sign. The function itself equals something—in this case, a return code. (Actually, a value is substituted internally.) In VB, that makes the two expressions equivalent. So this code:

```
C                         CALL   'GETARA'         99    Call failed

C                         PARM    DTAARA

C     *IN99               IFEQ    *OFF

C                           .

C                           .

C                         ENDIF
```

is the same as this code:

```
GETARA(DTAARA)   IFEQ    *OFF


                 ENDIF
```

You can pass a parameter to a function, and the function can pass a value back, but it passes it as the value of the function itself. For example, these common BASIC language statements are functions that receive an argument (parm) and *become the value* of the function's operation on the argument:

```
T = Time                  ' returns the time of day

X = Asc("A")              ' returns the ASCII value for the letter A

N = Chr(10)               ' returns the character assigned ASCII 10.

Name$ = Ucase$(Name$)     ' returns the uppercase equivalent of name$
```

The last example is of interest because the variable "Name$" is used as both the argument and the variable to receive the returned value. Very economical code.

OK, that explains functions (or more properly, function procedures). Not so hard, really.

Calling a General Procedure

A general procedure is called with the VB statement "Call," or you can omit the "Call" part and just type the procedure name without it.

For example:

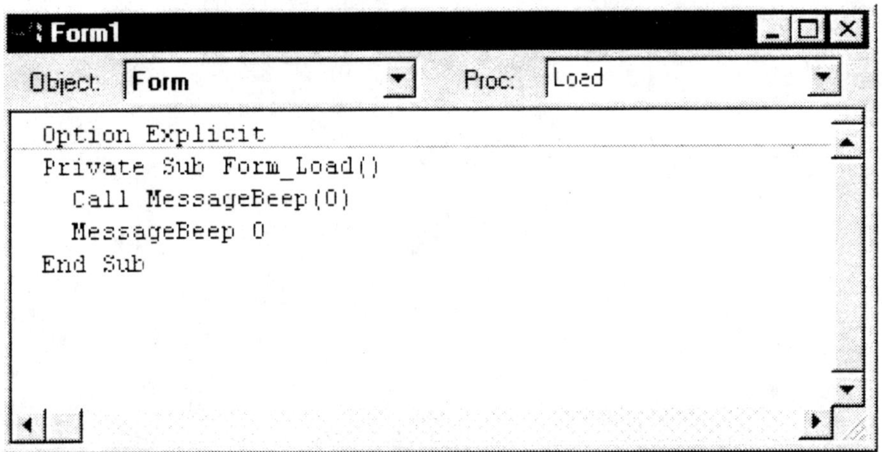

The procedure "MessageBeep" is called twice—once with Call and once without. They are equivalent. The value "0" after the procedure name is the parm passed, or, in VB terms, the *argument*.

Notice that when Call is used, the argument is enclosed in parentheses. When Call is not used, the parentheses are omitted.

Call is not to be confused with AS/400 program-to-program calls. Calls within a VB program are calling procedures also within the program. The RPG analogy to Call is "EXSR *subroutine-name.*"

Executing a Function

You don't call functions like you do procedures. They are considered to be a value (remember the equal sign?), so they can be part of an expression. For example, this is an expression:

```
Name = UCase(NameInput)
```

and "UCase(NameInput)" is a value like "JOHN" or "MARY." So, you just insert functions into expressions as if they were a value because that's what they represent.

Modules

Standard modules are like the calculations area of an RPG program, you remember, and have their own source file with an extension of ".BAS."

You've seen how general procedures and function procedures are created in the general area of a form. They can also be put into modules, which, for us AS/400 programmers, is a better place.

You are probably accustomed to having your subroutines all together in one place, available to any other part of the program. In VB, if you define a procedure in the general part of a form instead of a module, it is not available to code that's in other forms or modules.

A loose AS/400 analogy: Let's say you've coded display file attributes in DDS to control user keying, field exit, etc. The RPG program that is driving the display file has no idea of the editing process that is taking place at the screen. The process is unavailable to the RPG program—it can't be seen.

> ***Note:*** *For your purposes, and also because of the way you're accustomed to thinking, it is recommended that you keep nearly all general procedures, functions, and declarations in a single module.*

Step by Step: Adding a Code Module

1. Bring up the default project. Click on the "New Module" button on the toolbar: .

   You should see:

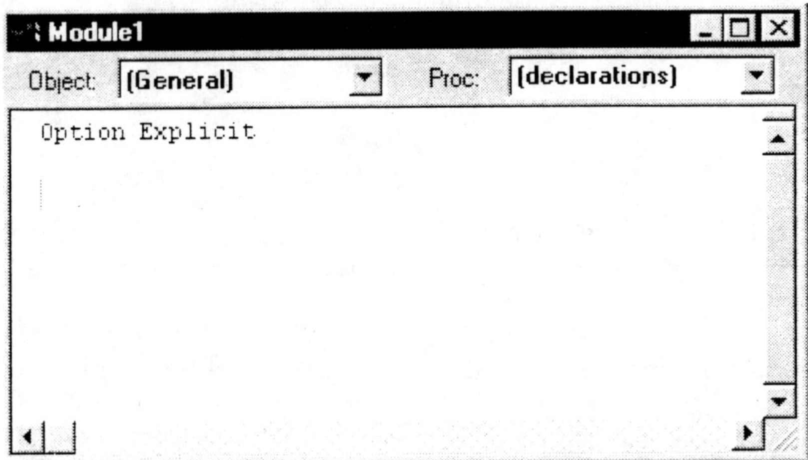

You've created a new module that VB has already given a default name of Module1.bas.

Take a look at the project box.

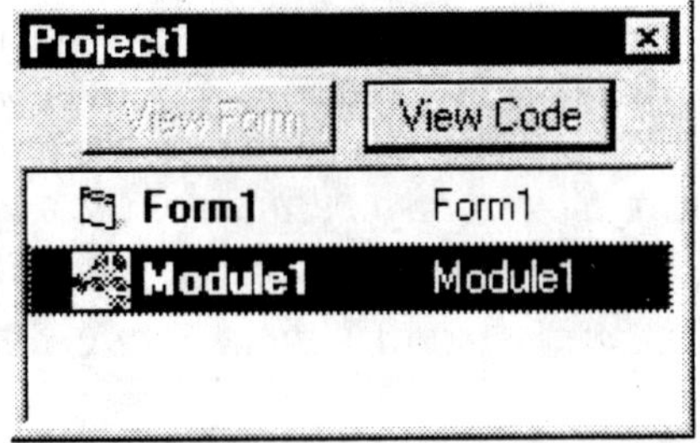

A new source file has been added. Observe also that of the two buttons "View Form" and "View Code," only "View Code" is available. That's because there are no forms in modules. They only contain code.

2. From the Insert menu select "Procedure..."

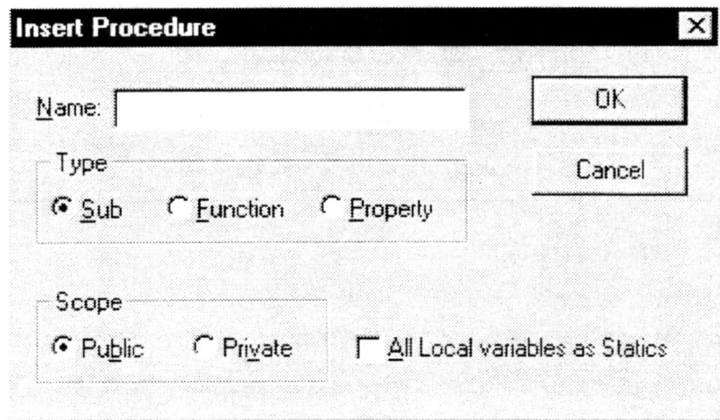

3. Key "test" into the name box and click on "OK." You should see:

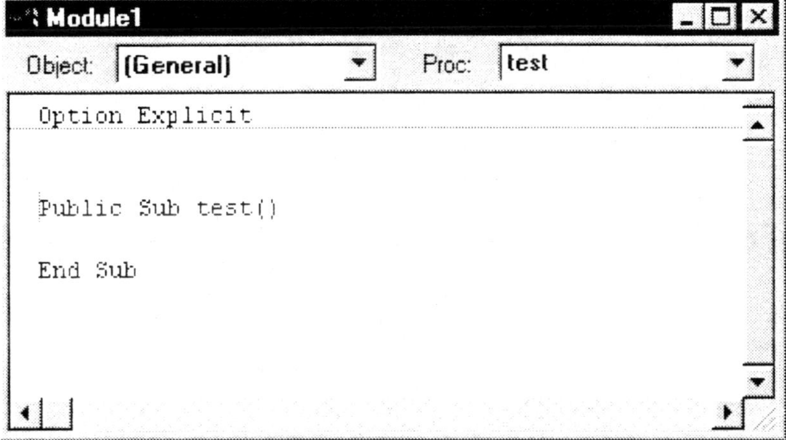

This is the same effect as was achieved previously. You've created a new procedure named "test," and you're ready to code.

In a real project, you would rename your new module using "Save As..."

4. Open the procedures list.

5. Click on "(declarations)."

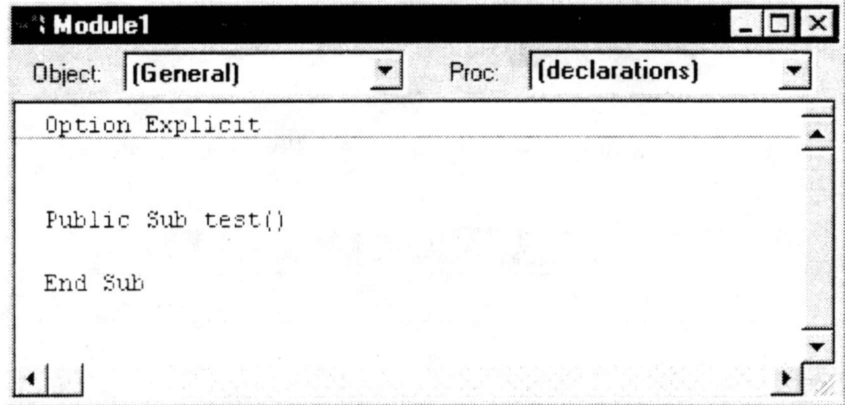

The declarations area of a form or module is where you define variables and constants that are used in your program. Examples of variable declarations are:

```
Private intIndex as Integer

Dim TodayDate as Date

Static lngRunningTotal as Long

Public CustomerName as String
```

A discussion of variable types follows in Chapter 5.

Forms

You know a lot about forms already. You know that they are the display screens in a VB application, and that each form has its own source file.

Step by Step: Adding Forms

1. Bring up VB's default project.
2. Click on the "New Form" button on the toolbar: [New Form button]. You should see a new form—"Form2." Reposition the new form so you can see the old one. You should see something like:

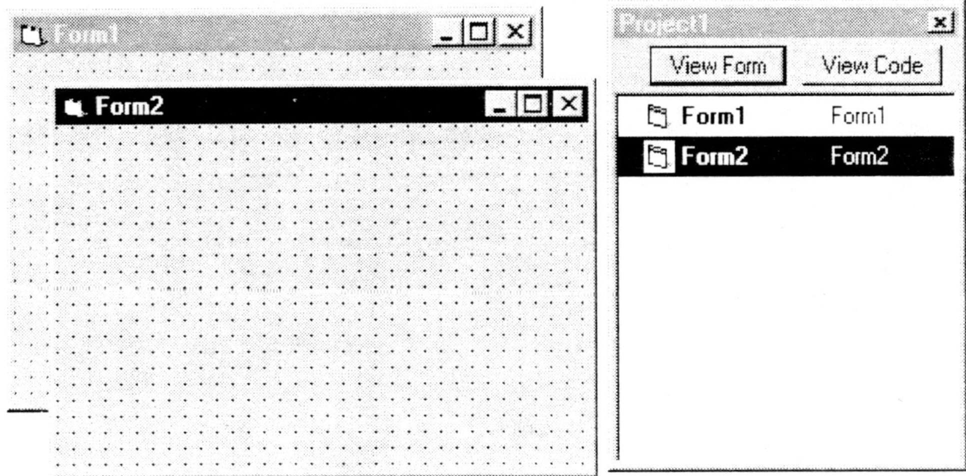

You've got a new form, a new entry in the project box, and, when saved, a new source file.

3. Click on "Form1" to bring it to the front.
4. Add a command button. Click on [command button] in the toolbox and draw the button on the form.
5. Add another command button to Form1. (Notice the default captions "Command1" and "Command2.")

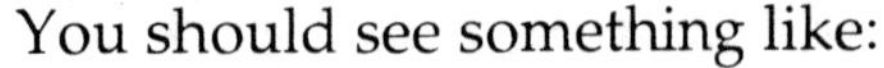

You should see something like:

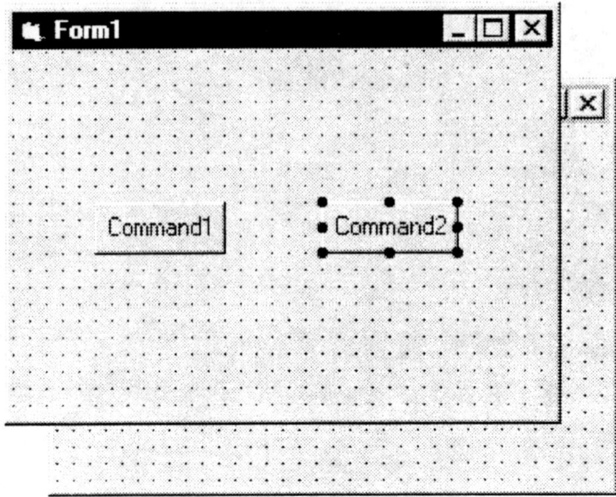

Notice the black frame around the "Command2" button. This indicates that this object is currently selected. You select an object on the form (or select the form itself) by clicking on the object. The selection marks appear around whatever is selected. The little black squares that are used to resize the button are called *handles*.

6. With "Command2" still selected, delete it from the frame by choosing the "Cut" command on the Edit menu, or by pressing the delete key. You should see:

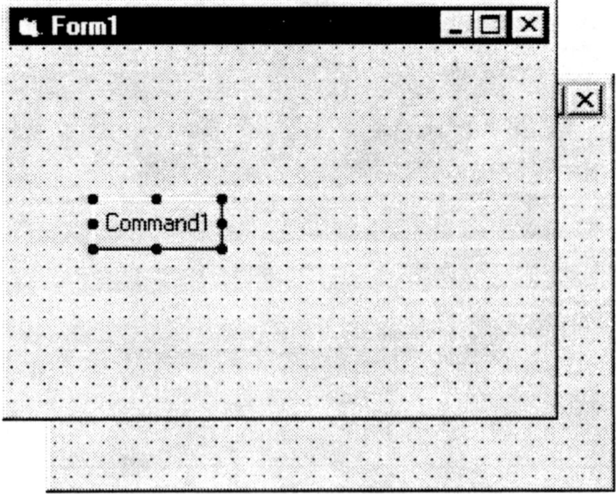

As "Command2" is removed from the form (and put into the clipboard) the VB Development Environment automatically selects another object—in this case, "Command1."

7. Click on "Form2" to select it, then select "Paste" from the Edit menu:

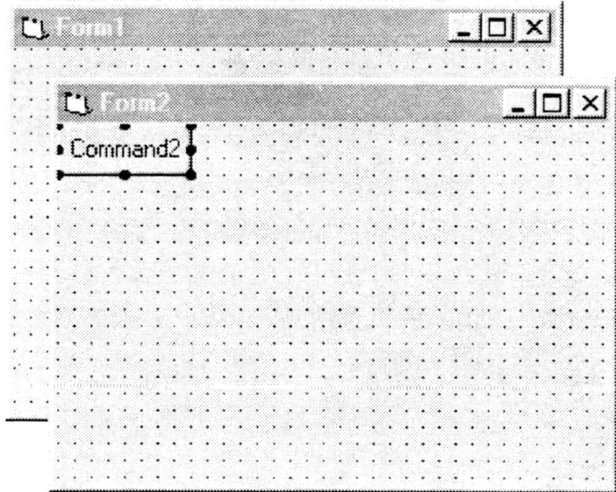

You've cut an object from one form and pasted it to another. Cut and paste is a familiar Windows method for manipulating text and graphics, and it is used in VB.

Example Project: A Text File Editor—EditText

Simple example programs that have worth are hard to come by. This example starts out as simply as possible, and then additions are made to illustrate upcoming concepts.

This program ends up being a simple version of Windows Notepad. It opens a selected file, copies its contents into an edit area for modification, and saves the file.

Step by Step: Establish Your Folder, Windows, Environment, and Files

1. Create a folder for projects in general—"C:\VB\PROJECTS" for 16-bit environments or "C:\Program Files\Microsoft Visual Basic\Projects" for 32-bit environments.

2. Create a folder for this project—"C:\VB\PROJECTS\EditText" (16 bit); "C:\Program Files\Microsoft Visual Basic\Projects\EditText" (32 bit).

3. Open VB or click "New Project" on the File menu.

4. Resize your windows now if desired—the dimensions are saved with the project.

5. Click on "Save File As..." on the File menu.

6. Scroll through the folders box until you get to "PROJECTS."

7. Double click on "PROJECTS."

8. Double click on "EditText."

   Now the name of the form file can be changed from "Form1.frm" to something else. Use "EditText1.FRM" to indicate that this is form one of the project EditText.

9. Change the name of the form file to "EditText1.Frm" and click on "OK."

   The file has been saved under its new name. The project box reflects the change:

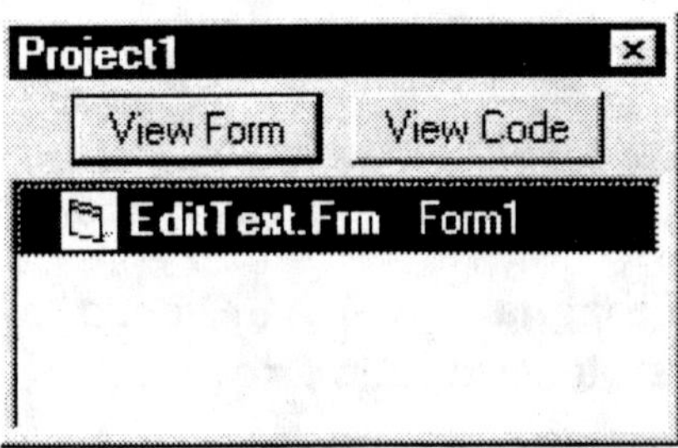

   Notice that, although the name of the source file for the form has changed, the name of the form itself remains "Form1." On the AS/400, you can have a DDS source file member named one thing, and the screen format defined within the member named something else. This is the case with form files.

10. Select "Save Project As..." from the File menu.

11. Change the project name to "EditText.Vbp" and click on "OK."

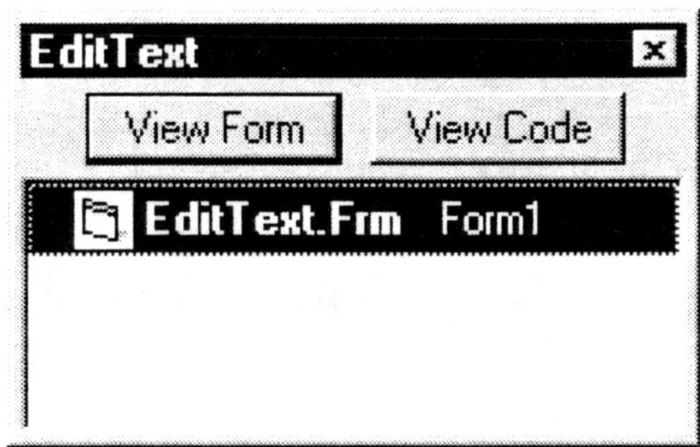

In its title, the project box now shows the new project name as well.

Okay. The project folder has been created, the renamed files have been created, and the environment has been set.

A brief presentation of a couple of controls is needed now, although controls in general are covered in Chapter 4.

Text Box

A text box is to a VB form what an input-capable field is to an AS/400 display screen. When you want to provide a simple field for the user to key an entry, use a text box.

Step by Step: Continue the EditText Project

12. With Form1 as the active window, double click on the text box button: 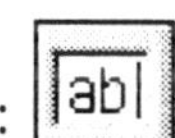 .

You should see:

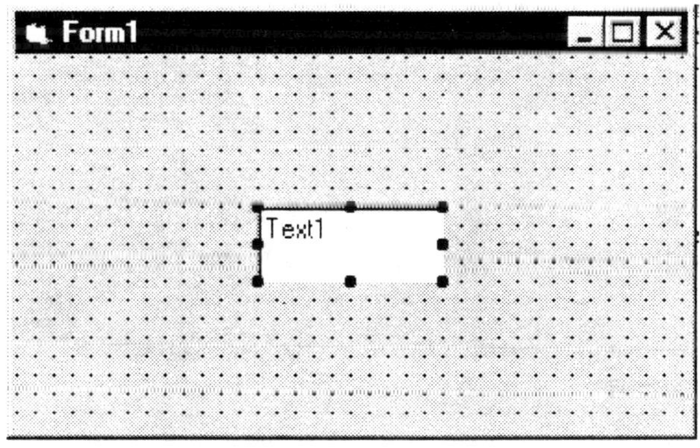

The default name "Text1" has been assigned by the VB Development Environment.

13. Reposition and resize the text box so it looks more like:

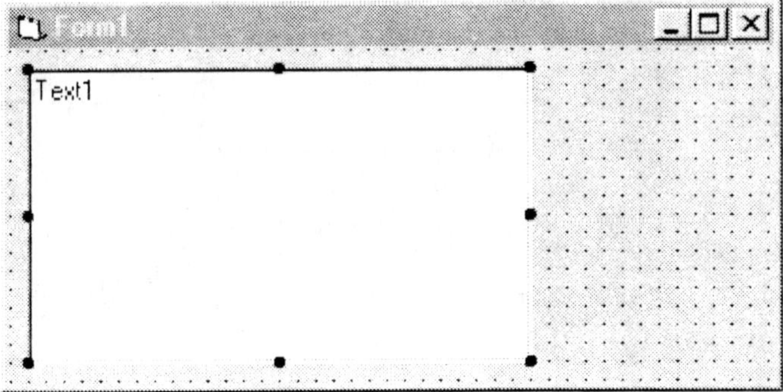

A command button is like the Enter key or F3 to an AS/400 screen. The user can click on a command button to specify OK (Enter,) or End (F3), etc.

14. Double click on the command button control in the toolbox: 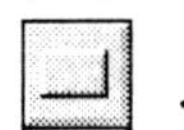 .

15. Reposition and resize the command button:

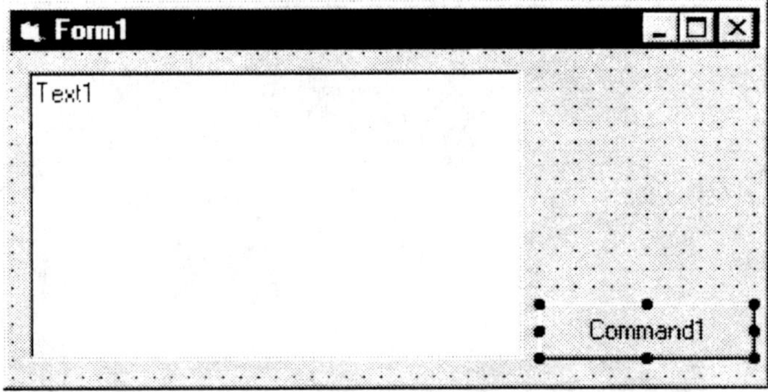

The Properties Box

Properties are like field attributes on AS/400 display fields. Each VB object has properties that are appropriate for the type of object. Some VB objects are not observable—that is, they are not a form or control but rather an internal entity (like the "Printer" object for interfacing with the Windows print manager). Objects that you can put on a form (and forms themselves) are called *insertable* objects. The *properties box* is where their properties are specified for design time.

This is the properties box for the command button "Command1." If the properties box is not on your screen, press F4, or click the "Properties" button on the toolbar, or select "Properties" on the View menu. There are several things to notice here:

- The names of the control ("Command1") and the control class (CommandButton) at the top of the box indicate which control you're working on.

- This information appears in a list box. See the little arrow? If you open the list box, you see all the insertable objects associated with the form "Form1:"

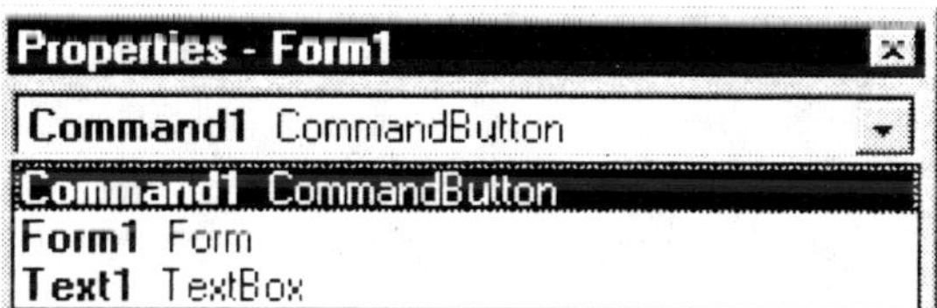

  You could select a different object from the list and bring up the properties box for it.

- The properties box contains two columns. The column on the left describes each property, and the column on the right displays the current setting.

Step by Step: Continue the EditText Project

16. Double click on the property "Caption." You should see:

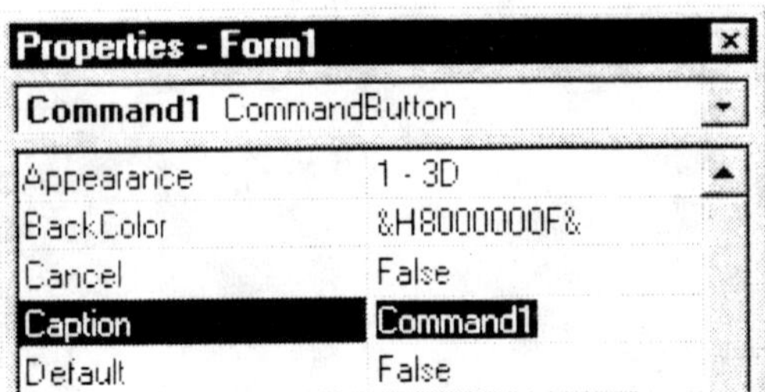

The name "Command1" has been highlighted in both the properties column and in the text box where it can be edited. The caption for a control is what identifies it to the user.

17. Type "OK" as the new caption for the button and click on the form. You should see:

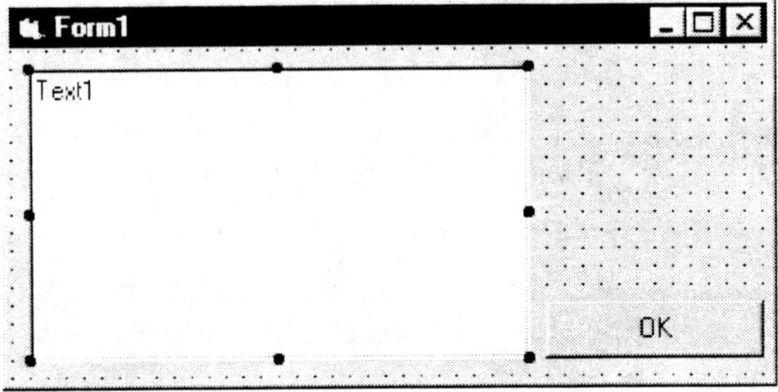

The caption for the command button is now "OK."

18. While the properties box for the "OK" button is open, scroll down to the property "Name," double click on it, and rename the button "cmdOK" (all one word).

There are many other properties that you may specify, like font, font size, and background color, that are a matter of personal choice. Other properties are presented later.

19. Click on the text box "Text1" to select it. Notice the change to the properties box. It now displays the properties for "Text1."

20. Change the name of the text box from "Text1" to "txtEditArea".

The names that you create for objects in VB are words and abbreviations put together without spaces, but with upper- and lowercase. *It's a good idea to put the object's class into its name.* For example:

```
For a text box:          txtCustomerName    (preferred)

                         TextCustomer

                         CustomerText

                         txtAddressLine     (preferred)


For a command button:    cmdCloseDialog     (preferred)

                         OKButton

                         ButtonOK

                         CancelButton
```

Names must start with an alpha character and have a maximum length of 40.

> ***Note** the preferred naming convention. It's preferred by Microsoft (and others) as an effort to establish some consistency between coders. The first three characters indicate the class of the control.*

Look for the caption property for the text box. There isn't one. The content of a text box is set by the property "Text." Remember that different objects have different properties? The caption property is not appropriate for text boxes, but it is for command buttons.

21. Double click on the text property for "txtEdit" to highlight it. Press the Backspace key to remove the entry and render the text box empty. Your form should look something like this:

22. Open the objects list in the properties box and click on "Form1:"

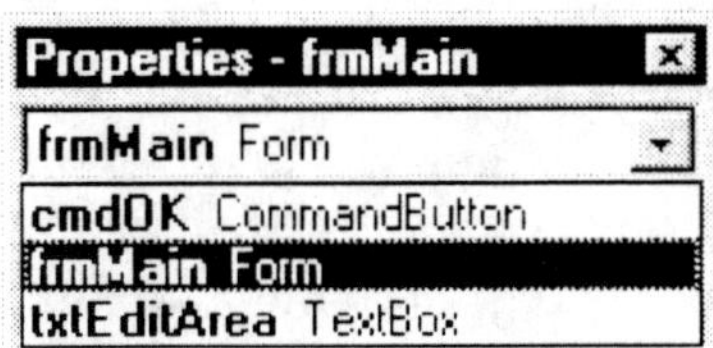

23. Scroll to the "Name" property and change the form's name to "frmMain".

24. To demonstrate a previous point, from the Tools menu select "Options" and click on "Project."

    The VB Development Environment has automatically changed the startup form to your new name.

25. Close the project options box and return to the properties box for frmMain. Forms can have a caption and it appears in the title bar for the form.

26. Double click on the caption property and change it to "Text File Editor."

    Although this program won't do anything, it will run.

27. Click on the "Run" button on the toolbar: ▶. You should see:

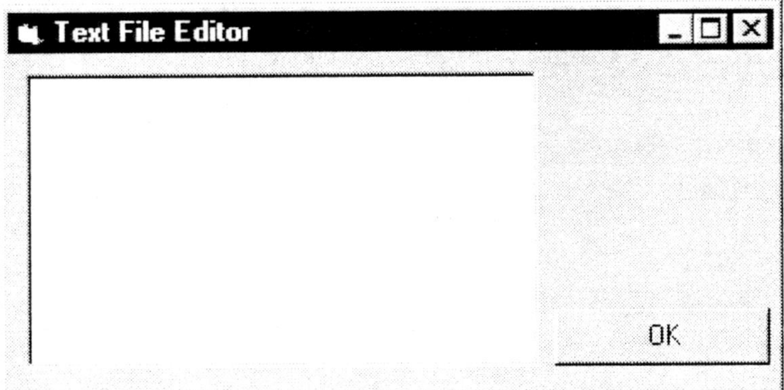

28. Alright. That was nice. Click on the "Stop" button on the toolbar: ■ .
29. Save the project. Click on the "Save Project" button on the toolbar: .

    Notice that you didn't have to specify any file names. You've already taken care of that by doing the "Save File As..." and "Save Project As..." steps earlier.

    We will reopen this project in subsequent chapters to add the specs to make it a functional program.

Objects

You remember that objects are forms and controls. (Objects also include other things, but you don't need to consider them now.) For a while, at least, *objects* means forms and controls.

To identify a form in code—that is, within VB statements—you simply use its name:

```
FormName
```

For controls, the qualified name is:

```
FormName.ControlName
```

When referring to a control, you may omit the form name. If you do, the current or *active* form is assumed. If you try to refer to a control only by its name and that control isn't on the active form, VB says it can't find it. Frequently, because it's more specific, less confusing, and more RPG-like, the whole name is used in this book.

Changing Property Settings

You've already set some properties for a form and a couple of controls. You recall that properties are similar to display attributes for screen fields on the 400. VB, however, allows you to change property settings at run time. In fact, there are some properties that cannot be changed at design time, and must be changed with code statements.

Imagine that, on the AS/400, you can change the attributes for a screen field as the program is running. Instead of coding DDS specs:

```
A*  Input field "CUSIN" . . .

A                     CUSIN 6A 0 6 8

A     21                             COLOR(GRN)

A     22                             COLOR(BLU)

A     23                             COLOR(RED)
```

and setting indicators, in the RPG code, you could specify:

```
C              'GRN'        COLOR  CUSIN
```

if COLOR was an RPG op code.

An example of a VB language statement that changes a color property is:

```
frmMain.txtEditArea.ForeColor = &HFFFF&
```

In VB code, properties for controls are identified in this format:

```
FormName.ControlName.PropertyName
```

The general syntax for changing property settings is:

```
FormName.PropertyName = [argument1, argument2...]
```

for forms, and:

```
FormName.ControlName.PropertyName = [argument1, argument2...]
```

for controls.

The form name may be omitted, but if it is, the active form is assumed.

In RPG, changes to screen fields and indicators made by the program aren't seen by the user until the screen is written. In VB, changes take place as soon as the statements are executed, and no write to the screen is required. It's as if an implicit write is executed after each VB statement.

Other Properties

There are other property settings that control the appearance and function of objects. You can set the color of both the background and foreground, change the font style and size, etc. You can also change settings for functional properties like nondisplay (the *visible* property) and protect-field (the *enabled* property). Rather than present all possible properties for all objects, they are discussed as they are needed.

Step by Step: Getting Help on Properties

1. Open project EditText.
2. Bring up "frmMain" in the form design window by clicking "View Code" in the project box if it's not already displayed.
3. Select the command button "cmdOK" by clicking on it, and open the properties box by pressing F4.
4. Highlight the property "Default."

5. Press F1. You should see:

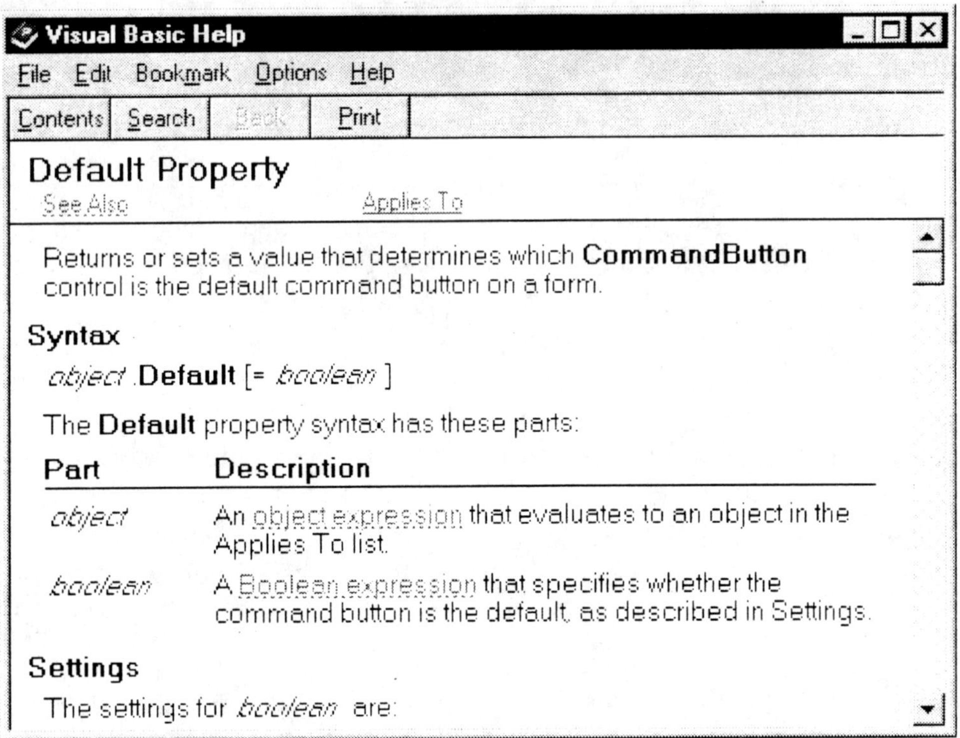

You've pulled up the help text for the property "Default." (Default determines which command button, if any, should be associated with the Enter key. On the form, the current default button gets a black border around it.)

"False" is the default for this property and the proper setting for this occasion. There's a text box on the same form that will require the Enter event. (Setting this property to "True" would take the "next line" capability away from the text box.)

6. Close the project. You needn't save the code.

Methods

A *method* is a procedure or function that operates on an object. Built-in methods come with Visual Basic—you don't have to create them. Just as a VB-supplied function (like UCase) operates on a variable, methods operate on a form or control.

For example, you control whether or not a form is visible with the *show method* and the *hide method*.

The syntax for methods, like properties, is:

```
FormName.MethodName   [argument1 argument2...]
```

for forms, and:

```
FormName.ControlName.MethodName   [argument1 argument2...]
```

for controls. Also like properties, the form name may be omitted.

Think of methods as being more like processes and properties as being more like attributes. Properties are set; methods are run.

An AS/400 analogy: When you cause a screen field to be highlighted by changing its display attribute to high intensity, that's like changing a property. When you cause a process to a screen to take place, like SFLINZ (subfile initialize), that's a method.

Examples of VB methods for forms:

```
frmMain.Hide                        ' hides a form

frmMain.Show                        ' shows a form

frmMain.PrintForm                   ' send a bit image of the form

                                    ' to the printer - like printkey
```

Examples of VB methods for controls:

```
frmMain.txtEditArea.Refresh         ' repaints the text box

frmMain.cmdOK.SetFocus              ' makes the OKButton the

                                    ' currently selected control
```

```
frmMain.lstPickOne.AddItem CustomerRecord        ' adds a record to a
                                                  ' subfile-like list box
```

An argument (parm) was only required for the last example.

Menus

Menus are like other controls, except they aren't drawn on the form—they're defined and then they appear along the top of a form, below the title bar.

Step by Step: Adding a Menu

1. Open the project EditText.
2. If "frmMain" is not in the code window, bring it up by selecting it in the project window and selecting "View Form."
3. Click on the "Menu" button in the toolbar: . You should see:

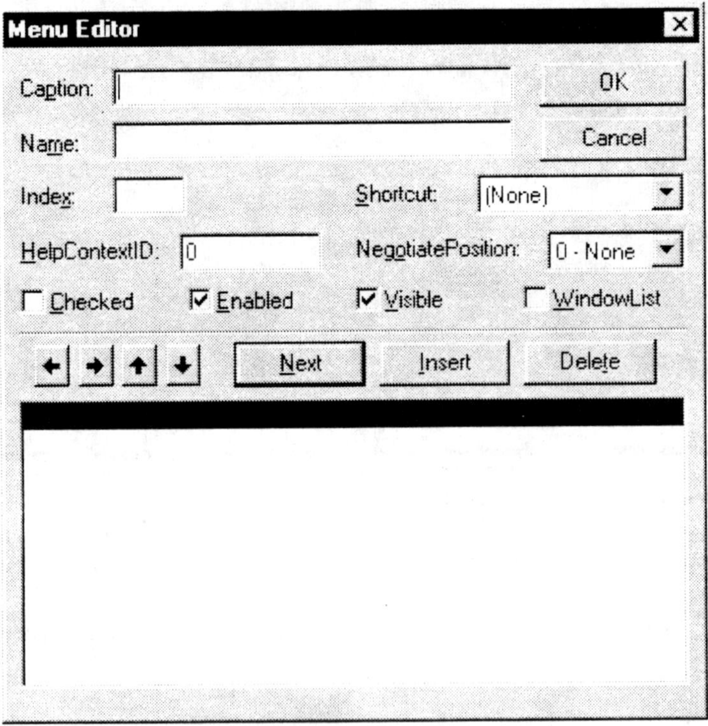

This is the menu design window. It's kind of an oddity in that there are no other code or design windows like it. The specs that define the menu are built outline-style in the box at the bottom.

4. Fill in the caption box with "File". The word "File" also appears in the box.

5. Fill in the name box with "mnuFile"—again using the preferred naming convention of a three-letter prefix identifying the control's class, and a descriptive suffix.

   These entries identify the caption that appears to the user on the menu (File) and the name of the menu ("mnuFile"). (The name is how you refer to this menu selection as well as how you refer to it in code.)

6. Click on the "Next" button to advance to the next outline item.

7. Click on the indent arrow located in the middle of the menu design window: .

   Notice the four little marks that indicate the indentation:

8. Fill in the caption box with "Exit".

9. Fill in the name box with "itmExit." Your screen should look like:

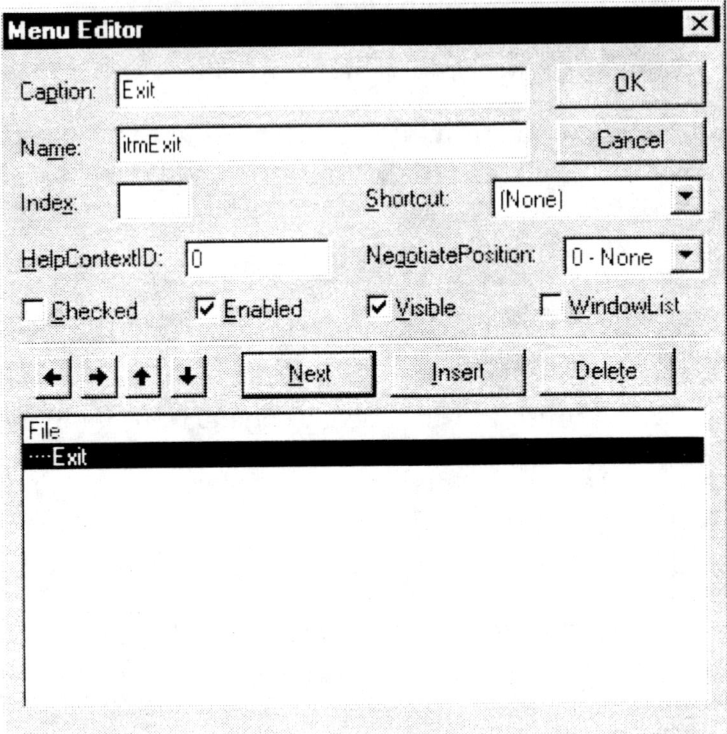

10. Click on "OK."

Now your form should have a menu along the top named "File," with one item in the menu named "itmExit" that has a caption of "Exit." Your form should look like:

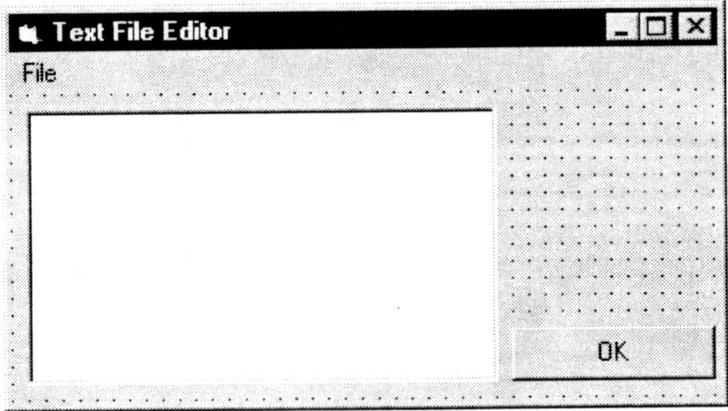

11. Click on the File menu. It should look like this:

What you have done is create a control, like a command button, that has a name and events.

12. Click on the item "Exit" to open the code window. You should see:

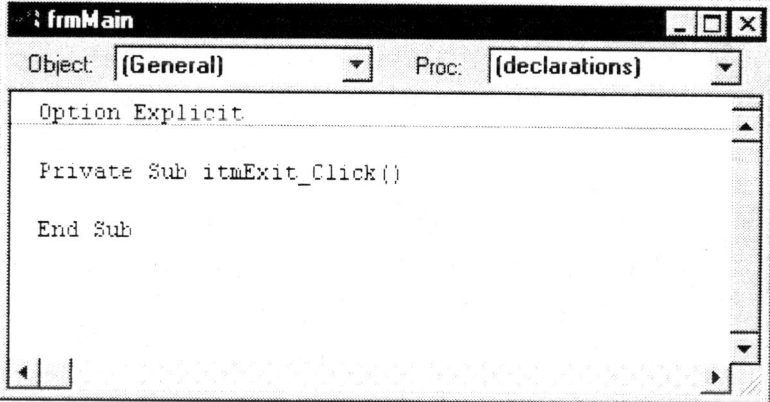

13. Add the BASIC statement "End" within the procedure:

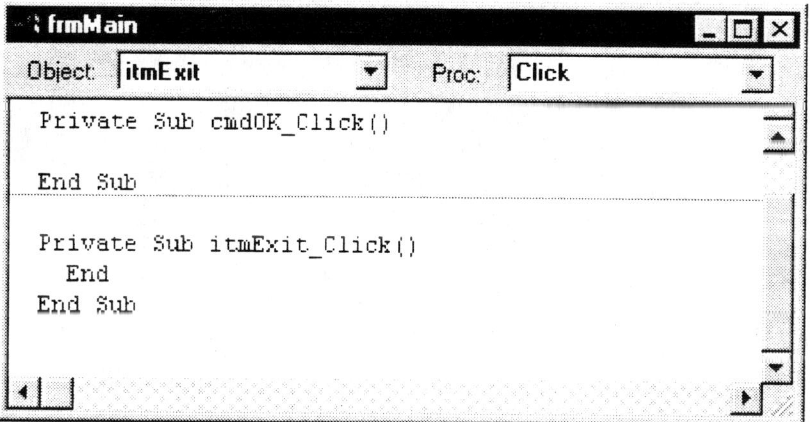

14. Click on the "Run" button on the toolbar.

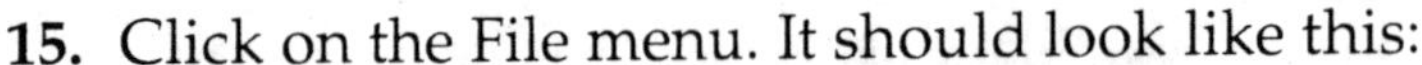

15. Click on the File menu. It should look like this:

16. Click on the menu item "Exit" to end the program.

17. Open the menu design window again.

18. In the caption box, the word "File" should be highlighted. Change it to "&File" to give the user shortcut access (Alt-F) to the menu, and to cause a little underline to appear under the F of "File." This is a Windows convention.

19. Click on "OK." Now, the File menu caption should look like this:

If you want another shortcut letter instead of F, insert the ampersand immediately before the letter. For example: Fi&le for the letter l.

20. Click on the "Run" button.

21. Hold the Alt key and press F to open the File menu.

22. Click on "Exit."

23. Open the menu design window again.

24. Highlight the line in the box for the entry "——Exit."

25. Open the list box labeled "Shortcut:" You should see:

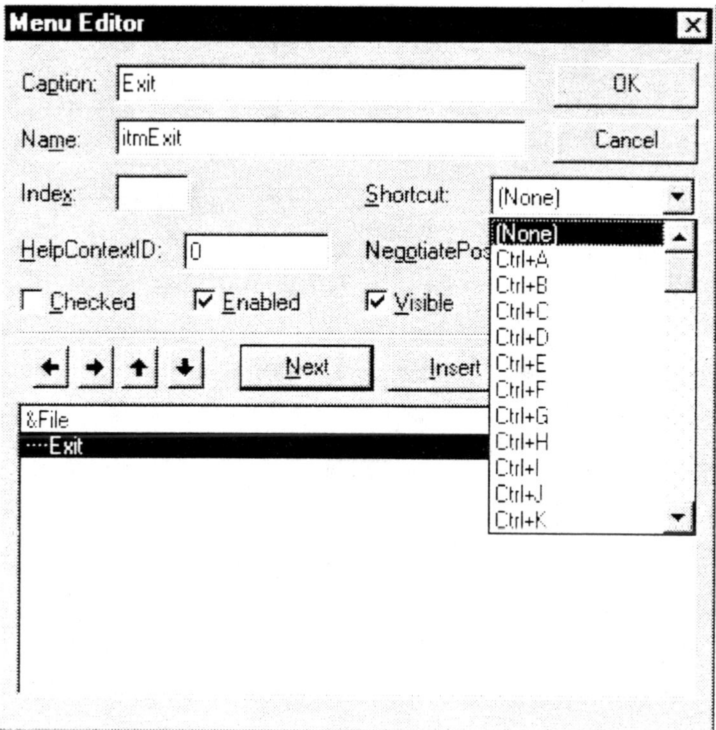

This is a list of the shortcut key combinations available for the Exit item.

26. Scroll down to "F3" and select it:

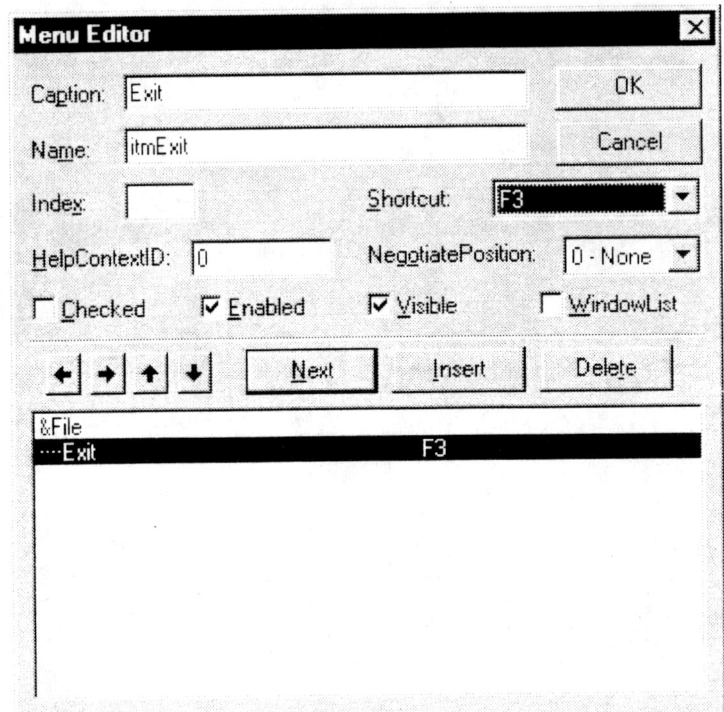

Note that the association between the exit item and "F3" is shown in the box.

27. Save your project. Other menus, items, and menu features will be added later.

Summary

Event-oriented Processing and Event Procedures

An *event* is an action the user takes, like clicking a mouse or pressing a key.

For each event, there is a corresponding procedure. You can bring a control's most common event procedure into the code window by double clicking the control.

All procedures within a module can be accessed from the object and procedures lists at the top of any code window.

General Procedures

Procedures are like RPG subroutines that you create. They're created by keying "Sub" or "Function" and "End Sub" or "End Function".

There are three kinds of general procedures—*Sub* procedures, *Function* procedures and *Property* procedures.

You can pass parms (arguments) to a procedure, and a procedure can change the value of the parm, or any other variable visible to the procedure.

Functions are procedures that return a value in the form of the function itself.

Sub procedures are called with the Call statement. Functions, because they become a value, are used in expressions.

Modules

Modules are like the calculation spec area of an RPG program. They are created by clicking the "New Module" button on the toolbar.

You can create procedures and functions in a module.

You can declare variables and constants in a module.

Objects and Properties

Objects are forms and controls. Objects have properties that are like attributes.

Properties are edited through the properties box.

Methods

A method is a procedure or function that operates on an object.

Whereas properties are set, methods are run or executed.

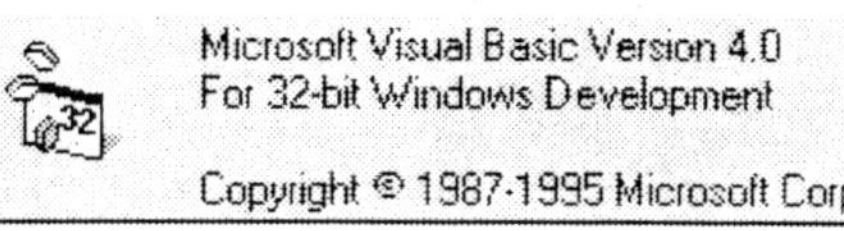

4

Controls

This chapter covers one of the most important components of a VB program—controls. The more common controls are presented here and more advanced controls are discussed later in Chapter 8.

What is a Control?

A control is an object that you draw on a form to enable or enhance user interaction with an application. You add menu controls to a form using the Menu Editor; all other controls appear in the Toolbox and are placed on a form by double clicking them or by clicking and then drawing them onto a form.

Controls accept user input or display output. Controls have properties that define aspects of their appearance, such as position, size, and color; and aspects of their behavior, such as how they respond to user input.

Controls can respond to events initiated by the user or triggered by the system. For example, you can write code in a button's click event procedure that loads a file or performs a calculation and then displays the result.

In addition to properties and events, you can use methods to manipulate controls from code. For example, you can use the Move method with some controls to change their location and size.

Each control has its own set of properties, events, and methods.

You recall that controls are the things you put on an otherwise blank form. Controls are command buttons, menus, text boxes, labels, plus a bunch more. They're represented by buttons in the toolbox:

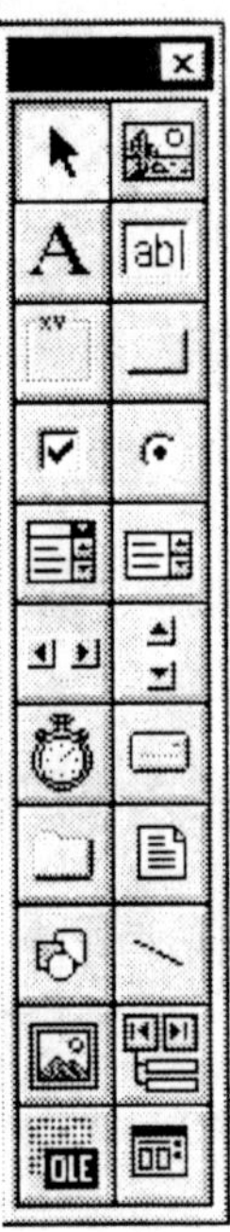

You've already worked with three important controls:

- The *command button*—a button on which the user can click to cause an action; use like the Enter key or command keys on the AS/400.
- The *text box*—a screen input or output field.
- The *menu*—more things on which to click to cause an action; presented on a drop-down list.

Some important points in understanding controls:

- The actions that can take place in a VB application (like clicking on a button or dragging the mouse) are called *events*. Each control has associated events that are appropriate for it. You can access the code area for events (procedures) by selecting from the procedures list above the code window.
- Each control has *properties* that are like attributes that you can set. Properties include settings for things like color and font size, plus settings for items such as visibility (like nondisplay), enable (like protect field), and caption (the text describing the control). Each control has only the properties that are appropriate for it. You access the properties for a control by selecting the control and then opening the properties box. You can also set control properties dynamically within code.
- A *method* is a process that can be called to act upon a form or control. Consider this analogy: An AS/400 operation such as SFLINZ (Subfile Initialize) is to a display screen what a Visual Basic method is to a form or control. SFLINZ isn't really an AS/400 screen attribute, and it's not really an RPG op code. It's more of a process you invoke to act on the display file, as is a VB method. You access methods in code.

Step by Step: An "Open File..." Form

1. Open the project EditText.Vbp.
2. Click on the "New Form" button: .
3. Resize and reposition the new form so it overlays nicely:

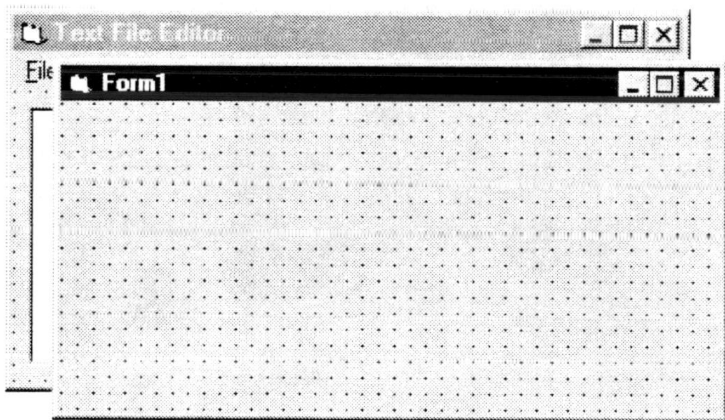

4. Select "Save File As..." from the File menu and save the source file for the new form as "OpenFile.Frm."

   The project box reflects the new form and its new source filename. Remember that the name of the source file for the form and the name of the form itself are two different things.

   When you clicked on the "New Form" button, the VB Development Environment gave the new form the name "Form1."

5. Select the new form by clicking on it, then press F4 to open the properties box for "Form1."

6. Scroll down to the "Name" property and change it to "frmOpen".

7. Scroll up to "Caption" and change it to "Open a File..." You should see:

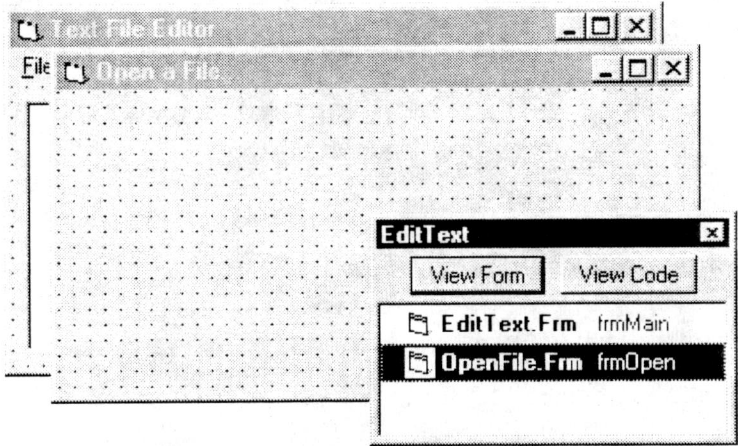

   The purpose of this new form, as its caption suggests, is to locate and load a file into your editor program.

8. Select form "frmOpen" to bring it to the front if it's not already there.

9. Double click on the "Drive List Box" button in the toolbox: .

10. Reposition the drive list box toward the bottom of the form:

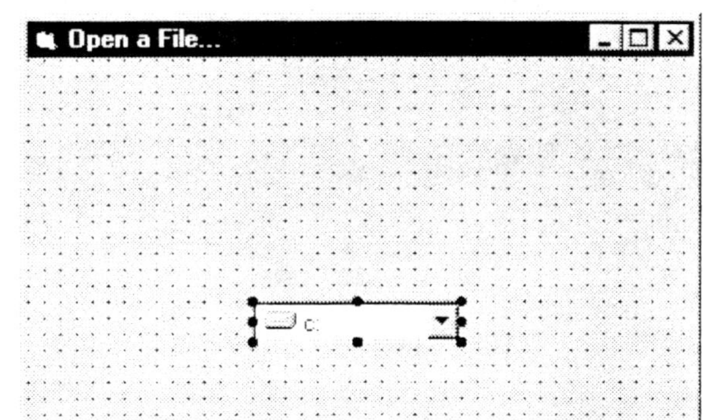

This control, called a *drive list box*, has only one function—to present a list of your disk and CD drives for selection. All of the function to accomplish this task is built into the control. You don't have to do anything.

11. Open the properties box for this control and change its name from "Drive1" to "drvBox".

12. Click on the "Folder List Box" (dir list box) control: .

13. Draw the control on the form, something like this:

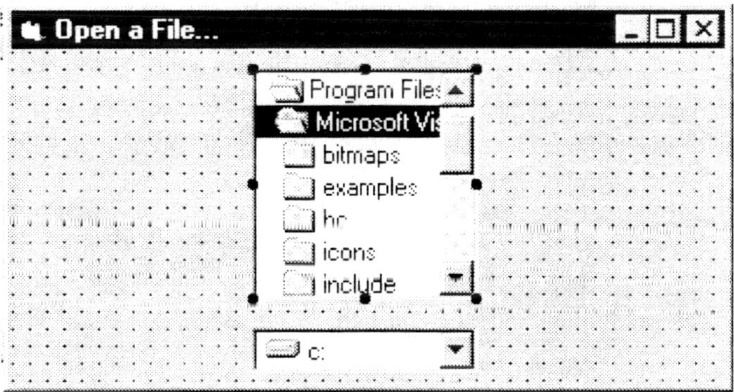

This control, the "*Folder List Box*," also has only one purpose—to display the folders in the selected drive. Notice that, even though you've only just placed the control on the form, it already is displaying actual folders.

14. Open the properties box for this control and change its name from "Dir1" to "flrBox".

15. Click on the "File List Box" control, [icon], and draw it on your form like this:

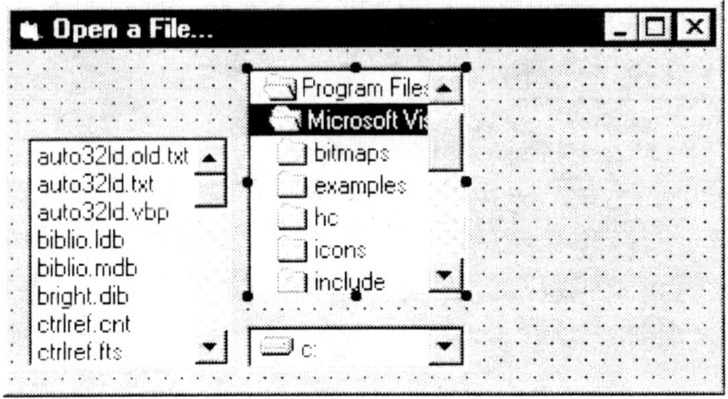

16. Open the properties box for this control and change its name from "File1" to "filBox".

17. Click on the "Text Box" button, [ab|], and draw it on your form.

18. Open the properties box for this control and change its name from "Text1" to "txtFileName".

19. Also in the properties box, scroll to "Text" and clear the entry "Text1."

20. Using the "Command Button" tool in the toolbox, [icon], draw two command buttons like this:

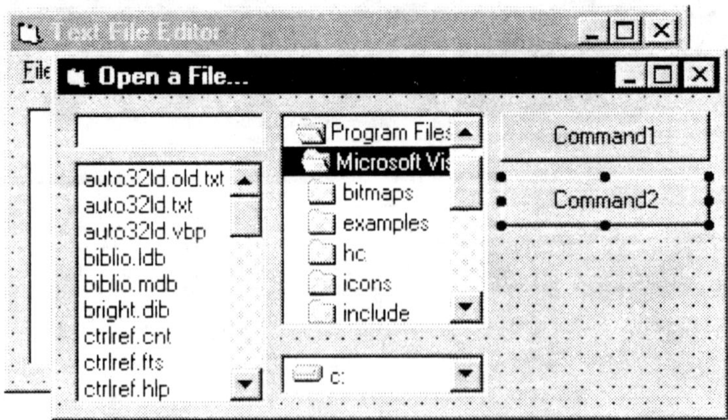

21. Select the top button, open its properties box, and change its name to "cmdOK".

22. Change its caption to "OK".

23. Change the property "Default" to "Yes". (This attaches this button to the Enter key. Notice the black border around the button.)

24. Select the bottom button, open its properties box, and change its name to "cmdCancel".

25. Change its caption to "Cancel". Your form should look like this:

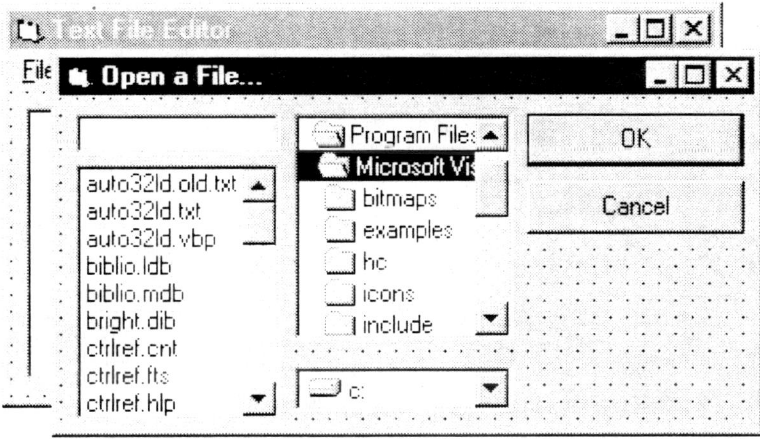

Starting to look pretty good, isn't it? Better save it.

26. Save your project.

These three new controls—Drive List Box, Folder List Box, and File List Box—have each, through built-in mechanisms, availed themselves of their respective system information. They must be associated with each other, though, so that when you click on a new drive, the folder box and the file box know about it. When you click on a new folder, the file box knows about it. But first, a little housekeeping.

Step by Step: Setting a Tab Index

1. Open the EditText project and bring "frmOpen" into the code window.

2. Press the Tab key on your keyboard. Press it again and again. The selected control advances as you press the key, but in the order that you created them. Unless changed, this is the order presented to the user.

3. Select the text box "txtFileName."

4. In the properties box, find "TabIndex" and change it to "0". (In VB, indices start with 0, not 1.)

5. Do the same for:

```
filBox          TabIndex 1

flrBox          TabIndex 2

drvBox          TabIndex 3

cmdOK           TabIndex 4

CmdCancel       TabIndex 5
```

   Notice that, as you select the different controls, the properties box displays the same property for editing for each control (where possible).

   Now as you tab around your form, the progression from control to control is logical. It's also what the user expects to see.

6. Save your project.

Step by Step: Associating the Drive, Folder, and File Boxes

1. Open the EditText project and bring "frmOpen" into the form design window.

2. Double click on the drive box, c: , to open the code window for the event "drvBox_Change."

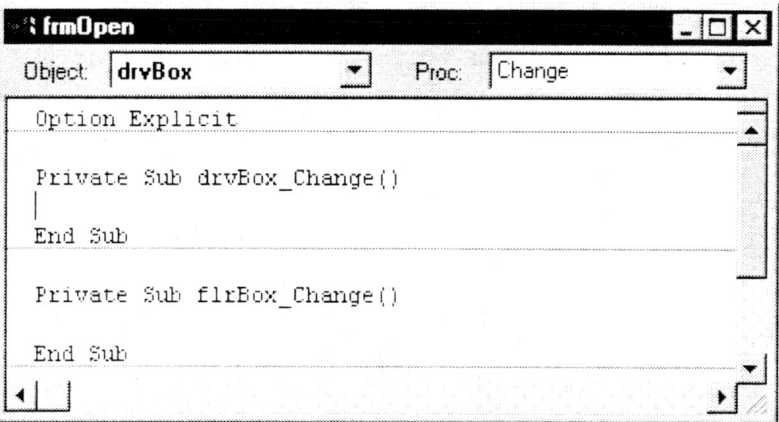

There are a couple of points worth mentioning. Recall that, when you double click on a control, the VB Development Environment opens the code window for the most commonly used event for that control. In this case, it's the change event.

The change event is like the CHANGE keyword for an AS/400 display file. When CHANGE is specified in the DDS for an AS/400 display file, and the user changes anything about a field, the indicator associated with the CHANGE keyword comes on. It's pretty much the same thing in VB, except that a change event for a control can be caused by the program as well as the user.

Other events are valid for a drive box. You can see the list and select event procedures from it by opening the procedures list box at the top of the code window.

3. Key in the following line of code between the Sub and End Sub statements (indenting looks good here):

```
Private Sub drvBox_Change()

  frmOpen.flrBox.Path = frmOpen.drvBox.Path

End Sub
```

It has been stated that there is a distinction between design time and run time. Only some properties for a control are available at design time; all are available at run time. The ones available at design time are listed in the properties box. For the drive box the property "Drive" is available only at run time, as is the case for the folder box property "Path."

4. Close the drvBox_Change code window and double click on the folder box:

This opens the code window for the most common event for a folder box—flrBox_Change.

5. Key in the following line of code between the Sub and End Sub statements:

```
Private Sub flrBox_Change()

  frmOpen.filBox.Path = frmOpen.flrBox.Drive

End Sub
```

So, you've set up kind of a small chain of events here. Whenever the drive selection is changed, the folder box property "path" gets changed, which causes the change event to register for the folder box control. When the change event happens to the folder box, it informs the file box by changing its property "path." Remember that the change event can be caused programmatically as well as by a user.

Okay, frmOpen is in pretty good shape. What is needed now is a means of accessing the form.

6. Close the code window and the form design window.

7. Select the first form "frmMain" in the project box and open its form design window.

8. Open the menu design dialog box.

9. Highlight the line "——Exit F3" in the box at the bottom like this:

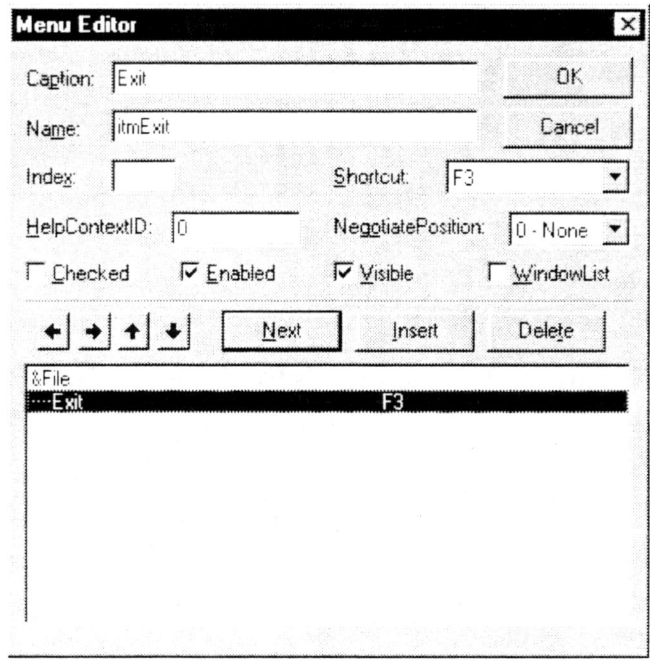

10. Click on the "Insert" button to provide a space for a new command.

11. Click on the caption box at the top and key "Open a File..."

12. In the name box, key "itmOpen"—all one word. That becomes the name of the control.

13. Click on "OK."

14. Click on the File menu on the form "frmMain." It should open and look like this:

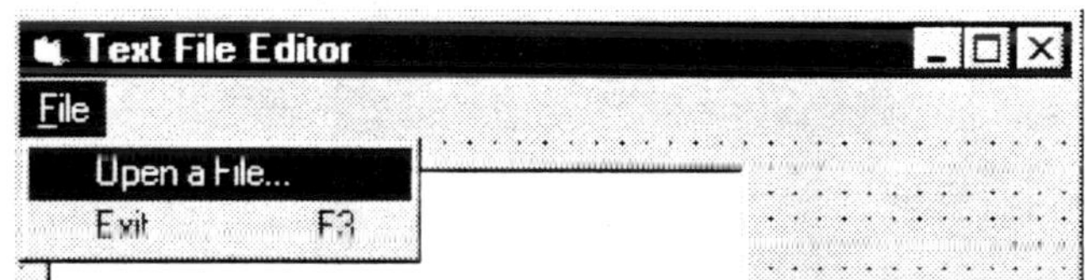

15. Click on the menu item "Open a File..." to open the code window for the click event. Add the following line of code:

```
Private Sub itmOpen_Click()

  frmOpen.Show 1

End Sub
```

The ".Show" part of this statement is a *method*—the *show* method. Recall that a method is a process that operates on a form or control. In this case, the process is to make the form visible.

The "frmOpen" part of the statement is the object of the operation.

Remember that some methods have arguments, some don't. The "1" part of the statement is the argument. It tells the show method to require the user to close the form in order to return to the prior form. You've seen this many times in Windows. Sometimes you can freely click on a window to bring it to the top of the underlying forms. Sometimes when you try to click an underlying form, you get a beep and are required to close the top form before you may return. The terms for these two types of show styles are "*modal*" and "*modeless*." The modal style requires the form to be closed. The modeless style does not require that the form be closed. The default is "0" for modeless.

Okay, so that's how you bring up the second form. You click on the menu item and that executes the statement that shows the form. As this is a form that opens a file to be edited on the first form, it only makes sense that the form be modal. Why let the user return to editing with a file load still pending?

Now what is needed is a way to get back from the second form to the first.

16. Bring up "frmOpen" in the form design window:

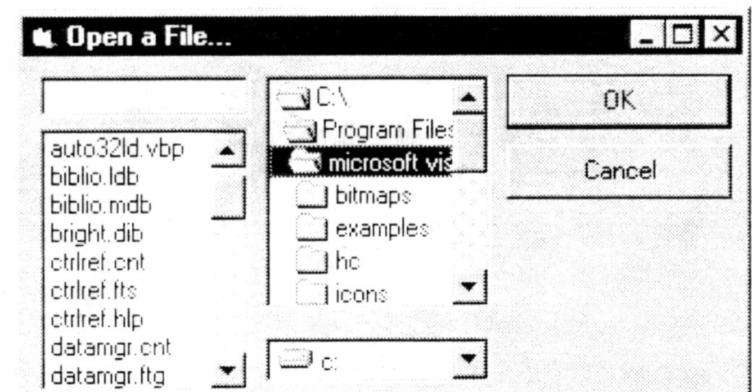

17. Double click on the "Cancel" button and open the code window for the event "Click."

18. Add the line between the "Sub" and "End Sub" statements:

```
Private Sub cmdCancel_Click()

  frmOpen.Hide

End Sub
```

Hide, as you might expect, is the opposite of Show. There are no arguments.

19. Save your project.

Although the functions behind the screens are yet to be added, the program runs well enough to illustrate how frmOpen is shaping up and how the drive, folder, and file controls are working.

20. Click on the "Run" button.

21. Open the File menu and click "Open a File...." You should see something like:

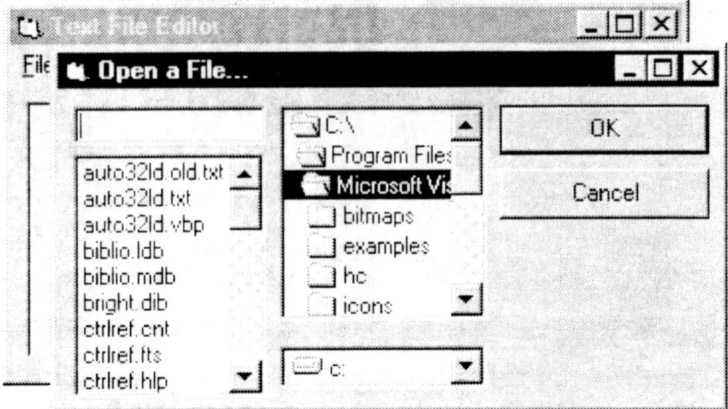

22. Double click on various folders in the folder box. The files in the file box should change correspondingly.

23. Put a diskette in drive A: and open the drive list box. Double click on the A: drive and see if both the folder box and the file box change.

24. While "frmOpen" is displayed, click on part of form "vermin sticking out underneath." It should beep.

25. Click on the "Cancel" button. You should return to screen "vermin.

26. Open the File menu and exit the program.

All of the functionality required to interface with the PC's drives, folders, and files has been built in to these controls. No wonder VB is popular.

In Chapter 8, you'll see how an add-in custom control called the *Common Dialog Box* can provide all this same functionality in one control.

The Label Control

VB labels are used like constants on an AS/400 display file. They identify fields, make titles, give information about available command keys, etc. There is a difference, though. The content of the label, or caption, is a property, and can be changed at any time. So, instead of the AS/400 way of putting multiple constants in the same place on the screen, all conditioned by indicators, you can just assign a new message to the same label. In this respect, a label is more like an output-capable field on the AS/400.

So the VB label control fills these two purposes. When you need a screen constant or an output-only field, use a label.

Step by Step: Adding a Label Control

1. Open the EditText project.
2. Bring "frmOpen" into the form design window. Make some room at the bottom of the form by dragging the form's edge down (about an inch).
3. Click on the "Label" control: A .
4. Draw the control on the form like this:

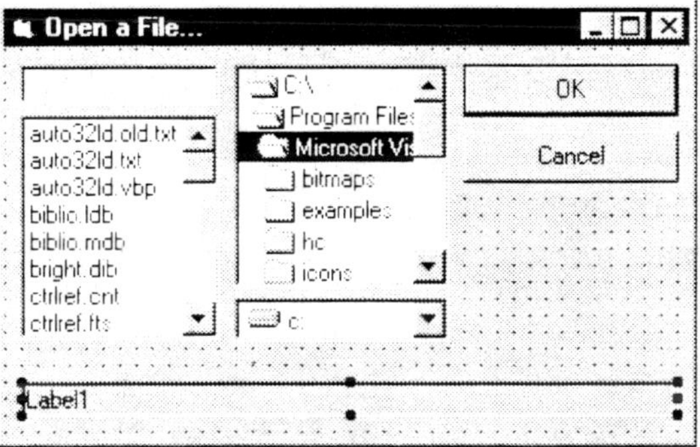

5. Open the properties box for the label and change its name to "lblFolder."
6. Scroll up to the "Border" property and change it to "1-Fixed Single."
7. Clear the contents of the caption property.

8. Add another label above the first like this:

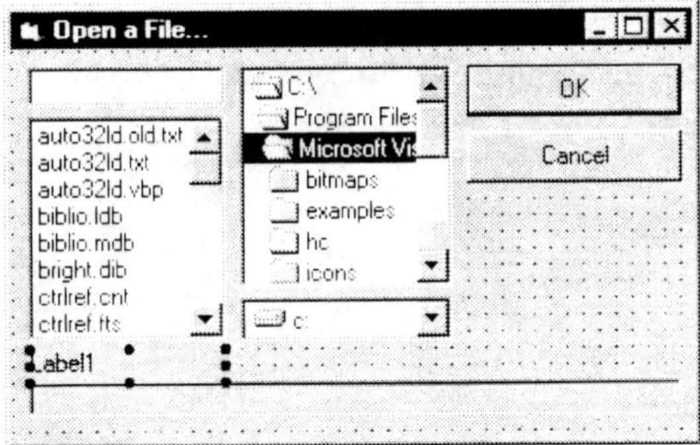

9. Change the caption of the label to "Folders:".

   The labels are used to display the currently selected folder like this (once some code is added to the project):

One label is being used as a constant (Label), and the other is being used as an output-capable field where the caption will change (lblFolder).

You may notice an inconsistency here. The label being used as a constant has not had the benefit of a name change. It's still named "Label." Customarily, VB programmers allow the VB Development Environment to name controls that are not referenced in code.

Design Logic Presented

There has been a lot presented that may not seem obvious, such as when to add a screen, how to overlay screens to show reference, and where to put access to other screens.

When to Add a Screen

As a programmer, you already know intuitively when to add a screen. You logically group related things on a screen, and display another screen when needed. There's nothing special about VB—you do it the same way.

The forms that ask for further information about something the user requests are called *dialog boxes*. You've used them many times in Windows applications. When you click on "Open a Project..." you get a dialog box asking for the name of the project. Remember the ellipsis—the "..." at the end of some captions? The "dot dot dot" means that a dialog box is opened when this control is clicked.

Some forms require that they be dealt with or canceled before the user may go on. You show these forms with an argument value of "1" and they are called modal.

How to Overlay Screens to Show Reference

With Windows style forms at your command, you can present more meaningful displays to the user. You can show a progression from screen to screen, and the path back. If a form seems to be an extension of another, present it that way. Try not to obliterate the underlying form. The forms should work together to achieve ease of use and present a good appearance.

Where to Put Access to Other Screens

On the AS/400, it is common to present access to other screens with command keys. The user presses F5, let's say, to see the customer inquiry display. With VB, access is more varied, and you have to make a decision as to where to put it. You could put access on a command button. If a screen is commonly displayed in the normal flow of your application, you may want to use the OK button to go to that screen. If access to a screen is exceptional or out of the normal flow, you may be better off putting access on a menu.

You don't want to clutter your screen with a bunch of buttons. Windows users are accustomed to seeing captions like "OK," "Go On," "Next," "Cancel," or "Close." However, if a lot of buttons are placed on a form, it gets confusing. If many buttons are presented, they should be related, as in a choice or "select one" situation.

Image and Picture Controls

One of the advantages of VB screens is presentation—what the user sees. Picture and image controls allow you to add bitmaps and icons to your forms. The two controls (image and picture) are very similar. The image control is the simpler of the two, and probably the most commonly used. The picture control has capabilities the image control doesn't (like displaying output from graphics methods and grouping controls), but it requires more overhead and doesn't stretch to fit the picture.

Step by Step: Adding a Picture to a Form

1. Open the EditText project and bring vermin up in the form design window.
2. Click on the image control button at the bottom of the tool box:  .
3. Draw the control on the form like this:

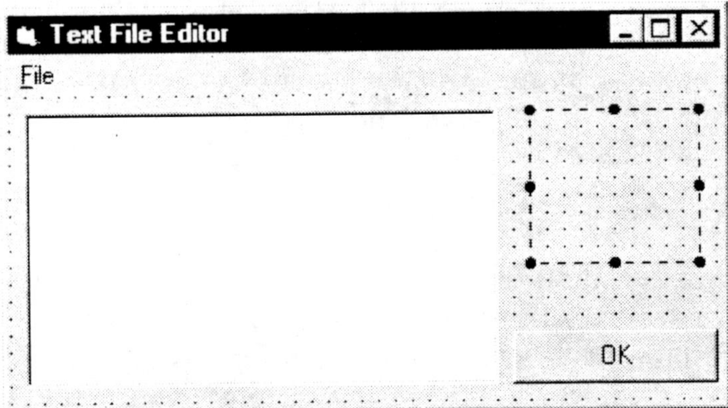

4. In the properties box for the image control, double click on "BorderStyle" to make it "1-Fixed Single." Lends a nice touch.

   The image control has a property called *stretch*. It controls whether the control changes size to fit the bitmap, or the bitmap changes size to fit the control. The default value is "False"—make the control fit the bitmap.

5. Change the stretch property to "True."
6. Scroll down the properties box until you get to the "Picture" property. This is how you load a graphic image into your control.

7. Double click on the property to open a dialog box asking for the name of a picture file. You may load a graphic supplied on the companion diskette (A:\VBBITMAP.BMP) or load one of your own.

   Okay, after centering the image a bit, the form should look like this:

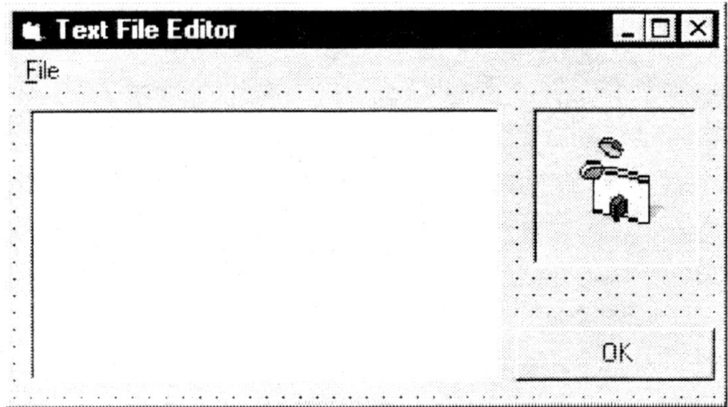

8. If all is well, save your project.

Text Box Control

A *text box* is the VB program's means of accepting keyed input. It is equivalent to an input/output-capable screen field on the 400. A text box is quite flexible— it may be too flexible.

Text in Windows applications is presented in a choice of fonts. Most fonts employ proportional spacing, that is, the letter i takes less space than the letter w. This makes it difficult to restrict the user to a certain length at the screen level by providing a field, say, 30-blanks wide. Maybe 30 blanks fit in there, but not as many Ws. You can use nonproportional fonts in limited situations (like columnar data,) but proportional fonts look much better.

This means that you can't provide input string length editing "by the inch." There is a property for text boxes, however, called "MaxLength" that limits the maximum number of characters input, regardless of width. You may also write code to perform edits on input strings. String handling techniques for VB are presented in Chapter 8.

A text box can be single-line, like an AS/400 screen field, or multiline. The difference is set in the *MultiLine* property. "False" is single-line and "True" is multiline. If a text box is multiline, it can either wrap the text or extend the text beyond the visible area by scrolling over as needed. Single-line text boxes extend the one line and automatically scroll over.

An example of wrapped text in a multiline text box:

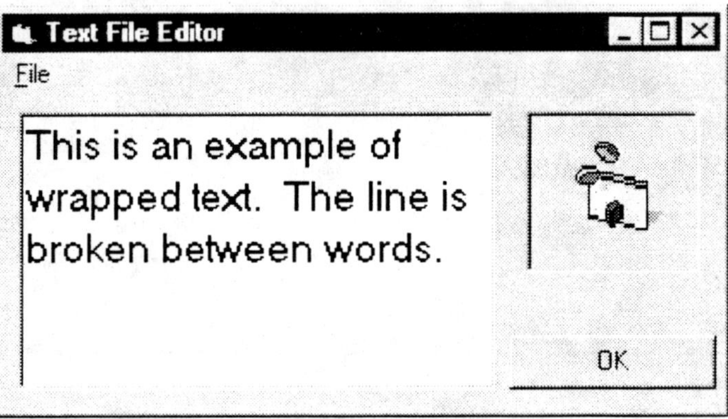

An example of nonwrapped text in a multiline text box:

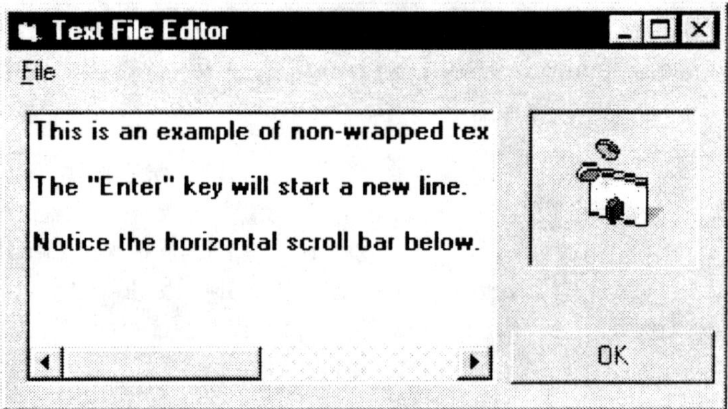

In the second example, the text disappears off to the right. The window scrolls over as you type. The Enter key starts a new line and brings the window back to the left. The"*ScrollBar*" property for the text box determines line wrapping. If the property is set to "1 - Horizontal," the text box acquires a scroll bar and the text won't wrap. If set to "0 - None," the text wraps.

So, you've already worked with a text box in the EditText project. You placed it on a form, named it "txtEditArea" and cleared it. A bit more is required to get the box ready for its text editor function, however.

Step by Step: More Text Box Settings

1. Open the EditText project and run the program.
2. Key more text into the "txtEditArea" text box than will fit. Observe how the box behaves. Try pressing the Enter key. Nothing happens, does it? There is no new line.
3. Use the arrow keys to move back and forth along the text. Press the Home key. Now the End key.
4. With the mouse, select some of the text.
5. While holding down the Ctrl key, press the letter X (this is the keyboard equivalent of selecting "Cut" from the Edit menu).

   The text box control has the capability of interacting with the clipboard. The text that you selected has been cut from the text box and placed in the clipboard.
6. Move the cursor to another part of the line. While holding Ctrl, press the letter V (this is the keyboard equivalent of selecting "Paste" from the Edit menu).
7. End the program and return to editing.
8. Select the "txtEditArea" box. Change the "Multiline" property to "True."
9. Run the program again and overfill the text box.

   See the difference? The text now wraps onto multiple lines. The Enter key acts as you would expect.
10. End the program and return to editing.
11. Select the "txtEditArea" box. Double click the "ScrollBar" property to change it to "1 - Horizontal."
12. Run the program again.

Now when you overfill the text box, it behaves as it did before it was multiline-capable, scrolling to the right automatically.

13. Press Enter to start a new line.

    Note that when a line is wrapped, it's only a display technique. Actual carriage-return and line-feed characters are not being inserted to start new lines. The string is considered to be one long, multiline string, not a series of one-line fields. If you stretch the box to a longer shape, the text takes advantage of it and stretches out as well.

    When you press Enter to start a new line, you are inserting a carriage-return and a line-feed character into the text. Stretching the text box does not change the text. It is being displayed according to the carriage-return and line-feed instructions.

14. End the program and return to editing.

15. Select the "txtEditArea" box. Double click on the "ScrollBar" property twice to change it to "3 - Both." Your form should look like this:

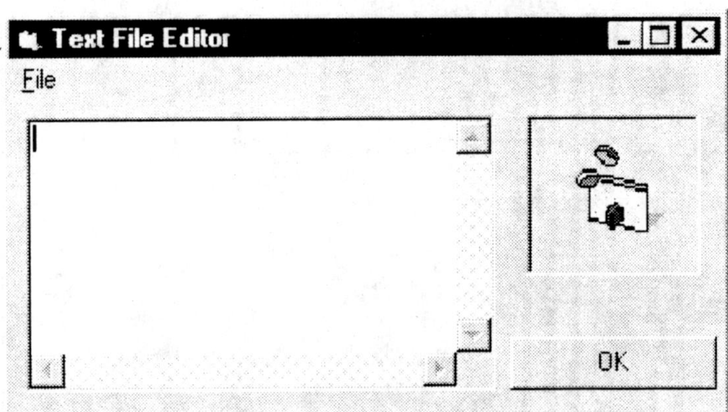

The vertical scrollbar doesn't work the same as the horizontal scrollbar. It does, however, give you the ability to scroll with the mouse. (You could do this before using the arrow keys.)

16. Save your project.

It was stated that, when you are placing a multiline text box on a form and you need the use of the Enter key to start new lines, you must make sure that no command button on the form has its "Default" property set to "True." (You recall that the "Default" property attaches the Enter key to a command button.)

There are more controls that haven't been discussed yet—obviously, there are more buttons in the tool box that haven't been discussed yet. These include the check box, option buttons, the list box, the combo box, and frames. They are presented, but rather than describe controls that you aren't ready to use yet, it is probably better to present the code that turns the controls you've learned so far into a real program. First, the fields used in a VB program.

Summary

In this chapter, you have learned the following about controls:

- Controls are the objects that you place on an otherwise blank form.
- Controls are represented as buttons in the tool box. You click the button and then draw the control on a form.
- The text box is the main method of accepting keyed user input. The text may be single-line or multiline, unwrapped or wrapped. The text box provides some of the functionality required for editing (e.g., cut, paste).
- The Command Button control is like the Enter key or F3 on an AS/400 screen. It's what the user clicks on to start an action.
- The Menu control is a drop-down version of command buttons. The user clicks on an item to initiate an action.
- The Drive List Box, Folder List Box, and File List Box controls interact with the operating system to provide access to stored files.
- The label control is used for descriptive on-screen text.
- The image control can be used to contain a picture (graphic). The picture may be loaded from the clipboard or from a ".BMP" file.
- Tab indices determine the order of keys as the user presses the Tab key.
- Forms are presented with the Show method, hidden with the Hide method.

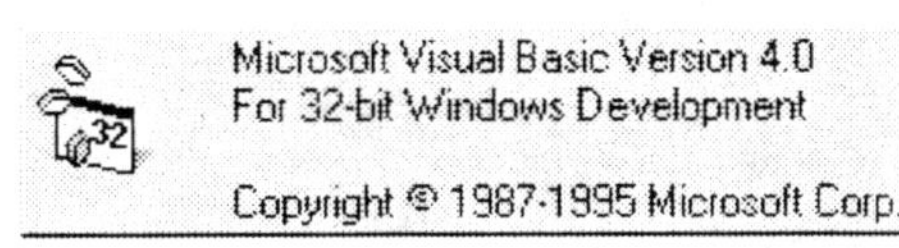

5

Fields Used in a Visual Basic Program

Just as in any other programming language, VB uses named fields to hold values. This chapter presents the fields available to a VB programmer (called data types), together with the concepts of *variable scope* and *lifetime*.

Variables

Variable Data Types

There are multiple data types available in VB. Some are familiar, some are not.

Although several data types are presented in this book, the ones that most resemble RPG are more useful to us and receive more extensive discussion.

You already know about AS/400 data types:

- Numeric fields
- Alphanumeric fields

For the purposes of illustration, also consider these to be data types:

- Data structures
- Arrays

Visual Basic has no less than 12 data types. The following exercise shows how to set a bookmark on the data type summary within VB help.

Step by Step: Online Data Type Summary

1. From the Help menu, select "Search for Help On..."
2. Key "data types, su" in the text box where the cursor is to bring up the listing for the data types summary. Press Enter.

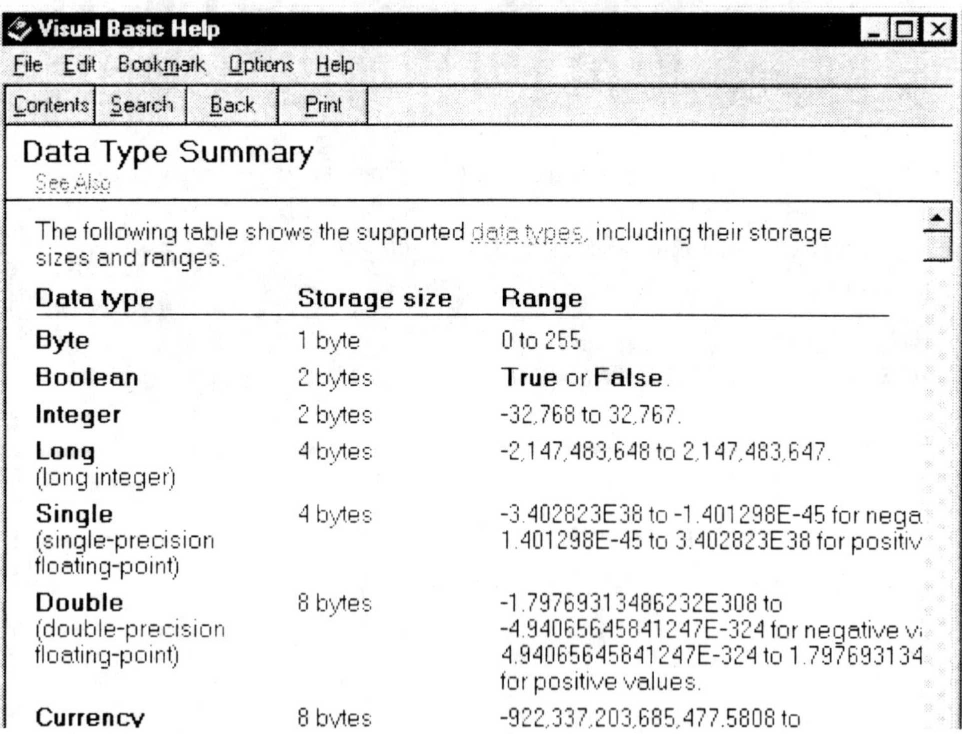

Visual Basic Help

File Edit Bookmark Options Help

Contents Search Back Print

Data Type Summary

See Also

The following table shows the supported data types, including their storage sizes and ranges.

Data type	Storage size	Range
Byte	1 byte	0 to 255
Boolean	2 bytes	**True** or **False**.
Integer	2 bytes	-32,768 to 32,767.
Long (long integer)	4 bytes	-2,147,483,648 to 2,147,483,647.
Single (single-precision floating-point)	4 bytes	-3.402823E38 to -1.401298E-45 for nega 1.401298E-45 to 3.402823E38 for positiv
Double (double-precision floating-point)	8 bytes	-1.79769313486232E308 to -4.94065645841247E-324 for negative v 4.94065645841247E-324 to 1.797693134 for positive values.
Currency	8 bytes	-922,337,203,685,477.5808 to

This is a summary of all the VB data types, storage size, and range of values. This is handy to keep available.

5. Open the Bookmark menu and click on "Define..."

   What this does is create a quick path through help to the data types summary. You can define bookmarks at other places as well. Just get to the spot you want and then create a bookmark. Bookmarks are defined to the VB Development Environment's help system itself, not to a project. That means that the bookmark will be there for all projects, in both the 16- and 32-bit environments, until you remove it.

6. Click on "OK."
7. Return to the VB Development Environment.
8. To see if the bookmark works, go into any help topic by pressing F1.
9. Open the Bookmark menu. You should see:

10. Click on "1 Data Type Summary." You should see the data types summary.

Numeric Data

Back to data types. RPG programmers are used to defining numeric data as being so many bytes long, with so many of those bytes being post decimal (to the right of the decimal point). Being able to define numeric fields precisely allows you to manipulate data within them.

For example, consider the following RPG code:

```
   *  Add to TOTAL ( a 9 byte, 3 post decimal position field) . . .

 C                    ADD   AMOUNT      TOTAL          93
```

```
      *  Trim the post decimal positions for summary display . . .

C                   Z-ADDTOTAL         DSPTOT        60
```

Of course, there are other ways to do the same thing in RPG, like in a data structure, but you get the point.

In VB, you are given several rigid choices for numeric fields and you must select from them. The numeric data types are:

- *Integer Data Type*—Integers (also called short integers) are whole numbers ranging from -32,768 to 32767. You can't express a fraction with an integer.
- *Long Data Type*—The long type (also called long integers) are whole numbers ranging from about negative 2.1 billion to about positive 2.1 billion. Again, you can't express a fraction with a long integer.
- *Single and Double Floating-Point Data Type*—Single and double floating-point variables are similar. Single can accommodate any value you're likely to use. Double can accommodate much more. The term *floating-point* means the decimal point floats around to accommodate whatever value the variable contains. That's why manipulation like you're used to is not as easy. You have to use different methods, which are presented later in this book.
- *Currency Data Type*—A currency variable is like the single and double type in that any value not found in astronomy is accommodated, but the decimal point is fixed. Currency is approximately the equivalent of a 19-byte field with four post-decimal positions. Obviously, it's intended for calculations involving money.

Character Data

String Data Type

String variables are character fields. They can be fixed or variable length, depending on how you define them. Both have their useful occasions. If defined with no length specified, the length is variable and limited to about 65,000 bytes.

Although there is nothing similar to a VB variable-length string in RPG, it can be very handy when you get used to using it. In RPG or CL, since variables are of fixed length, finding the last nonblank character is often required for concatenation. With a variable-length string, the field is automatically lengthened or shortened to fit, so concatenation is easy.

Variant Data

Variant Data Type

There is a data type within BASIC that is both numeric and alpha, called a *variant*. If a variant field contains numbers, it's numeric. If it contains alphanumeric data, it's a string. The length, naturally, is variable. VB likes the variant type. It's the default type for variables.

With all that flexibility comes a certain amount of confusion. For example, if you specify the plus sign (+) between two variants that contain strings, you get concatenation. If you specify the plus sign between two variants containing numeric data, you get addition. What happens when one variant is characters and the other is numeric? Well, if VB can convert the string variant into a number, then you get addition. If not, you get concatenation. So the content of the variable determines the operation performed. Not acceptable, really.

However flexible and convenient the variant data type may be, its worth to us as RPG programmers is limited. You're used to working with variables of fixed type and length and make efforts to match things up accordingly. Explicit declaration and control are preferred whenever possible—especially when dealing with AS/400 client/server applications.

Special Data Types

Date Data Type

As its name suggests, the *date* data type is for holding a date and time. Date variables display dates according to the short date format recognized by your computer. Times display according to the time format (either 12- or 24-hour) recognized by your computer.

- *Byte Data Type*—The byte data type is new to VB. It's a means of manipulating binary data, usually in an array.
- *Boolean Data Type*—A Boolean variable is like an indicator in RPG. It can have a true or false, on or off status. Also new to VB, the Boolean data type is really an integer. Previously, a true/false value was kept in an integer. You could set an integer to "false" and it would get a value of "0," or "true" and it would get a value of "-1" (any nonzero value is considered to be true). Now there is a specific data type for this purpose. When you need a switch, like an indicator, use a Boolean variable.

Object Data Type

In PC programming, there is the concept of an *object*. The concept exists on the AS/400 as well, but the PC developers take it a bit further. On the 400, an object is anything that has been created and given a name. That is, it's anything you can put into a library, including libraries themselves. Among PC developers, an object is anything that is defined, but not necessarily named. An object can be anything that you can conceive of as a unit. An example of an object with no name is a range of cells in an Excel spreadsheet. If this set of fields is logically connected, it can be an object. At the other end of the spectrum, an entire application, like Excel or Word, is an object, as well.

Objects don't always have a name, so you may declare a variable to represent a reference to them. That variable is of the object data type.

User-defined Data Type

In VB, the programmer is allowed to define a mix of singular types into a new, more complex type.

The user-defined data type is very similar to an RPG data structure. You can assemble simple data types (like integers and strings) into a complex unit with its own name, just like in RPG. But where, in RPG, the data structure is used like a complex field, VB considers it to be a definition for a data type. From then on, you can declare a variable and specify that its type is the one defined by the programmer.

Here is an AS/400 analogy: In RPG you can specify an externally described data structure. Consider this RPG input specification:

```
I DSNAME1  E  DSFILENAME

I DSNAME2  E  DSFILENAME
```

The data structures named "DSNAME1" and "DSNAME2" are defined by reference to an externally described file "FILENAME." A user-defined data type in VB is the same, except the description for the structure is contained inside the VB program. So you could define a structure as a user type named "Record," and then define variables that are of type "Record."

Arrays

An array in BASIC is just like an array in RPG. It's just multiple fields, all with the same name, that are referred to by index. All the elements are of the same type except variant arrays, which can vary. (Imagine having an array that is part numeric and part alpha. Another reason to stick to nonvariant types.)

There's an important difference between RPG and BASIC arrays. Unless you specify otherwise, the index for a VB array starts with element zero. In other words, if you define an array with 100 elements, the VB index for that array goes from 0 to 99. In RPG, the first element of an array is element 1, and referring to element 0 causes an array index error. Again, you can make VB behave just like RPG by specifying that the index for an array start at element 1 when the array is defined. Defining data types is presented later in this chapter.

BASIC is capable of something that RPG is not—multidimensional arrays. In fact, you can declare an array with up to 60 dimensions (but you're more properly limited by memory restrictions). Multidimensional arrays are not explored in this text. See the *Visual Basic Programmer's Guide* for more information.

Arrays can be dynamically redefined in VB. That is, you can define an array with, say, 10 elements to start, and then redefine it with more elements as needed. A word of caution, though. When you redefine an array in VB, the contents of the array are cleared unless you specify that the contents be preserved. (See the ReDim statement and the Preserve clause.)

Data Type Suffixes

Each data type, except the user type, can have a suffix that defines the type. For example, to implicitly declare a string variable named "CustomerName," you could refer to it in code like this:

```
CustomerName$ = TextBox.Text.
```

The "$" at the end of the name makes it a string when implicitly defined. A suffix of "none" or no suffix, causes a variable of type variant to be defined. Use of this feature of VB is not recommended, and is not used in this book, but you should be aware of it.

Scope

Scope refers to the extent to which a variable or procedure is *visible*. You can make VB act like the different parts of a program are unknown to each other (an essential element of object-oriented programming). If you define a variable within a procedure, it is only known to that procedure. If you try to refer to the variable elsewhere in the program, you get an error. This gives you the latitude to use the same name for distinct variables used in different parts of your program.

Using an AS/400 analogy: This is like calling an RPG program from within another RPG program. The fields used in the called program are not available to the calling program. The *scope* of the fields is limited to the programs they're in, even if fields in the two programs share the same names. Suppose that subroutines within an RPG program behaved the same way. Fields in one subroutine are not *visible* to another subroutine.

Variables that are only visible to their own procedure are said to be *local variables* and are defined with the Dim or Static statement. Variables that are visible to all forms and modules are called *public* or *global variables,* and are defined with the Public or Global statement.

There's a third level of scope called *module level* that is kind of a mix. It's visible to all procedures in a module, but not to other modules or forms. Module-level variables are defined using the Private, Dim, or Static statement in the declarations area of a module. They are not used in this book because things are confusing enough, but they're useful nonetheless.

The following illustration shows how scope works.

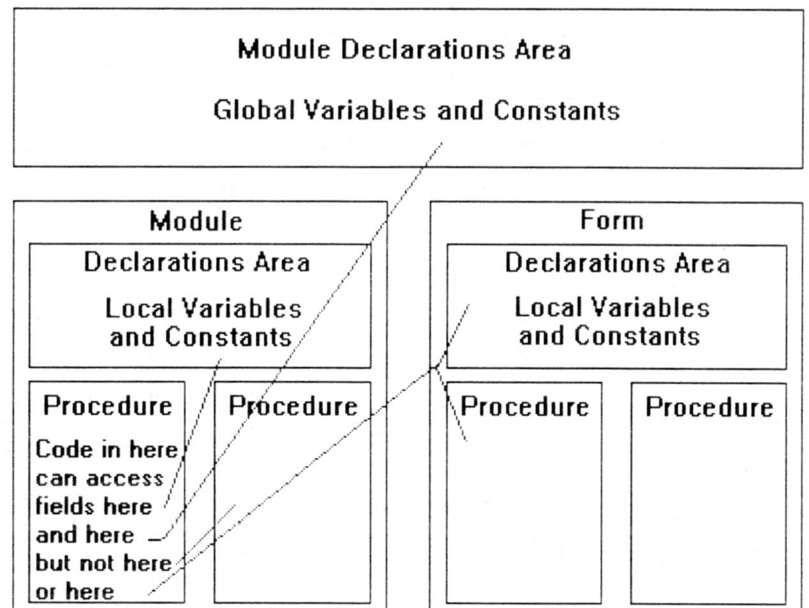

The code in each box can "see" the fields in the boxes above it, if you will. The code can't see fields below or on either side.

In RPG, it's common to use the same work field throughout your program. You might clear the field before reusing it, but you're using the same field nevertheless. In VB, you could use the same name in different procedures, but the field would be different. This is probably a feature of VB that you don't want to take advantage of at this time. Again, the reason is to keep VB as familiar as possible and to minimize confusion.

Dealing with scope in an RPG manner means that you have to have a program area that can be accessed by all other program areas. The declarations and general procedures area of a *form* won't do. It is not visible to other forms or modules.

You recall that *modules* are like AS/400 calculation specs. Modules, as they are not part of a form, are visible to all forms and other modules. For now, this is where the declarations and general procedures should be kept. One exception is made for work fields. The contents of a work field only matter while it's being used within a procedure, and the declaration of the variable equivalent to clearing it.

Lifetime of Variables

Variables in VB procedures are thought to have a *lifetime*. That is, they keep losing their contents. What happens is they keep getting a new assignment in memory. If a variable is declared within a procedure using the Dim statement, the variable is cleared every time the procedure is executed. You can prevent the variables from being cleared again and again by substituting Static for Dim (see "Declaring Variables" later in this chapter).

Constants

The RPG statement:

```
I                    'Error Message'   C              CONNAM
```

defines a constant named "CONNAM" with a value of "Error Message." Constants in VB, like other languages, are named references to a declared value. A constant can't be changed by the program.

Symbolic Constants

In VB, constants take on more of a role than in RPG. Consider this RPG code:

```
I              '1'                C        HEADER

I              '2'                C        DETAIL

I              '3'                C        TRAILR
```

This defines three constants "HEADER," "DETAIL," and "TRAILR." Now, if you coded like this (assume "RECTYP" to be a record type field from one of three record formats):

```
        C            RECTYP                IFEQ     HEADER
```

instead of:

```
        C            RECTYP                IFEQ  '1'
```

you would be using constants like VB does. It's much more descriptive. If you define two VB constants called MODAL—equal to "1" and MODELESS—equal to "0," then you could say:

```
FrmOpen.Show MODELESS
```

which is more descriptive than:

```
FrmOpen.Show 0
```

Constants defined for this purpose are called *symbolic constants*.

Of course, VB also uses constants for the usual reasons like holding message text and long literals.

Names for Constants

As a convention, VB programmers usually declare constants in all uppercase letters with the underscore character used to separate words. That way, you immediately know what kind of field it is.

Examples of constant names are:

```
BAD_RETURN_CODE

ERROR_MESSAGE_1

DEFAULT_CAPTION

RESET_VALUE
```

Additionally, constants supplied by the VB Development Environment have names beginning with "vb," and then a regular upper- and lowercase VB name. Examples of VB-supplied constant names are:

```
vbRed

vbKeyF3

vbMaximize

vbShapeCircle
```

VB-supplied Constants

Constants are liberally used in VB to allow more descriptive code than is possible with literals. As a convenience, a collection of values has been assigned to descriptive constant names included with Visual Basic.

Instead of coding:

```
frmMain.BackColor = &HFF&
```

you can code:

```
frmMain.BackColor = vbRed
```

with the help of the constant.

VB-supplied constants are made available through additions to the VB Development Environment called *references*. Objects contained within these references are in turn made available to you through the *object browser*.

Step by Step: A First Look at the Object Browser

1. Bring up VB or start a new project. Double click form1 to bring up the code window for the click event. Key in this partial statement:

```
Form1.BackColor =
```

2. Click on the object browser button on the toolbar:  .

   This is the object browser dialog box:

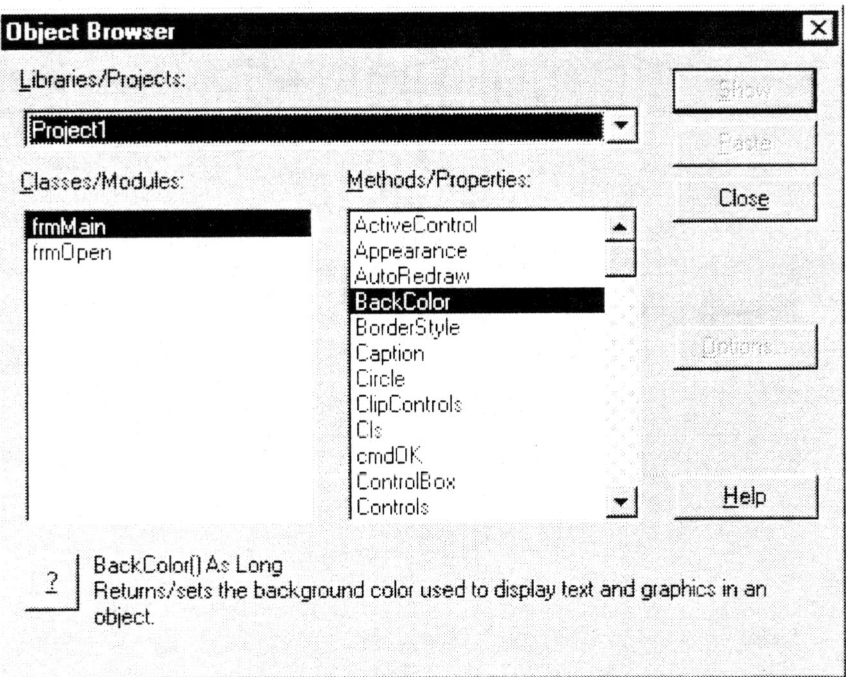

3. In the Libraries/Projects box select "Visual Basic objects and procedures." In the Classes/Modules box, you see the different objects that are available to your program by reference—that is, things that can be referenced.

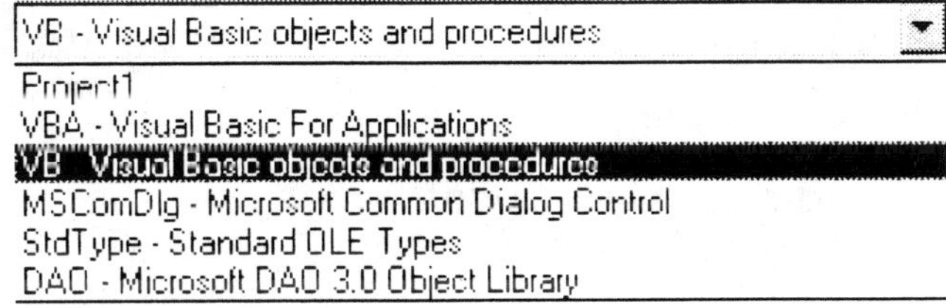

4. Select "ColorConstants" in the Classes/Modules box and "vbRed" in the Methods/Properties box.

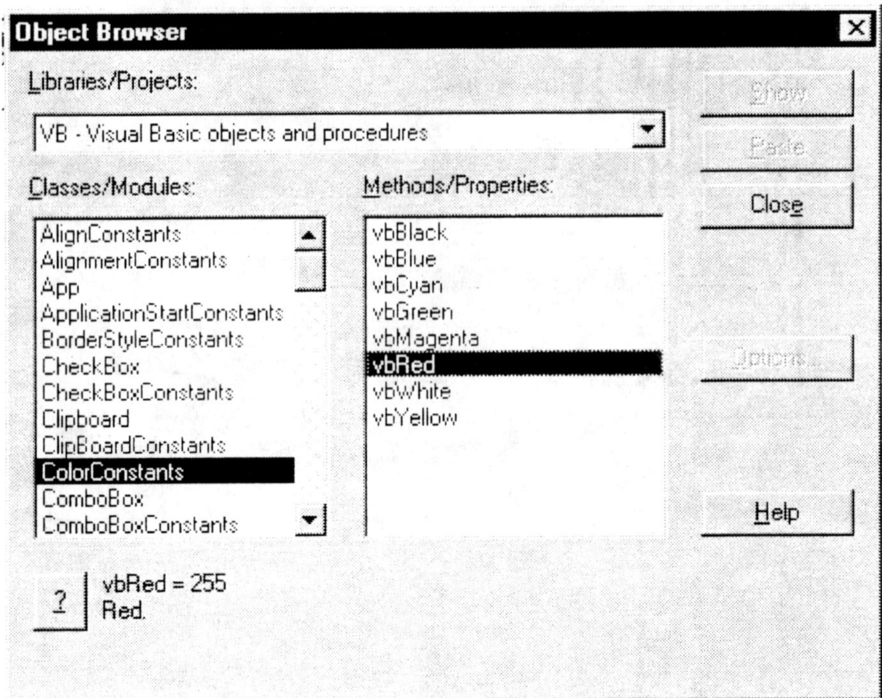

Notice the brief explanation of the purpose and value for the constant in the lower-left corner of the box. Also notice the "Paste" button. You may copy the name of the constant (vbRun) to your program.

5. Click on "Paste" to copy the constant to your code.

   These constant names are available to your program without further definition—like "UDATE" in RPG.

6. To complete the illustration, run the program. You should get a big red square.

7. End the program and discard the code.

Declaring Variables

Fields within Controls

Let it first be said that many of the fields you use in a VB project are built in to the controls. A label, for example, has the caption property, which is really a field; a text box has the text property, which is also really a field. Instead of defining the fields with statements, they are provided intrinsically as properties.

When referring to a property in code, you must do it like this:

```
FormName.ControlName.PropertyName
```

For example, the text field (property) in a text box named "txtCustomerName" on a form named "frmInput"is referred to like this:

```
frmInput.txtCustomerName.Text
```

Recall that, when you're coding *within a form module* (not a *standard* module) you may omit the form name.

Additionally, each class of control has a default property. That is, a control, referred to only by its name, with no property specified, defaults to its most common property. For a text box, the default property is "Text," for a label the default property is "Caption." The code:

```
TestString = txtCustomerName
```

is the same as:

```
TestString = txtCustomerName.Text.
```

You recall that fields in a VB program are of two scoping types—local and global. Global variables and constants provide the most RPG-like code.

Some constants and a variable are needed in the EditText project. These constants and the variable are defined as Global in scope to be more RPG-like.

Global variables are defined in the declarations area of a *module*, using the Public statement. So the next step in the EditText project is to add a module. For most of your projects, one module is enough. There, you can keep all your general procedures as well as the field definitions.

Step by Step: Creating a Standard Module

1. Open the EditText project.
2. Click on the "New Module" button on the toolbar:  . You should see:

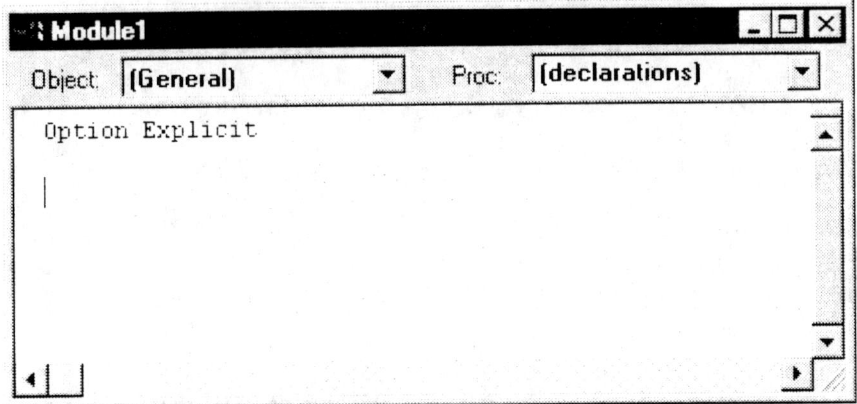

This is the area for declaring variables and defining procedures.

3. Click "Save File As..." on the File menu.
4. Save the new module file in your EditText directory under the name "EditText.Bas."

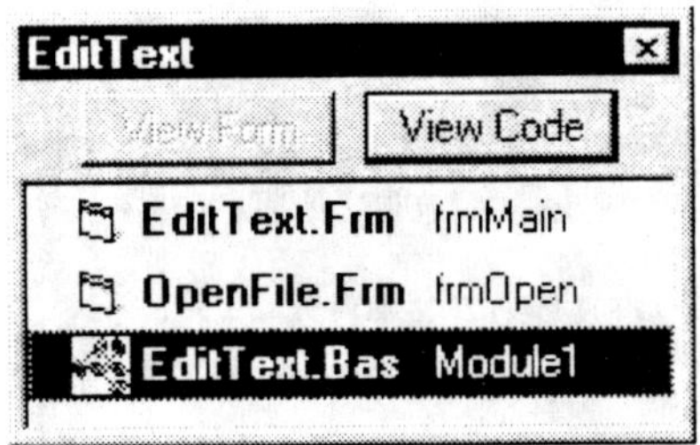

The new module has been added to your project under its new source file name "EditText.Bas." Notice that the "View Form" button is disabled. That's because there are no forms associated with standard modules.

5. Save your project.

Scoping Variables

Scope

Scope, as was previously explained, is the extent to which a variable is visible to other parts of a program. *How and where you define your variables determine their scope.* Variables may be declared as either local or global, in either procedures or modules.

Scope	Local	Global
Procedure Level	All fields are local to the procedure in which they appear.	Not applicable. You cannot declare public variables within a procedure.
Module Level	Fields are available to the procedures in the module in which they appear only.	Variables are available to all procedures in all modules.

Fields Defined in Procedures—Dim and Static

All fields defined within a procedure are local to that procedure. No other procedures can access them.

Use the keyword Dim to declare a variable within a procedure. Public and Global are not valid for a procedure variable.

Dim declares a variable that is only visible to the procedure (or module), in which it's defined. (Dim is short for dimension, which isn't very descriptive, so the word Private was provided as the preferred equivalent for module-level declarations.)

If declared with Dim within a procedure, the content of the variable is cleared each time the procedure is run. Dim, then, is well suited for work variables used within a procedure.

Static works like Private or Dim, except the variable isn't cleared each time the statement is encountered. Only the first time.

Fields Defined in Modules—Public and Private

Recall that there are both form and standard modules. Both types have a declarations area where variables may be declared as either Private or Public.

If you define a variable with Dim in the declarations area of a form or module, it will be visible to all procedures in that form or module, but not to other forms or modules.

Public declares a global variable. You may only declare public variables in the declarations section of a module. (Using this approach gives you the most RPG-like access to variables.)

The only place it makes sense to declare a global variable is in a standard module. If you put one in a form module, it's still only visible to the procedures in that module anyway—the same result as declaring it as private.

Examples of global declarations (made within the declarations area of a standard module):

```
Option Explicit

Public CustName as String           'Customer name

Public CustNumber as Long           'Customer number

Public CustBalance as Currency      'Customer balance
```

These fields are available to all procedures in all modules.

Examples of local declarations for work fields (made within a procedure):

```
Private Sub Form_Load()

 Private ArrayIndex as Integer      'Work field for arrays

 Dim WorkSubTotal as Double         'Work field for totals

 etc....
```

These fields are only available within the procedure for which they are defined, and they are cleared each time the procedure is executed.

> ***Note***: *The keyword Private on the Sub line refers to the procedure itself. It has nothing to do with the scope of the variables inside.*

One more example for completeness.

```
Private Sub Form_Load()

 Static RunningTotal as Currency    'Work field - doesn't get cleared

 etc....
```

This field is local to the procedure in which it's defined, but it isn't cleared each time the procedure is executed.

Fixed-length Strings

Visual Basic is capable of fixed-length definitions for strings. This feature makes manipulating the contents of the variable more familiar to RPG programmers.

A variable-length string, however, is handy for text handling in that the length of the variable is altered to fit the value it contains. This is convenient when joining strings.

Fixed-length strings are defined like this:

```
Private WorkString as String * 10

Static HoldName as String * 35

Public CustomerName as String * 35
```

The syntax is pretty obvious. A string becomes fixed in length when defined with "*" and a value to indicate the number of bytes.

The last definition in the above example is of particular interest. This definition:

```
Public CustomerName as String * 35
```

renders a fixed-length alpha field that is available to all parts of the program. This is the type of character field with which RPG programmers are most comfortable.

Declaring User-defined Data

The user-defined data type is really just simple variables grouped together like an RPG data structure and given a name. There is a distinction, though. The definition name is not a variable—it's just a description that serves as a format or model for defining a real variable. A proper analogy to RPG is not found, but defining a user data type in VB resembles defining an internally described file in RPG. A large block of data is described by defining subdivided fields within it.

This is an example of a user type definition:

```
Type CustomerLayout

      CustomerNumber As Integer

      Customer Name as String * 35

      CustomerStreet As String * 35

      CustomerCity As String * 25

      CustomerState As String * 2

End Type
```

The reserved word *"Type"* is followed by the name of the definition. Subfield specs come next, and the definition is concluded by *"End Type."*

This example structure represents a user-defined data type called *CustomerLayout*. CustomerLayout is not a variable, it's a definition. Once a format for a user type of data is defined, you may declare the variable:

```
Public CustomerRecord As CustomerLayout
```

Now there is a variable called CustomerRecord that is of type CustomerLayout.

Note that the definition for the user type must come before the variable that refers to it. That is, CustomerLayout must precede CustomerRecord in the specs.

Referring to Subfields in a User Type

You may refer to the components within the CustomerRecord like this:

```
CustomerRecord.CustomerName = "Lindsey Hoover"
```

The syntax follows the same format as you've seen before, going from the general to the more specific, separated by periods:

```
UserTypeVariableName.SubfieldName
```

A reference to a subfield must include the user type variable name. Using the preceding example, you can't refer to "CustomerName" alone. It has to be specified as "CustomerRecord.CustomerName" or you get an error.

Step by Step: Declaring Variables

1. Bring up your EditText project.

2. Select "EditText.Bas" in the project box and click on "View Code." You should see:

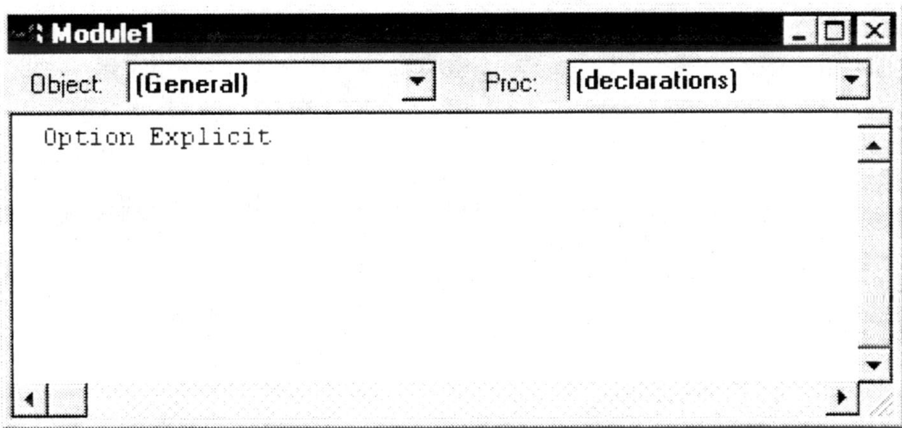

Recall that the environment setting "Require Variable Declaration" will insert the line "Option Explicit" in all new modules.

A standard module may have a name other than the name of its source file. It's like a form module, which can have a source file named one thing and the form itself named another. Rename a module by pressing F4 while a code window for the module is active.

Okay, you've brought up the declarations area of the module "EditText.Bas." This is where global variables and constants are defined.

3. The keyword Const designates a field as a constant. Add the following lines of code:

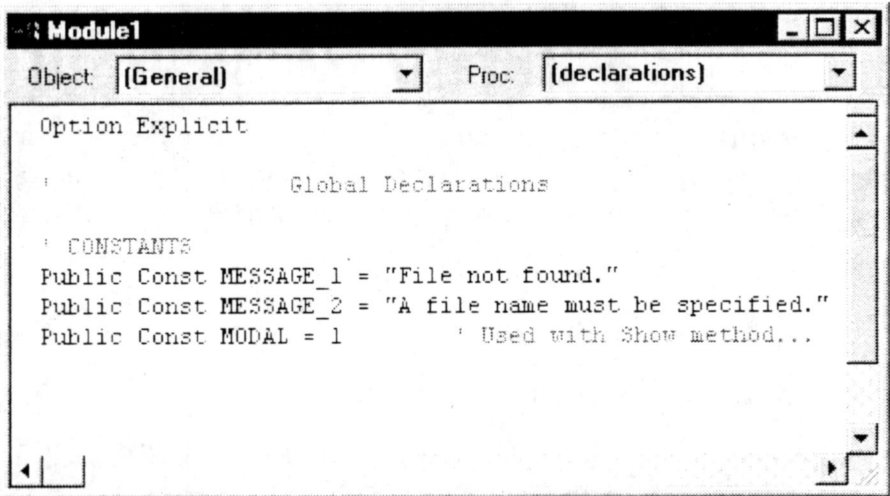

This defines two error message constants and one symbolic constant that are accessible to any part of the program. Notice that these statements are keyed into the module in general. They are not placed between "Sub" and "End Sub" statements. This is the only place global fields are allowed.

Notice also that an apostrophe identifies comments. A comment can be placed at the end of a statement or on a line by itself, just like in AS/400 CL.

Constants, as a matter of convention, are defined in all uppercase. The underscore character is allowed, and is often used to separate words.

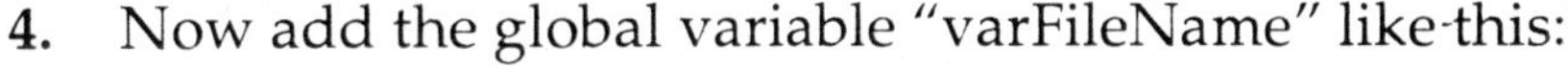

4. Now add the global variable "varFileName" like this:

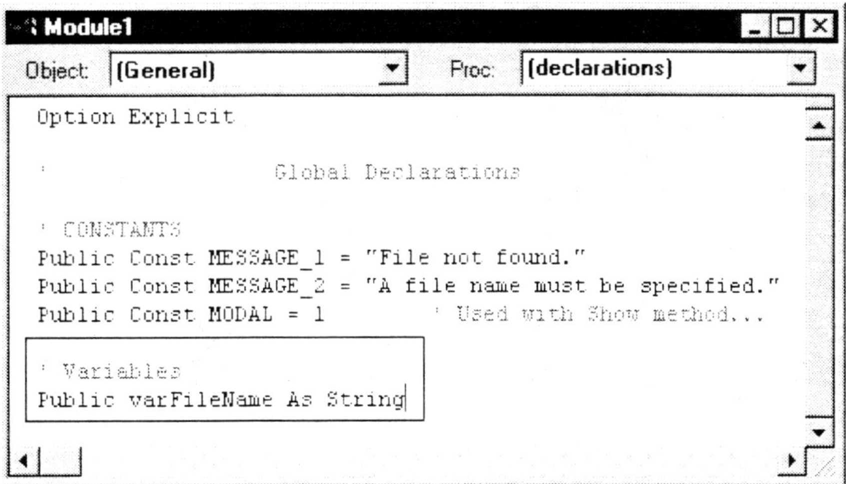

This string (varFileName) is declared as variable length—there is no "*" or number at the end of the statement. Remember that variable-length strings are handy for string concatenation. That's what this field will be used for, so that's how it's defined. The reason that this is defined as a global variable and not as a work field is the field will be used in more than one procedure, on more than one form. It will be used to open a file from the frmOpen form and then to save the file from the frmMain form.

Normally, variables are defined using upper- and lowercase to make words. No spaces and no underscores. In this case, the prefix "var" has been used to stay away from the property named "FileName."

5. For now, those are all the global variables that are required. Close the code window for the module.

6. To take advantage of the symbolic constant MODAL, bring the form frmMain into the form design window by selecting it in the project box and clicking "View Form."

7. Change the line:

```
frmOpen.Show 1
```

to:

```
frmOpen.Show MODAL
```

Now you don't have to remember that modal is 1 and modeless is 0. Not a revolution to programming, just an illustration of symbolic constants.

8. Save your project.

Summary

Data Types

There are several more data types in BASIC than there are in RPG.

VB allows implicit definitions of variables. You should disable this feature by specifying "Option Explicit" in a form or module. That line of code may be inserted automatically by specifying "Require Variable Declaration" in the VB environment settings. ("Options" command on the Tools menu.)

VB Help contains an online summary of data types and a description of each. You have seen how to set a bookmark for quick access.

Numeric Data

Numeric variables are of predetermined length and decimal positions. The types are:

- Integer
- Long
- Single and double floating-point
- Currency

Character Data

Character data is stored in strings. Strings can be of fixed or variable length.

Variant Data

Fields of the variant type can be either character or numeric, depending on what they contain.

Special Data Types

- Boolean
- Date
- Object
- Byte

User Data

You can combine regular VB data types to form a more complex structure called a user data type. The structure, once created, is used to define other variables of the same type.

Arrays

You can define an array with up to 60 dimensions in VB. The first element of an array has an index of "0," not "1" like in RPG.

Arrays in VB are capable of being resized dynamically, but the contents are cleared unless "Preserve" is specified on the ReDim statement.

Data Type Suffix

If you choose to allow implicit data definitions, you may specify the data type with a special character (like %, $, @) at the end of the variable name. If you do not specify any data type suffix, the variable defaults to a type of variant. Use of implicit data definitions, even with data type suffixes, is not recommended.

Scope

Scope is the degree to which a variable is available to procedures in other forms and modules. A variable is said to be *visible* if it is available.

The scope of a variable can be local, global, or module level.

VB allows the use of the same name for distinct fields. If their scopes intersect, the local variable is considered first.

Lifetime of a Variable

Local variables cease to exist each time the procedure they're defined in ends unless "Static" is specified on the variable definition.

Constants

A constant is a named reference to a declared value.

A symbolic constant is one that replaces a literal with a more meaningful word when used in code.

Constants may be defined by the programmer or defined by using the Object Browser.

User constant names, by convention, are all uppercase with the underscore as a word divider.

Names of constants supplied by the VB Development Environment begin with lowercase "vb."

Declaring Variables

Variables are declared with:

- Dim. A variable defined in a procedure—a local variable.
- Private. A variable defined in the general declarations area of a module—local to the module.
- Public. A variable defined in the general declarations area of a standard module—available to all procedures.

- Static. A variable defined in a procedure in place of Dim—contents of the field are preserved when the procedure ends.
- Type. Defined in the general declarations area of a module—consists of simple data types collected into a data structure definition.

Declaring Fixed-length Strings

Fixed-length strings are defined with an "*" and a value declaring their lengths.

Fixed-length strings are better suited to client/server applications.

Declaring a User Date Type

The user data type is declared with "[Public | Private] Type" and "End Type." Regular data types make up the elements between.

The definition of a user data type is not a variable—it's a format or pattern for other variables declared as that type.

Subfields in a user data type are referenced as:

```
"VariableDefinedAsType.Subfield"
```

Microsoft Visual Basic Version 4.0
For 32-bit Windows Development

Copyright © 1987-1995 Microsoft Corp.

6

VB Starter Code

You'll find that coding in VB is much like coding in the languages you already know. You have a task in mind, you consider the programming tools at your disposal, and you decide on a solution. The tools available may be unfamiliar to you, but mostly in terms of syntax. This chapter deals with the BASIC language as adopted and extended by Visual Basic.

If you haven't seen BASIC lately, you may expect statements to look like this:

```
10  CLS

20  CM$ = "com1:09600,n,8,1,rs,cs,ds,cd": CR$ = CHR$(13)

30  OPEN CM$ FOR OUTPUT AS #1

40  B$ = TIME$

50  LOCATE 6, 5: PRINT B$

60  OPEN "TEST.TXT" FOR INPUT AS #2
```

```
70  a$ = INPUT$(1, #2)

80  PRINT #1, a$

90  GOTO 70

100 END
```

BASIC has evolved into a well structured, easy to work with language. Gone are the line numbers, most of the "goto's" and what little screen abilities the language had.

Take a look at what Visual Basic looks like now:

VBSPL021

Object: (General) Proc: GetOutqs

```
Private Sub GetOutqs()

Private Index As Integer
Request = "*ALL       Q"
SendReceive (Request)
Message = Mid$(Record, 945, 80)

Do
 For X = 1 To 90
  If Mid$(Message, 1, 9) = "(INVALID)" Then
   MsgBox "Access denied. Possible authority problem.", 48, "AS4(
   Exit Do
  End If
  OutqTemp = Mid$(Record, ((X * 10) - 9), 10)

  If OutqTemp = "          " Then
   Exit For
  End If
  OutqForm.OutqList.AddItem OutqTemp
 Next X

 SendReceive (Request)
 Message = Mid$(Record, 945, 80)
Loop
```

VB has become a viable, structured language. There are do loops, if-else conditionals, leave and select equivalents that operate just like they do in RPG. If anything, it's easier to achieve structured code in VB. So your programming skills are quite transferable to Visual Basic. Things are done in pretty much the same way.

VB code is free-form in nature, like AS/400 CL, as opposed to the columnar approach used in RPG. You are allowed, indeed encouraged, to indent code contained in For, If and Do groups (see example above).

The Visual Basic Language

The Visual Basic programming language is made up of statements, functions, operators, procedures, methods, and properties. All are built in, like the op codes within RPG.

You're already familiar with most of these, but to review:

- *Statements* are declarations and definitions (like Dim), and op codes (like If...End If) that perform actions within a program.
- *Functions* are procedures that return a value. It is common to speak of a function as being *something of* a passed argument. For example, the function "UCase" can be said to be the *uppercase of* the passed argument.
- *Operators* are the action or comparison elements of an expression. The plus sign, the minus sign, and the equal sign are operators. So are the greater than sign, the less-than sign, etc. Operators are basically grouped as either *arithmetic* operators (+, -, *, /), *comparison* operators when used with "If...End If" or "Do While...Loop" (<, >, =, <=, >=, <>), *concatenation* operators (&, +), and *logical* operators (And, Eqv, Not, Or).
- A *method* is a process that may be invoked on an object. An example of a method is the *Show* method that causes a form to become visible. Methods are subroutines that are built in to objects.
- *Properties* are attributes of a form or control. You may set properties at design time or while a program is running. An example of a property is the *caption* property attendant to several controls.

The Difference between Statements and Functions

A statement performs an action; a function returns a value. This is sometimes a confusing difference, especially when, in VB, there are statements and functions with the same name.

Take the function *and* statement "Time$." "Time$" the function returns the date and time. "Time$" the statement *resets* the computer's clock. Quite a difference.

Another case is the "Mid$" statement and function. "Mid$" the function returns a substring of a longer string. "Mid$" the statement *replaces* a substring of a longer string.

The Object Browser

Perhaps you recall a vague definition of an object, presented earlier, as being just about anything that can be conceived as a logical unit. Certainly anything that's actually been defined is an object. So it is.

Now that you've defined some things (forms, controls) they are available for access through the *Object Browser*.

Step by Step: The Object Browser

1. Open the EditText project.
2. Press F2. You should see:

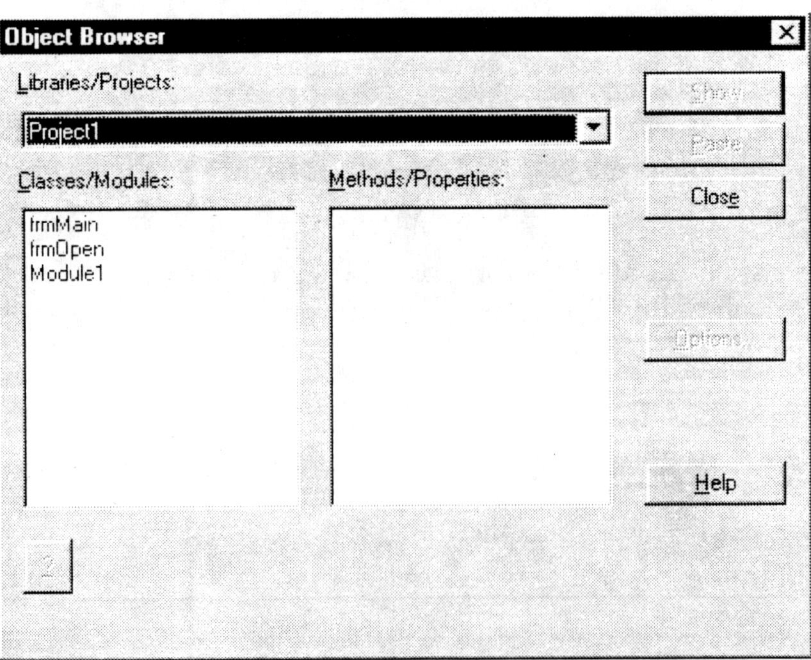

The Object Browser displays the classes, properties, and methods available from object libraries, and the modules and procedures in your project. You can use it to find and use objects you create, as well as objects from other applications.

You've already seen how VB-supplied constants (yes, constants are objects in this environment) are available to your program through a referenced object library. (In a preceding exercise, the object library "Visual Basic Objects and Procedures" was accessed through the Object Browser to obtain the constant "vbRed.")

The object browser can display elements of your project as well as reference library objects. If you select your project—in this case it's "Project1," you see the modules in the project (remember, forms are modules too), and the properties, methods, and procedures contained in the module.

3. Click on "frmMain" in the Classes/Modules box.

4. In the "Methods/Properties" box, scroll down and click "cmdExit_Click." (This is the menu item that you created previously.)

5. Click on the "Paste" button to go directly to the procedure's code window:

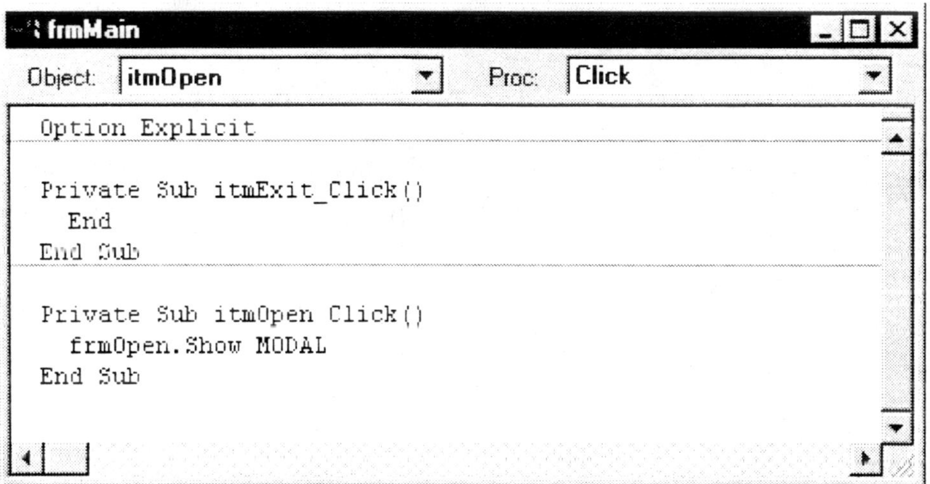

Visual Basic Statements

Examples of Visual Basic statements:

```
Private ArrayIndex As Integer          'declares a work variable
frmMain.Text = ""                      'an assignment statement
On Error Resume Next                   'a "monitor message" statement
Do While ArrayIndex < 100              'do-while statement
If txtEditArea.Text = "" Then          'if-then statement
  Exit Do                              'a "leave" statement
End If
```

Without too much imagination, you can see how statements in BASIC are similar to statements in RPG, and how you can follow pretty much the same process in developing a program.

Please refer to the following chart illustrating some Visual Basic statements and their RPG equivalents.

Some BASIC Statements	RPG Equivalents
Do While Index < 100	INDEX DOWLT 100
Exit Do	LEAVE
Loop	ENDDO
If Index = 100 Then	INDEX IFEQ 100
End If	ENDIF
Select Case VariableName	SELEC
Case Value	VNAME WHEQ VALUE

You get the idea. First think of what you want to do in a program; think of what mechanisms must be used and then figure out how to do that in VB. The problem solving process is the same as you're used to, except the final expression of the solution is in VB, not RPG. *It's reasonable to operate on the premise that you don't have to learn how to program again.*

Step by Step: Code for "frmOpen"

1. Open the EditText project. Bring "frmOpen" into the form design window.
2. Double click on "cmdOK," and bring the procedure "cmdOK_Click" into the code window.
3. Key in the following code:

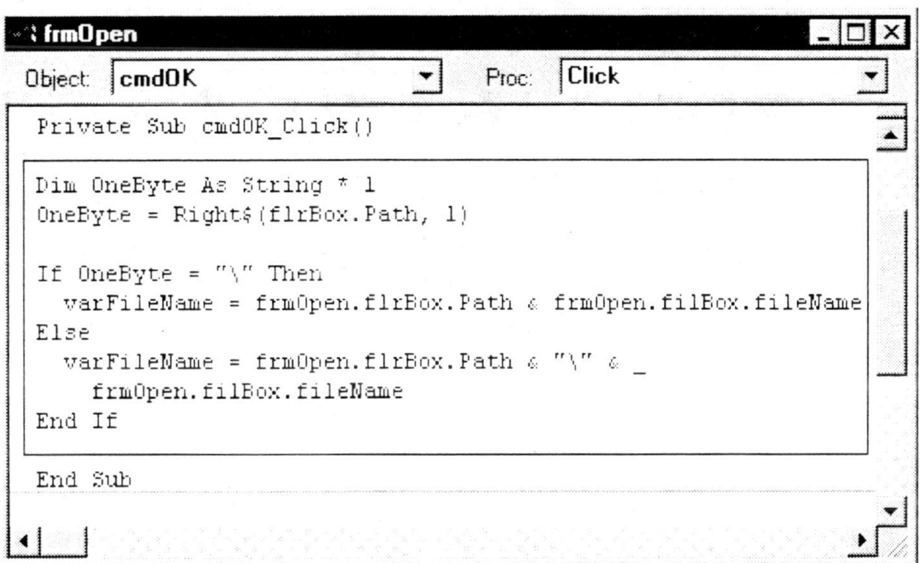


```
Private Sub cmdOK_Click()

Dim OneByte As String * 1
OneByte = Right$(flrBox.Path, 1)

If OneByte = "\" Then
  varFileName = frmOpen.flrBox.Path & frmOpen.filBox.fileName
Else
  varFileName = frmOpen.flrBox.Path & "\" & _
    frmOpen.filBox.fileName
End If

End Sub
```

What's new in here? There's a function called "Right$," for one.

4. Place the cursor on "Right$" and press F1. This brings up a general information help screen. Click on "Right$."

   It says, "Returns a specified number of characters from the right side of a string." This is like the SUBST op code in RPG.

Remember functions return a value, so you can combine a function with the assignment ("something equals something") statement:

```
OneByte = Right$(flrBox.Path, 1).
```

In fact, you don't really need the variable "OneByte." A function is a value, so everywhere you find "OneByte" you can substitute "Right$(flrBox.Path, 1)." The two are equivalent.

5. Simplify the code by removing "OneByte" and substituting the "Right$" function.

   Notice the line continuation character—the underscore. This behaves like the line continuation characters in CL.

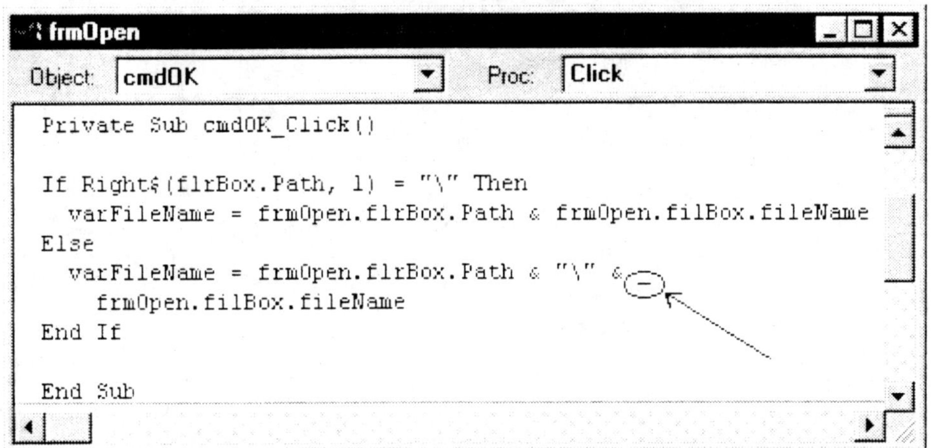

Now notice the assignment statement (varFileName = frmOpen....). The variable "varFileName" that you defined previously is being assigned the values in the Path and FileName together. The ampersand (&) is being used to join the strings. The equivalent in CL is "*CAT;" in RPG "CAT."

You can use the plus sign (+) to perform the same function, but the plus sign is also used to add numbers. The plus sign can behave like *CAT for strings and like the arithmetic operator for numerics. VB decides which to use, based on the type of variables involved in the operation.

For clarity, use the ampersand to concatenate strings.

6. The user is presented with a text box (txtFileName) to key a file name rather than selecting from the list boxes, so add an "If...Else...End If" around the existing code like this:

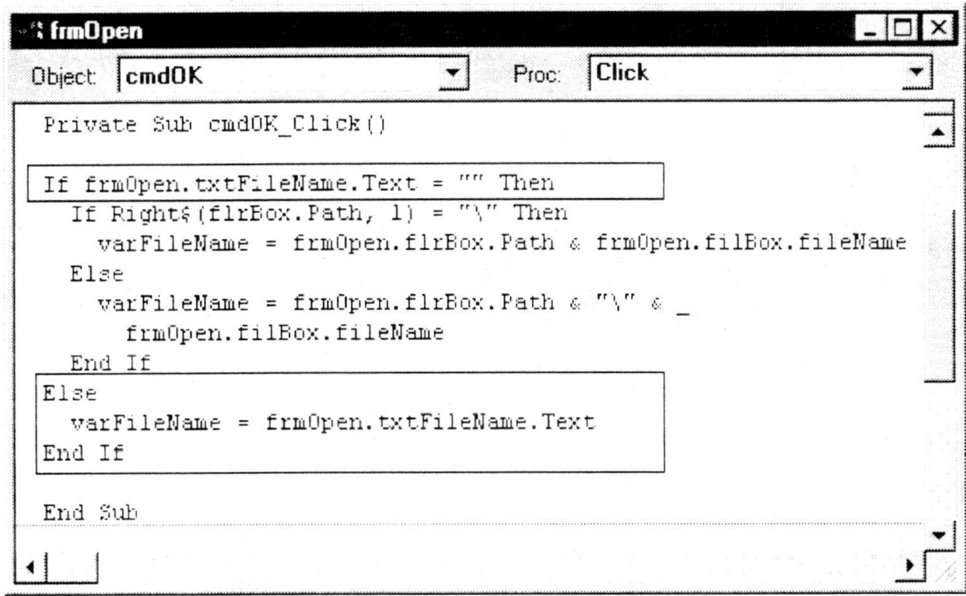

```
Private Sub cmdOK_Click()

If frmOpen.txtFileName.Text = "" Then
  If Right$(flrBox.Path, 1) = "\" Then
    varFileName = frmOpen.flrBox.Path & frmOpen.filBox.fileName
  Else
    varFileName = frmOpen.flrBox.Path & "\" & _
      frmOpen.filBox.fileName
  End If
Else
  varFileName = frmOpen.txtFileName.Text
End If

End Sub
```

The "txtFileName" text property is a variable length string. When it is empty, the length is zero.

The comparison in the statement—If frmOpen.txtFileName.Text = ""—is to an *empty string*. It doesn't have a value of blanks, like in RPG—it has no value at all—so you must compare it to "". This doesn't hold true for fixed-length strings, however.

7. Add the code to open the file and load its contents into the "txtEditArea" text box on the form frmMain:

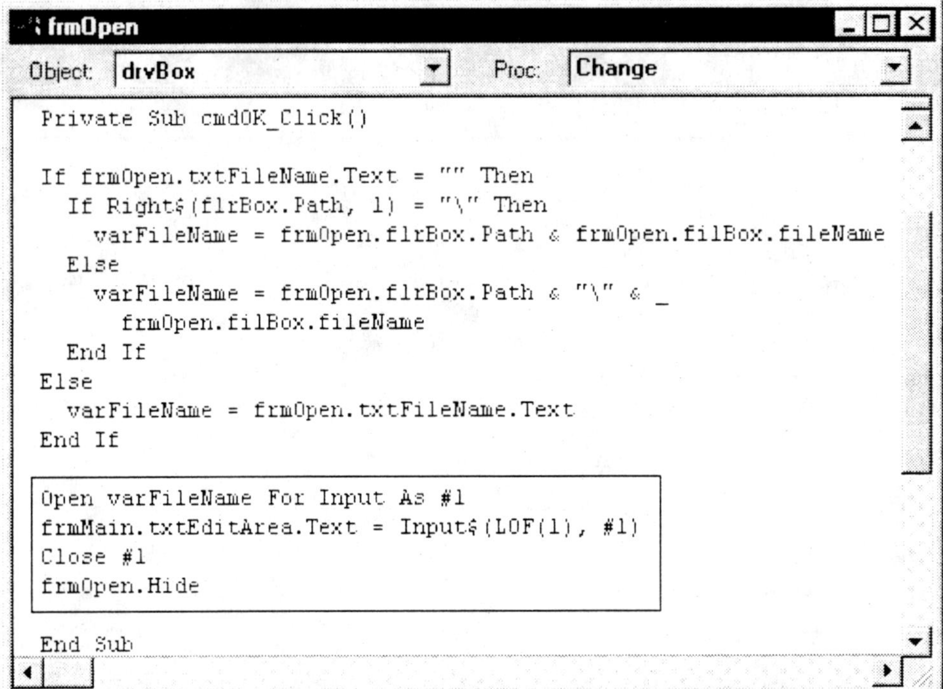

```
Private Sub cmdOK_Click()

If frmOpen.txtFileName.Text = "" Then
  If Right$(flrBox.Path, 1) = "\" Then
    varFileName = frmOpen.flrBox.Path & frmOpen.filBox.fileName
  Else
    varFileName = frmOpen.flrBox.Path & "\" & _
      frmOpen.filBox.fileName
  End If
Else
  varFileName = frmOpen.txtFileName.Text
End If

Open varFileName For Input As #1
frmMain.txtEditArea.Text = Input$(LOF(1), #1)
Close #1
frmOpen.Hide

End Sub
```

Note: The fully qualified name "frmMain.txtEditArea.Text" must be used because the txtEditArea control is on another form—frmMain.

The *Open* statement is fairly self-explanatory, except for the "#1" part. In BASIC, a file name is assigned a number when opened, and thereafter, references to the file are by number, not name. (A similar situation is found in the AS/400 OPNQRYF syntax for joining files.)

You can open a file for *append, input, output, random,* or *binary*. Detailed PC file handling is not within the scope of this book, but you should be aware that append *adds* to a file, output *replaces* the file.

Input$ reads from file #1, sequentially—byte by byte, not record by record—for the specified number of bytes in the expression ((LOF) 1). "*LOF*" is an intrinsic function that returns the "*length of file*" in bytes, so the whole file is read into the variable length string "Text."

The fact that BASIC deals with files by the byte, and not by the record, may be worth mentioning. A record, as you're used to thinking of it, with a fixed number of bytes, only exists for files opened for random access. A record, in this case, is the data between newline characters (ANSI code 10).

Notice that the *Close* statement references the file number.

Finally, "frmOpen" is hidden and control returns to "frmMain."

8. To finish the "frmOpen" code for now, bring "frmOpen" into the form design window.

9. Double click on the "flrBox" to bring up the event procedure "flrBox_Change."

10. Add the following line of code to put the currently selected folder in the caption of "lblFolder:"

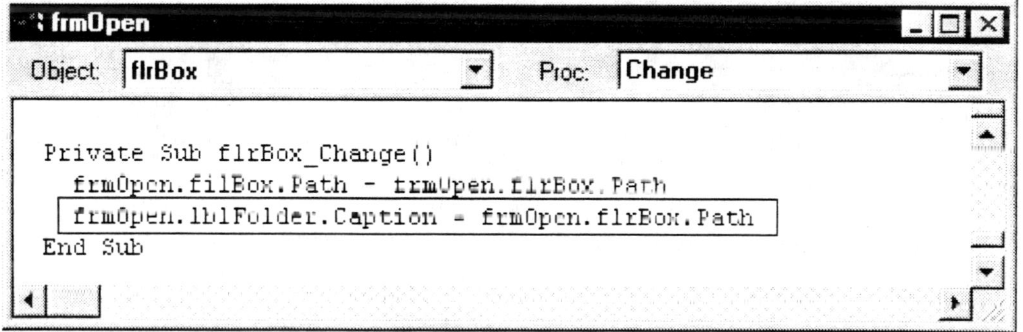

This simply updates the caption of the "lblFolder" control (the little box at the bottom of "frmOpen").

Now, to initially load the caption, go into the equivalent of the *INZSR subroutine in an RPG program—the load event for the first form of the project.

11. Bring "frmMain" into the code window. Open the objects list at the top of the window and click on "Form:"

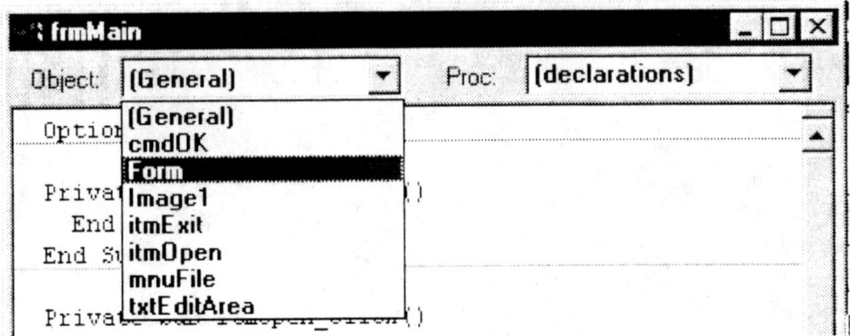

This starts a new procedure for the form (again the most common procedure is assumed—the load event).

12. Add the following line of code:

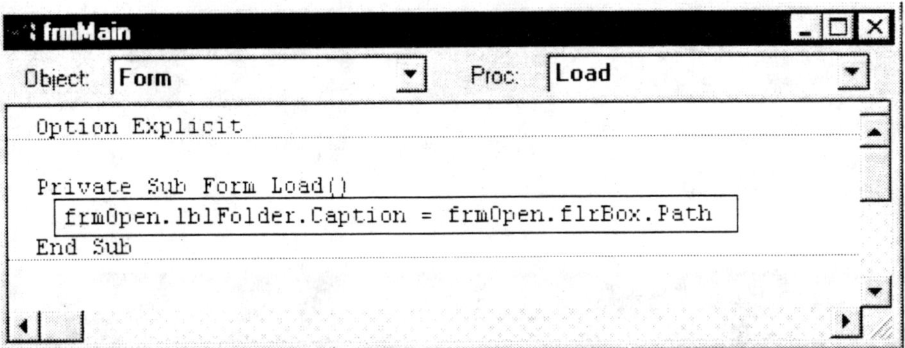

Again, the full, qualified name of the control, "frmOpen.lblFolder.Caption," has to be used because the control is unknown to this form.

In normal practice you will very likely omit the form's name where allowed. This affords you a bit of portability of code because the statements will operate in another form without having to be modified with the new form name.

13. Run your program. Open the File menu and click on "Open a File..." You should see:

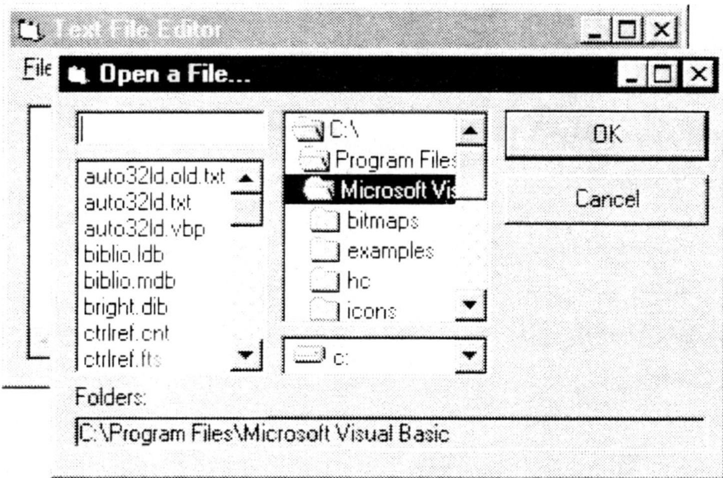

The label in the lower corner should display the current folder.

14. Double click on another folder like icons. The label should reflect the change.

15. Go to the root folder and select the file "autoexec.bat" or "config.sys" and click on "OK." You should get something like this:

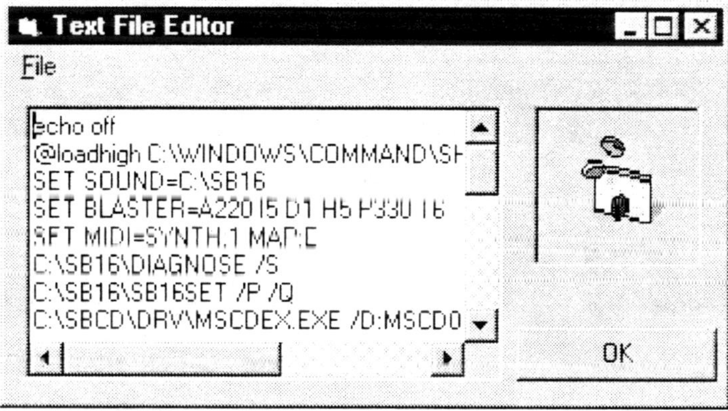

The contents of the file have been loaded into the text box for editing. End the program.

Note: If you received a run-time error message ("62 - input past end of file"), it's because the file that was loaded had no end-of-file character. Try bringing the file into NotePad and saving it. This adds the EOF character. In Chapter 7, you'll see how to trap the error yourself.

16. If all is well, save your project.

The project is almost finished for now. The file contents have been loaded into the text box for editing. The text box control handles the actual editing. Now what's needed is a means to save the file.

Step by Step: Saving the File

1. Bring up the EditText project.

2. Bring "frmMain" into the form design window. Double click on the "OK" button and bring the event procedure "cmdOK_Click" into the code window. Add the following code:

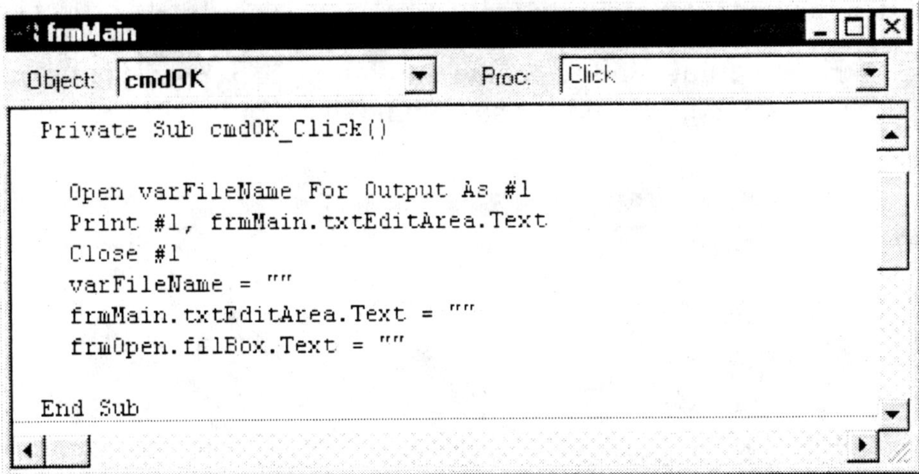

```
Private Sub cmdOK_Click()

  Open varFileName For Output As #1
  Print #1, frmMain.txtEditArea.Text
  Close #1
  varFileName = ""
  frmMain.txtEditArea.Text = ""
  frmOpen.filBox.Text = ""

End Sub
```

Important! *This code opens the file for output, which* clears *the file.*

The *Print #* statement writes the contents of the EditText box to the file.

The program then closes the file and clears fields.

Note: The Editor program is now "live." It will update your files, and doesn't make a backup copy!

Suppose the user wants to cancel out. There should be a means for her/him to do that.

3. Bring "frmMain" into the form design window. Add a command button and name it "cmdCancel." Give it a caption of "Cancel." Shift the existing controls ("OK" usually goes above "Cancel") for a better fit, like this:

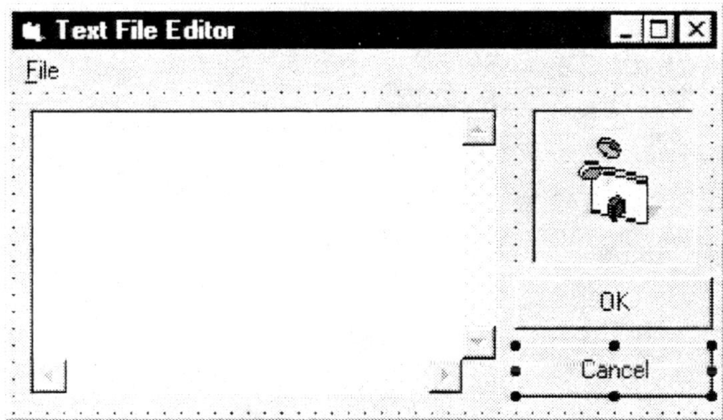

4. Double click on "cmdCancel" to bring the event procedure into the code window. Add an "End" statement. (This is the same as the "Exit" event on the File menu, but more conveniently placed.)

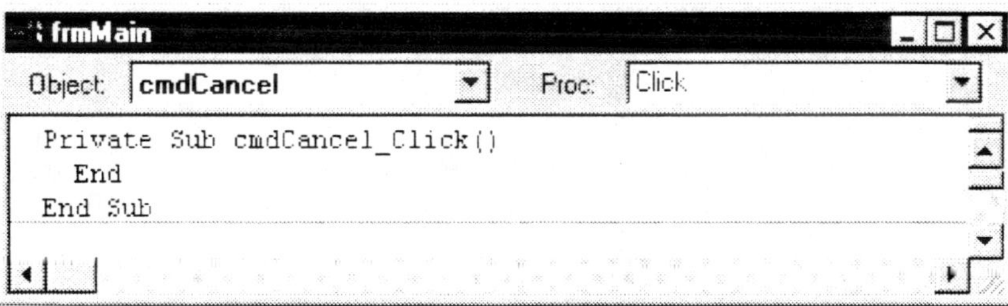

5. Run your program and try out the new code.

   ***Note:** Again, be careful! The editor is now "live," will alter your files, and doesn't make a backup copy.*

One last thing. If this program is to be a text file editor, it can be restricted to those kind of files.

6. Bring "frmOpen" into the form design window. Click on the "FileListBox" control to select it. In the properties box, find the "Pattern" property, and change it to "*.txt". This causes only the files with an extension name of ".txt" to be selected for editing.

7. Run the program and bring up "frmOpen." It should now look something like this:

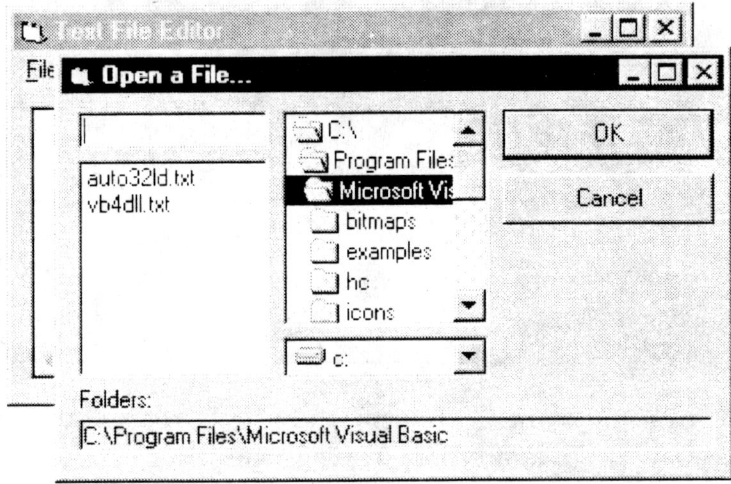

The files listed now are all ".txt" files.

8. End the program and save your project.

Summary

In this chapter, you have learned the following about Visual Basic Code:

- The process of formulation of logic into code can be the same as in RPG.
- VB code is made up of statements, functions, operators, methods, and properties.
- Statements are definitions, declarations, and op codes that perform an action.
- Functions are procedures that return a value.
- Operators are the comparison elements of an expression.

- A method is a process that can be invoked on an object.
- Properties are the attributes of a form or control.
- There is a distinct difference between statements and functions. Statements perform an action; functions return a value.
- Code is placed in procedures within forms and modules.
- Help is available for all VB code elements by placing the cursor on an op code and pressing F1.

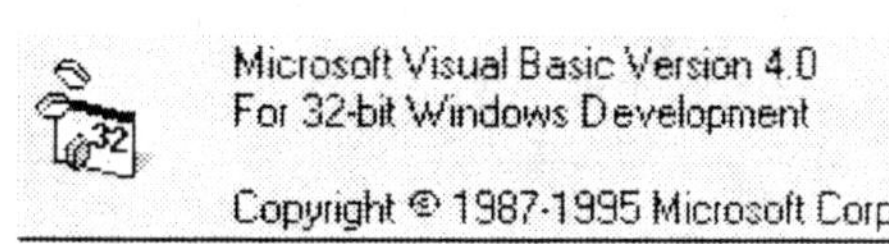

7

Error Handling and Debugging

Visual Basic, unlike RPG, has the ability to monitor for errors that occur within the program. In RPG, when an error occurs, the program stops and a C, D, G, or S (Cancel, Dump, Get-In, or System dump) message is sent. The only place to re-enter the executing program is at "GetIn" (Get Input)—the top of an RPG cycle program. Not really all that useful.

VB detects errors when they occur and presents them for individual handling. This chapter shows you how to set up run-time, error-handling routines.

One of the best features of Visual Basic is its extensive ability to assist with debugging. This chapter also shows how to use the VB debugging tools.

The Message Box

The message box is a VB function and statement that has a built-in dialog box. It's a lot like the AS/400 CL commands, SNDPGMMSG and SNDUSRMSG. With either of these commands, you can display a simple message to the user and, optionally, get a simple response.

In your AS/400 applications, you probably wouldn't include SNDUSRMSG in your main screen flow, but you might use it for displaying error or informational messages. That's the role that message boxes play in a VB program, and that's why they're presented together with error handling.

The message box is one of those VB things that can be both a function and a statement. Used in an expression, with an equal sign to return its value, it's a function. When used as a standalone informational message, it's a statement. The syntax is identical:

```
MsgBox(prompt[, buttons][, title][, helpfile, context])
```

MsgBox, the function, is like the SNDUSRMSG command in that a reply of some sort is requested. The reply takes the form of buttons on the box. Different values are returned to your program, depending on which button the user clicks.

MsgBox, the statement, is like the SNDPGMMSG command in that the message is informational and a reply is not required (beyond pressing Enter). No value is returned to your program.

The MsgBox Statement

You've already placed the MsgBox statement in your project, but without much explanation. As outlined in the preceding syntax diagram, you pass arguments to the MsgBox function to tell it what to display, and what responses to make available.

The first argument (parm) that is passed is the message itself. The message argument can be a literal, like "File not found...," or it can be a variable that contains the desired text.

Skipping the second argument for a moment, the third argument is the text that will appear in the title of the message box.

The second argument is the button type. The button argument specifies the way MsgBox displays the message and the options the user can click on.

The following table shows the values you pass and the type of message box displayed:

Symbolic Constant	Value	Function Performed
vbOKOnly	0	Display OK button only.
vbOKCancel	1	Display OK and Cancel buttons.
vbAbortRetryIgnore	2	Display Abort, Retry, and Ignore buttons.
vbYesNoCancel	3	Display Yes, No, and Cancel buttons.
vbYesNo	4	Display Yes and No buttons.
vbRetryCancel	5	Display Retry and Cancel buttons.
vbCritical	16	Display Critical Message icon.
vbQuestion	32	Display Warning Query icon.
vbExclamation	48	Display Warning Message icon.
vbInformation	64	Display Information Message icon.
vbDefaultButton1	0	First button is default.
vbDefaultButton2	256	Second button is default.
vbDefaultButton3	512	Third button is default.
vbApplicationModal	0	Application modal; the user must respond to the message box before continuing work in the current application.
vbSystemModal	4096	System modal; all applications are suspended until the user responds

Don't let that "Symbolic Constant" part of the listing throw you. Those constant names are defined in the object library that comes with VB. (See Object Browser.)

> **Note**: *As an information-only message box, the statement usage of MsgBox should only present the "OK" button for the user to click. After all, it only makes sense because no value is returned to your program.*

The MsgBox Function

If you give the user a choice beyond "OK," that choice must be related back to the program. That's where the MsgBox *function* comes in. It works the same way as the MsgBox statement, but remember, a function equals something, so the syntax goes like this:

```
ReturnCode = MsgBox("Prompt goes here", Buttons, "Title goes here")
```

To illustrate message box button types, let's look at the next example.

Step by Step: MsgBox Types

1. Start the VB Development Environment, but don't open any projects. This is just for illustration.

2. Double click on "Form1" to bring up the load event.

3. Key in the following MsgBox examples:

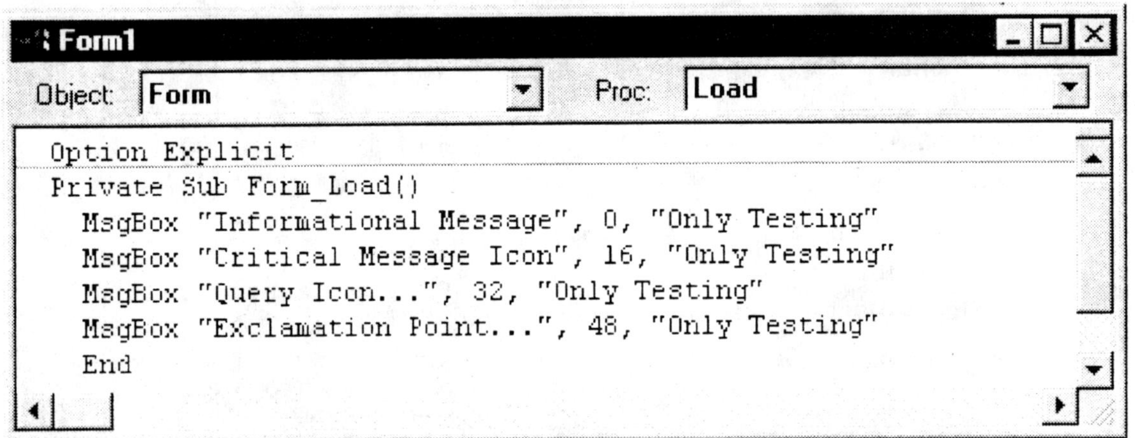

4. Click on the "Run" button. You should see:

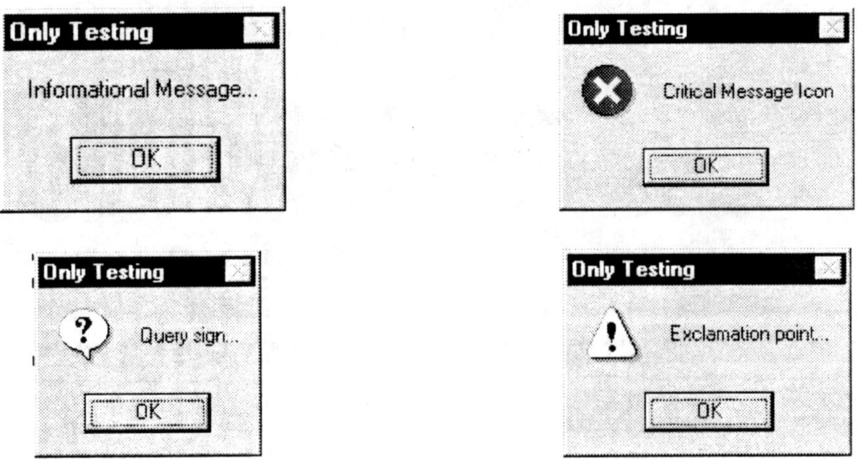

You get the idea.

You can also add type codes together and pass the sum to the MsgBox statement/function. For example, to get a "Yes, No, Cancel" type with query sign, you would add 3 (for Yes, No, Cancel), and 32 (for the query sign), and pass 35. To get a "Retry or Cancel" message with a "critical message" icon, add 5 (for Retry or Cancel), and 16 (for the icon).

5. Bring up the same code window—Form_Load event for Form1.

6. Change the code like this:

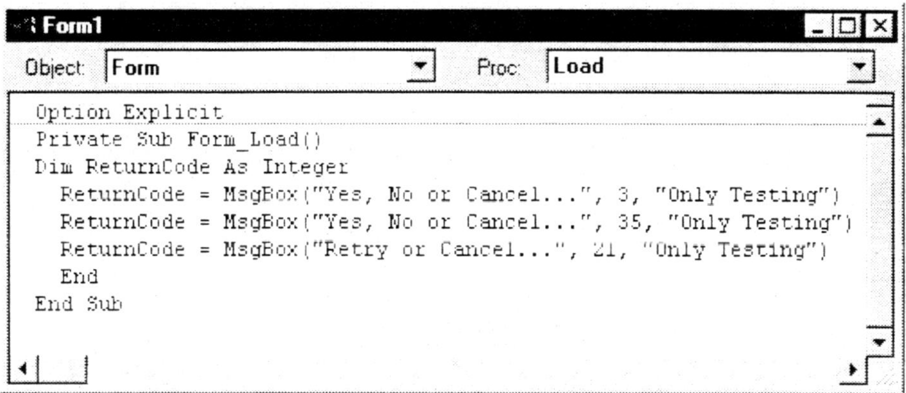

7. Run the program. You should get this:

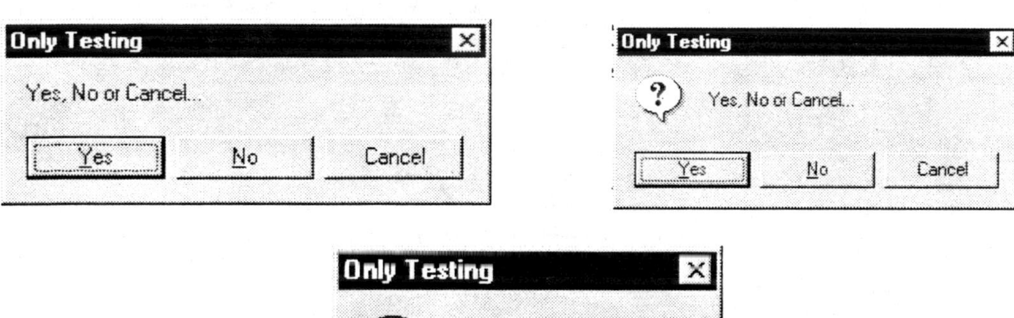

Only Testing

Retry or Cancel...

Retry Cancel

Now, these values that you've added together to produce a MsgBox with an icon and buttons can be expressed in terms of the corresponding symbolic constants. For example, the symbolic constant for "Yes, No, or Cancel" buttons is "vbYesNoCancel"—which has a value of 3. The symbolic constant for the exclamation point icon is "vbExclamation" and has a value of 48. To get a MsgBox with these two elements combined requires a value of 51 (48 + 3). You may also express this value like this:

```
vbYesNoCancel + vbExclamation
```

Obviously, the value expressed this way renders more lucid code.

MsgBox Return Codes

OK, you've set up the MsgBox as a function, to return a value. Now you need to know the value that corresponds to each button. Please refer to the following chart (copied from online help)

MsgBox Function

See Also   Example

Return Values

Constant	Value	Button chosen
vbOK	1	OK
vbCancel	2	Cancel
vbAbort	3	Abort
vbRetry	4	Retry
vbIgnore	5	Ignore
vbYes	6	Yes
vbNo	7	No

:

Let's do one last exercise to illustrate all that's been presented on the MsgBox.

Step by Step: MsgBox Return Values

1. Change the code to this:

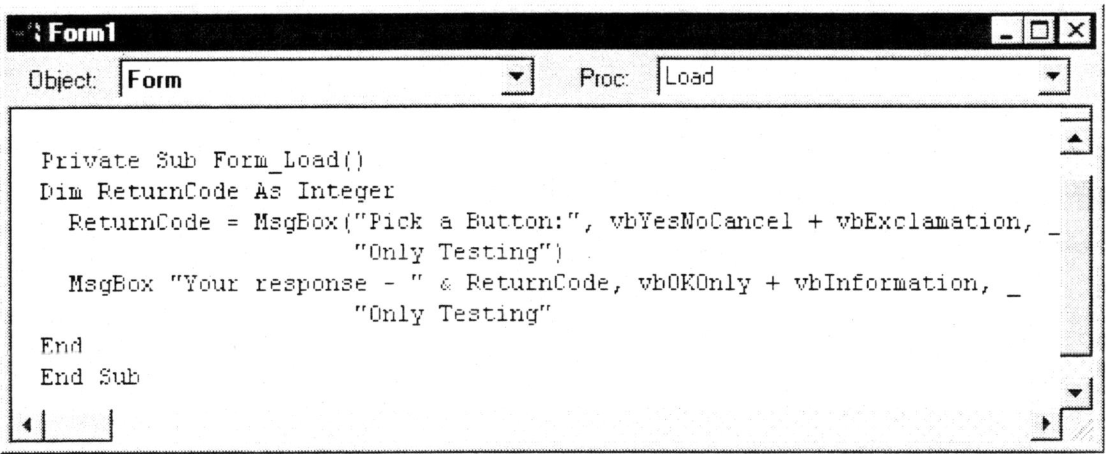


```
Private Sub Form_Load()
Dim ReturnCode As Integer
  ReturnCode = MsgBox("Pick a Button:", vbYesNoCancel + vbExclamation, _
                      "Only Testing")
  MsgBox "Your response - " & ReturnCode, vbOKOnly + vbInformation, _
                      "Only Testing"
End
End Sub
```

Here, MsgBox is used first as a function, to get a response, and then as a statement to display an informational message that includes the return code.

2. Run the program. You should see:

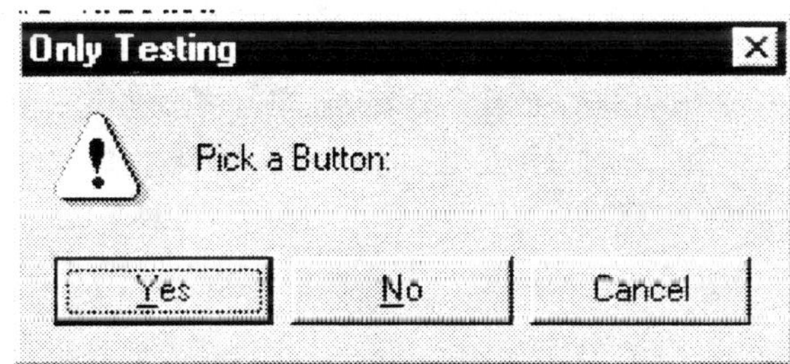

3. Click on "Yes." You should see:

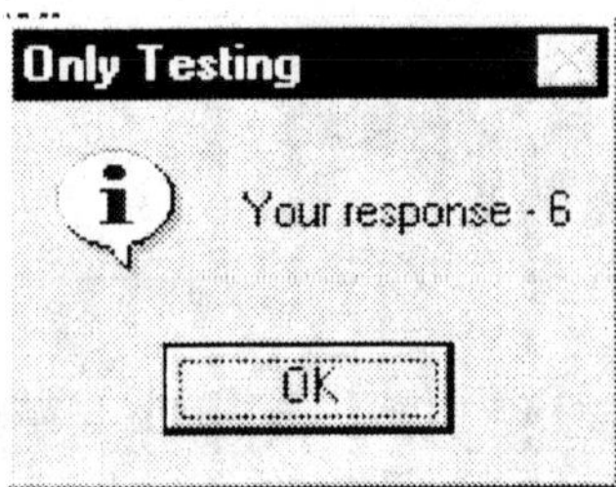

This is the return code for the "Yes" button.

4. Run the program again and observe the other choices.

5. Bring up the MsgBox statements again.

   Notice that a variable of type integer was defined to receive the return code. That's because the function itself is of type integer, and the type must match across the equal sign.

   Notice also that, if the type and title arguments are omitted from the MsgBox statement/function, type defaults to 0 and the title becomes the project name.

6. Discard the code.

Error Trapping

Error trapping is not new to you. You've used it before. In an AS/400 CL program, the command "MONMSG" is a glowing example. If you place it at the beginning of a CL program, error monitoring is in effect for the entire program. Error trapping in VB works in a similar way.

When an error is trapped, control is passed to a subroutine that you write. For our purposes, call it the *error-handling subroutine.* You deal with the error in there, and usually return control to the mainline calculations (with the "Resume" statement).

An AS/400 analogy is the error-handling subroutine that you can specify in the continuation lines (K specs) of an RPG program for an ICF file. If there's an error on the file, the subroutine is automatically invoked.

The Error Handler

The VB statement:

```
On Error GoTo ErrorSubr1
```

enables the *error handler*. Without this statement, errors aren't trapped and all errors cause a hard halt (called a fatal error).

In this example, "ErrorSubr1" is the name of a tag (called a label as in CL). Recall that labels are coded like this:

```
ErrorSubr1:     ' on a line by itself
```

or

```
ErrorSubr1: MsgBox "Error Message", 50, "Title" 'with a statement
```

When the "On Error...GoTo" statement is encountered, the error handler redirects errors to the label named in the statement. If another "On Error...GoTo" statement is encountered, the error handler redirects errors to the new label from then on. In this way, "On Error...GoTo" differs from MONMSG, which is capable of general monitoring and line-by-line monitoring at the same time.

Once enabled, the error handler becomes active when an error occurs. Control is directed to your error-handling subroutine. The error handler goes inactive and control is returned to the program when a "Resume," "Exit Sub," or "Exit Function" statement is encountered.

The error handler can't deal with more than one error. That is, if there's an error in your error-handling subroutine, you get a fatal halt.

You can disable previously set error trapping with the statement:

```
On Error GoTo 0
```

This is like having no monitoring at all in a program . All errors cause a halt.

You can bypass error trapping with the statement:

```
On Error Resume Next
```

This is like putting "MONMSG MSGID(CPF0000)" at the top of a CL program. No errors would cause a halt. When encountered, errors are ignored, the statement is not executed, and the program continues with the next line.

The following code:

```
On Error GoTo ErrorSubr

     .

     .

     On Error Resume Next          ' Bypass error trapping

     Kill "C:\WorkFile.Txt"              ' Delete work file if created

     On Error GoTo ErrorSubr             ' Resume error trapping

     .

     .

ErrorSubr:
```

is about the same as the CL code:

```
DLTF         FILE(QTEMP/WORKFILE)

MONMSG       MSGID(CPF0000)
```

Trappable Errors

Trappable errors are those for which you can monitor, exactly like in AS/400 CL. Also like in CL, each error has a message ID (like CPF0001 or RPG9001, except it's just a number) and a message description or message text.

The list of trappable errors is extensive and is not presented here. It is, however, available through VB help.

Step by Step: Trappable Errors List

1. Bring up the VB Development Environment, click on "Contents" in the Help menu.

2. Key in "Trap" to bring the search list to "Trappable Errors." Press Enter. Select "Trappable Errors - Visual Basic Help." This should bring up a pane about "Trappable Errors."

3. Scroll down a bit and click on "Miscellaneous Messages."

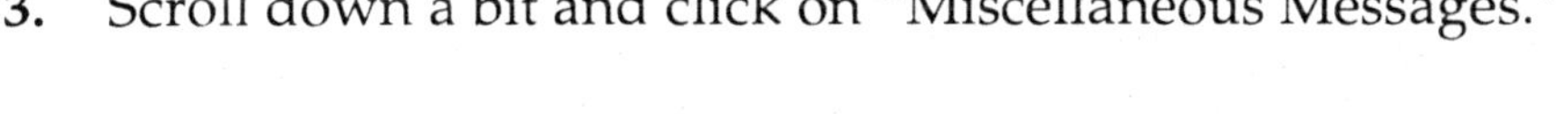

This is a partial list of the general VB errors for which you can monitor.

4. Scroll down the list to get an idea of the errors that can be trapped.

5. Find the error:

   9 Subscript out of range

   (This is the equivalent of the dreaded RPG "Array Index Error.")

6. Click on the "Subscript out of range" entry to see the help text for the error.

7. Close the list and exit help.

The Error Object

The *Error Object* is the error-handling mechanism within VB. When error trapping is enabled and an error occurs, the properties of the Error Object are set. You can then interrogate those properties and determine the cause.

Properties of the Error Object

The intrinsic objects in VB have properties and methods just like forms and controls. So it is with the Error Object.

The *Number property* contains the error code when an error occurs. (The error handler must be previously enabled by the "On Error...GoTo" statement.)

You can include the error code in the message text displayed to the user like this:

```
MsgBox "Error: " & Err.Number, 48, "Title Text"
```

The property "Number" is concatenated to the literal string "Error: ".

More informative yet would be to include the error number and its associated description. This is kind of like presenting DSPMSGD (Display Message Description) in a CL program. The *Description property* contains the error's text description (like "Subscript out of range").

The Description property added to the above example looks like this:

```
MsgBox "Error: " & Err.Number & " - " & Err.Description, 48, _
                    "Title Text"
```

Step by Step: Informative Error Messages

1. Open your EditText project and bring the click event for "frmOpen.cmdOK" into the code window.

2. Add the line to the program, at the topto enable error trapping:

```
frmOpen
Object: cmdOK                Proc: Click
Private Sub cmdOK_Click()

On Error GoTo ErrorSubr

If frmOpen.txtFileName.Text = "" Then
  If Right$(flrBox.Path, 1) = "\" Then
    varFileName = frmOpen.flrBox.Path & frmOpen.filBox.file
  Else
```

3. At the bottom add the "Exit Sub" statement and the error-handling routine:

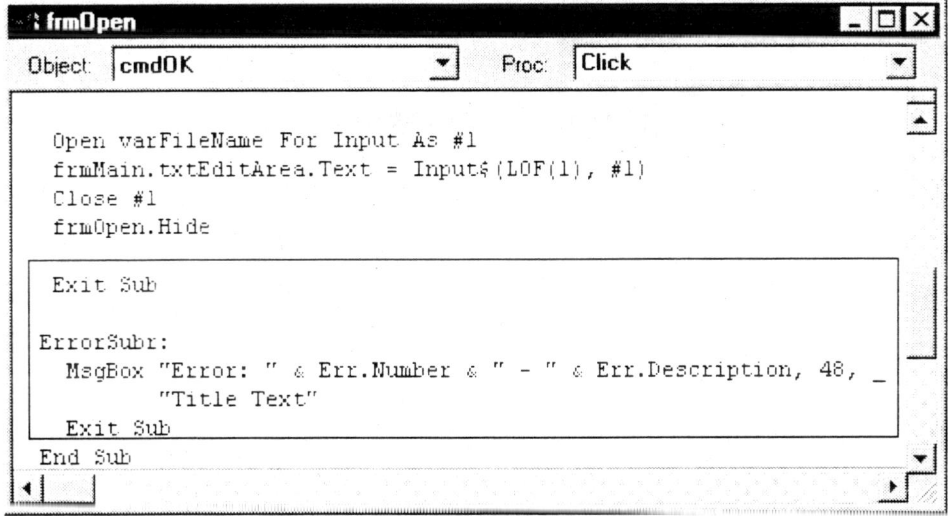

Note: The MsgBox statement has been folded. Notice the line continuation character—the underscore.

The first "Exit Sub" statement skips around the error routine when there is no error. The second drops out of the procedure when there's been an error.

The "ErrorSubr" statement is a tag identifying the error-handling subroutine.

4. Save your project.

5. Run the program. Open the File menu and click on "Open a File..."

6. In the text box, key some nonexistent file name:

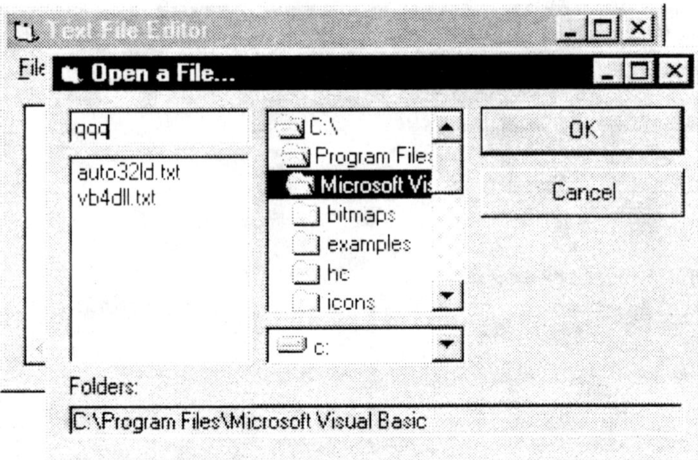

7. Click on the "OK" button. You should see:

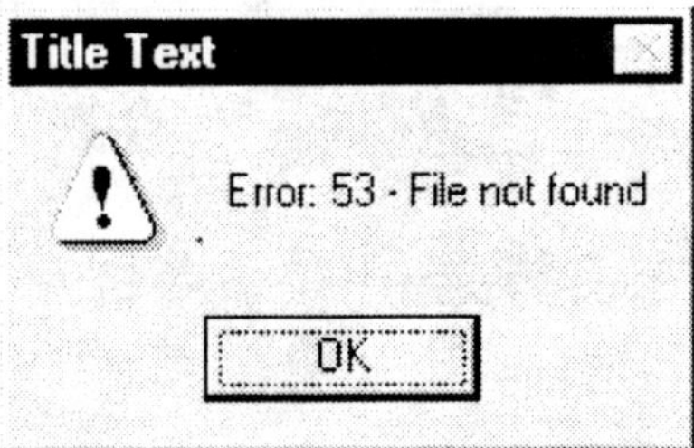

8. Click on "OK." End the program.

In Chapter 8, you'll see how the error-handling subroutine can be made smarter with the "Select Case" statement.

Errors in Called Procedures

In VB 4.0, errors in a called procedure are handled differently than they were in VB 3.0. In VB 3.0, if a called procedure had no error-handling routine of its own and an error occurred, a hard halt resulted. Now, in VB 4.0, the *calling* procedure's error-handling routine, if present, receives control. *Be aware of this new feature when you are calling procedures that don't have their own error routine.*

The Resume Statement

With no argument, or a "0," *Resume* causes control to return to the line where the error occurred—a "Retry" in essence. *Resume Next* causes execution to begin with the line following the line in error—like an "Ignore." Or, you can specify a label name. All in all, like this:

```
Resume [0]          ' Go to the line that caused the error

Resume Next         ' Go to the line following the line that caused the error

Resume LabelName    ' Go to a tag
```

> ***Note***: *The VB help system has the following to say about the Resume statement:*
>
> *"When an error-handling routine is active and the end of a procedure (an End Sub, End Function, or End Property statement) is encountered before a Resume statement is encountered, an error occurs because a logic error is assumed to have been made inadvertently. However, if an Exit Sub, Exit Function, or Exit Property statement is encountered while an error handler is active, no error occurs because it is considered a deliberate redirection of execution."*
>
> *This does not appear to be the case. In testing, VB doesn't seem to care if a Resume statement is present before encountering an Exit Sub, Exit Function, etc.*

Using the same CL monitor message example as before, the lines:

```
/*  Delete work files if present . . .                          */

        DLTF          FILE(QTEMP/WRKF001)

        MONMSG        MSGID(CPF2901)

        DLTF          FILE(QTEMP/WRKF005)

        MONMSG        MSGID(CPF2901)

        DLTF          FILE(QTEMP/WRKF01A)

        MONMSG        MSGID(CPF2901)
```

```
                    '

                    etc...
```

would be the same as:

```
Private Sub Form_Load

On Error GoTo ErrorSubr

            '

        Kill "C:\WRKF001.TXT"

        Kill "C:\WRKF005.TXT"

        Kill "C:\WRKF01A.TXT"

            '

Exit Sub


ErrorSubr:

        If Err.Number = 53 Then         ' 53 = File not found

            Resume Next

        End IF

        MsgBox "Error - " & Err.Number & " - " Err.Description & _

                    48, "Title Goes Here"

        Exit Sub


End Sub
```

(within the structure of an overall error trapping mechanism).

If error "53" is encountered (File not found), the error-handling subroutine goes to the next statement. Any other error displays a message and exits the procedure.

Debugging

If you've never worked with the VB debugging capabilities, you're going to like this. You recall that BASIC, like CL, can be compiled and run, or interpreted line by line.

Stepping through a Program

Your program can be interpreted without being compiled, so the VB Development Environment can run it, in debug mode, even as it's open for editing. On the AS/400, this is like having a program in SEU for editing, going into debug mode, and running the program without ever leaving the editor.

Step by Step: Stepping Through a Program

1. Bring up the VB Development Environment or start a new project. Double click on "Form1" to bring the load event into the code window.

2. Key in the following code to illustrate a point:

```
Private Sub Form_Load()

On Error GoTo ErrorSubr



  Kill "Z:\XXX.XXX"

  Kill "Z:\XXX.XXX"



  End



ErrorSubr:
```

```
    Resume Next

  End Sub
```

You probably don't have a Z: drive, so this should produce an error condition. The point here is to watch the code go round and round.

3. Click on the "Step Into" button on the tool bar: .

   This button starts your program like the "Run" button, but in a step-by-step mode. You should see:

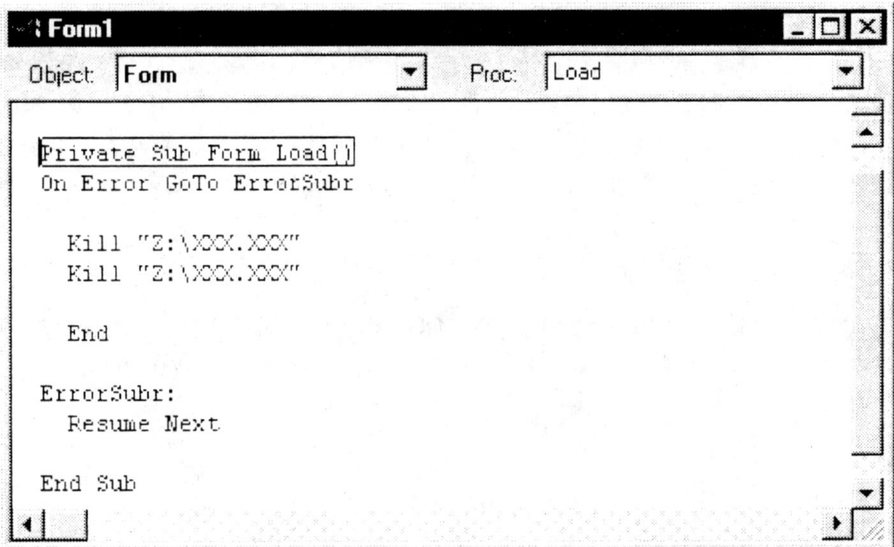

The rectangle signifies the current statement (before it's executed).

4. Click on the "Step Into" button again. The current line advances. Keep clicking the single-step button until the program ends. Discard the code.

In this manner, you can watch your program execute and check the flow of control.

The other button, [icon], is the "Step Over" command. Clicking on this button also steps through the program one statement at a time, but when a call to a *procedure* is encountered, it's treated as if it were a single statement. Use this button when you don't want to step through procedures with which you're not concerned.

You may use these buttons together. That is, you can click on "Step Over" until you reach a procedure you want to see, and then click on "Step Into" to go into it one statement at a time.

You may also click on the "Run" button at any time to run the program normally, or the "Stop" button to end program execution.

Breakpoints

Just like the AS/400, VB can set breakpoints that cause an executing program to pause. You can interrogate variables or properties, and then resume execution.

Step by Step: Setting Breakpoints

1. Bring up theEditText project. Bring the form "frmOpen" into the form design window and double click on the "OK" button to bring up the code for that event.

2. Scroll to "Open FileName for Input as #1." Place the cursor on that line and press F9. You should see:

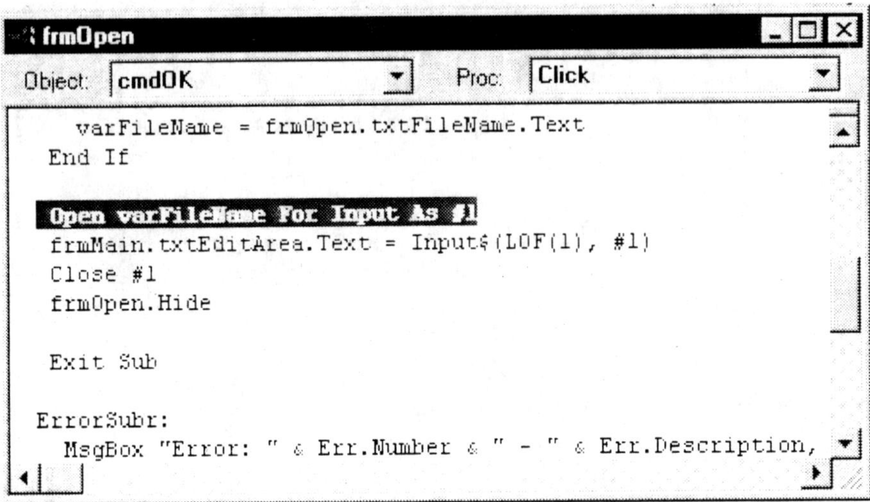

The red band indicates that a breakpoint has been set for the line.

3. Press F9 again. This toggles the breakpoint off and on. Press F9 again to reset the breakpoint.

4. Click on the "Run" button. The program should begin normally.

5. Click on "Open a File..." on the File menu to bring up "frmOpen." Select a file and click on "OK." You should see:

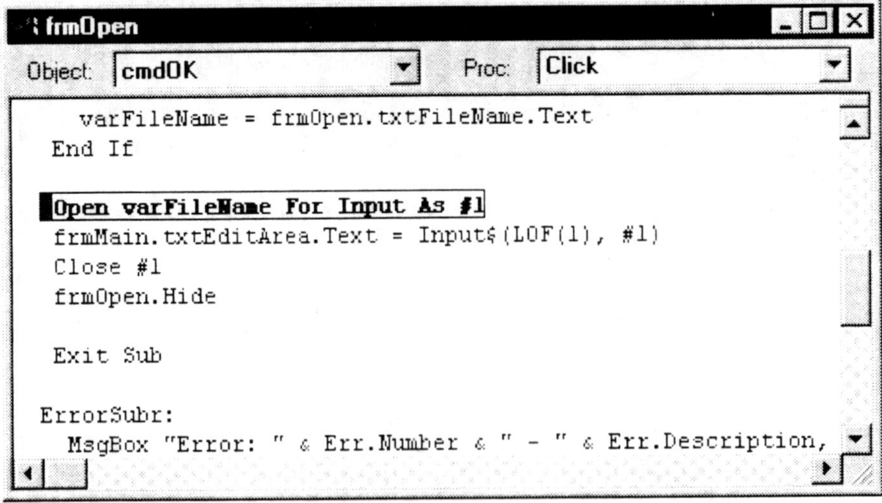

The program has paused on the breakpoint line and the rectangle showing the current statement confirms it.

6. With the mouse, highlight the variable name "varFileName" like this:

```
Open varFileName For Input As #1
```

7. Click on the "Instant Watch" button on the toolbar. You should see something like:

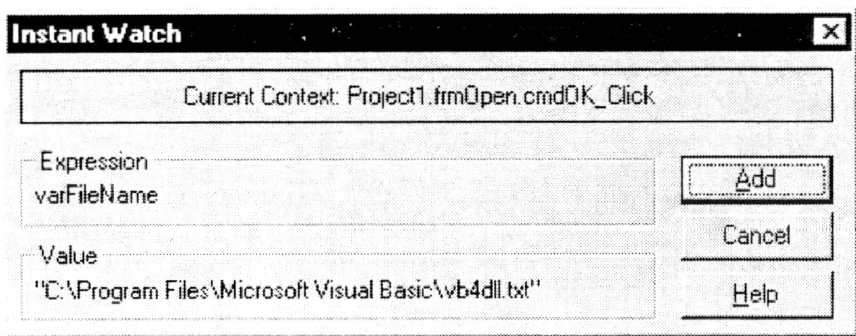

This is the *Instant Watch* window. The window allows you to view the contents of any variable that's visible to the current procedure. This is similar to specifying a variable to display on the AS/400 ADDBKP command.

This is, however, an *instant* watch, meaning that tracking of the variable ends as soon as you click on "Cancel."

8. Click on the "Add..." button. You should see:

This is the *"Debug Window."* The debug window lies underneath the code window. Bring it to the front by clicking on it.

> ***Note**: You can highlight and display any variable or property that is currently visible. The variable or property doesn't have to be on a breakpoint line.*

The top line in the window displays the contents of the variable "varFileName." The *context* of the watch is also shown:

```
"frmOpen.cmdOK_Click"
```

Now as the program executes and the watched variable is changed, you can monitor it in the debug window.

9. In the debut window, double click on the line containing the variable name "varFileName" to bring up the "Edit Watch" dialog box. You should see:

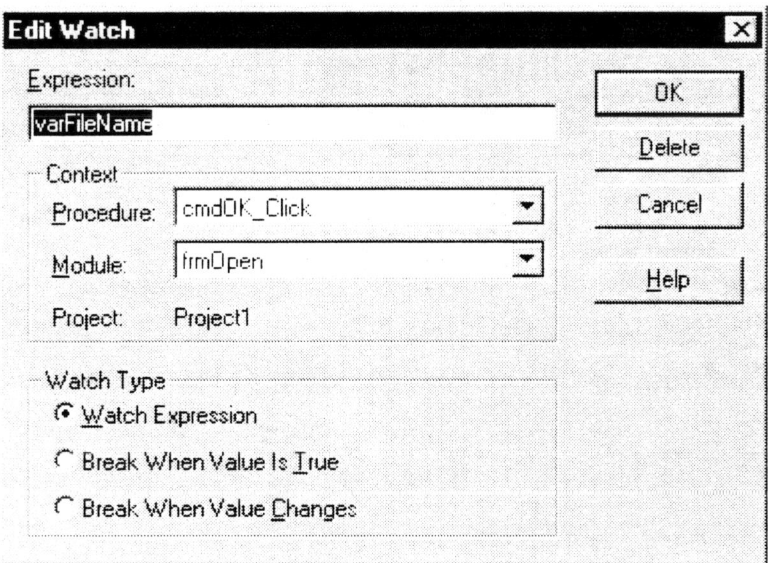

This dialog box allows you to specify how the watch is set up. You can specify a variable at the program level (Project), within the form or module (Form/Module), or only for the current procedure.

10. Notice that there is a "Delete" button available.

11. Click on the "Delete" button to remove the watch.

12. Open the Run menu.

13. Click on "Clear All Breakpoints." The red band goes away.

All of this has been going on while the program is active. Fact is, within limits, you can actually add or change statements while the program is running, and the new or altered statements will be executed.

14. While the program is paused, with the code window for "frmOpen" procedure "cmdOK_Click" open, place the cursor on the line "Exit Sub."

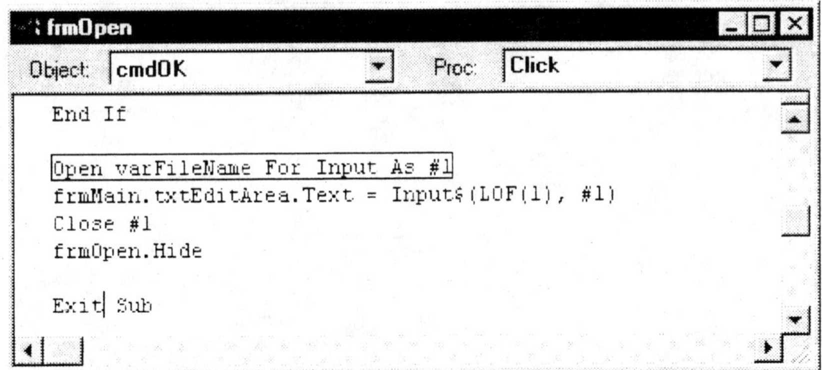

Notice that the "Open varFileName For Input As #1" statement is still current, as designated by the rectangle.

Open the Run menu again and click on "Set Next Statement."

Suddenly, the "Exit Sub" statement is current and has the rectangle. So, if your program is choking at a certain point, you can circumvent the problem and exit gracefully. Let's see you do *that* in RPG.

15. Click on the "Run" button and then end the program. No need to save the project.

The Stop Statement

Another way to suspend program execution is with the "Stop" statement. (It differs from the "End" statement in that the program is still loaded, files are not closed and variables are not cleared.) You put the "Stop" statement in the code and, when it's encountered, the program pauses, like with a breakpoint. You can resume program execution by clicking on the "Run" button, the "Step Into" button, or the "Step Over" button.

The Debug Window

You probably have noticed that, whenever you run a program from the VB Development Environment, the debug window opens. It lies inconspicuously at the bottom of your screen.

The debug window is like the AS/400 command entry screen that is available by pressing F10 from a program breakpoint. It is a means of keying statements directly for immediate processing. In fact, in VB version 1.1, the debug window was called the "immediate" window.

In order for the debug window to accept statements, the program must be paused. The program pauses between single steps, procedure steps, at breakpoints, or when the "Pause" button is pressed: .

Step by Step: Keying Statements into the Debug Window

1. Bring up your EditText project and run the program.
2. Click on the debug window to make it active and try to key something into it. It shouldn't let you because the program is still active.
3. Click on the "Pause" button. Now you should be able to key text into the debug window.
4. Key the following and press Enter:

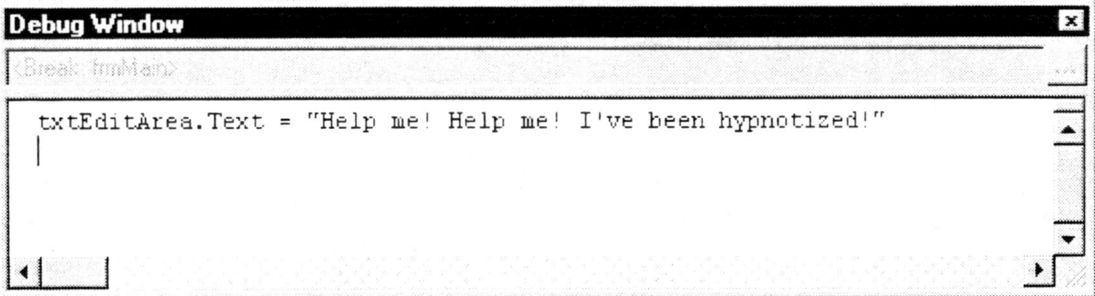

This statement is executed immediately. It loads the text property on the "frmMain" screen with a phrase. Note that the fully qualified name of the control doesn't have to be specified because the control is on the current form.

Okay, one more feature of the debug window. Instead of using the instant watch feature to see the contents of a field, you can ask for it directly through the debug window if you know its name. You ask for it like this:

```
?VariableName
```

5. Click the "Run" button to resume the program.

6. Bring up the "Open a File..." form and load a text file into the editor.

7. Click on the "Pause" button. In the debug window, key "?varFileName" on the second line and press Enter. You should see:

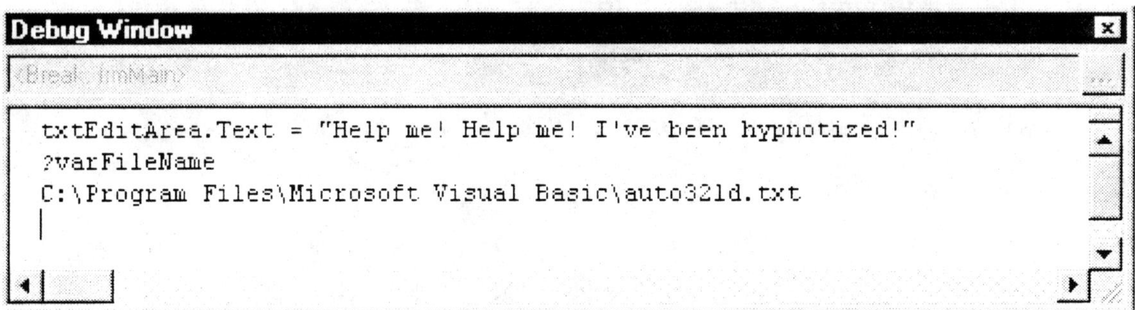

The contents of the variable "varFileName" (a global variable) is returned on the next line.

8. Click the "End" button. No need to save the project.

So, all in all, you can see that the debugging tools available in VB are very extensive and easy to work with.

Summary

The Message Box

The "MsgBox" statement and function are used for error message display and user response.

The MsgBox statement pauses the program and displays a message. The only button available to the user is "OK."

The MsgBox function pauses the program, displays a message, and returns the user's response. Several choices of buttons are available.

An icon may be added to the MsgBox by adding the designated value for the icon to that designated for the buttons.

Symbolic constants are well suited for use with the MsgBox.

Error Trapping

Error trapping is your method of monitoring for error situations and taking appropriate action.

Trappable errors each have an error code available with the Number property of the "Err" object.

The Description property returns the descriptive text for an error.

The Error Handler is enabled with the "On Error" statement, and activated when an error is encountered.

The "Resume" and "Exit Sub/Function/Property" statements deactivate the error handler.

Debugging

VB programs can be compiled or interpreted from the VB Development Environment.

You can step through your code one statement at a time with the "Step Into" button or one procedure at a time with the "Step Over" button.

You can set or clear breakpoints in your code by putting the cursor on a line and pressing F9. You can also set and clear breakpoints from the "Run" menu.

The "Watch" feature allows the contents of a field to be displayed.

The "Stop" statement can be used to pause a program, like a breakpoint.

The debug window displays watched variables and provides access for immediate execution of statements.

You can display the contents of a variable by pausing the program and keying "?VariableName" in the debug window.

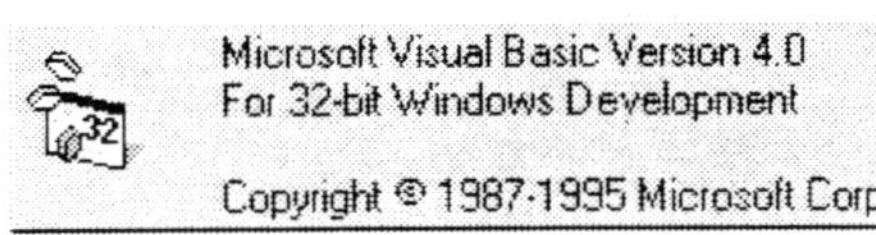

8

More Advanced Controls and Code

This chapter describes many of the more advanced controls and code. These more advanced features are not used in the example project. The intended purpose is to make you aware of what they are and when to use them.

In-use examples of the controls and code can be found in the AS/400 Report Download Utility. The descriptions of the code and controls are presented, wherever possible, with AS/400 comparisons and analogies.

Controls

There are a few valuable controls in the intrinsic set within Visual Basic that haven't been discussed. They are the list box, the combo box, the check box, the frame, option buttons, and the data control.

List and Combo Boxes

The list box and the combo box are so similar that they are presented together.

The List Box 

You've seen and used list boxes many times. They're all over the place in Windows. The example below is from the VB Development Environment.

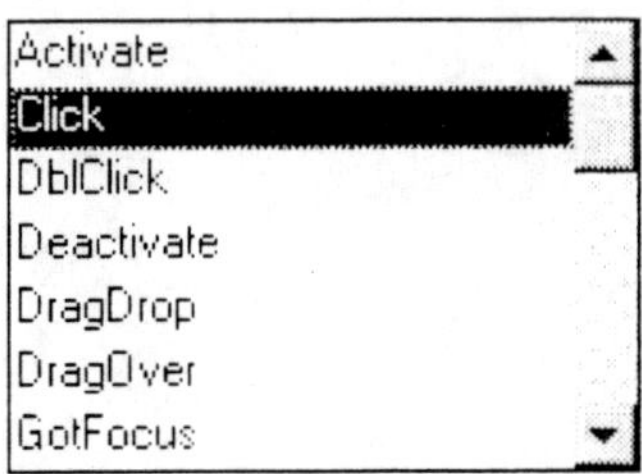

The list and combo boxes are the VB equivalents to an AS/400 subfile. When you have several items to present to the user for selection, use a list or combo box. Adding and deleting records is easy using the list box properties "AddItem" and "RemoveItem."

Items in the list are like array elements and are tracked and referred to by *index*. The index is just like an array index. (Remember that VB array indices start with 0, not 1.)

Notice the similarities between manipulating list/combo boxes and AS/400 subfiles. A portion of the VB-to-AS/400 Cross Reference is reprinted here:

VB List and Combo Boxes Property/ Method	AS/400 Subfile Equivalent
AddItem method—adds a list item	WRITE to record format subfile
Clear method—clears list	Subfile clear, Subfile initialize
Index property—pointer to a list item	RRN of subfile record
ListCount property—total items in the list	Total number of subfile records
ListIndex property—Index value of current list item	RRN of selected record (cursor position)

VB List and Combo Boxes Property/ Method	AS/400 Subfile Equivalent
RemoveItem method—deletes a list item	DELET a Subfile record
Sorted property—sort alphabetically as items are added	N/A

The Combo Box

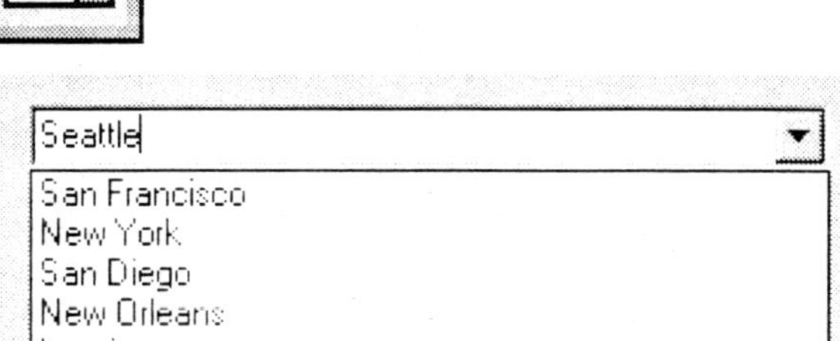

The combo box is a list box and a text box combined. It's a list box with a space at the top for the user to key a selection directly, rather than choose from a list.

Use a combo box when the user is allowed to select from a list of existing items or key the name of one.

Combo boxes come in three styles:

- **Style 0** Drop-down combo (the preceding example is a drop-down combo).

  This is the type normally used in applications. A list is combined with a text box that is input-capable. The list is opened by clicking the arrow. The text box and the list work together; that is, by clicking a selection in the list, the text box is filled with the corresponding value.

- **Style 1** Simple.

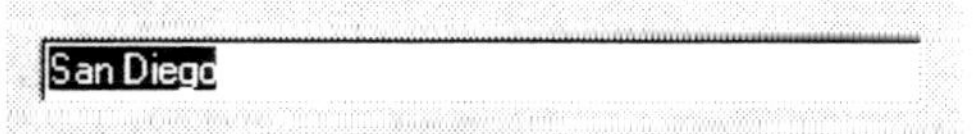

The text box is all you see, but the list is behind there. You can move through the list by pressing the arrow keys (each item appears in succession). The text box is input-capable.

- **Style 2** Drop-down List.

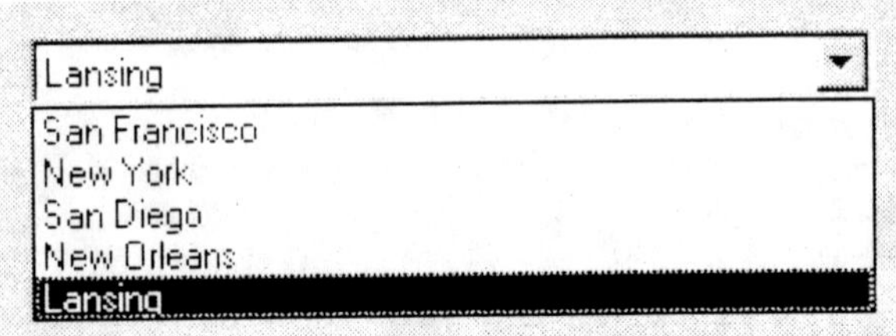

This isn't really a combo box even though it's called one. It would be better to call it a "drop-down list box." Although it has a text box, it's like a list box in that the user must select an item from a list and can't key their own item. The list isn't visible until the user clicks on the text box or the accompanying arrow. The text box is not input-capable.

Note: The properties and methods for combo boxes include all those of the list box plus the "Text" property.

The Check Box

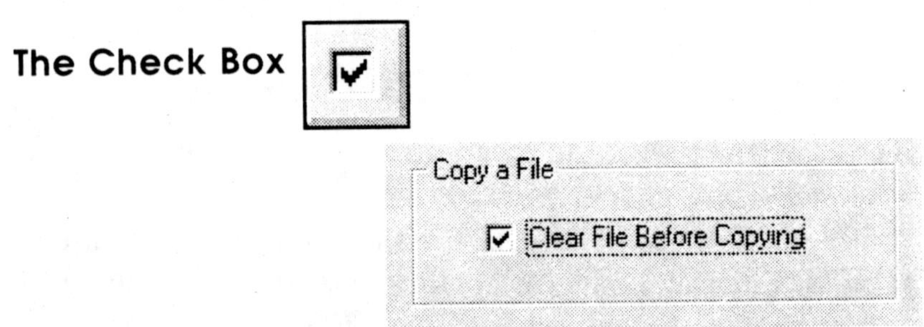

Use a check box when you want the user to specify "Yes" or "No." A check box control has only three states—true, false, or disabled, as kept in the "Value" property:

```
FormName.CheckBoxName.Value = 0          ' Unchecked

FormName.CheckBoxName.Value = 1          ' Checked

FormName.CheckBoxName.Value = 2          ' Dimmed (disabled)
```

You can test for the user selection like this:

```
If FormName.CheckBoxName.Value = 0 Then          ' Unchecked
```

You can have multiple check boxes on a form, and they are independent of each other; that is, clicking one on doesn't turn another off.

Control Arrays

A control array is not a control, it's an array of controls. Many controls can be defined as an array. For example, suppose you had an application that called for five command buttons, like this:

If the buttons are defined as an array, each button can be referred to with an index, instead of "Command1" or "SanDiegoButton."

Step by Step: Defining a Control Array

1. Bring up the VB Development Environment. (The default project will do, this code will be discarded.)
2. Click on the text box control and draw it on the form.
3. Click on a second text box and draw it on the form, like this:

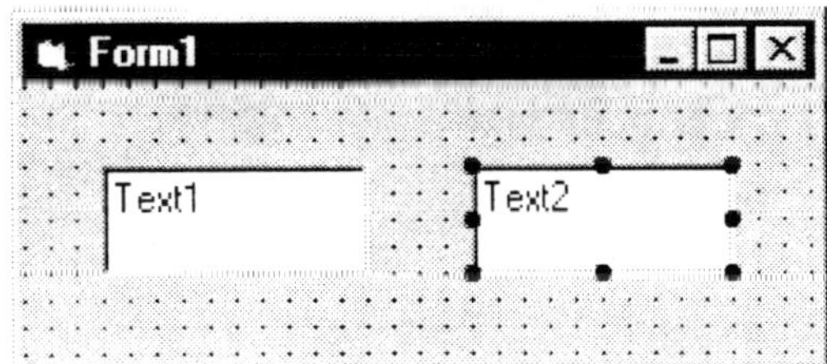

4. Select "Text2" (if not already selected) and, in the properties box, change its name to "Text1" (the same name as the first text box). You should see:

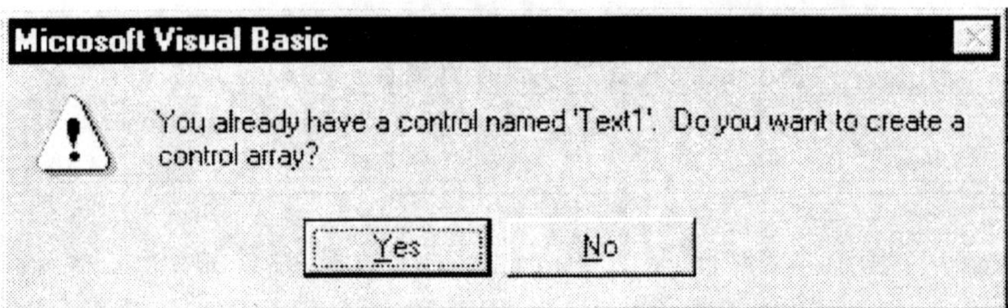

5. Click on "Yes."

   Now the text box controls are defined as a control array. It's that easy. Their name, "Text1," now has an index associated with it. The first text box is "Text1(0)" and the second is "Text1(1)."

6. Double click on the left text box to bring up the change event.

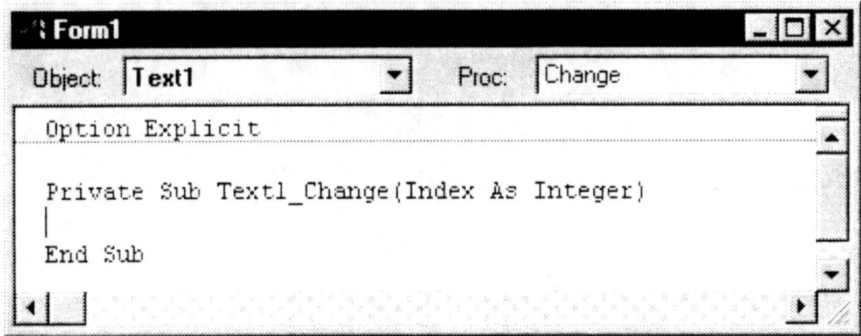

   Notice that now there is an argument associated with the procedure—"(Index As Integer)." When this procedure is called, the index of the changed text box will be passed in the "Index" argument.

7. Close this code window and double click on the other text box. You should see the very same code window you saw before.

   The text boxes, because they're part of an array, share all their event procedures; all the procedures now have arguments.

8. Discard the project.

The Frame Control 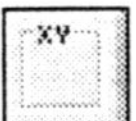

A *frame* can be thought of as a container that holds other controls, particularly control arrays. A frame can also group controls by function or for convenience.

Option Buttons 

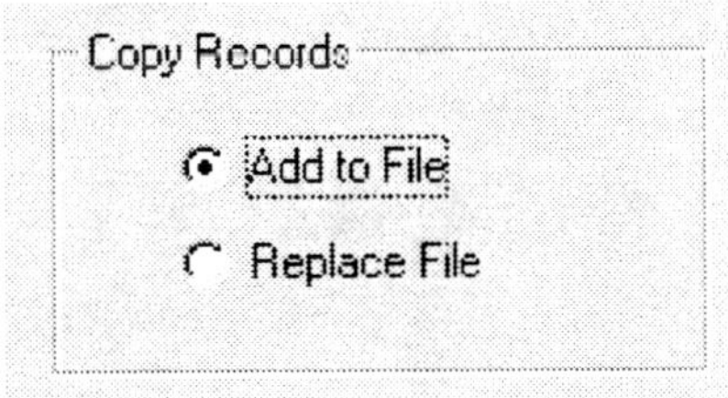

Option buttons are like check boxes in that they may be on or off only. However, option buttons are usually assigned in mutually exclusive multiples. In other words, only one option button of a group can be clicked on at a time. Clicking one button on turns the rest in the group off. The group, as you might have guessed, is a control array of option buttons.

Even if defined as a control array, *check boxes* are not mutually exclusive; that is, they can *all* be checked if desired. Another difference between option buttons and check boxes is that check boxes toggle, option buttons don't.

Step by Step: Defining Frames and Option Buttons

1. Bring up the VB Development Environment or start a new project. This won't be saved.

2. Click on the "Frame Control" button in the toolbox.

3. Draw the frame over about half the form like this:

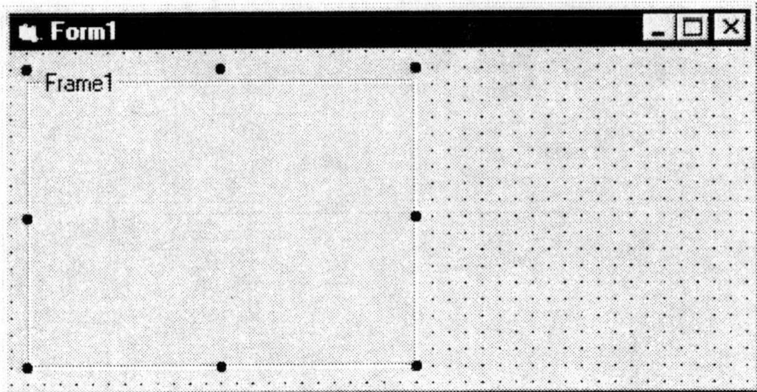

4. With the new frame as the active control, click on the "Option Button" button in the toolbox.

5. Draw the option button *on the frame*, like this:

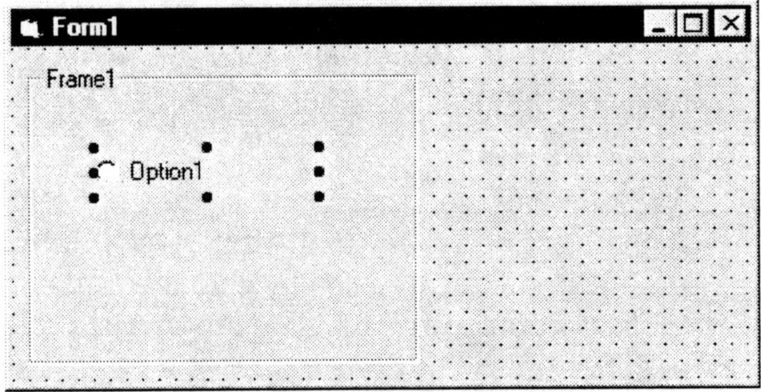

The option button is affixed to the frame, not the form.

6. Click on the frame to select it and drag it to the other side of the form. The option button should have gone along with it. If it didn't, it's attached to the form instead of the frame.

7. Click on the "Option Button" tool again and draw a second option button on the frame:

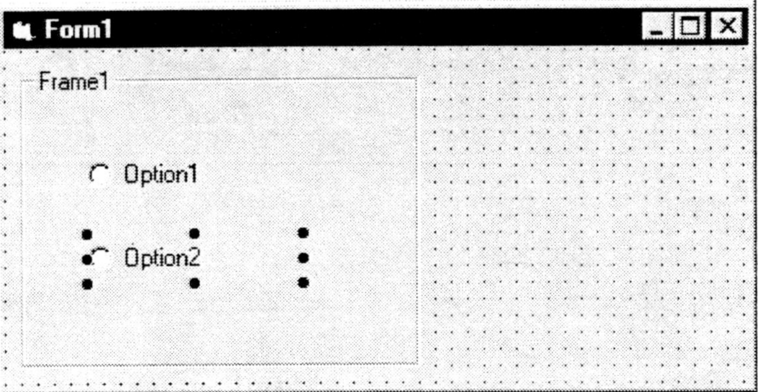

8. Run the program and click the option buttons.

   Because they're on the same frame, they work together. "Option1" (index 0) is selected by default when the program is started. Click on "Option2." "Option1" should turn off.

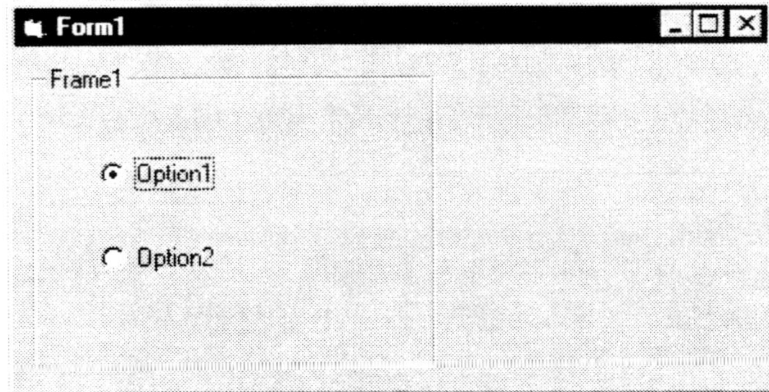

9. End the program and rename the "Option2" button "Option1." You should get the "Do you want to create a control array?" message. Say "Yes."

10. Select the "Option1" option button and try to drag it off the frame onto the form. If the button is fixed to the frame, you can't drag it off.

11. Select the "Option1" button, if you haven't already, and click on "Cut" on the Edit menu. The button should go away.

12. Click on the form itself, outside the frame, to select it. Click on "Paste" on the Edit menu. You should see:

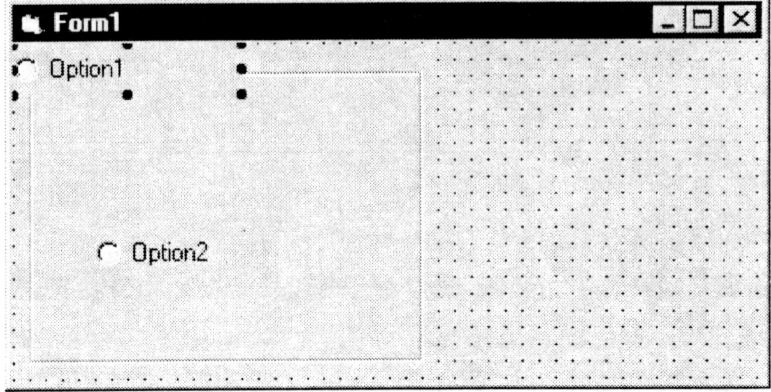

The control "Option1" is cut from the frame and pasted to the form.

13. Now try to drag the "Option1" button to the right side of the form. You should be able to do it now.

14. Run the program, and click on the option buttons. You see that they are now independent of each other. They don't work together.

    Even though the two buttons are elements in the same control array, they lose contact with each other when not on the same frame or form.

15. End the program.

16. Now cut the other option button, "Option2," from the frame and paste it on the form. Drag it to the right side of the form and run the program.

    Now that the option buttons are together again on the same form or frame, they work the way they're supposed to.

    If you haven't already done so, note that "Cut & Paste" is a valuable tool that you can use for controls and code.

17. Discard the project.

The Common Dialog Control 

The Common Dialog control provides a standard set of dialog boxes for operations such as opening, saving, and printing files or selecting colors and fonts.

The Common Dialog control provides an interface between Visual Basic and the routines in the Microsoft Windows Dynamic Link Library COMMDLG.DLL. To create a dialog box using this control, COMMDLG.DLL must be in your Microsoft Windows SYSTEM directory.

You create dialog boxes for your application by adding the Common Dialog control to a form and setting its properties. The type of dialog box displayed is determined by the methods of the control. At run time, a dialog box is displayed when the appropriate method is invoked; at design time, the Common Dialog control is displayed as an icon on a form. This icon can't be sized.

Under Microsoft Windows 95, the Common Dialog control automatically provides context-sensitive help on the interface of the dialog boxes by clicking:

- The "What's This" help button in the title bar, then clicking the item for which you want more information.
- The right mouse button over the item for which you want more information, then selecting the "What's This" command in the displayed context menu.

In the tutorial project EditText, a common dialog box could have been used instead of "frmOpen" to open a text file. This is a custom control, which is a separate file with an ".OCX" extension. To use the Common Dialog control in your application, you must add the COMDLG16.OCX or COMDLG32.OCX file to the project. To automatically include this custom control in new projects, add the file you need to AUTO16LD.Vbp or AUTO32LD.Vbp. When distributing your application, install the ".OCX" file in the user's Microsoft Windows SYSTEM directory. For more information on how to add a custom control to a project, see the *Visual Basic Programmer's Guide.*

> **Note:** *You can't specify where a dialog box is displayed.*

Record-level Access to a Database

In the overall direction taken in this book—that VB will be used as a PC language for an AS/400 client/server environment—it is assumed that the data and data handling are the responsibility of the AS/400. The goal for this section is that you be aware of the record-level access capabilities within VB.

Unlike standard BASIC, Visual Basic applications can be made *data aware*. That is, VB can deal with a database (either local or remote), at the record level. The database can be local on the PC, defined with a PC package like MS Access, FoxPro, dBASE, Paradox, or Btrieve; or accessed remotely through an Open Database Connectivity (ODBC) driver.

The ODBC Driver

The AS/400 is capable of being a remote database and there is an ODBC driver available that allows a VB program to access record sets. However, use of the ODBC driver as a c/s platform usually represents only a two-tier model. That is, all the rules of business and all of the processing logic to enforce those rules must reside on the PC, written in VB, or in stored SQL procedures. A more acceptable three-tier model is achieved with an RPG partner program in the middle, doing most of the work.

That's not to say that the ODBC driver doesn't have merit—it does. With V3R1 of OS/400, the ODBC became an excellent conduit for simple record retrieval where complex rules of business are not a concern.

> ***Note:*** *For complete instructions on Installing and Using the ODBC Driver, see Appendix B.*

PC Databases

PCs are capable of keeping a *relational database*. A *database* is defined as a collection of tables (files), indices, and queries centering around related information. You can define a PC database using a package like Microsoft Access or one of the others mentioned previously.

Visual Basic has a database access engine built in called the *Jet Engine*. It's the same engine that runs the Microsoft Access PC database package. You may also define a PC database using the VB database object.

The Database Engine Object

The database engine object (call DBEngine Object) is the interface between your VB application and a database. The DBEngine object maintains the description of the database structure (tables, indices and queries). The DBEngine object controls the Jet Engine. The database object supports several VB methods that you can use to manage the database.

Data Controls and Bound Controls

As was mentioned, VB has a database access engine built in. Further, VB has controls that can be connected to a specific database through that engine. This means that you can get access to, and maintain, a database with little or no code.

There are two controls that come into play—the data control and the bound control. The data control provides record-level access to a database, and bound controls are regular controls (like text boxes) that are bound to the fields within the database record. In each case, properties are used to connect the data control to a database, and bound controls to their respective fields.

Again, PC record-level access is not within the scope of this book; but if you're interested in a good overview of the concept, see Chapter 22 of your *Visual Basic Programmer's Guide.*

VB Code—Controlling Program Flow

> ***Note**: All VB code presented here is also listed in the "AS/400 and VB Cross References" chart for quick look up.*

Some Visual Basic common code has yet to be presented. As with controls in the first part of this chapter, code, for the most part, is only described and not used in the example project EditText. In-use examples of most of the code presented here can be found in the "AS/400 Report Download Utility" in Chapter 14.

The If...Then Statement

The "If...Then" statement is the equivalent of the RPG op code IFxx...ENDIF.

The RPG code:

```
C                  FIELD1       IFEQ  VALUE1
C                               .
C                               .
C                               ENDIF
```

is expressed in VB as:

```
                   If Field1 = Value1 Then
                          .
                          .
                   End If
```

The RPG code:

```
C                  FIELD1       IFLE  VALUE1
C                               .
C                               .
C                               ENDIF
```

is expressed in VB as:

```
                   If Field1 <= Value1 Then
                          .
                          .
                   End If
```

The RPG code:

```
C                  FIELD1       IFGT  VALUE1
C                  FIELD2       ANDLT VALUE2
```

```
C                    FIELD3       OREQ   VALUE3
C                                 .
C                                 .
C                                 ENDIF
```

can be expressed in VB as:

```
If Field1 > Value1 And Field2 < Value2 Or Field3 = Value3 Then
    .
    .
End If
```

In VB, you can substitute an expression for the fields and values:

```
If Field1 * Field2 <= (Field1 + Field2) * Field3 Then
    .
    .
End If
```

Note: *Parentheses are used for determining the order of calculations.*

The Select Case Statement

The VB "Select Case...End Select" statement is the equivalent of the RPG op code "SELEC...ENDSL."

Consider the following RPG code:

```
C                                 SELEC
C                    REPLY        WHEQ   'YES'
C                                 .
C                    REPLY        WHEQ   'NO'
```

```
C                              .
C                              OTHER
C                              .
C                              ENDSL
```

The VB way of saying the same thing is:

```
Select Case Reply
  Case "Yes"
      '
  Case "No"
      '
  Case Else
      '
End Select
```

Notice that, in RPG, the "WHxx" statements don't all have to refer to the same variable. You could have code like this:

```
C                  SCREEN      WHEQ  '01'
C                  REPLY       ANDEQ 'YES'
C                              .
C                              .
C                  REPLY       WHEQ  'NO'
```

The VB statement ties the variable to the "Select Case" statement, so only one variable may be involved. VB can be very flexible with the one variable, though.

The code for the RPG "OREQ" condition:

```
C                 REPLY       WHEQ  'Yes'
C                 REPLY       OREQ  'All Right'
C                 REPLY       OREQ  'OK'
C                 REPLY       OREQ  'You Win'
C                             .
C                             .
C                 REPLY       WHEQ  'No'
C                 REPLY       OREQ  'Not Now'
C                 REPLY       OREQ  'Sorry'
```

The VB equivalent is:

```
Case "Yes", "All Right", "OK", "You Win"
                .
Case "No", "Not Now", "Sorry"
```

The "OR" condition is set up with a list of valid values, separated by commas.

You can use a range of values in the expression, like this:

```
Select Case Reply
  Case "A" To "L"
      .
  Case "M" To "Z"
      .
  Case Else
      .
```

```
End Select
```

You can use a comparison expression (like ">4" or "<=8") with this syntax:

```
Select Case Reply
  Case Is < "A"
      .
  Case Is > "Z"
      .
  Case Else
      .
End Select
```

Notice the keyword *"Is."* If omitted, VB inserts it automatically.

Finally, you can combine expressions and ranges:

```
Select Case Reply
  Case "A" To "C", "H" To "J", Is > "T"
      .
  Case Else
End Select
```

Plenty of ways to express your logic.

Step by Step: The Select Case Statement

The "Select Case" statement is commonly used in error-handling routines to take appropriate action based on the error code (*Number property* of the *Error Object*).

1. Bring up your EditText project.

2. Run the program. Go into "Open a File..." and, without clicking on any file names in the File Box or keying anything into the text box, click on "OK." You should see:

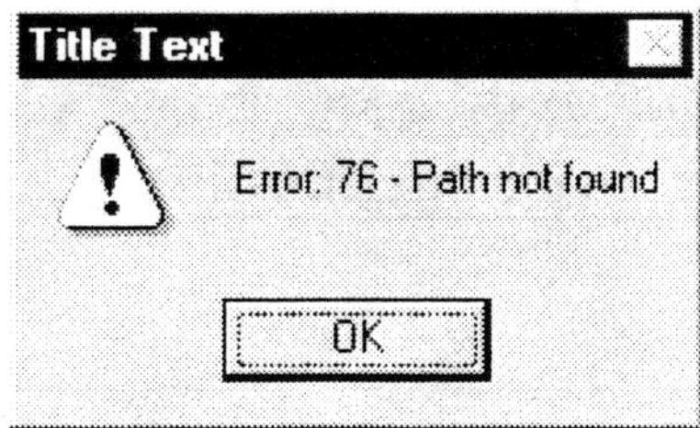

Well, that's really not true. Because of the way the property "FileName" is concatenated from the folder box path and the file box name properties, the "FileName" property contained "c:\vb\" (16 bit) or "C:\Program Files\Microsoft Visual Basic\" (32 bit). This was interpreted as a bad path, and the error handler was invoked with an Err.Number value of 76. The real problem was that no file name was specified.

You can make error messages more informative and useful by substituting your own text.

3. Bring "frmOpen" into the form design window. Double click on the "OK" button to bring the "cmdOK_Click" procedure into the code window.

4. Change the "ErrorSubr" error-handling subroutine to read like this:

frmOpen

Object: cmdOK   Proc: Click

```
ErrorSubr:
  Select Case Err.Number
  Case 53
    MsgBox MESSAGE_1, vbOKOnly + vbExclamation, "Open a File"
  Case 76
    MsgBox MESSAGE_2, vbOKOnly + vbExclamation, "Open a File"
  Case Else
    MsgBox "Error: " & Err.Number & " - " & Err.Description, _
           vbOKOnly + vbExclamation, "Open a File"
  End Select
  Exit Sub
```

Now, the messages that were loaded into the global constants defined earlier are used to give the user a better chance of solving the problem.

The messages are displayed for a specific error code by the "Select Case" statement. "Case Else" displays the general error message.

5. Run the program. Go into "Open a File..." and, without clicking on any file names in the File Box or keying anything into the text box, click on "OK." You should see:

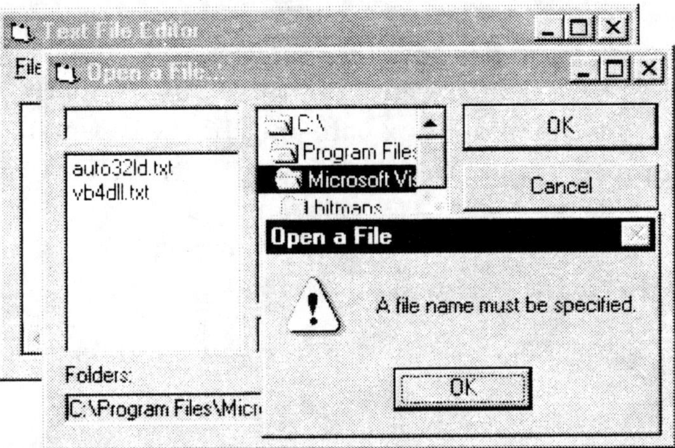

A more accurate message.

6. Click on "OK." Click on the txtFileName box in the upper left of "frmOpen."

7. Key in a nonexistent file name. Click on "OK." You should get the "File not found" message. (Admittedly, this message is the same as the Err.Description message.)

8. End the program.

9. Save your project.

10. Now, as the last addition to the EditText project, add error checking to the DriveChange event.

    With "frmOpen" up, double click on the drive box, [c:], to bring "drvBox_Change" into the code window.

11. Add the following code:

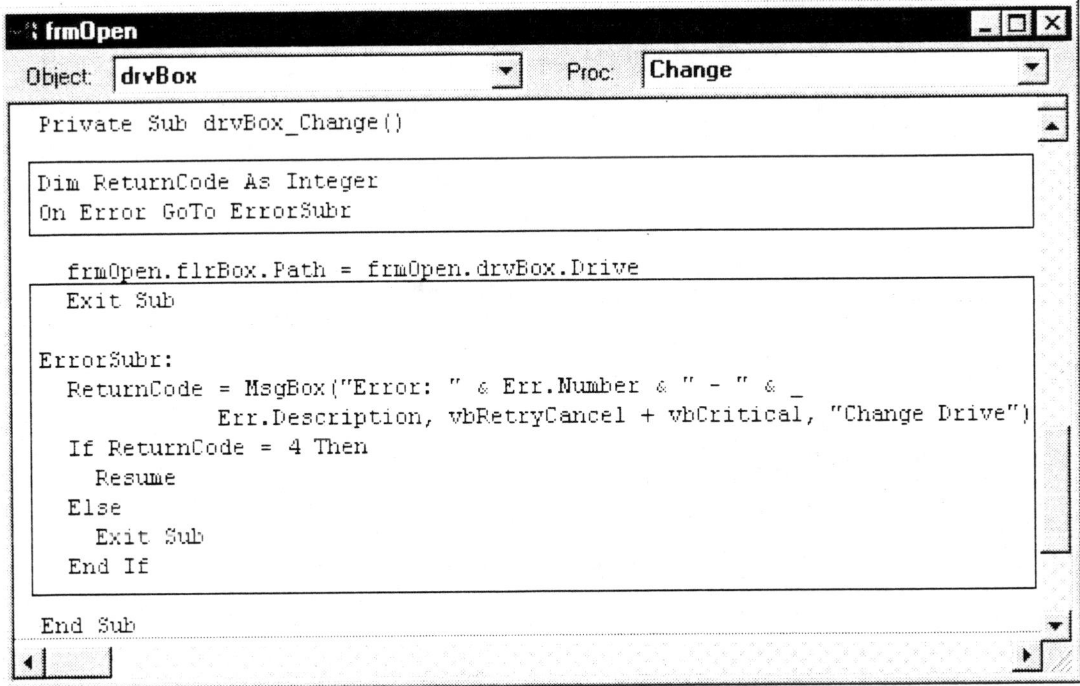

```
Private Sub drvBox_Change()

Dim ReturnCode As Integer
On Error GoTo ErrorSubr

  frmOpen.flrBox.Path = frmOpen.drvBox.Drive
  Exit Sub

ErrorSubr:
  ReturnCode = MsgBox("Error: " & Err.Number & " - " & _
              Err.Description, vbRetryCancel + vbCritical, "Change Drive")
  If ReturnCode = 4 Then
    Resume
  Else
    Exit Sub
  End If

End Sub
```

With this code, the user responds to an error message with "Retry" or "Cancel." The response is placed in the variable "ReturnCode," and appropriate action is taken. The value returned when the user clicks on "Retry" is 4.

> ***Note:*** *The MsgBox used here is the function, not the statement. In order to get a response, you must use the function.*

12. Run the program. Bring up "frmOpen." With no diskette in drive A:, click on the drive box arrow to open it. Click on the entry for the A: drive. You should see:

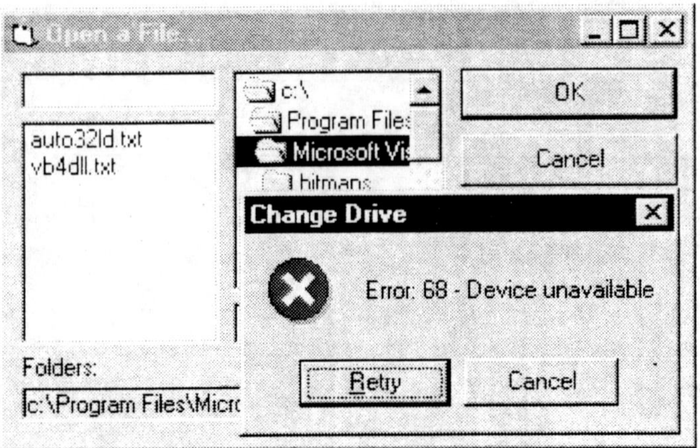

13. Put a diskette in drive A: and click on "Retry." The "Retry" button is associated with the statement "Resume," which tries the errored statement again. All should be well, now.

14. End the program and save your project.

The For...Next Statement

The VB "For...Next" statement is the equivalent of the RPG op code "DO (number of times)."

Consider the following RPG code:

```
C                START       DO      ENDAT         CURENT
C                            .
C                            .
C                            .
C                            ENDDO
```

Assume START = 1, ENDAT = 10. This structure executes 10 times. The variable "CURENT" has a value of 1 to 10, depending on the iteration.

The VB equivalent is:

```
For Current = Start To EndAt
      .
      .
Next Current
```

If, for some reason, you need the equivalent of the RPG code:

```
C                START       DO    ENDAT        CURENT
C                            .
C                            .
C                            .
C                            ENDDO 2
```

where the value of CURENT is incremented by 2 on each iteration (see "ENDDO 2"), add "Step" to the "For" statement, like this:

```
For Current = Start To EndAt Step 2
      .
      .
Next Current
```

The Do...Loop Statement

You've seen that the equivalent of the RPG op code "DO (number of times)" is the "For...Next" statement. The equivalent of the RPG op code "DOWxx...ENDDO" is the VB "Do While...Loop" or "Do Until...Loop" statements.

The RPG code:

```
C                FIELD1      DOWLE VALUE1
C                            .
```

```
C                             LEAVE
C                             .
C                             ENDDO
```

is expressed in VB as:

```
Do While Field1 <= Value1
 .
 Exit Do
 .
Loop
```

or

```
Do Until Field1 > Value1
 .
 Exit Do
 .
Loop
```

Notice that the "Do Until...Loop" is not the equivalent of the RPG op code "DOUxx;" it's just another way of saying "Do While." The test for the do loop is at the top in both cases. To keep the two "Do" statements equivalent in the above examples, the operator "<=" in the first had to be changed to ">".

The "DOUxx" example follows. The RPG code:

```
C                 FIELD1      DOULE VALUE1
C                             .
C                             LEAVE
C                             .
C                             ENDDO
```

is expressed in VB as:

```
Do
  .
  Exit Do
  .
Loop While Field1 <= Value1
```

or

```
Do
  .
  Exit Do
  .
Loop Until Field1 > Value1
```

In both the RPG and VB examples, the test for the iteration is done at the bottom of the loop. Just as in RPG, this is the less preferable form.

Obviously, the VB equivalent of the "LEAVE" op code is "Exit Do."

You can approach RPG's op code "ITER" in one of two ways—you can use the dreaded "GoTo" statement:

```
Do1:        Do While Field1 <= Value1
              .
              GoTo Do1
              .
            Loop
```

or

```
            Do
             .
             GoTo Loop1          ' Like "ITER"
             .
Loop1:      Loop Until Field1 > Value1
```

Or you can use the "Next" statement in a "For...Next" loop:

```
            For Field1 = 1 To Value1
             .
             Next Value1         ' Like "ITER"
             .
            Next Value1
```

VB Code—String Handling

String handling is frequently called upon in VB, especially when dealing with an AS/400 in a client/server environment, in order to get data in a form the 400 can deal with, and for efficient data transport. VB has a number of functions for string handling.

Bear in mind that both functions and statements of the same name exist in VB. (For example, "Time" the function, which returns the time of day, and "Time," the statement that *sets* the time of day.) Functions and statements are presented together, where applicable.

Many functions come in two varieties—one that returns a variant data type and one that returns a string data type. The variant type function has no "$" at the end, the string type does. String-type functions are more appropriate for client/server applications and receive preference.

Substringing

Substringing is extracting or replacing a portion of a string. The following VB functions and procedures handle substringing:

VB Function or Statement	What it Does
Left/Left$, Right/Right$	Returns a substring from the left or the right of a larger string.
LTrim/LTrim$, RTrim/RTrim$, Trim/Trim$	Returns a string with leading, trailing, or leading and trailing blanks trimmed off.
Mid/Mid$	Returns a substring from a larger string.

The Left/Left$, Right/Right$ Functions

"Left$" and "Right$" functions are like specialized versions of the "Mid$" function. Substrings are returned, but only from the ends of the larger string. In a situation where you might need code like this:

```
C                   MOVEL LONGER      SHORTR  10
```

or

```
C                   MOVE   LONGER     SHORTR  10
```

to get the leftmost or rightmost 10 bytes of "LONGER," use this VB code:

```
Shorter = Left$(Longer, 10)
```

or

```
Shorter = Right$(Longer, 10)
```

There are no Left/Left$ or Right/Right$ *statements*. You have to use Mid/Mid$.

The LTrim/LTrim$, RTrim/RTrim$, Trim/Trim$ Functions

All these functions do the same thing. When passed a string as an argument, they return a value that has leading or trailing blanks trimmed off. The RPG equivalent would be an array-handling routine to determine the last nonblank character, lop off the blanks, etc.:

"LTrim$" returns a value with leading blanks trimmed.

"RTrim$" returns a value with trailing blanks trimmed.

"Trim$" returns a value with both leading and trailing blanks trimmed.

The syntax goes like this:

```
TrimmedField = Trim$(UnTrimmedField)

TrimmedField = RTrim$(UnTrimmedField)
```

The first example trims blanks from both ends, the second only from the right.

The "Trim$" function is especially useful when comparing a string to a literal or another string. For instance, suppose you are checking a text field for user input with the following statement:

```
If txtUserInput.Text = "" Then
```

This works fine most of the time, but suppose the user keyed something into the text box, changed his/her mind, and keyed blanks to remove the input. The above statement would fail. The "Trim" function saves the day:

```
If Trim(txtUserInput.Text) = "" Then
```

An empty string or a string of blanks produces the same result.

For all of the substringing functions, if the receiving field is a variable length string, the results are predictable:

Trim$("bbbXXXbbb")—comes back as "XXX."

Rtrim$("bbbXXXbbb")—comes back as "bbbXXX."

Mid$("bbbXXXbbb, 3, 3)—comes back as "XXX."

Less obvious is the value returned to a *fixed* length variable. Assume the string to receive the value to be 8 bytes long and fixed:

Trim$("bbbXXXbbb")—comes back as "XXXbbbbb."

Rtrim$("bbbXXXbbb")—comes back as "bbbXXXbb."

Mid$("bbbXXXbbb, 3, 3)—comes back as "XXXbbbbb."

The function is performed on the string and the returned value is left justified into the receiving field. If the receiving field is longer than the returned value, the field is padded with blanks.

The Mid/Mid$ Functions

The "Mid" and "Mid$" functions return a substring of another string. The syntax goes like this:

```
ShorterString = Mid$(LongerString, FromStart, ForLength)
```

For example, the RPG code:

```
C                   10           SUBST   LONGER:5   SHORTR  10
```

extracts 10 bytes from the field "LONGER," starting at position 5, and puts them in the field "SHORTR." The same thing in VB is:

```
Shorter = Mid$(Longer, 5, 10)
```

The Mid/Mid$ Statements

The "Mid" and "Mid$" statements *replace* part of a longer string with a substring.

The syntax is:

```
Mid$(LongerString, FromStart, ToLength) = ShorterString
```

Notice that this is practically the reverse of the "Mid$" function. This code replaces the contents of the variable "LongerString," starting at position 5, for a length of 10, with the contents of the variable "ShorterString." There is no RPG equivalent.

The length argument may be omitted. If it is, the length defaults to the length of the variable "ShorterString," less the characters before the start position.

VB Code—Data Conversion and Formatting

Frequently in RPG, data needs to be converted from one type to another, or from one format to another. For instance, a numeric field is converted to alpha in RPG (with the "MOVE" op code):

```
C               MOVE   NUMFLD         ALPFLD
```

or with a data structure:

```
I      DS
I                              1      90NUMFLD
I                              1      9 ALPFLD
```

Or, in output specs, data is reformatted with edit codes or words:

```
O                              NUMFLD Z   68
O                              NUMFLD     68    'bb0000*'
```

In VB, there are several functions and statements for data conversion and formatting:

VB Function or Statement	What It Does
Asc	Returns an ASCII value for a character (opposite of Chr$).
CCur, CDbl, CInt, CLng, CSng, CStr, CVar	Converts expressions into a specific data type.
Chr/Chr$	Returns character for an ASCII value from 0 to 255 (opposite of Asc).
Format/Format$	Returns a formatted numeric or string variable according to instructions.
InStr	Returns the position of the first occurrence of a scanned-for string within another string.
LCase/LCase$	Returns lowercase string.
Len	Returns the length of a string.

VB Function or Statement	What It Does
LSet statement	Left aligns a string.
RSet statement	Right aligns a string.
Space/Space$	Returns a string of a specified number of blanks (opposite of Val).
Str/Str$	Returns a string for a numeric variable.
UCase/UCase$	Returns an uppercase string.
Val	Returns the first numbers found in a string (opposite of Str$).

The Asc Function

Just as each character is represented internally in the AS/400 as a value in EBCDIC, characters are represented in a PC as a value in ASCII. The "Asc" function returns the ASCII value of a character. For example, on the 400, a blank is represented internally by the value 64 (hex 40). If you had an AS/400 command that would tell you what the internal value was for a character, that would be like the "Asc" function.

In this example, the integer variable "I" ranges from 65 (the ASCII value for A) to 90 (the ASCII value for Z):

```
Dim I As Integer

For I = Asc("A") To Asc("Z")

   .

Next I
```

The compliment of "Asc" is the Chr$" function.

The CCur, CDbl, CInt, CLng, CSng, CStr, and CVar Functions

All of these functions convert any valid data expression to another specific data type. For instance, suppose you have a numeric variable that you want to put in a currency format. You could convert the value of the numeric variable using the CCur function and put it into another variable.

The following table lists the common conversion functions and the type of conversion they perform:

Function	Conversion Type
CCur	Currency
CDbl	Double
CInt	Integer
CLng	Long
CSng	Single
CStr	String
CVar	Variant

The Chr/Chr$ Functions

"Chr$" is the opposite of "Asc." As was stated, each character has an internal value. The value can range from 0 to 255. "Chr$" returns the corresponding character for a value. This is handy because not all 256 values can be represented with a character, and some have special meanings.

For instance, to add the "New Line" ("LineFeed") character to the end of a string:

```
SomeString = SomeString & Chr$(10)
```

This is something new to AS/400 programmers—being able to access special characters.

The Format/Format$ Functions

As edit codes and edit words are to an RPG numeric field, the "Format$" function is to a VB variable. You pass a number or string variable and formatting instructions to the Format$ function and the formatted string is returned. Notice that you can format both numeric variables and string variables.

For example, this code:

```
Today = Format$(Now, "ddddd") & " " & Format$(Now, "ttttt")
```

loads the string variable "Today" with the date and time formatted according to the instructions "ddddd" (date) and "ttttt" (time):

```
01/11/9X 12:10:06 PM
```

Like an RPG edit word is instructions for formatting printed output, these are instructions to the Format$ function. The codes and their meaning can be brought up in the VB Development Environment through "Help" —search on "Format."

Additionally, the instructions argument can be a *format name*. There are several predefined format descriptions available, and you call them by name. Think of them like the Z or Y edit codes in RPG output specs.

Expressions:

```
TodaysDate = Format(Now, "general date")
```

and

```
Money = format(1084.25, "currency")
```

return values of "01/11/9X 12:10:06 PM" and "$1,084.25," respectively.

The InStr Function

The "InStr" function is the equivalent of the RPG "SCAN" op code. It returns the position of the first occurrence of one string within another.

The syntax goes like this:

```
PositionNumber = InStr(StartPosition, LookAt, LookFor, 1)
```

If the "LookFor" string is found, "PositionNumber" receives the position within "LookAt" where it is found. If "LookFor" is not within "LookAt," zero is passed back to "PositionNumber."

If a value for "StartPosition" is omitted, the scan starts at the first position of "LookAt."

You may also specify whether or not the scan is case sensitive. The argument "0" (case sensitive) or "1" (not case sensitive) is appended as the fourth argument. The default is "0"—case sensitive. (Also, see the *Visual Basic Language Reference* as to how to change the default compare method with the "Option Compare" statement.)

The LCase and LCase$ Functions

"LCase$" returns the lowercase equivalent of a string:

```
StringVariable = LCase$(StringVariable)
```

In this example, the variable is both the argument and the receiving variable, so it is converted to lowercase. There is also a "UCase" function.

The Len Function

"Len" returns the length—in terms of storage bytes—for a variable. BASIC numeric data types are predefined, so the "Len" function's main use is to determine the length of a variable length string or of a user data type.

Syntax for the "Len" function:

```
StringLength = Len(OfAString)
```

The LSet Statement

The "LSet" statement is like the RPG op code "MOVEL." It left aligns a value into a variable. The variable must have a nonzero length for it to work.

For example, this code places the 6-byte literal "<-Left" in the left-most positions of 10-byte "TempString:"

```
Dim TempString As String * 10

LSet TempString = "<-Left"
```

Again, the "TempString" must have a nonzero length.

The RSet Statement

The "RSet" statement is the compliment to "LSet." As you would expect, "RSet" is like the RPG op code "MOVE." It right aligns a value into a variable. The variable must have a nonzero length for it to work.

"RSet" syntax:

```
RSet TempString = "Right->"
```

The Space/Space$ Functions

The "Space$" function returns a specified number of blanks. Use it to clear fixed-length string variables:

```
CustomerName = Space$(30)
```

The Str/Str$ Functions

The "Str$" function returns a string version of a numeric variable or expression. It's the equivalent of the RPG:

```
C                    MOVE  NUMFLD       ALPFLD
```

Syntax for "Str$:"

```
StringVariable = Str$(NumericVariable)
```

The opposite of "Str$" is the "Val" function.

The String/String$ Functions

The "String$" function returns a string of all the same character. As the "Space$" function returns a number of blanks, "String$" returns a specified character.

Like this:

```
AllZs = String$(30, "Z")
```

The UCase and UCase$ Functions

"UCase$" returns the uppercase equivalent of a string:

```
NewString = UCase$(OldString)
```

In this example, "NewString" gets the uppercase version of "OldString." The value in "OldString" remains unchanged.

The Val Function

The "Val" function returns a numeric value for a string of characters. You might well ask, "How can a string of characters have a numeric value?" It doesn't. What the "Val" function does is scan the string for numerals, stripping out blanks, tabs, and linefeeds. It does not, however, strip out other characters. It just stops looking.

For instance:

```
NumbersOnly = Val("  75.98 for set of 4")
```

renders 75.98 in NumbersOnly. The 4 at the end is not seen because the letter f is encountered.

This statement:

```
NumbersOnly = Val("  $75.98 for set of 4")
```

returns a value of 0. Zero is returned when no numbers are found before a non-numeric character (the "$").

The "Val" function is the opposite of the "Str$" function.

VB Code—Date and Time

There are three functions and statements within VB for returning date/time information:

VB Function or Statement	What It Does
Date/Date$ function	Returns the current system date.
Date/Date$ statement	Sets the system date.
Now function	Returns the current date and time.
Time/Time$ function	Returns the current system time.
Time/Time$ statements	Sets the system clock.

The Date/Date$ Functions

"Date$"—the function—returns the current system date:

```
TodaysDate = Date$
```

The Date/Date$ Statements

"Date$"—the statement—resets the current system date.

For example:

```
Date$ =  "01-11-1996"

Date$ = TodaysDate
```

The Now Function

Returns the current system date and time as a date data type or a variant data type "7" (date). Variant data is to be avoided, so when you need the date and time for display purposes, you can use the date data type.

Like this:

```
Dim Today As Date

  Today = Now
```

Also, once the information has been captured, you can convert the information into a string with "CStr."

The Time/Time$ Functions

Returns the current system time:

```
TimeRightNow = Time$
```

The Time/Time$ Statements

Resets the current system time:

```
Time$ = TimeFromAS400
```

These are by no means all of the VB functions and statements, but it's an adequate working set.

Summary

Controls

The list box and combo box controls are used like AS/400 subfiles—to list several like records for display or selection.

A check box is used to get a yes or no answer from the user. It can only be on or off.

Control arrays are multiple controls of the same type, with the same name referenced by index, like a regular array.

Control arrays are created by defining a second control with the same name as the first.

A frame is a container for grouping other controls.

Option buttons are like check boxes, except that they are grouped together and a selection of one deselects all others in the group.

VB Code

Statement structures to control program flow:

```
If...Then

Else If

Else

End If

Select Case

Case

Case Else

End Select

Do While

Exit Do

Loop

For

Exit For

Next
```

String Handling statements and functions:

```
Left$, Right$

LTrim$, RTrim$, Trim$

Mid$
```

Data conversion and formatting statements and functions:

```
Asc

CCur, CDbl, CInt, CLng, CSng, CStr, CVar

Chr$

Format$

InStr

LCase$

Len

LSet, RSet

Space$

Str$

UCase$

Val
```

Date and time statements and functions:

```
Date$

Now

Time$
```

Microsoft Visual Basic Version 4.0
For 32-bit Windows Development

Copyright © 1987-1995 Microsoft Corp.

9

Procedure Calls, Functions, and APIs

Before additional Visual Basic topics are presented, the subjects of procedure calls, functions, APIs, linking to external routines, and, ultimately, the AS/400, merit discussion.

Procedure Calls

An *argument*, it's been said, is a parameter that is passed to a procedure or function. Arguments are passed after the procedure name, within parentheses, separated by commas. For illustration, perform the following steps.

Step by Step: Passing Arguments

1. Bring up the VB Development Environment.

2. Double click on the default form "Form1" to bring up the code window for the "Load" event. Notice the "Sub" statement:

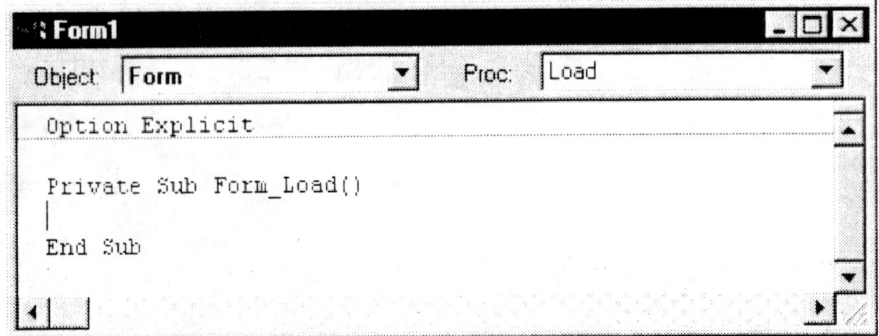

See the parentheses on the "Sub Form_Load" statement? That's where the arguments for a procedure are placed. This procedure, then, accepts no arguments.

3. Click on the procedures list at the top of the code window to open the procedures list for "Form1."

4. Scroll up until you come to the event procedure "KeyPress." Click on "KeyPress."

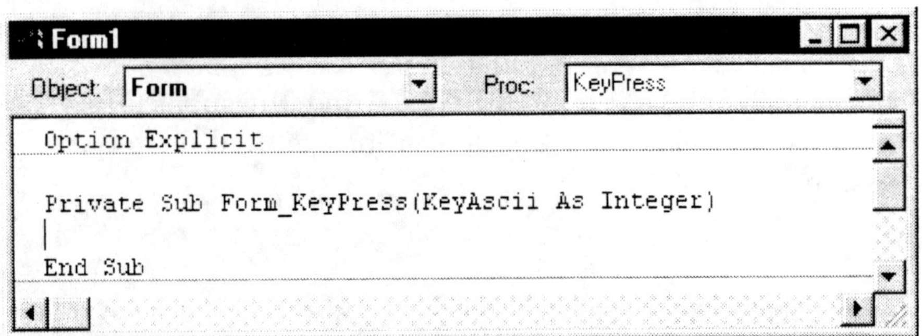

"KeyPress" is the event that takes place when the user presses a key—any key.

Now, there is an argument inside the parentheses. That's because the event "KeyPress" has an associated argument—the key that was pressed.

What is passed is the ASCII value of the keystroke that caused the event. For example, when the user presses the Enter key, VB passes the corresponding ASCII value for that key—13—to the procedure.

Here is typical code for the KeyPress event:

```
Private Sub Form_KeyPress(KeyAscii As Integer)

  If KeyAscii = 13 Then

    Call Form_Click

  End If

End Sub
```

In this procedure, only the Enter key is considered. Any other key press is ignored. If the user presses the Enter key, the procedure "Form_Click" is called.

5. To further illustrate arguments, open the procedures list again. Click on "KeyUp" to bring that event procedure into the code window:

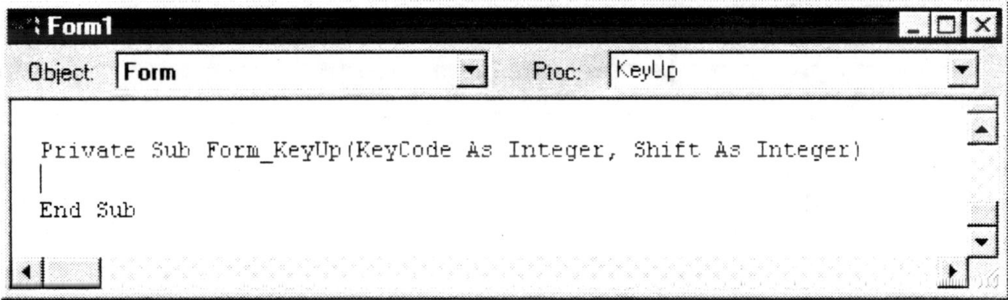

This event has two arguments, separated by commas. The first is the same as before—the key that was pressed. The second is the status of the Shift, Ctrl, and Alt keys, as expressed in an integer. This event, by the way, occurs when the user *releases* a key.

In the two examples above, VB invokes the procedures and passes the arguments when the corresponding event occurs. Those same procedures can be called by code in your program, but you have to pass the parms.

6. Start a new project. Bring the procedure for the KeyPress event into the code window, as before.

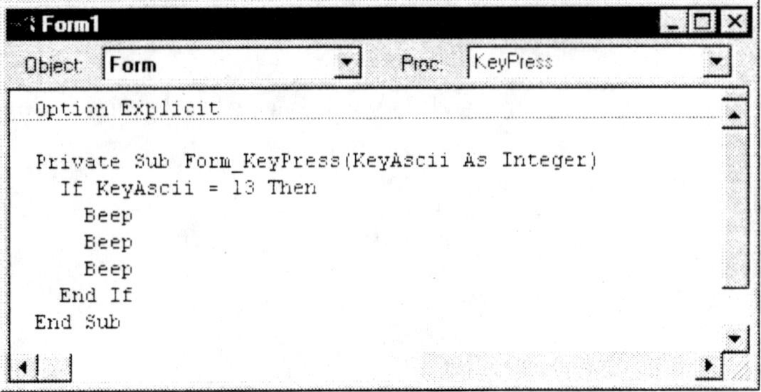

7. Key the following code into the procedure:
8. Run the program. Press the Enter key. You should hear a little chirp.
9. With the mouse, click inside the form. Nothing, right?
10. End the program. Open the procedures list and bring up to the click event.
11. Key in this one line of code:

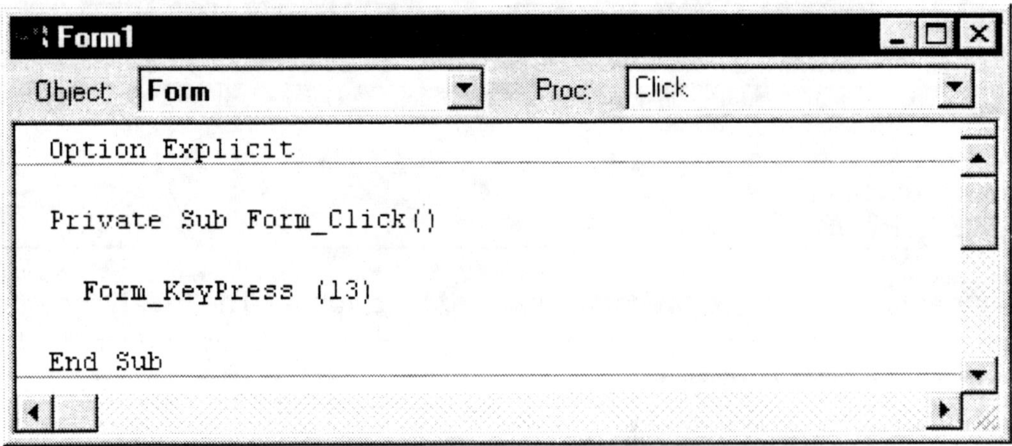

One of the points of this exercise is to show that you can invoke an event procedure just as readily in code as through user action. The "KeyPress" procedure is executed when called from within the "Click" procedure, although no KeyPress *event* took place. In other words, all procedures are alike. They can be invoked by an event or they can be called explicitly.

12. Run the program. Click inside the form. You should hear beeps this time.

13. End the program. You should be back to the code window for the click event.

The other point to be made: The value "13" was passed as an argument from procedure "Click" to procedure "KeyPress." (You know it got there because that's the only value that causes a beep.)

In RPG and CL, you have to make parameters match between the calling and the called programs. They must match by data type, length, and number. In VB, the same holds true, but the process is simpler. Recall that numeric variables available in VB do not allow you to specify decimal positions or length. So all the calling and called procedures have to agree upon is "Integer," "Long," or "Currency." Strings, if defined as fixed-length, require matching by length.

Step by Step: Matching Arguments by Variable Type

1. Change the code in the "Click" procedure (don't forget the double quotes):

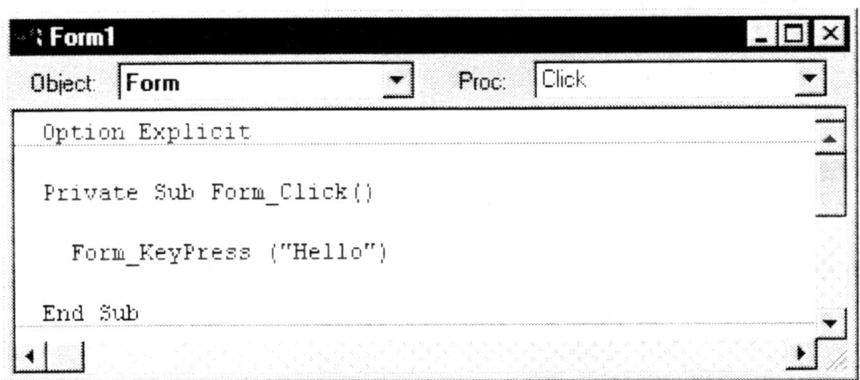

VB considers the literal "Hello" to be of data type *string*.

2. Run the program and click the form. You should see:

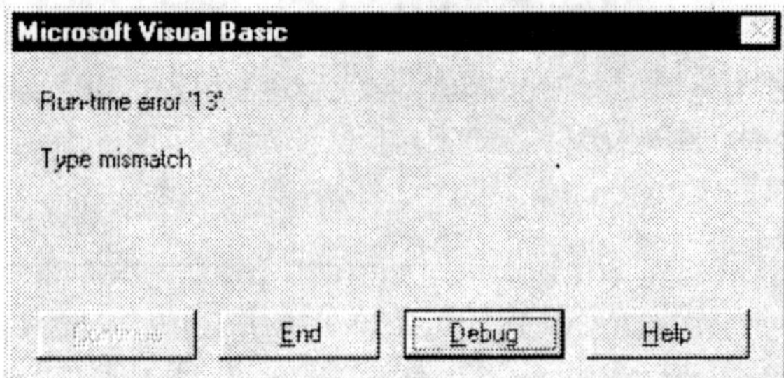

This message is telling you that the argument you're trying to pass doesn't match the type expected in the called procedure.

3. Discard the project.

If there were multiple arguments to pass, each has to match in type and in the order passed.

Creating Procedures That Accept Arguments

In this code:

```
Private Sub Form_KeyPress(KeyAscii As Integer)

    .

End Sub
```

"KeyAscii" is a local variable—that is, known only to this procedure. It's defined as an argument with the "KeyAscii As Integer" clause. (A *clause* is a part of a statement.) Recall that the default type for a variable is *variant*. The "As Integer" part of the statement defines the variable as an integer.

Creating and Calling Your Own Procedures

You can, of course, create your own procedure. If that procedure requires parameters, you define it like this:

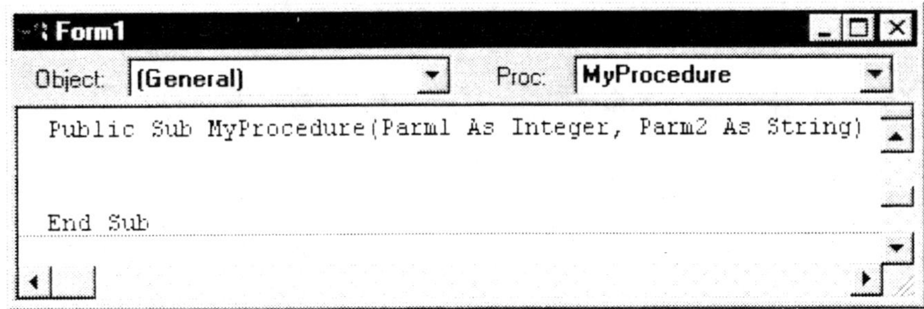

Just as in RPG or CL, the variables "Parm1" and "Parm2" are there to receive values passed. They are not the variable names from the calling procedure. Arguments are matched up by position, just like on the 400.

The statements that call this procedure look like this:

```
Call MyProcedure(IntegerToPass, StringToPass)
```

or

```
MyProcedure IntegerToPass, StringToPass
```

There are two forms of the "Call" statement—one with the word "Call" and arguments enclosed in parentheses, and one without. VB allows the keyword "Call" to be omitted. If you omit the "Call" keyword, you're left with this:

```
MyProcedure(IntegerToPass, StringToPass)
```

which is the syntax for a *function*. So, in order to differentiate between the sub procedure and the function, an alternate syntax is required. All in all, the more explicit form is preferred when arguments are passed. Including the "Call" keyword leaves no doubt as to the intent of the statement. Here then, over and under, is the calling statement and the called procedure:

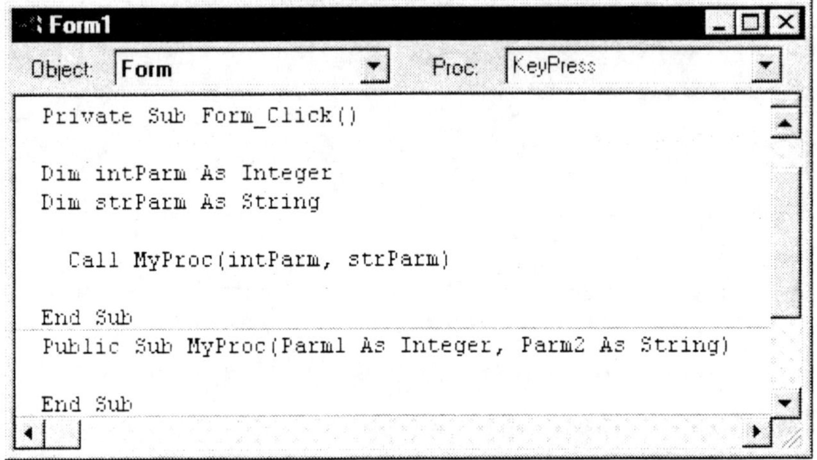

"intParm" in the calling statement matches up with "Parm1" in the called procedure. Likewise, "strParm" matches up with "Parm2."

Notice that the variables "Parm1" and "Parm2" are defined within the argument list of the "Sub" statement. If the "As Integer" or "As String" clause is omitted, the arguments are defined as type variant.

The ByVal Keyword

It is said in VB that when the *ByVal* keyword precedes an argument, the argument is passed by *value* instead of by *reference*. What does that mean?

On the 400, when parms are passed, what is really passed is the *address* of the variable. If the called program changes the value of the parm, it's being changed at the address as defined to the calling program. (That's why you can't use an incoming parm in an RPG data structure.)

The same thing is true in VB. That's what by *reference* means—by *address*.

Consider this RPG code:

```
C                              .
C                              MOVE   'ABCD'        PARM1
C                              CALL   'CLPGM'
C                              PARM                 PARM1
```

and the called CL program:

```
PGM        PARM(CLPARM)
DCL        VAR(CLPARM)    TYPE(*CHAR)    LEN(4)
CHGVAR     VAR(CLPARM)    VALUE('1234')
ENDPGM
```

An RPG program calls a CL program, passing it the parm "PARM1." The CL program receives the parm into its variable "CLPARM," changes it, and ends.

Question: "What is the value of "PARM1" in the calling RPG?"

Answer: "1234." The called program changed its variable named "CLPARM" and the RPG program's variable "PARM1" is changed. They have the same address—and VB works the same way.

If you specify "ByVal" along with the argument, VB makes a temporary copy of the argument and passes the address of *that*. Therefore, the contents of the original variable are not changed.

The calling statement that includes the "ByVal" keyword looks like this:

```
Dim intParm As Integer
Dim strParm As String
  Call MyProc(ByVal intParm, strParm)
```

Notice in this example that the first argument is passed by value, the second is not. "ByVal" is specified for each argument individually.

The called procedure statement must match the call statement:

```
Public Sub MyProc(ByVal Parml As Integer, Parm2 As String)
```

Again, only the first parm is passed by value.

Step by Step: Defining and Illustrating the ByVal Keyword

1. Start a new project. Bring the "load" event into the code window for "Form1."
2. Key in the following code:

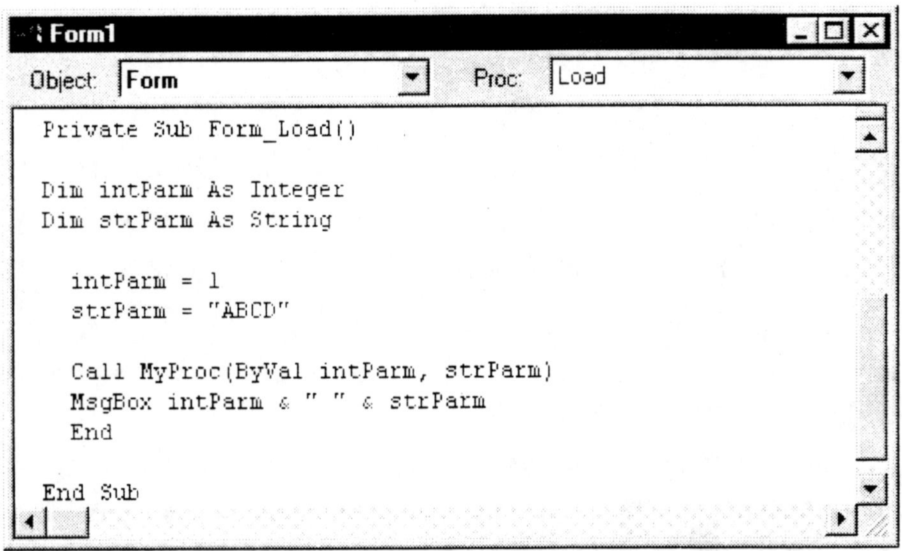

Notice that the ByVal keyword is only specified for the first argument.

3. Press the Page Down key on your keyboard. This should move your cursor beyond the last "End Sub" statement.
4. Key in "Sub MyProc" and press Enter. The VB Development Environment takes this to be a new procedure, places an entry in the procedures list, and supplies the "End Sub" statement.

5. Key in the following code:

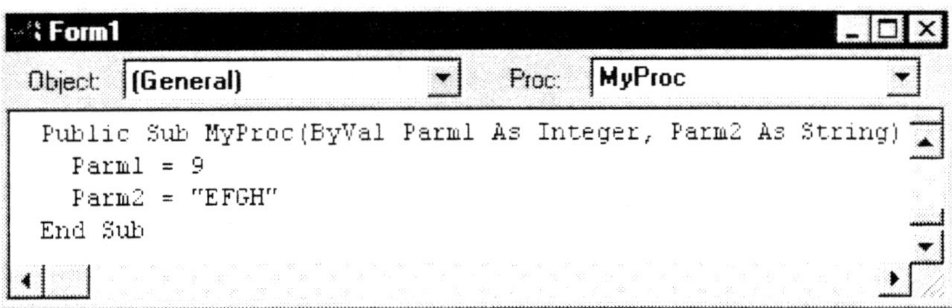

Again, the ByVal keyword is only specified for the first argument, matching the calling statement.

So, you've set up a general sub procedure, and a statement that will execute it. The point here is to observe the values in the variables as the program runs.

6. Click on the "Single Step" button, , four times. You should see:

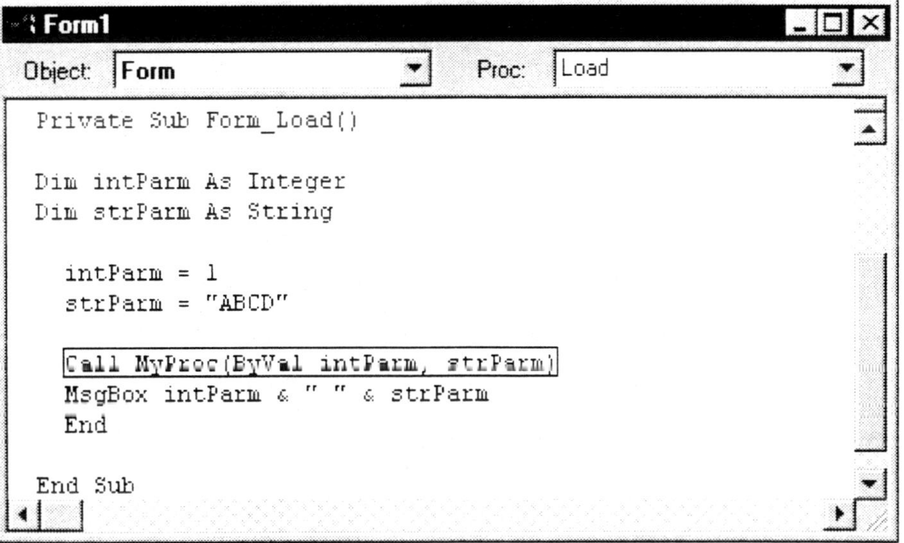

The rectangle shows the line that is about to be executed. At this point, "intParm" contains the value "1" and "strParm" contains the value "ABCD."

7. Click the "Single Step" button and watch the code execute until you get to this:

The message box is displaying the current contents of the variables "intParm" and "strParm." Although the called procedure changed both incoming parms, only the change to the second parm—"Parm2"—is seen back in the calling procedure (in "strParm"). That's because the two variables— "Parm2" and "strParm"—share one and the same address.

In a nutshell, use "ByVal" when you don't want your parms changed by a call.

8. End the program and discard the code.

Creating Your Own Functions

Suppose you had a need for a routine that accepts an argument and produces a result based on that argument. For example, suppose you need a routine that accepts the number of minutes past the current hour and returns the equivalent in hundredths of an hour, for billing purposes.

Knowing what you do about Sub procedures, you could pass two arguments to a procedure—one being the minutes, the other, hundredths. The procedure would accept minutes and place the corresponding value in hundredths. This is how you would probably do it on the 400. In VB, a better way is to create a *function* because a function can be used in an expression.

As you know by now, a function has a value. In the above example, the function has a value of hundredths of an hour expressed as a single precision floating-point variable. For instance, if the value 15 is passed to this new function, the function becomes the return value of 25—one quarter of an hour expressed in hundredths.

Nearly everything that can be said of passing arguments to a Sub procedure holds true for functions—arguments passed must match by type and position, and arguments may be passed by reference or by value.

Now let's see how functions are created.

Step by Step: Creating a Function

1. Start a new project. This code will not be saved.

2. Bring "Form_Load" into the code window. Key in this code:

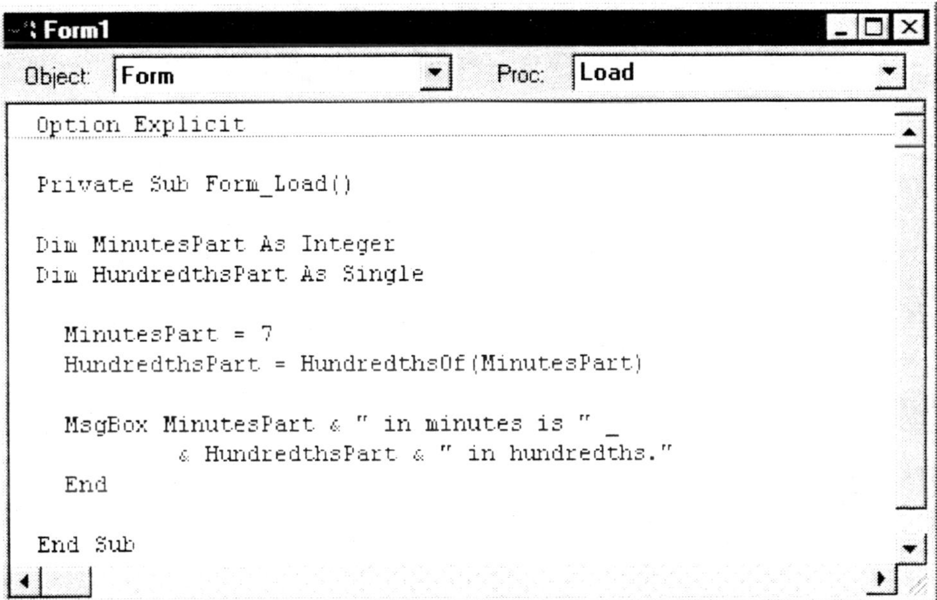


```
Option Explicit

Private Sub Form_Load()

Dim MinutesPart As Integer
Dim HundredthsPart As Single

  MinutesPart = 7
  HundredthsPart = HundredthsOf(MinutesPart)

  MsgBox MinutesPart & " in minutes is " _
          & HundredthsPart & " in hundredths."
  End

End Sub
```

   This code sets an environment to illustrate a function. Now for the function itself.

3. Position the cursor between "Option Explicit" and "Private Sub Form_Load". This is part of the declarations area for the form where a new Sub may be created.

4. Key "Private Function HundredthsOf" and press Enter to start a new function.

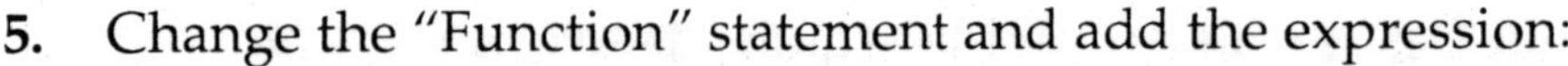

5. Change the "Function" statement and add the expression:

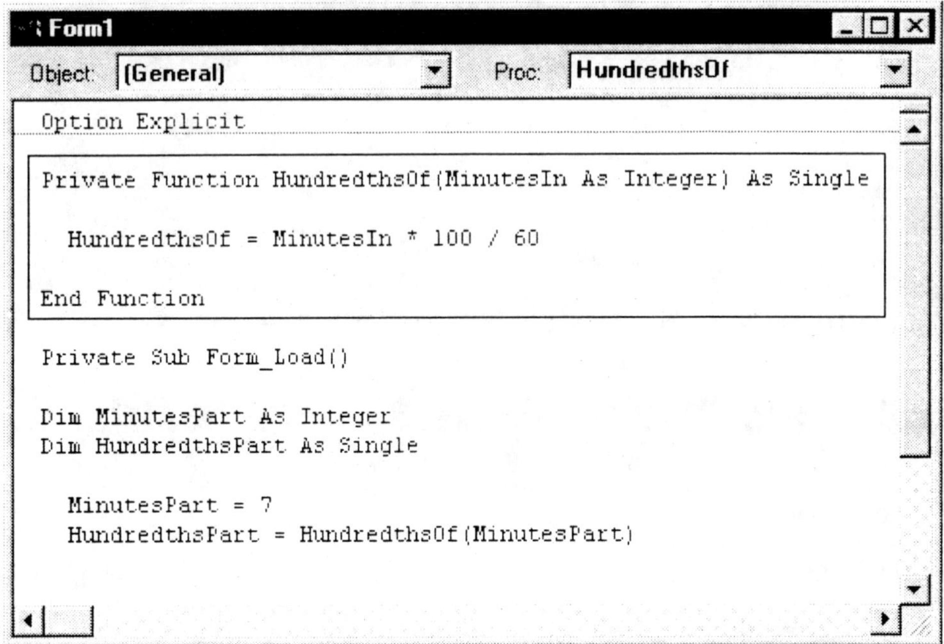

You've defined a function named "HundredthsOf." The function has an incoming argument defined as "MinutesIn"—an integer. Because functions are capable of being a value, the function itself has to be given a data type. In this case, this function is a single precision floating point. Notice that this matches the data type for "HundredthsPart" in the calling procedure.

The statement within the procedure merits inspection. The right side of the equal sign is simply an arithmetic expression. But notice the left side. It's the name of the function itself. In this way, the function acquires its value. All functions should acquire a value, even if it's just a zero or a blank to signify that the function couldn't be completed.

6. Run the program. You should see:

7. End the program and bring "Form_Load" into the code window. Now, because "HundredthsOf" is a function, it can be substituted in an expression like any other value:

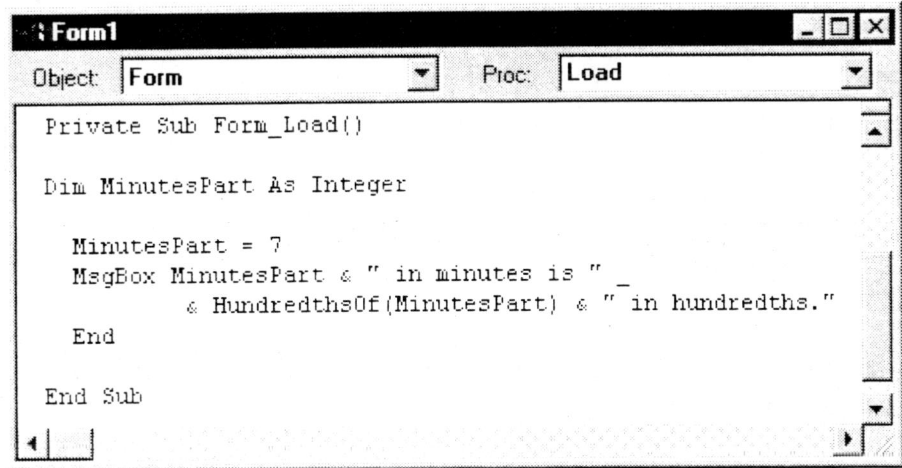

The MsgBox statement sees "HundredthsOf(MinutesPart)" as a value like any other. Indeed, it is.

8. Run the program. You should get the same result.

9. End the program. Discard the code.

APIs

RPG is a very capable language, but there are some things that it doesn't do very well. For example, it is much more difficult to submit a job from within an RPG program than a CL program. You can't clear a tape or send a message to the system operator or look at a device status. Ah, but you're getting ahead, here. You're thinking, "We do this all the time by calling a CL program from within the RPG program." Right you are. Whenever faced with the need for something that can't be had in RPG, you can call an external program.

You hear about APIs (Application Program Interfaces) all the time. The AS/400 is full of them. They are your means of getting at something that would otherwise be inaccessible, like data queues for instance. You call an API program, maybe pass it some parms, and it does something black-box style that you want.

There are APIs on your PC, too, and they're the exact same thing. They are programs and routines that are called to perform a task that couldn't otherwise be done easily.

Dynamic Link Libraries

In the DOS days, there were DOS API routines available, as well. Access to the operating system was accomplished through interrupt 21 calls to DOS. When the program was compiled, the linker looked for references to external routines and copied their code into the linked object from a group of external routines called a library. This process is known as *static linking* because the addressing for external routines is fixed within the executable, and remains unchanged (static) while the program is running.

Static linking takes place when the program is compiled. With Windows multitasking, Microsoft introduced *dynamic linking*. Dynamic linking takes place when the program is run. That way, only a single copy of a routine need be resident in memory, even though several multitasked applications may be using it.

Dynamic routines are collected into a file called a *dynamic link library* (DLL). These files usually have an extension name of "DLL," but there are exceptions. Windows system routines are kept in files that end with "EXE." Those files make up the *Windows API*. The API routines on your PC that allow a VB program to run and allow an APPC link to the AS/400 are also collected into DLLs.

Visual Basic is a very capable language, but it can't do some of the things that C can. VB is unable to directly interact with Windows, for example. But just as RPG is capable of calling a CL program, Visual Basic is capable of linking to external routines written (usually) in C.

DLL files are not stand-alone application programs. They're only a collection of program fragments that have a very specific purpose. If you were to look at the files on your PC that end in ".DLL," you would see something like:

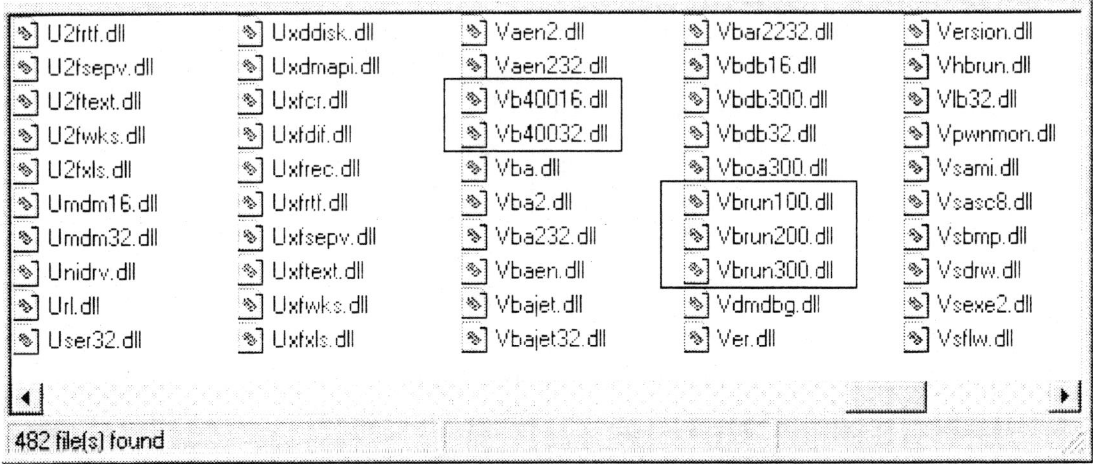

These are some of the DLLs in the WINDOWS\SYSTEM folder. They each provide a set of routines that can be linked to a VB program.

Of particular interest are the special VB run-time DLLs, "Vb40032.dll" (version 4.0, 32 bit), "Vb40016.dll" (version 4.0, 16 bit) and "VBRUNxxx.DLL" (where "xxx" is the VB version—1.00, 2.00, or 3.00), as these are the routines that allow a Visual Basic program to operate. Even the simplest VB program uses routines contained in one of these DLLs. You don't need all of these DLLs, only the one that matches your version of VB. (VB 4.0 comes with both 16- and 32-bit versions.)

Visual Basic does not compile into a standalone executable. VB compiles into an intermediate form called "Pseudo Code," or "P-Code." At run time, P-Code statements are interpreted by the run-time DLL.

Each of the above run-time DLL files represent a different version of Visual Basic. When it comes time to make distribution diskettes for your executable VB program, you'll see that Vb40016.Dll accompanies your program, and installs in the WINDOWS\SYSTEM folder.

Now look into your CA/400 or PC Support folder for files that end in ".DLL":

Ehnapmn.dll	Ehnclcfg.dll	Ehndtwm.dll	Ehnrtrw.dll
Ehnappc.dll	Ehncln1.dll	Ehnec.dll	Ehnsfcw.dll
Ehncfdq.dll	Ehncln2.dll	Ehnhaw.dll	Ehnsfmn.dll
Ehncfflr.dll	Ehnclp1.dll	Ehnlqw.dll	Ehnsfw.dll
Ehncfprt.dll	Ehnclsys.dll	Ehnndmn.dll	Ehnsrmn.dll
Ehncfstr.dll	Ehnclt1.dll	Ehnnetw.dll	Ehnsrw.dll
Ehncfsys.dll	Ehnddmn.dll	Ehnnrmn.dll	Ehntfmn.dll
Ehncfupd.dll	Ehndqmn.dll	Ehnrqw.dll	Ehntfw.dll
Ehncl01.dll	Ehndqw.dll	Ehnrqwm.dll	Ehnvpw.dll
Ehncl02.dll	Ehndtw.dll	Ehnrtmn.dll	

These are some of the DLLs that make up the Client Access/PC Support API. They allow you to get at the PC Support router, data queues, virtual printing, file transfer, message queues, remote commands, etc. The features of Client Access, running under Windows, are made available by this API. These DLLs are installed on your disk when you install Client Access/PC Support for Windows. They are copied from the AS/400 QIWSFL2 folder through the I: drive.

> ***Note:*** *Your version of CA/400 may include an intermediate folder "QDLS."*

These are the DLLs that allow a client/server relationship with the AS/400. All the low-level interaction with the Client Access router is accomplished by calling the routines within these files.

Linking to external subroutines allows Windows programs to share routines so each program needn't carry all that baggage. Fact is, DLLs even call other DLLs for the same reason.

API routines of a like nature are collected together in a group called a *library*. When you link to a library, the routines in that library are available to your program and may be called. The library isn't a collection of *files*—it's a collection of *routines*, all in one file.

Dynamic means that the routines located in the library are not included in the compiled program but, rather, are called at execution time. You're familiar with this—it works the same way on the 400. You can compile a CL or an RPG program that has a call to another program that may not even exist. Of course, when you try to run the CL program, you get an "Error found on call" message.

To restate:

- APIs are routines that you can call from within a program to perform functions that are not possible otherwise.
- Like API routines are grouped together in an object called a DLL or Dynamic Link Library.
- The link between your program and a DLL is established at run time.

Declaring a Link to External Code

Since DLL routines are external to a VB program, some sort of definition is required to tell the VB program where to find them. Also, DLLs contain multiple routines, and you have to specify which routine you want to use. Once known to the VB program, the external routines may be used as if they were defined inside the program. A routine is called if it is a Sub procedure, and used in an expression if it is a function.

The Declare Statement

To define an external routine, use the "Declare" statement. The routine needs to be defined only once. Thereafter, it can be called wherever needed.

A "Declare" statement can only be placed in the declarations area of a standard or form module. If the "Declare" statement appears in a form module, it must be preceded with "Private," as "Public" is the default and not allowed in a form. Additionally, declaring the routine in a standard module makes it available to the whole program.

The declare statement has four parts—the *function* or *procedure clause*, the *routine name*, the *library*, and the *argument list*. Consider this example "Declare" statement for an external APPC function:

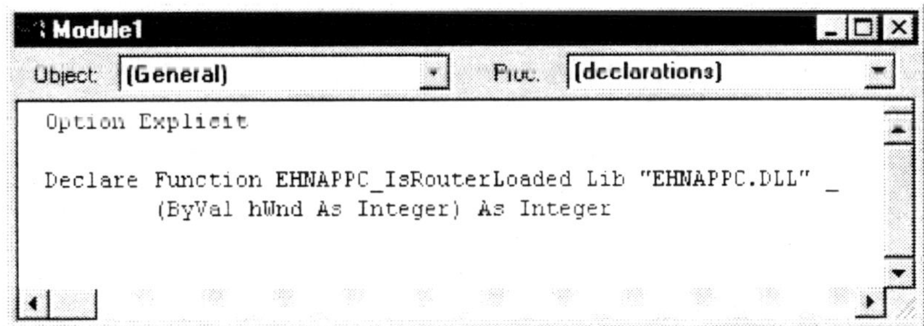

The first part, "Declare," says that what follows is external to your program. ("Declare" is not used on an internal function or procedure.) "Function" defines this routine as a function. You have to know what the external routine is—a function or a procedure—and declare it to match.

Second comes the name of the routine that you want to use. In this case, it's "EHNAPPC_IsRouterLoaded." "EHNAPPC_IsRouterLoaded" is a routine that does two specific things—it checks to see if the Client Access/PCS router is loaded, and if the program PCSWIN is loaded. If either is not active, a value of zero is returned.

The third part, 'Lib "EHNAPPC.DLL,"' tells where the routine can be found. Remember, a library is a PC file that contains a collection of like routines. The routine declared in the example is among others in the library (DLL file) "EHNAPPC.DLL." In this case, as no folder is specified, the current path is searched.

The fourth part, "(ByVal hWnd as Integer)," is the *argument list*. This is where the parms that are passed to the external routine are placed. In this case, there is only one argument—"hWnd."

"hWnd" is a thing called a *Windows Handle*. It's what allows Windows to keep track of all the windows that are open. Think of a handle as the equivalent of an AS/400 Job number. Each form and control in your VB program has a Windows handle, under the covers, that is stored as a property. It is available to you without being defined. You'll see it illustrated shortly.

Nearly all arguments passed to an external routine are passed *by value*, hence the *ByVal* keyword. You recall that the ByVal keyword causes VB to create a copy of the argument and pass that. The copy is made in a standard Pascal format that matches what the external routine expects. (That is, for all data types except arrays or a user data type.) For the purposes of this book, assume that all arguments are passed to external routines by value.

The rest of the statement, "as Integer," defines the data type for the function itself, just like you saw in internal functions.

There's a lot in the "Declare" statement. To restate:

- The "Declare" statement has four parts: the function or procedure *clause*, the routine *name*, the *library*, and the *argument list*.
- The function or procedure clause identifies the routine as either a "Sub" or a "Function" procedure.

- The routine name is the name of the function or procedure in the DLL that you want to use.
- The library is the name of the DLL file that contains the routine (like EHNAPPC.DLL).
- The argument list is the parms, or arguments, that are passed to the external routine.
- "hWnd" is the Windows handle for a form or control when the routine is called.

Calling an External Routine

Once declared in the declarations area of a form or module, an external function or procedure can be referred to in an expression (if it's a function), or called (if it's a procedure). The code needed to access an external "Sub" or "Function" procedure is the same as that of an internal one. It can be referred to or called from any other procedure that can "see" it (that is, within the routine's *scope*).

As a rule, make your external routines available to all parts of your program by declaring it as public in the declarations area of a *standard module,* not a form.

Most external routines are functions, not "Sub" procedures. The following example defines a variable to accept the value of the function ("ReturnCode"), and then refers to the external function "EHNAPPC_IsRouterLoaded" to run it.

Once declared, to run an external function, refer to it in an expression:

```
Dim ReturnCode As Integer

ReturnCode = EHNAPPC_IsRouterLoaded(ByVal hWnd)
```

If the PC Support router and program PCSWIN are loaded, a Boolean value of -1 (true) is returned; otherwise 0 (false) is returned.

Boolean Values

You may wonder why -1 is returned when the test for the router is true. It's a convention used in VB called a *Boolean* value. There are two built-in constants in VB: "True" and "False." "True" has a value of negative one; "False" has a value of zero. This allows a comparison in the code to "True" or "False."

Note: From this point on, elements of the Client Access/PCS API will be required in this book. These are files that should be in the Client Access/PCS folder of PCs that are running CA400/PCS under Windows. **Additionally, as this API is made up of 16-bit DLLs, the 16-bit version of Visual Basic must be used.**

Step by Step: Declaring an External Function

1. Bring up the 16-bit version of the VB Development Environment. (This code will not be saved.)
2. Click on the "New Module" button, , to start a module, "Module1." The code window opens automatically, showing the "Option Explicit" statement.
3. Add the following "Declare" statement:

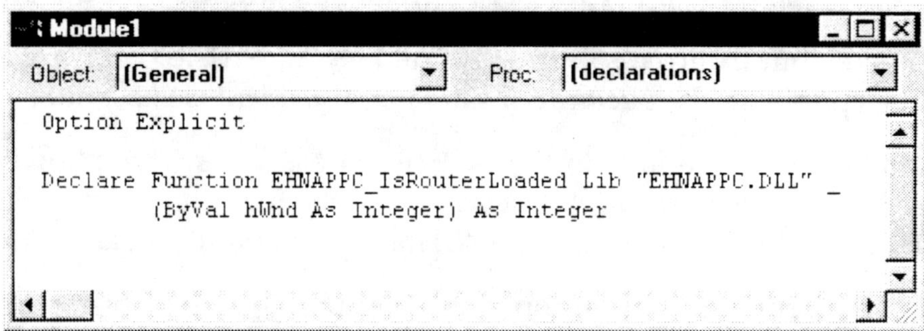

This Declare statement links the external function "EHNAPPC_IsRouterLoaded" to your VB program. The function is part of the routines in the file "EHNAPPC.DLL." One argument is passed—"hWnd" by value. The function itself is of type integer.

Admittedly, creating a new module for a program that has only one form isn't necessary; it is done to emphasize recommended placement of "Declares."

4. Close the code window for "Module1." Open the code window for the "Form_Load" procedure in "Form1." Key in the following code:

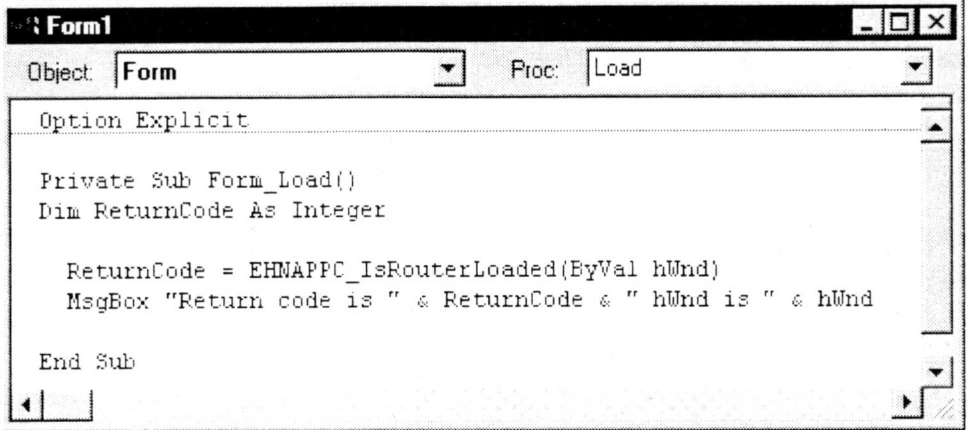

This code defines a variable to receive the function's value, "ReturnCode," runs the function by referring to it in an expression, and displays the result in a message box. Additionally, the Windows handle is displayed, just to show what it looks like.

5. Run the program. You should see something like this:

If your Client Access router is not loaded, or if you are not running PCS for Windows, your return code is "0." Of course, the value for "hWnd" is different on your PC.

6. Click on "OK," end the program, and discard the code.

So in just these few lines of VB code, you have accomplished something very significant. You have gained access to low-level CA/400 elements by linking to a powerful DLL.

Although there are several more DLL routines involved, it is in just this manner that all Client Access features are accessed to accomplish a full and capable client/server application.

As a development effort proceeds, programs grow in size and complexity, but they're still made up of simple components. On the AS/400, large, complex applications are made up of smaller programs or routines. The same is true of your VB programs as presented from here on. The amount of code increases significantly to allow interaction with the Client Access router and the AS/400, but the individual elements are no more complex than what you've seen already.

At this point, if you've hung in through the book, you have enough tools to start your first true client/server application.

Summary

Procedure Calls

An argument is a parameter passed to a procedure or function.

Arguments must match by data type. Passing an argument as data type "Any" overrides data type checking.

You can create and call your own "Sub" and "Function" procedures. Those procedures can pass arguments.

The "ByVal" keyword preceding an argument in an argument list causes the argument to be passed by value rather than by reference.

A function procedure represents a value, so you create a function when you need to use the result in an expression.

APIs

An API (Application Program Interface), is a routine or program, external to your application, that can be called to perform a function that would otherwise be unavailable.

APIs exist on the AS/400 and on the PC.

Similar PC API routines are collected into files called Dynamic Link Libraries or DLLs.

Links to external routines are established at run time with the VB "Declare" statement.

External "Sub" and "Function" procedures can be called or used in an expression just like internal procedures.

Boolean values are often used to represent return codes for called procedures. Boolean values are -1 = "TRUE", 0 = "FALSE."

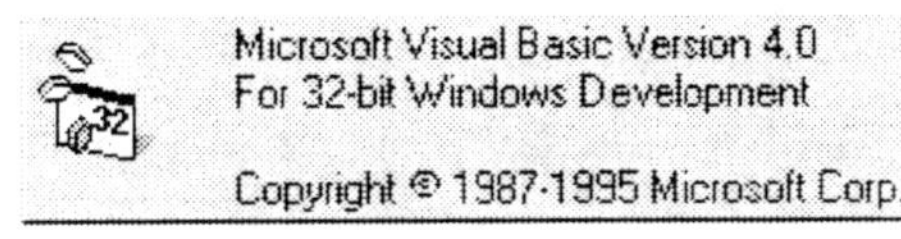

10

IBM-supplied Client/Server Tools

Fortunately, IBM has provided some tools that make development of a client/server application easier. You've already seen one of those tools—the EHNAPPC Dynamic Link Library. Also of value are two other tools provided by IBM—the *APPC Declarations file,* which contains templates of all the declare statements for EHNAPPC routines, and sample VB code, which shows how to call those routines and what to pass. All of the client/server applications presented in this book are based on APPC (Advanced Program to Program Communications) functions that are provided by IBM. These functions are contained in the Dynamic Link Library "EHNAPPC.DLL" (the same DLL used in the last chapter).

The APPC Declarations File

This is a file of predefined VB code that provides all of the constants and declarations needed to use the routines in the EHNAPPC DLL. In other words, the "Declare" statement used in the last chapter didn't have to be keyed from scratch; it's already available and could have been copied. For the purposes of this book, call this file the "APPC Declarations File." This file was developed prior to VB 4.0, when constants and declare statements were imported into your application in a text file.

This file can be included with your VB projects, eliminating the need for keying the declarations and definitions that it contains. The name of the file is "RTRSAMP.GBL," but it probably isn't on your PC—yet.

Here's what a portion of the APPC declarations file looks like:

```
'*****************************************************************
' Global declarations
'*****************************************************************

Global SysName As String * 8
Global ConvID As Long

'*****************************************************************
'          Router DLL Global Definitions                          *
'************************************************************ *******
'  PURPOSE:
'    This file contains global constants, data structures and DLL
'    declarations to be used to interface with AS/400 Client Access/PCS APPC
'    router from a Microsoft Visual Basic application.
'    All string inputs are expected to be in ANSI ASCII character set,
'    and all output strings are in ANSI ASCII.
'  ROUTINES:
'    EHNAPPC_Allocate
'    EHNAPPC_ExtendedAllocate
'    EHNAPPC_SendData
'    EHNAPPC_ReceiveAndWait
'    EHNAPPC_ReceiveImmediate
'    EHNAPPC_Deallocate
'    EHNAPPC_Confirm
'    EHNAPPC_SendError
'    EHNAPPC_PrepareToReceive
'    EHNAPPC_Confirmed
'    EHNAPPC_RqsToSend
'    EHNAPPC_Flush
```

```
'    EHNAPPC_QuerySystems
'    EHNAPPC_GetCapabilities
'    EHNAPPC_IsRouterLoaded
'    EHNAPPC_QueryConvState
'    EHNAPPC_QueryUserId
'    EHNAPPC_GetAttribute
'    EHNAPPC_GetDefaultSystem
'    EHNAPPC_RemoteProgramStart
' Global constants for "type" on Allocate requests
Global Const EHNAPPC_BASIC = 0
Global Const EHNAPPC_MAPPED = 1
' Global constants for "whatReceived" on Receive requests
Global Const EHNAPPC_DATA = 0
Global Const EHNAPPC_DATACOMPLETE = 1
Global Const EHNAPPC_DATAINCOMPLETE = 2
Global Const EHNAPPC_RECEIVEDCONFIRM = 3
Global Const EHNAPPC_RECEIVEDCONFIRMSEND = 4
Global Const EHNAPPC_RECEIVEDCONFIRMDEALLOC = 5
Global Const EHNAPPC_RECEIVEDSEND = 6
'*********************************************************************
Declare Function EHNAPPC_Allocate% Lib "EHNAPPC.DLL" (ByVal hWnd%, ByVal
nBufferLength%, ByVal bType%, ByVal bSynchLevel%, ByVal lpszLocationName$,
ByVal lpszTpn$, ByVal nPipLength%, ByVal lpPipData As Any,lpdwConversation&)

'  PARAMETERS:
'    HWND               hWnd                 Caller's Windows handle
'    unsigned           nBufferLength        Size of buffer to be allocated by
'                                            router.  It must be at least 271.
'                                            If it is less than 271, a 271 byte
'                                            buffer will be allocated.
'    ConversationType   bType                Basic or Mapped conversation
'    SyncLevelEnum      bSynchLevel          None or confirm
'    LPSTR              lpszLocationName     ASCIIZ string specifying host system
'                                            name.
'                                            Set to NULL to use default system.
'    LPSTR              lpszTpn              ASCIIZ string specifying partner
'                                            program name.
'                                            If first character is less than 0x40
'                                            ASCII to EBCDIC translation is not
'                                            done.
'    int                nPipLength           Length of PIP data.  Set to 0 to
'                                            not send PIP data.
'    LPVOID             lpPipData            no translation done, must be in GDS
'                                            format
'    LPDWORD            lpdwConversation     Pointer to a double word handle
```

```
'                                                    returned by router to be used on
'                                                    subsequent calls.
' RETURN VALUE:
'   int         Use the ReturnCode enumeration to determine the meaning
'               of the return code
' USAGE NOTES:
'   procedure Allocate is used to start a conversation with a partner
```

So, what's in here? There is a list of the functions that are contained in the EHNAPPC Dynamic Link Library (like *"EHNAPPC_IsRouterLoaded"),* there are some symbolic constants (constants with names that describe what their values mean), and there is a "Declaration" statement for each APPC function together with an explanation of usage. In fact, the only thing that isn't in the file is the syntax for executing the functions. Be aware that this is only a portion of the file.

Don't let the apparent complexity of the things in this file throw you. It's not as bad as it looks because along with this file comes sample code that shows you how to use it. All you have to do is provide values for the arguments that are passed to the APPC functions, and then use the functions in expressions.

APPC and ICF as a Client/Server Platform

At the very beginning of this book, it was stated that you're not going to see a lot of fancy stuff in here. The method chosen to accomplish a client/server relationship is perhaps the least fancy of all—APPC and ICF. ICF stands for Intersystem Communication Function. It's been around for a long time—all the way back to bisync communications in plain old SNA. What does this mean to you? Good question. It doesn't mean that you have to become an APPC/ICF programmer to use these tools any more than you have to be an auto mechanic to drive a car. All you have to do is copy a few APPC routines into your code (both VB and RPG) and execute them. These routines will perform the APPC functions to establish a c/s link, start a partner program (your RPG) on the 400, pass transactions back and forth, and end.

This sort of application represents an example of a three-tier, device-independent client/server model. That is, there are three entities involved:

- The user interface, as accomplished by a VB program.
- An AS/400 HLL program, which enforces the rules of business.

- The AS/400 native database, acting as a server to the HLL program, and in turn to the PC.

Each contributor to the application does what it does best, at the appropriate level. There is a contemporary, easy-to-use interface at one end and the native AS/400 database at the other. The key to the arrangement is the HLL program in the middle.

This HLL program, written in RPG in this book, takes the place of SQL, stored procedures, the ODBC, and the like. It's a traditional AS/400 program, where accustomed rules of business and database relationships are utilized to derive information from the database and serve it up to the client. It's the most important piece of the application, and, fortunately, the one with which you're most familiar.

One more point in favor of using APPC and ICF—everything you need is already on your AS/400, as included with your operating system, except Client Access/PCS. There's nothing further to buy.

> ***Note:*** *Client Access/PCS has multiple options that can be selected when it's installed on the AS/400. You should find out if the Client Access/PCS tools folder,"QIWSTOOL," is on your system. On an AS/400 command line, key "GO LICPGM" for the licensed program menu. Display installed licensed programs for Client Access/PCS (product code 5738PC1). Look for "Client Access/PCS Tools Folder." If it's not installed, you will not have access to the IBM- supplied tools. You can, however, copy them from the diskette that came with this book.*

Getting the APPC Declarations File to Your PC

As was mentioned, the APPC Declarations file is on your AS/400 along with some other useful things (assuming Client Access/PCS "tools" is installed—the "QIWSTOOL" folder). They are kind of hard to get at, but once copied to your PC they are available for all future projects.

The APPC declarations file is downloaded to your PC as part of the sample VB application "WVBSAMP" that comes with Client Access/PCS.

Here's how you do it.

Step by Step: Downloading the APPC Declarations File

1. Create a new folder to hold the files being downloaded. A good place to keep them is in a folder named "TOOLS" off of "C:\VB\PROJECTS" (remember, if you're using VB 4.0 you should be using the 16-bit version.) You may create the new folder at a DOS prompt with Make Folder (MD) like this:

   ```
   MD C:\VB\PROJECTS\TOOLS.
   ```

2. Start Client Access/PCS (running under Windows).

3. You should have an I: drive. Bring up the Windows File Manager (Win3.1) or "Explore" (Win95).

4. Switch to the I: drive. Select the "QIWSTOOL" folder. It should look something like this:

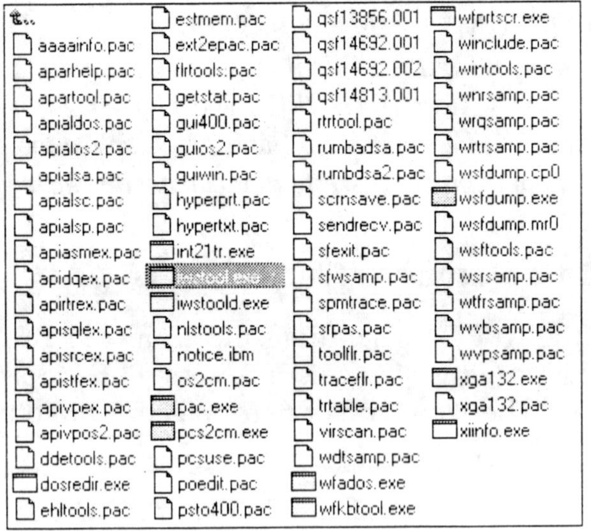

   What is all this? Do you see all those files that end in PAC? Each one is a package of sample programs and files to be included. There are samples for Assembler, Modula, C, and Visual Basic. Unfortunately, there is only one VB package, but it contains three sample programs. (Only one is needed here, but you get all three.)

5. Find the program "iwstool.exe." This program gives you access to all the sample packages and copies selected packages to your PC.

6. Run the "iwstool.exe" program (by double clicking on it). The program churns a while as it examines all the ".PAC" files. Eventually a list of the available packages is presented.

7. Scroll down until you come to the WVBSAMP entry (toward the bottom):

```
WSFTOOLS Work Station Function Tools and Circumvention Programs.
WSRSAMP  PC Support/400 Submit Remote Command Windows API Example
WTFRSAMP Example Using PC Support/400 Transfer API for Windows
WVBSAMP  PC Support Sample Programs using Microsoft Visual Basic
WVPSAMP  Example Using PC Support/400 Virtual Print API for Windows
XGA132   Switch Mode of XGA display to 132 columns
```

8. With "WVBSAMP" selected, press Enter. You should see:

```
PC Support Sample Programs using Microsoft Visual Basic

This package contains example Visual Basic source programs detailing the
use of some of the PC Support/400 APIs for Windows.

The following sample programs and their associated files are listed below:

* WVBSAMP.ABS  ; Visual Basic Abstract File

Router sample program:

* RTRSAMP.MAK  ; Visual Basic Make file
* RTRSAMP.GBL  ; Contains global definitions specific
                 to this sample and general Router DLL global
                 definitions to be used by any Visual Basic
                 application wishing to communicate to the Router.
* RTRSAMP.FRM  ; The form used by this sample program. It contains
                 the controls used to interact with the program plus
                 numerous routines in the "general" object that make
                 it easier to communicate to the router routines.
```

This screen, called an *abstract*, is an explanation of the samples that are contained in the package.

9. Page down to the bottom of the abstract where you'll find a place to key in a folder for the downloaded files. Key in the name of the folder you created for this purpose: "C:\VB\PROJECTS\TOOLS" and press Enter. If all is well, the files are copied to the specified folder.

10. End the "iwstool" program.

    You now have a powerful tool, useful in writing a client/server application.

The RTRSAMP Program

The APPC Declarations file is just one of the items downloaded to your PC. If you look at your "Tools" folder, you'll see three VB projects: a Client Access/PCS router program, a file transfer example program, and an SQL example program. Each project has a project file with a pre-VB4.0 extension name of ".MAK", and source files.

Of the three, the one that provides general-purpose access to the AS/400 is the router program "RTRSAMP." The other two are not discussed in and of themselves, but they're similar to RTRSAMP.

RTRSAMP is an example program that connects to the PCS router, starts a conversation with the AS/400, talks to a partner program running on the 400, makes requests, and receives transactions. These are the basic requirements of this sort of c/s relationship. Once this framework is built, many c/s applications are possible.

The APIRTREX Package

If you read the abstract for the WVBSAMP package, you see that, in order to run the sample programs, you have to do some other things.

Another package is required because that package has files that create objects on the AS/400 that in turn set up the demo environment. The package name is "APIRTREX."

Step by Step: Downloading the APIRTREX Package

1. Follow the same steps used to download "WVBSAMP" (use the same folder—"C:\VB\PROJECTS\TOOLS"):
   - Run "IWSTOOL" in the "QIWSTOOL" folder.
   - Select "APIRTREX," page to the bottom, and key in the folder for the download.
2. Look at the "TOOLS" folder in "Explore" (Win95) or "File Manager" (Win3.1). You should see these files:

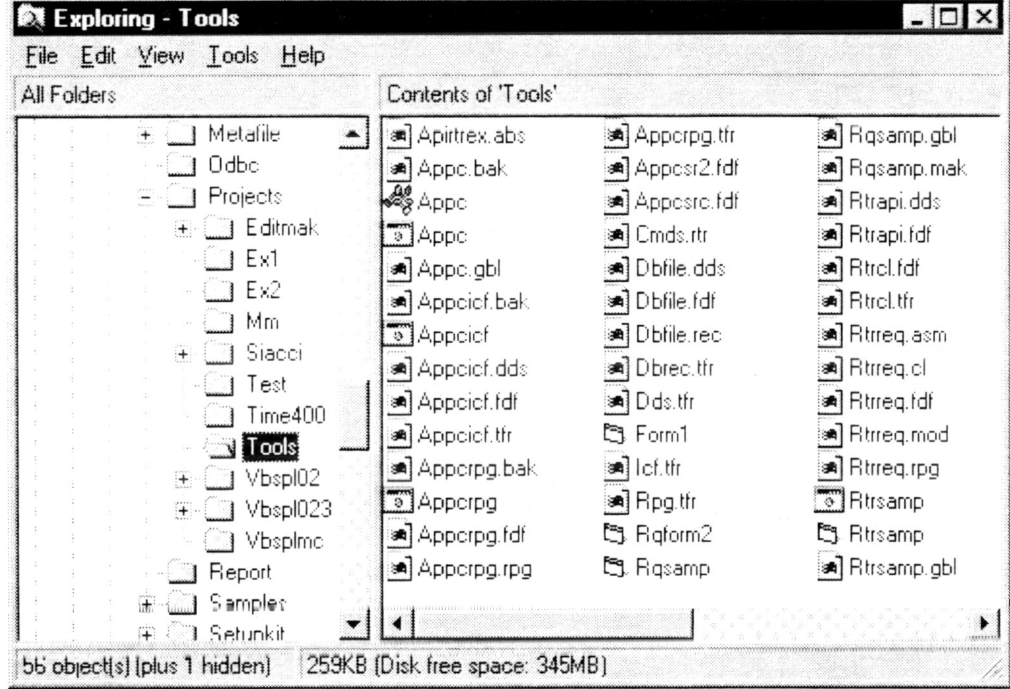

These are the files that have been downloaded to your PC from the two packages, "WVBSAMP" and "APIRTREX."

Note that several files came down to your PC that you probably can't use. These files are:

RTRREQ.C	Sample "C" program to make inquiries to AS/400 database.
APPCSUBS.C	Sample subroutine library for router APPC verbs.
APPCSUBS.H	Header file for above Library routines.
APPCTYPE.H	Header file that contains the record layout for verbs.
RTRREQ.MOD	Modula-2 sample program.
APPC.DEF	Definition module for library routines to access router.
APPC.MOD	Implementation module for above routines.
WRITERC.DEF	Routine that writes a message for error return codes.
WRITERC.MOD	Implementation module for above routine.
RTRREQ.ASM	Assembler program to make inquiries to AS/400 database.
CSAMP.BAT	BAT that compiles and links "C" sample using Microsoft "C" Version 6.0.
J.BAT	BAT that assembles and links assembler sample program.

All the other files that were downloaded from APIRTREX are used for uploading the sample program and files to the AS/400.

DBREC.TFR

RTRREQ.RPG

RTRAPI.DDS

DBFILE.DDS

DBFILE.FDF

DBFILE.REC

DDS.TFR

ICF.TFR

RPG.TFR

3. Stay where you are in Explore/File Manager for a moment. The contents of one of the files is of interest and requires some discussion.

Using Client Access/PCS Features to Create AS/400 Objects

There is a batch file called "RTRSAMP.BAT" that contains commands to upload source files; to create a physical file, a CL program, and an RPG program from those source files; and even put a little data into the file. This scheme is of particular interest because, when you get to creating distribution diskettes for your applications, you can use this same method to create your AS/400 partner programs and objects.

Here are the contents of the RTRSAMP.BAT file:

i:rmtcmd crtlib jdet	Creates a library on the 400.
i:rfrompcb rtrcl	Uploads CL source using a transfer request.
i:rfrompcb dds	Uploads DDS source for a physical file.
i:rfrompcb icf	Uploads DDS source for an ICF file.
i:rfrompcb rpg	Uploads RPG source using a transfer request.
i:rmtcmd /i cmds.rtr	Runs commands on the 400 as read from a file.
i:rfrompcb dbrec	Uploads some demo data.

These commands use regular Client Access/PCS features to:

- Create a library on the 400.
- Upload CL source using a transfer request.
- Upload DDS source for a physical file using a transfer request.
- Upload DDS source for an ICF file using a transfer request.
- Upload RPG source using a transfer request.

The sixth line uses the "rmtcmd" feature of Client Access/PCS just like line one, but it's reading commands from a file "cmds.rtr." The Client Access/PCS "rmtcmd" program is capable of reading entries from a PC file and issuing them as commands to the 400.

The contents of this file are:

```
addlible jdet

crtclpgm pgm(jdet/rtrreqcl) srcfile(jdet/qclsrc)

crtpf file(jdet/dbfile) srcfile(jdet/qddssrc)

crticff file(jdet/rtrapi) srcfile(jdet/qddssrc) share(*yes)

addicfdeve file(jdet/rtrapi) pgmdev(rqsdev) rmtlocname(*requester)+

      cmntype(*appc)

crtrpgpgm pgm(jdet/rtrreq) srcfile(jdet/qrpgsrc)
```

All of these commands are executed on the AS/400 by the "rmtcmd" feature of Client Access/PCS. Note that the commands are considered together, as if they are a CL program. The first statement adds the new library to the lib list, and the statements that follow have the advantage of it.

Finally, some data is uploaded into the physical file just created for demo purposes.

This batch file represents a powerful technique for installing a client/server system on an AS/400. Indeed, the AS/400 Download Utility included with this book creates all the AS/400 objects in just this manner. (You could even delete the source code once the programs and files are compiled by adding a couple more remote commands.)

> ***Note:*** *A lack of proper authority on the AS/400 can cause installation failure.*

Step by Step: Downloading the APPC Declarations File Continued

1. To run the RTRSAMP.BAT file you must have the I: drive assigned to the Client Access/PCS/400 folder ("QIWSFL2"). From a DOS prompt, go to the I: drive and see that it's at: "I:\QIWSFL2."

2. Go back to Explore/File Manager and double click "RTRSAMP.BAT" to run the batch file. (You must have proper authority to execute the AS/400 commands.) You should see Client Access/PCS messages as the statements execute.

3. End Explore/File Manager.

That's a lot of material covering largely unfamiliar territory. Fortunately, once done, you shouldn't have to do it again. (One exception might be after installing PTFs or going to a new release of OS/400—*maybe*.) In fact, downloading the APIRTREX package and running RTRSAMP.BAT need only be done from one PC per AS/400. The AS/400 objects that you created are in library "JDET" and available to any programmer. Another programmer, however, would have to either download the WVBSAMP package to get the main item of this whole discussion—the APPC Declarations file—or get it from you.

The IBM Sample Project—RTRSAMP (and the Error within)

In your "TOOLS" folder you now have three VB projects:

- RQSAMP   Remote SQL example
- TFSAMP   File transfer example
- RTRSAMP   PCS router example

The one of most use is RTRSAMP (even though the pre-V3R1 version of PC Support has an error in it—which will be fixed).

The RTRSAMP Error—OS/400 Pre-V3R1

The pre-V3R1 version (PC Support) of the RTRSAMP project is shipped with two errors in it. As of V2R3, the errors hadn't been corrected.

> ***Note:*** *If you're using Client Access/400, rather than PC support, skip the next exercise.*

Step by Step: Correcting the Error in the RTRSAMP Project

1. Bring up the 16-bit version of the VB Development Environment. Go into "Open Project..." and specify "RTRSAMP.MAK" in folder "C:\VB\PROJECTS\TOOLS." You should see a message like:

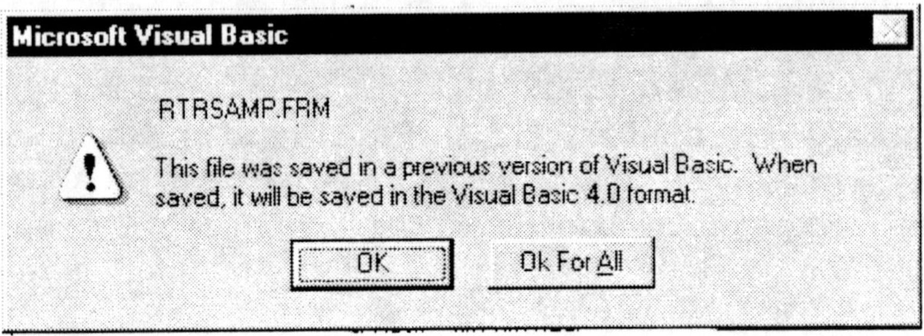

   These messages only indicate that the RTRSAMP project was developed on an earlier version of Visual Basic. No big deal.

   The project, however, was shipped with an error in the code. It's a small error (the letter S is used where a dollar sign should be), but it's enough to make you think you're doing something wrong.

2. Run the program. You should see:

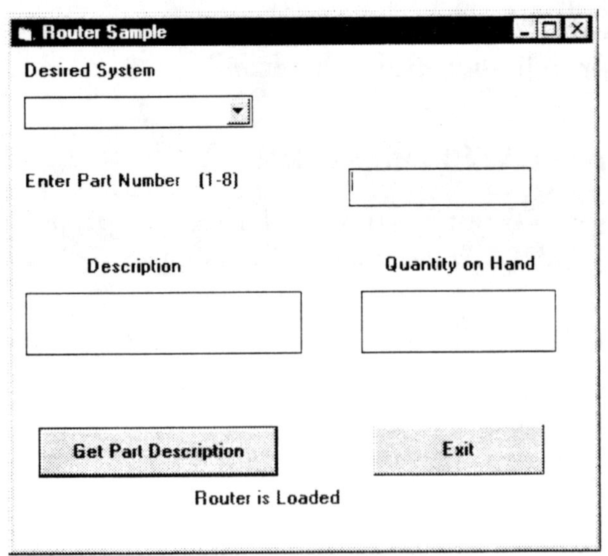

3. Key in a part number (1-8) and click on "Get Part Description." You get an error message. The content of the message depends on your version of VB. Respond to the message and end the program.

4. The statement that caused the program to fail should be displayed. If it's not, hold the Ctrl key and press F to bring up the search dialog box. Search on"PipDataS". The word "PipDataS" appears. It should read "PipData$" with a dollar sign in place of the "S."

5. Click on "OK." Change the "S" to a "$".

6. Run the program again. This time you should see:

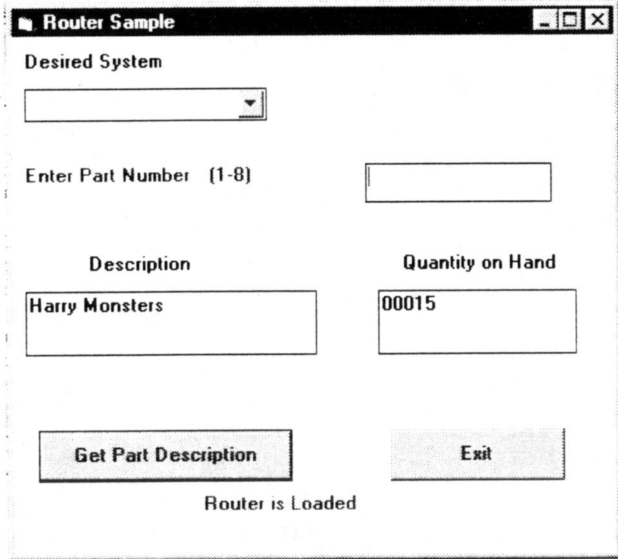

One other error is in the "EHNAPPC_Confirm" routine in "RTRSAMP.GBL."

7. Bring "RTRSAMP.GBL" into the code window. Bring up the "Find" dialog box.

8. In the "Find What:" box, key "Convirm"—yes, with a "v." That's the error—the word "Confirm" is misspelled.

9. Click on "OK." The "Find" effort should bring up this statement:

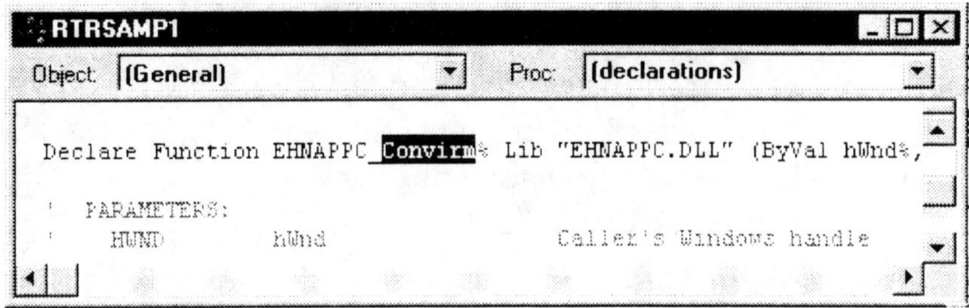

10. Correct the error.

11. Save the project.

APPC Procedures in RTRSAMP

The keys to the castle are contained in this project. Laid out here are the APPC steps required to establish a conversation with the AS/400. All you have to do is lift the code and use it in your own applications.

Note that in the sample application, some of the procedures are contained in the declarations area of the one and only form. While this makes sense when there is only one form, a more flexible setup is achieved by creating a code module and keeping these procedures in there.

These APPC routines will be set up as universal procedures, available to all your future projects. That is, the routines, once lifted, should be left alone and any application-specific code kept elsewhere (meaning in another module).

First, take a look at the APPC procedures in this project.

Step by Step: The RTRSAMP Procedures

1. Bring up the RTRSAMP project into the VB Development Environment. (It should load without any messages this time if you saved your project after making the "PipData" correction).

2. Select "RTRSAMP.FRM" in the project box and click on "View Code." This brings the declarations area into the code window.

3. Click on the procedures list at the top of the code window to open it. Scroll down one procedure. You should see:

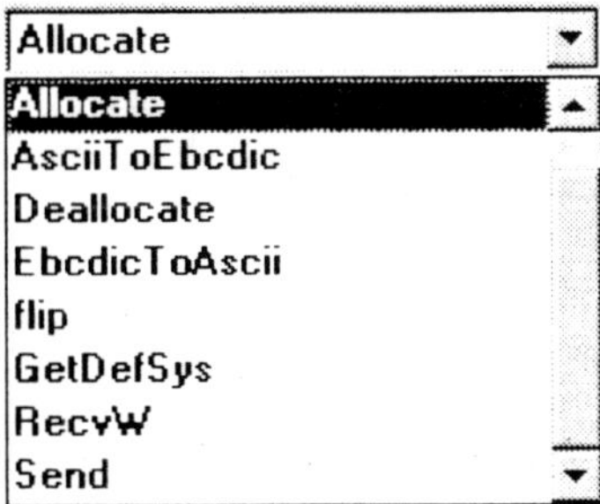

These eight procedures (one will be replaced) are most of the APPC functions that you use to perform the low-level client/server functions. There are a few more elsewhere that will have to be lifted as well.

- *Allocate* starts a conversation with the AS/400.
- *AsciiToEbcdic* converts data from ASCII (which the PC uses) to EBCDIC (which the AS/400 uses).
- *D eallocate* ends the conversation with the 400.
- *EbcdicToAscii* converts data the other way.
- The next procedure— *"flip"*—is intended to set a data length value for the conversation with the 400. "flip" is a procedure that works for the sample procedure but has some limitations. It will be replaced with a better routine.
- *GetDefSys* retrieves the system name of the AS/400. This routine is only used when there are multiple AS/400s to which you could connect.
- *RecvW* extracts transmitted data from the router and puts it in a string.
- *Send* puts data to the router for transmission to the AS/400.

4. Just to see what's in there, click on one of the procedures, like "Allocate:"

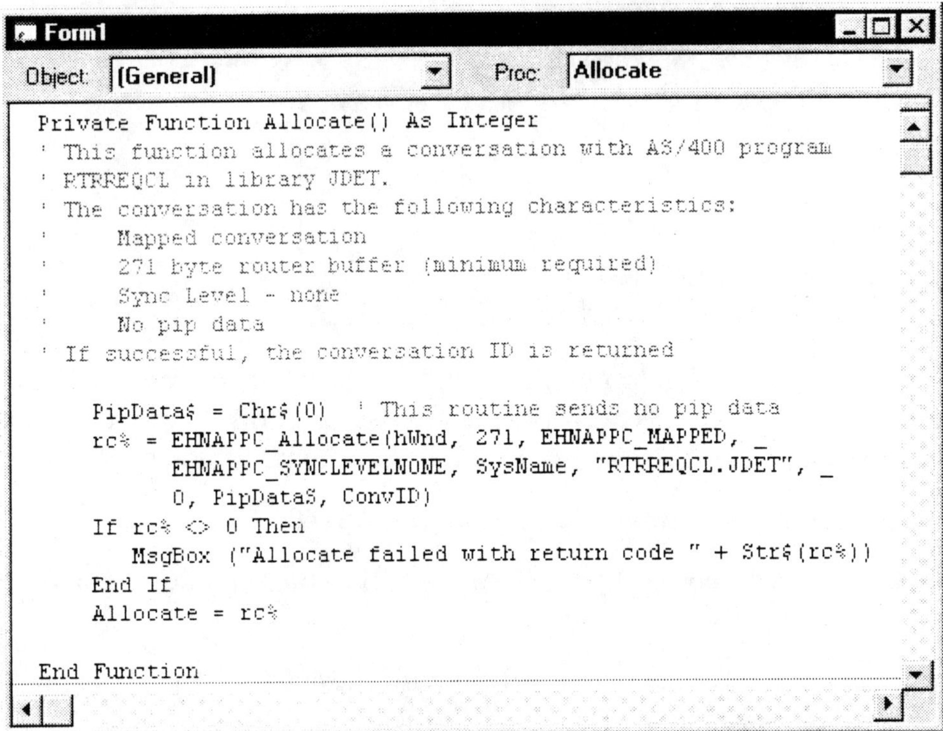

Notice that there is an application-specific reference in there (like "RTRREQCL.JDET"). This will have to be changed, later.

The remainder of this chapter deals with lifting the code from this sample program and putting it into other files so that it can be copied cleanly into your c/s applications.

The tools in these procedures need to be made generic. That is, not application specific. Once that is done, you have code upon which you can build your c/s projects.

Getting the IBM Tools Ready for Your Use

A little scrubbing and a different folder and the tools will be ready for the client/server project coming in the next chapter. The following are rather detailed, cookbook instructions for getting the tools ready. You need only perform them once.

This IBM sample code was written under VB 2.0, so you will see some keywords and conventions that are expressed slightly differently under VB 4.0. In most cases, the meaning of the VB 2.0 code is obvious. Where it is not, explanation is provided.

> **Note:** *The finished files are included on the diskette that comes with the book, and may be copied from there (see the note at the end of this chapter). If you choose to do so, please read through the following so you know how they got there.*

Step by Step: Copying the Tools

1. Start 16-bit VB and bring up the RTRSAMP project.
2. Click on "RTRSAMP.GBL" in the project box. This is the APPC Declarations file. (Or at least it will be in a moment.) Click on "View Code."
3. Delete all of the comments in the first part of the file down to where it says:

```
'****************************************************************

Global declarations specific to this sample program

'****************************************************************
```

   This should now be the first line of the file. The comments were specific to the sample project and are out of place now.

4. Change the comment above to read just "Global declarations".

   The VB keyword "Global" is the equivalent of "Public." "Public" is now the preferred substitute because it contrasts with "Private," but VB 4.0 accepts the "Global" keyword.

5. Remove the lines "Global SysName As String * 8" and "Global PartNo As String * 5." (The part number exists only in the sample program.) The other variable "ConvId" is fine as it is.

```
Global SysName As String * 8

Global ConvID As Long

Global PartNo As String * 5
```

Okay, that's it, but don't save the file yet—you don't want to overwrite the original. Instead, you should clone this file into another one.

6. Click on "Save File As..." on the File menu.
7. Specify a new name of "APPC.GBL" and a folder of "C:\VB\PROJECTS."

   This places the APPC Declarations file in the "PROJECTS" folder where all projects in subfolders have easy access to it.

8. Click on "OK" and save the file.

   As you know, the project will now point to the renamed file, so you want to discard the changes.

9. From the File menu, click on "New Project." You'll be asked if you want to save the changes to "RTRSAMP.MAK." Respond with "No."

   The preceding steps created a modified clone of the IBM-supplied APPC Declarations file in the folder "PROJECTS" without disturbing the original RTRSAMP project. Okay, next file.

10. Go into the File menu and open the RTRSAMP project again.
11. Start a new standard module by clicking on the "New Module" button. This is where code will be copied and become a universal module. It will not be kept as part of the RTRSAMP project.
12. The new module should have come up with "Option Explicit" already specified. Remove it.

    Unfortunately, "Option Explicit" won't work for this new module because IBM has freely used implicitly defined variables (you remember, those defined with a suffix like "$"). It is a good idea to switch this around, but not now.

13. Key in the following four definitions for constants in the declarations area of "Module1.Bas:"

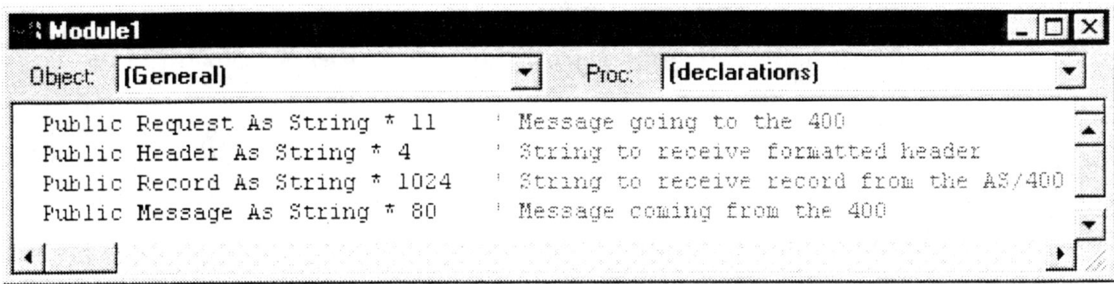
```
Public Request As String * 11    ' Message going to the 400
Public Header As String * 4      ' String to receive formatted header
Public Record As String * 1024   ' String to receive record from the AS/400
Public Message As String * 80    ' Message coming from the 400
```

These are the global variables used for passing requests and data back and forth between the 400 and the PC.

Note that this code window overlays the code window for the form "RTRSAMP.FRM." This is convenient as you'll be jumping from one code window to the other as procedures are copied.

The next task is to copy seven procedures from the general area of form "RTRSAMP.FRM" to the new code module.

14. Adjust the position of the top code window so that both can be seen (and clicked to select):

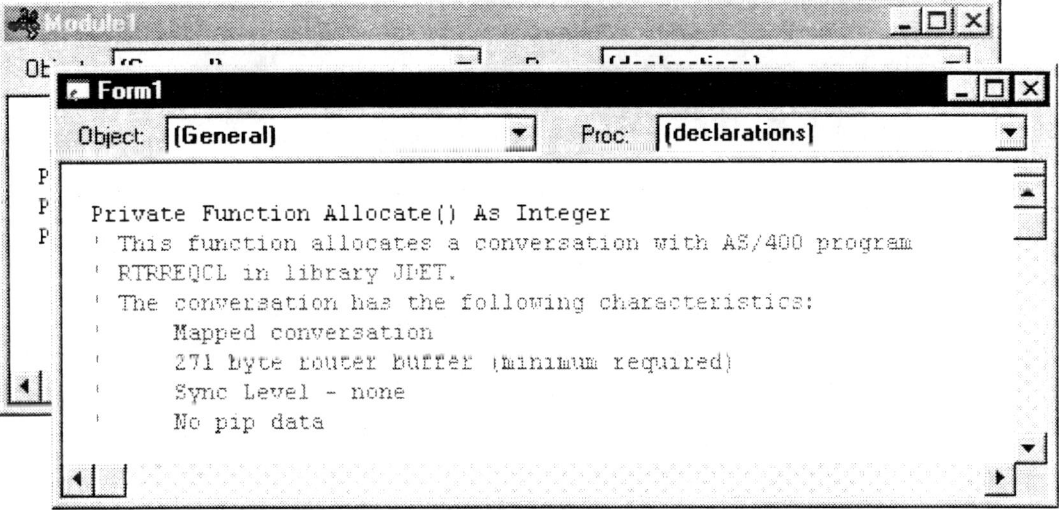
```
Private Function Allocate() As Integer
 ' This function allocates a conversation with AS/400 program
 ' RTRREQCL in library JDET.
 ' The conversation has the following characteristics:
 '     Mapped conversation
 '     271 byte router buffer (minimum required)
 '     Sync Level - none
 '     No pip data
```

The reason for having two code windows open is so procedures may be transferred, one at a time, to the new module. The module will then be saved under a new name to the PROJECTS folder.

The fact that the IBM sample code of interest is in a form instead of a module makes it unusable as a code engine for other applications, so it must be moved.

15. Click on "RTRSAMP.FRM" to bring it to the front if it is not already there. Click on the procedures box to open the list:

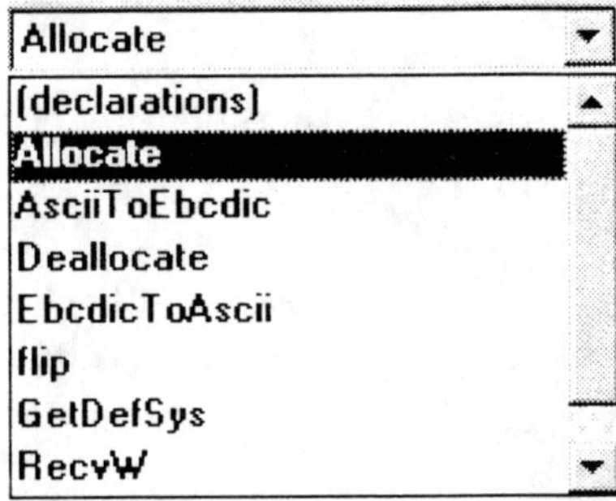

16. Click on the function "Allocate" to bring it into the "RTRSAMP.FRM" code window. With the mouse, highlight all of the code in this procedure—from "Function" to "End Function:"

Form1

Object: (General) Proc: Allocate

```
Private Function Allocate() As Integer
' This function allocates a conversation with AS/400 program
' RTRREQCL in library JDET.
' The conversation has the following characteristics:
'     Mapped conversation
'     271 byte router buffer (minimum required)
'     Sync Level - none
'     No pip data
' If successful, the conversation ID is returned

    PipData$ = Chr$(0)   ' This routine sends no pip data
    rc% = EHNAPPC_Allocate(hWnd, 271, EHNAPPC_MAPPED, EHNAPPC_SYN
    If rc% <> 0 Then
      MsgBox ("Allocate failed with return code " + Str$(rc%))
    End If
    Allocate = rc%

End Function
```

17. Go up to the Edit menu and click on "Copy." This places the highlighted information into the clipboard.

18. Click on the new module "Module1.Bas" to bring it to the front.

19. Open the Edit menu and click on "Paste" (or press Ctrl-V.) The copied code should flow into the new module.

    Note that because the code contains "Function" and "End Function" statements, the VB Development Environment recognizes it as complete and adds it to the module's list of procedures.

20. On your keyboard, press and hold the Down Arrow key. The cursor runs down the procedure until one line past the "End Function" statement. This sets the stage for the next procedure to be copied.

21. Click on the form ("RTRSAMP.FRM") to bring it to the front.

22. On your keyboard, press Page Down to page through the "Allocate" function and bring up the next—"AsciiToEbcdic:"

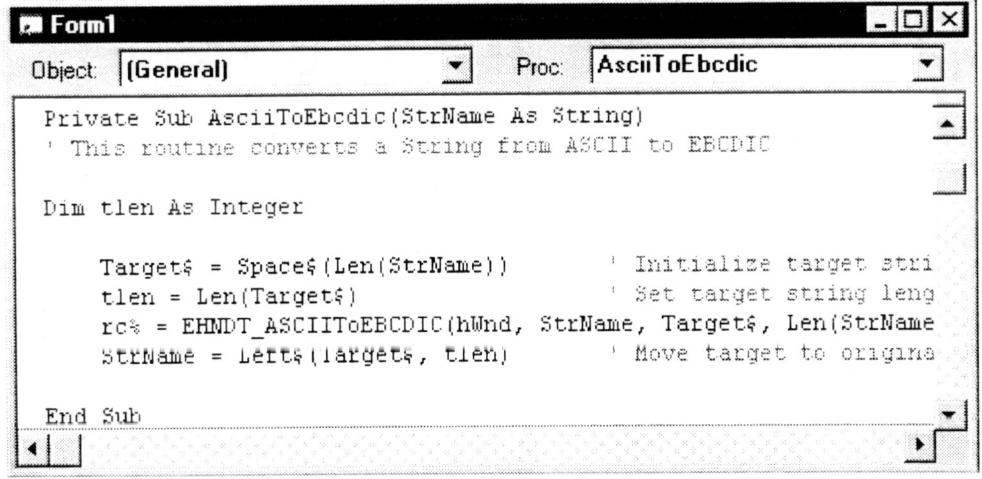

23. Highlight the code from "Sub" to "End Sub" (this is a Sub procedure, not a function) and copy it into the clipboard. Bring the module window to the front and paste the code in, as before.

24. Press and hold the Down Arrow key to get beyond this procedure, go back to the "form," press Page Down, and copy and paste the next procedure "Deallocate."

25. Repeat for "EbcdicToAscii" but *skip over the Sub procedure* "flip." "flip", as mentioned before, will be replaced with a few lines of more capable code.

26. Continue to copy the procedures:

    GetDefSys

    RecvW

    Send

27. When you're finished, open the procedures list for the new module. You should see:

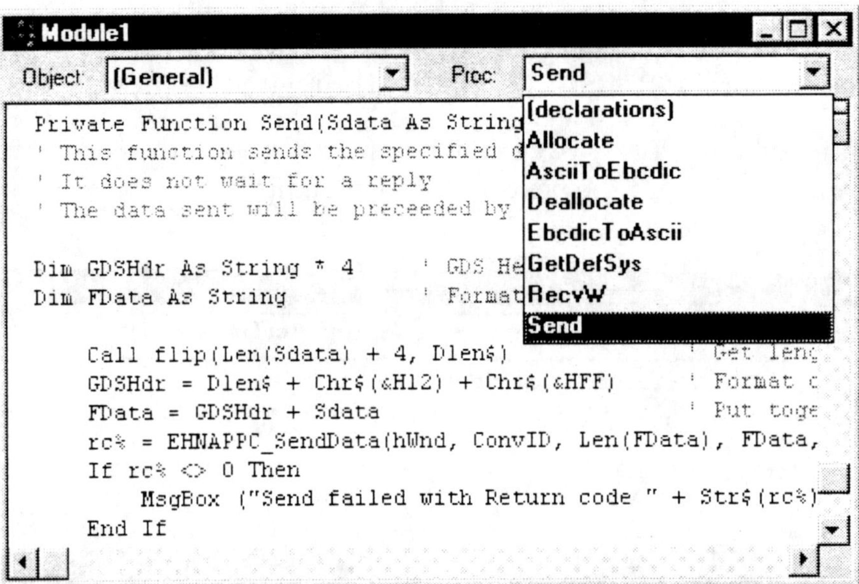

28. Click on the "RTRSAMP.FRM" code window to bring it to the front and close it leaving the code window for "Module1.Bas" the only one open.

To reiterate what you've done so far: You've created a new code module to hold the procedures from the sample program, and you've copied seven function and Sub procedures to the new module. The procedure "flip" was skipped.

You're well on your way to assembling a box of tools for client/server applications. Notice that it only takes a handful of routines to accomplish all the APPC functions of a basic c/s relationship. Each of these procedures (and one more,) is discussed as they're applied to the beginning c/s project in the next chapter.

Step by Step: The SendReceive Procedure

So there are all these procedures now but nothing to tie them together. Coding your c/s applications is simplified if you create a small procedure to run most of the mechanisms.

1. With any procedure in the "Module1.Bas" code window, press and hold the Down Arrow until you get past the "End Sub/Function" statement. From here you can start a new procedure.

2. Key:

```
Sub SendReceive(Request as String)
```

and press Enter. You should see:

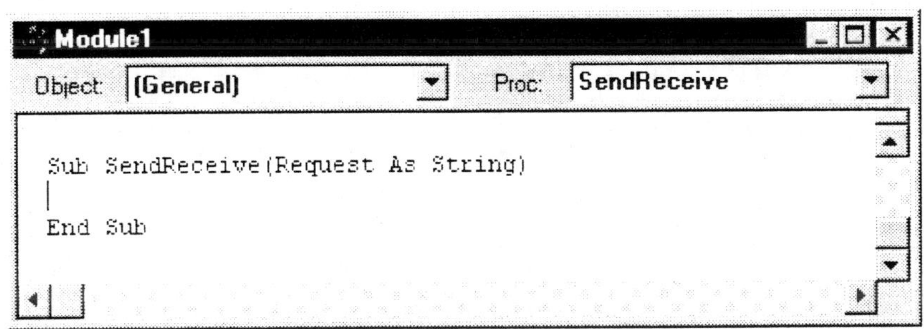

The new procedure "SendReceive" has been started.

3. Carefully key in the following code between the "Sub" and "End Sub" statements:

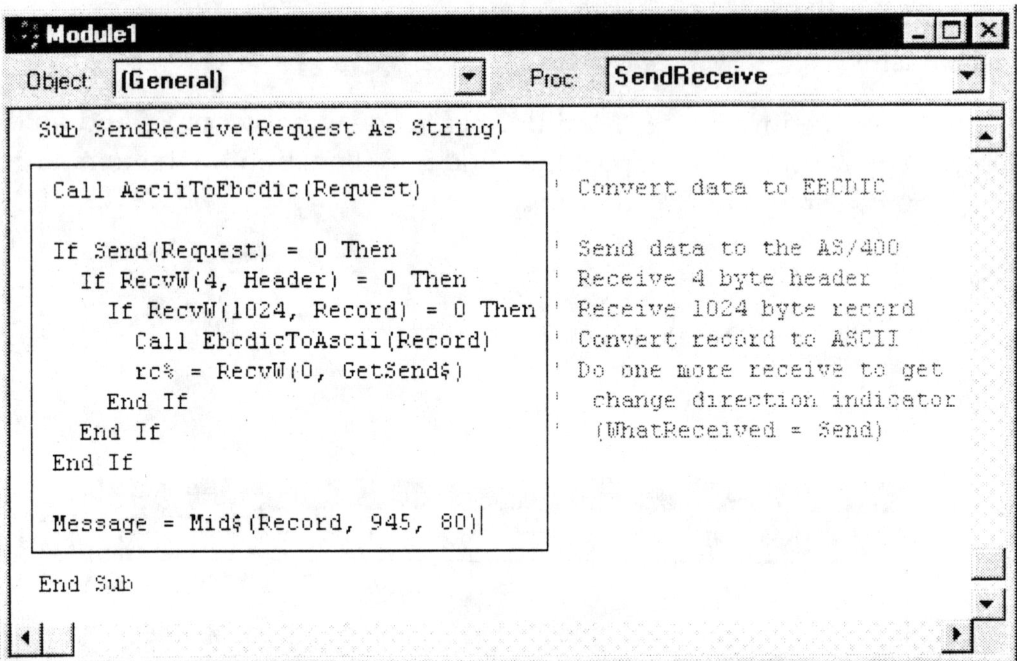

These statements tie most of the other procedures together so you can easily send requests and receive responses from the AS/400.

So far, the new code module hasn't been saved or renamed. It still belongs to the RTRSAMP program; you'll fix all that after one more step.

The code in the procedure "Send" has to be modified. The call to "flip" must be removed and replaced by a few lines of code.

4. Bring the procedure "Send" into the active code window.

5. Remove the line "Call flip(Len(Sdata) + 4, Dlen$)" by highlighting it and clicking "Cut" on the Edit menu (or pressing Ctrl-X):

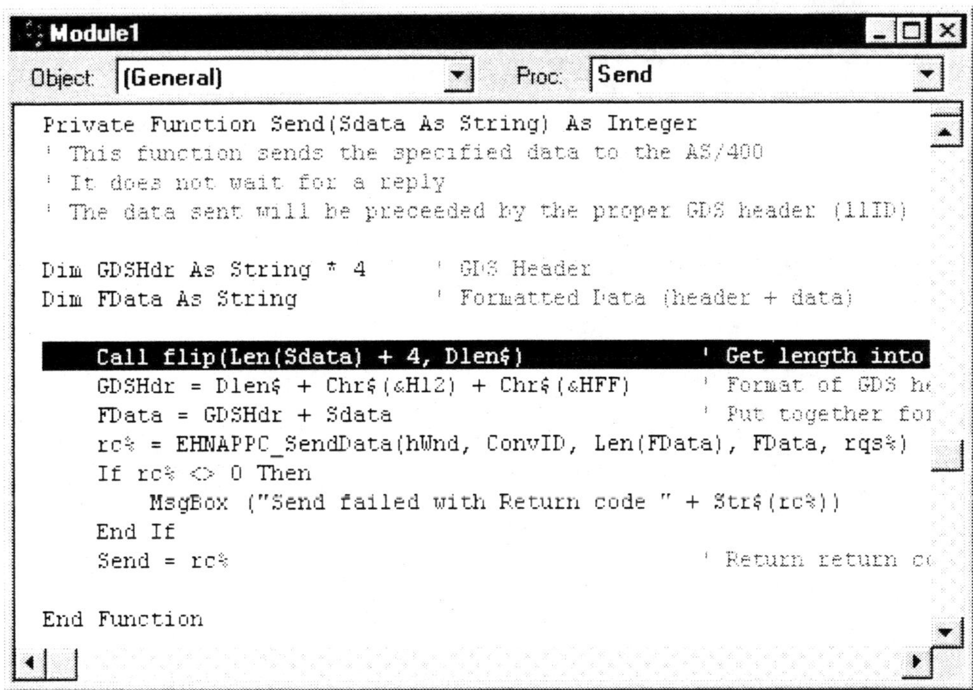

In its place, carefully add the following five lines of code:

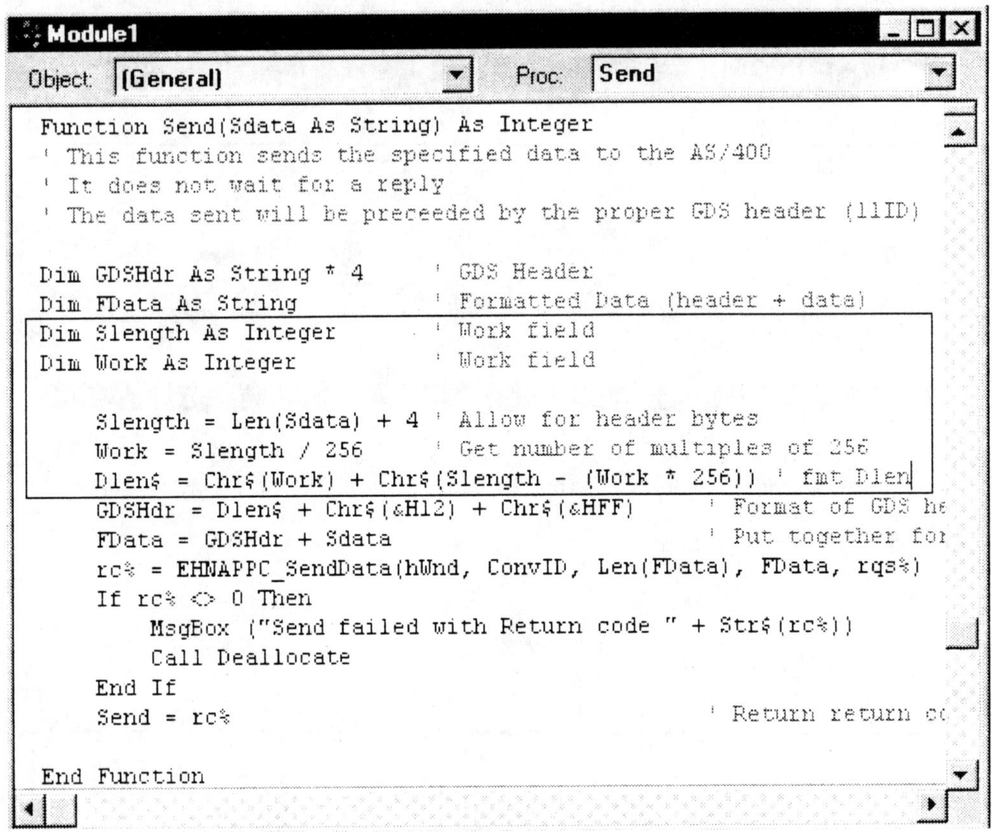

The function "flip" was supposed to determine the length of the data string to be sent to the AS/400 and prepare a record header that told the router how long the string is. "flip" only works for a string up to 10 bytes. This little routine handles any allowable data string length.

Now to doctor up the "Allocate" function. "Allocate" has a hard-coded reference to the CL partner program used in the example "RTRREQCL.JDET" (which, in turn, calls an RPG program). It should be replaced with an argument variable containing the program name that can be passed in. Also, the data string to the AS/400 can be increased to 1024 for better efficiency.

6. Bring the function "Allocate" into the code window.

7. Add a variable name "ProgramName as String" between the parentheses on the Function statement as a passed-in argument. This makes the function generic. In the line beginning "rc% = EHNACCP_Allocate," replace the literal "RTRREQCL.JDET" with the variable name ProgramName, no quotes:

```
Function Allocate (ProgramName As String) As Integer
' This function allocates a conversation with
' an AS/400 program xxxxxxxx in library xxxxxxxx.
' The conversation has the following characteristics:
'     Mapped conversation
'     1024 byte router buffer
'     Sync Level - none
'     No pip data
' If successful, the conversation ID is returned

PipData$ = Chr$(0)   ' This routine sends no pip data
rc% = EHNAPPC_Allocate(hWnd, 1024, EHNAPPC_MAPPED, _
 EHNAPPC_SYNCLEVELNONE, SysName, ProgramName, 0, PipData$, Convid)
If rc% <> 0 Then
  MsgBox ("Allocate failed with return code " + Str$(rc%))
End If
Allocate = rc%

End Function
```

this line is folded

8. Also change the buffer length of 271 to 1024—a better data transport.

Okay, all this valuable effort is at risk. Better save it, but under a different name.

9. Close the code window. Check that the selected file in the project box is "Module1.Bas."

10. Open the File menu and select "Save File As...."

11. Select the folder "C:\VB\PROJECTS," specify a name of "APPC.BAS," and save the file.

12. To preserve the original sample project, click "New Project" from the File menu and say "No to All" to the "Save your changes?" prompt.

Congratulations. Your toolbox, however basic, is complete enough to write a first client/server application. Now, there is a global declarations module named "APPC.GBL" and a code module of c/s functions called "APPC.BAS." These two files will be used, together with the Visual Basic forms and controls that you've already learned about, to create full-function client/server applications.

> **Note:** *This has been a long string of cookbook instructions to render the two files "APPC.GBL" and "APPC.BAS." If you're unsure of the success of your efforts, copy the two files from the accompanying diskette to your "C:\VB\PROJECTS\" folder.*

The next chapter takes you, step by step, through a first client/server application. Details on how to use your new tools are presented as they're put into the application.

Summary

The IWSTOOL Program

The "QIWSTOOL" folder on the AS/400 contains a program called "IWSTOOL" that presents a list of sample projects of all kinds.

The "IWSTOOL" program will also download project files to your PC.

The APPC Declarations File

The APPC Declarations file (APPC.GBL) contains the constants and declarations to use the routines in "EHNAPPC.DLL."

The file is meant to be shared by your c/s projects and shouldn't be altered once it is on your system in finished form.

The file is part of the IBM-supplied sample application "RTRSAMP."

> **Note**: *You can create the declarations file from the Client Access/PCS sample project or copy it from the accompanying diskette. Its name is "APPC.GBL" in folder "A:\PROJECTS." Copy it to folder "C:\VB\PROJECTS."*

The APIRTREX Package

This package contains files that create objects needed to demo the "RTRSAMP" project. The package also contain examples of methods used to create objects on an AS/400 from a PC distribution diskette.

The RTRSAMP Package

The "RTRSAMP" VB project is the place where examples of how to use the "EHNAPPC" API may be found.

> **Note**: *A template file available to your c/s projects may be created from this example project or copied from the accompanying diskette. Its name is "APPC.BAS" in folder "A:\PROJECTS." Copy it to folder "C:\VB\PROJECTS."*

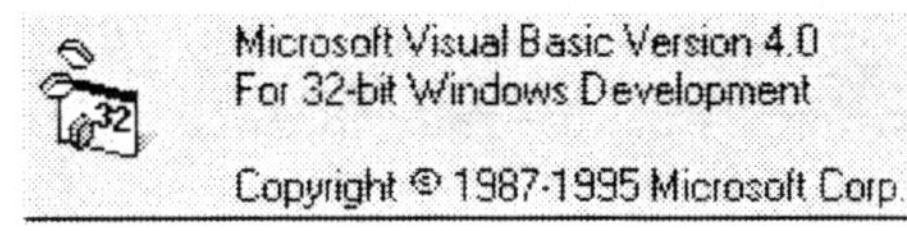

11

A First C/S Application

TIME400

This chapter deals almost entirely with a simple client/server application called TIME400.

Topics presented in this chapter include:

- A simple design method for the application.
- The Visual Basic code.
- The RPG partner program template.
- How the ICF file fits in.
- Step by step, how to code the application.

Tools Provided on the Accompanying Diskette

Within this chapter, you are given the choice of uploading AS/400 source code for this project from the accompanying diskette, or keying it in. If you prefer to upload the source code, you may upload part or all of it. Here are the upload batch files for this project that are on the accompanying diskette:

APPC.BAT	Creates library VBLIB and source files.
APPCALL .BAT	Uploads all templates and all elements of the TIME400 project (calls all other template and "TIME400" batch files).
APPCICF.BAT	Uploads template ICF file source code.
APPCRPG.BAT	Uploads template RPG source code.
TIME400.BAT	Uploads "TIME400" RPG source code.
TIME400C.BAT	Uploads the "TIME400" CL source code.
TIME400D.BAT	Uploads the "TIME400"" ICF file source code.

Note that you may create the library "VBLIB," create the source files, and upload all AS/400 template and TIME400 source code by calling the one batch file "APPCALL.BAT" in folder "A:\TOOLS" on the accompanying diskette.

What TIME400 Does

TIME400, a VB program, is started on the PC. The program tests for the Client Access/PCS router and, if loaded, starts a conversation with the AS/400.

An RPG program is started on the 400 as the *partner* to the VB program.

The VB program issues a request to the RPG program for the current date and time of day, as known to the AS/400.

The RPG program gets the current date and time and returns it to the VB program.

The VB program sets the PC's clock to match the AS/400.

The VB program issues a request to detach from the 400, and both programs end.

This little application, aside from being a good way to ease into client/server, may even have a use in your shop. If your PC users are sharing files, say through

Client Access/PCS shared folders, and a PC has an incorrect date, any document that is changed by that PC and saved back to the shared folder may cause an incorrect overwrite by another user. (The second user may think a file is older or newer than it really is.)

Even without sharing files, having all your PCs (that are attached to the 400) set to the AS/400's clock provides reliability for date and time stamping, whether that be at the 400 or at a PC. Changes for Daylight Savings time, etc., are automatic and reliable.

The Approach for TIME400

This project is meant to be an introduction to establishing a client/server system with an AS/400. VB code extraneous to that purpose is kept to a minimum. In other words, an effort has been made to keep this project as simple as possible from a VB point of view.

There are no forms, and the user has no interaction with the program. Either the VB program can get the date and time from the AS/400 or it can't.

In the full-blown VB client/server application—"The AS/400 Report Download Utility," presented in Chapter 14—all the elements of VB and client/server are brought together.

Step by Step: Setting Up for the TIME400 Project

1. Create a new folder to hold the source files off of the "VB\PROJECTS\" folder. Call it "TIME400."

   The next step is to properly arrange and name the source files. To do this, you must remove the default form file from the project, add a code module, and rename the project file.

2. Bring up the 16-bit VB Development Environment. Look to see that "Form1.Frm" is selected in the project box. From the File menu, select "Remove File."

   Now, a new module for code that is specific to this project is needed.

3. Start a new module and select it in the project box.

4. From the File menu, select "Save File As..." Specify a folder of "C\VB\PROJECTS\TIME400\" and a file name of "TIME400.BAS."

   This is a c/s project, so you need the APPC tools you built (or copied) in the last chapter ("APPC.GBL" and "APPC.BAS"). These files, although attached to this project, are meant to be shared and unaltered by any one project. That's why they're kept in the common folder "PROJECTS."

   Now, add the files to the project.

5. From the File menu, click on "Add File..."

6. In the dialog box, open the "List files of type:" list box at the bottom. Scroll down the list and click on "All Files (*.*):"

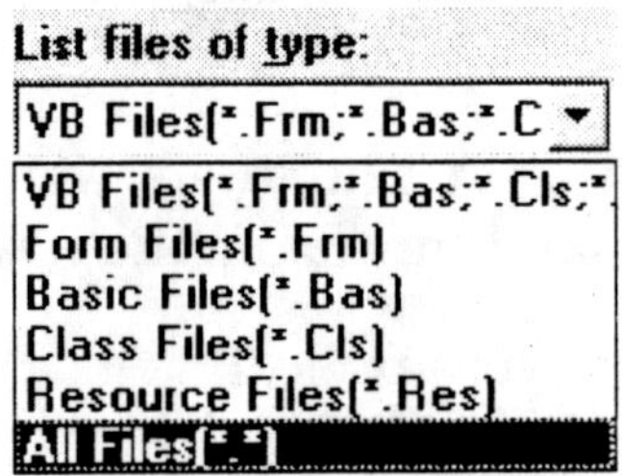

   This brings these two files into the files box:

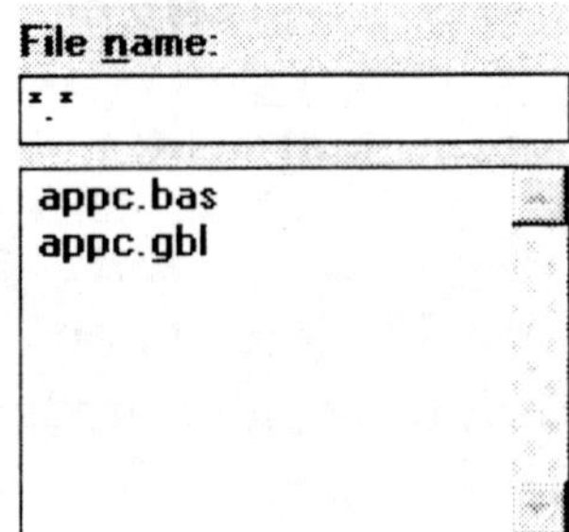

7. Select "appc.gbl" and click on "OK." The file is added to the project box.

8. Repeat steps 5 and 6, this time selecting the other file, "appc.bas."

Your project box should look like this:

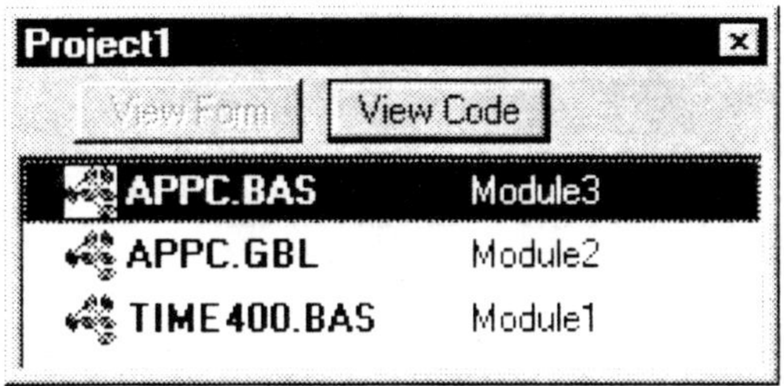

There's a code module for the project statements, and the APPC tool files. Now, save the project file itself under a new name.

9. Select "Save Project As..." from the File menu. Again, specify a folder of "C:\VB\PROJECTS\TIME400\" and a project file name of "TIME400.Vbp."

   The project box reflects the project's new name and its source files:

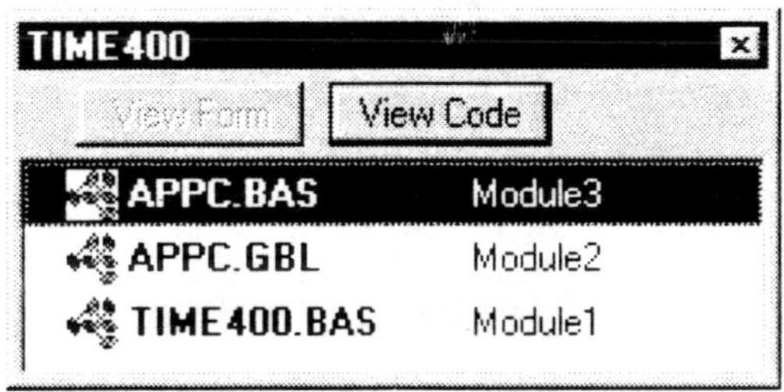

Step by Step: The Initialize Procedure

OK, time to code. In this straight-ahead approach, logic suggests that the next thing needed is a routine like the RPG INZSR subroutine that runs once only at the beginning of the program to initialize things.

1. Open the code window for the module "TIME400.BAS." In the declarations area of the module, key these two variable declaration statements:

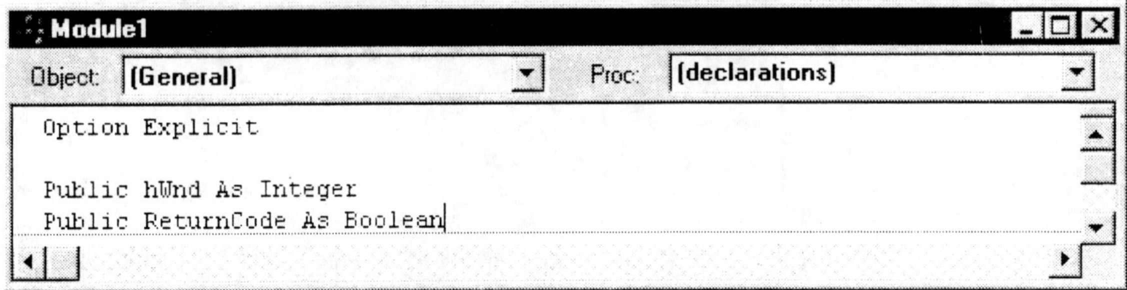

The first global variable is the windows handle for calls to external routines. The second is a variable to receive general-purpose return codes, and that is only defined as global for convenience. Because you placed these variables in the declarations area of a module, they are visible to the whole program.

Now, the new initialize procedure.

2. From the Insert menu click on "Procedure..." Select "Sub" and "Private." Name the new procedure "Initialize."

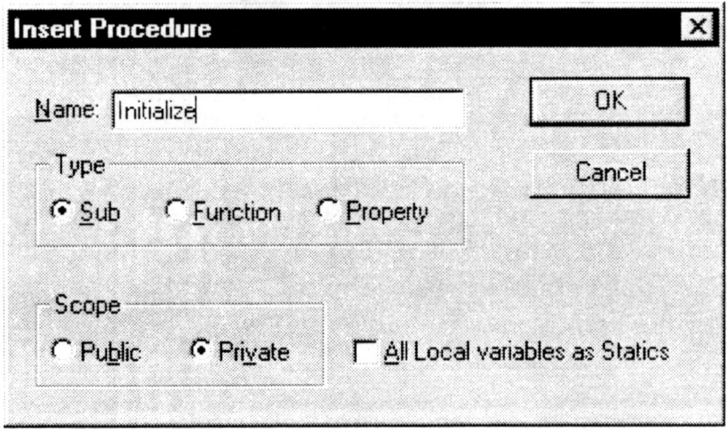

3. Key in the following code:

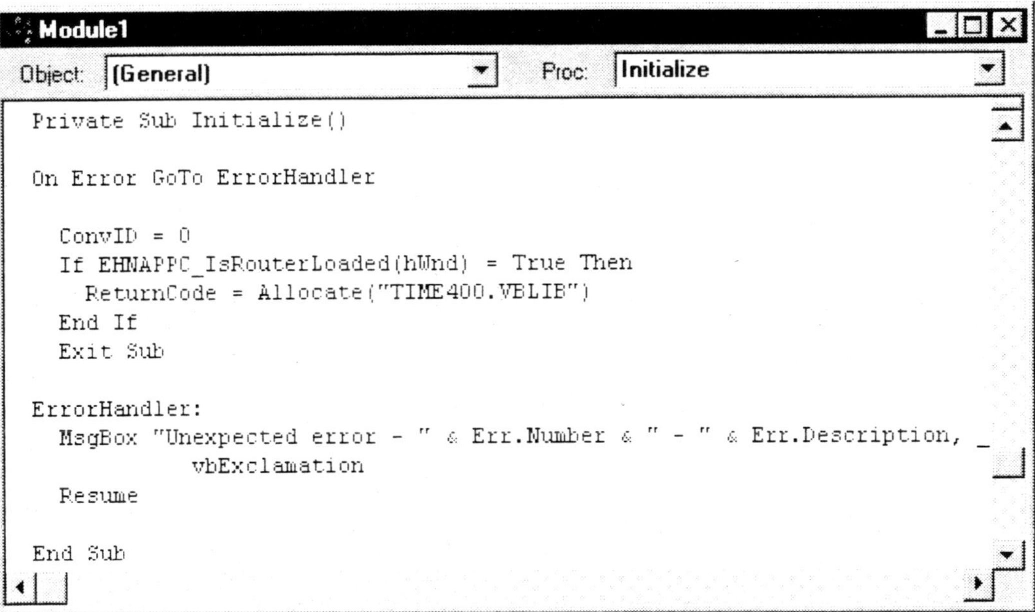

```
Private Sub Initialize()

On Error GoTo ErrorHandler

  ConvID = 0
  If EHNAPPC_IsRouterLoaded(hWnd) = True Then
    ReturnCode = Allocate("TIME400.VBLIB")
  End If
  Exit Sub

ErrorHandler:
  MsgBox "Unexpected error - " & Err.Number & " - " & Err.Description, _
            vbExclamation
  Resume

End Sub
```

Notice that the partner program name—"TIME400C.VBLIB"—is in S/38 format. This is a lingering characteristic of ICF files.

4. Save your project.

   As its name suggests, this procedure is called when the program is started, but not automatically as is *INZSR. It must be called explicitly—which is shown in a moment.

   Line by line, here's what the procedure does:

   - The error handler has been enabled with the "On Error" statement.
   - A global variable "ConvId" is initialized. All APPC conversations receive a "conversation id" when the two computers start talking. If they don't start talking, the conversation ID remains zero.
   - The next statement is a call to the external routine "EHNAPPC_IsRouterLoaded," which checks for the presence of the Client Access/PCS router and the PCSWIN program, as was presented previously.

Note: The function itself is being treated as if it is either "True" or "False" in the statement "If EHNAPPC_IsRouterLoaded..." Recall that many functions return a Boolean value. This is one of them.

- The function "Allocate" is among those lifted from the sample project into your tools file "APPC.BAS." It sends a request for a conversation to the AS/400.

Several parameters are passed to the 400 that establish the particulars under which the conversation is struck. Those parameters are required by APPC to define the conversation. Most are provided for you by your tools routines, but some are peculiar to the individual application and you must pass them.

Among the parameters is the name of the AS/400 *partner program* that you want loaded. APPC on the 400 accepts this parm and starts the program. The partner program is what works with your VB program to service requests. In the illustration, the program "TIME400C.VBLIB" is specified. (Remember, an RPG program is presented shortly.)

Note: APPC conversations come in as communications jobs. As such, they have no job description, so they adopt the AS/400's system-level library list—"QUSRLIBL" and "QSYSLIBL." If you keep your system library list free of production libraries, you'll have to hard code a library name, as in the example.

If the router is loaded and if there's a problem starting the conversation, "Allocate" displays a message identifying the code number of the error.

If the conversation is successfully started, the variable "ConvId" receives a nonzero value in the "Allocate" routine. You can use the value in ConvId throughout the program to test for the presence of a conversation with the AS/400.

The next step is to call the initialize procedure when the program is started. This initialize procedure is not like the RPG *INZSR. It must be called explicitly.

Recall that the project options specify a startup form. Normally when your program is started, a form is automatically loaded. But in this case, because there are no forms, you must create a Sub procedure called "Main." VB runs it when the program is started, in place of loading a form. You can call the "Initialize" procedure from there.

5. In the project box, highlight "TIME400.BAS." Click on "View Code" to bring up the declarations area for the module.

6. Start a new procedure called "Main" in the same manner that you started the procedure "Initialize."

7. Key in the following code:

```
Private Sub main()

Dim WorkDate As String * 8

Dim WorkTime As String * 8


 ' Test for the router and get a conv. id...

 Call Initialize


 If ConvID <> 0 Then

    ' Send request to the AS/400 and receive a reply...

    Request = "DATEANDTIME"

    SendReceive (Request)

    ' Check the message from the 400...

    If Message = "(OK)" & Space$(76) Then

       ' Parse the date & time from the returned string...

       WorkTime = Mid$(Record, 1, 2) & ":" & Mid$(Record, 3, 2) _

                & ":" & Mid$(Record, 5, 2)

       WorkDate = Mid$(Record, 7, 2) & "/" & Mid$(Record, 9, 2) _

                & "/" & Mid$(Record, 11, 2)

       ' Set the PC's clock...
```

```
      If WorkDate > "00/00/00" And WorkDate < "99/99/99" Then
        Date$ = WorkDate
      End If
      If WorkTime > "00:00:00" And WorkTime < "24:00:00" Then
        Time$ = WorkTime
      End If
    Else
      MsgBox "Unexpected error - " & Err.Number & " - " & _
               Err.Description, _vbExclamation
    End If

    ' End the conversation with the AS/400...
    Call Deallocate
  End If
  End
End Sub
```

8. Again, save your project. Here's what happens in the "Main" procedure:
   - Two work fields are defined (remember that fields defined inside a procedure are only visible to that procedure).
   - The "Initialize" procedure is explicitly called to establish a conversation with the AS/400.
   - If the initialization renders a conversation ID, a request is sent to the 400.
   - The AS/400 has a chance to communicate with the VB program through a portion of the string that is returned—called "Message" in

the program. If the message is "(OK)," meaning the request has been completed, the returned string is substringed into the work fields.

- The values are checked again, and, if okay, are used to set the PC's date and time.
- Finally, if a conversation is active, the procedure "Deallocate" is called to end the conversation with the 400, and the VB program ends.

9. To check your efforts, use the "Step Into" button on the toolbar to step through your code.

The CL Partner Program

At the other end of the client/server relationship is the AS/400 program. Very often that program will be a CL program that sets the library list and calls an RPG program to handle the actual transactions.

In this project, the AS/400 partner program is "TIME400C" in library "VBLIB" as specified in the "Allocate" procedure. "TIME400C" just adds "VBLIB" to the job's library list and calls "TIME400," an RPG program that does all of the work.

There is no template included on the accompanying diskette for such a simple CL program. The source code for the actual program—"TIME400C"—for this application is, however, available for uploading from the accompanying diskette (or just key it in):

```
/ *- - - - - - - - - - - - - - - - - - - - - - - - - - - - - - - - - - -/
/*                                                                     */
/*  CL program TIME400C                                                */
/*              This program sets the liblist for the C/S              */
/*              program TIME400.  TIME400 gets the date & time         */
/*              from the AS/400 and passes it to the VB program.       */
/*                                                                     */
/*   Revisions                                                         */
/*     Date       Pgmr       Revision                                  */
/ *- - - - - - - - - - - - - - - - - - - - - - - - - - - - - - - - - - -/
             PGM
             ADDLIBLE    LIB(VBLIB)
             MONMSG      MSGID(CPF2103)
             CALL        PGM(TIME400)
             ENDPGM
```

The code may be uploaded by running the batch file "TIME400C.BAT" in folder "A:\TOOLS" on the accompanying diskette.

The RPG Partner Program Template

The RPG code will be cloned from a template and then modified to fit the "TIME400" application. As with the VB code, the RPG program is kept as simple as possible.

The RPG template shows how to code two kinds of transactions—one where only one transmission will fulfill the VB program's request, and another where multiple transmissions are required to get all of the data to the PC.

Here, then, is the RPG template as included on the accompanying diskette:

```
 *- - - - - - - - - - - - - - - - - - - - - - - - - - - - - - -
H
 *- - - - - - - - - - - - - - - - - - - - - - - - - - - - - - -
 *                                                                 *
 *   Program - APPCRPG                                             *
 *             This program is a template for RPG client/server   *
 *             partner programs to a Visual Basic PC program.     *
 *                                                                 *
 *   Revisions                                                     *
 *     Date       Pgmr       Revision                              *
 *                                                                 *
 *                                                                 *
 *- - - - - - - - - - - - - - - - - - - - - - - - - - - - - - -
FAPPCICF CF  E                    WORKSTN
F                                             KNUM        1
 *  Data structure to receive information about the ICF file . . .
F                                             KINFDS FEEDBK
 *  Error handling subroutine for ICF operations . . .
F                                             KINFSR EXCPTH
 *- - - - - - - - - - - - - - - - - - - - - - - - - - - - - - -
 *  Messages to the VB program . . .
E                    MSG     1  10 80
 *  Array to load data base records into the outgoing ICF record
E                    REC        8110
*- - - - - - - - - - - - - - - - - - - - - - - - - - - - - - - -
IICDATA      DS
I                                      1 880 REC
IFEEDBK      DS
```

```
     I                                          38  45 FMTNM
     I                                         401 404 MAJMIN
     I                                         401 402 MAJCOD
     I                                         403 404 MINCOD
      * Constant(s)
     I              'request 1 '          C         @RQ1
     I              'request 2 '          C         @RQ2
      *- - - - - - - - - - - - - - - - - - - - - - - - - - - - - - -
      *  Indicators defined in the ICF file DDS:
      *    66  -  RCVFAIL
      *    82  -  RCVDETACH
      *- - - - - - - - - - - - - - - - - - - - - - - - - - - - - - -
      * Read from the Client Access/PCS router . . .
     C                     READ RQRECORD                 88
B001 C           *IN82     DOWEQ*OFF
      *
      * Incoming requests . . .
B002 C                     SELEC
      *
      * Requests where only one transmission is required . . .
   2 C           RQDATA    WHEQ @RQ1
   2 C                     EXSR SINGLE
      * Request where multiple transmissions are required . . .
   2 C           RQDATA    WHEQ @RQ2
   2 C                     EXSR MULTPL
      * Return an "Invalid" message when request can't be determined...
   2 C                     OTHER
   2 C                     EXSR NVALID
      *
E002 C                     ENDSL
      *
      * Get next request . . .
     C                     EXSR WR
E001 C                     ENDDO                             *in82
      * When ReceiveDetach is received, release ICF file and end
     C                     EXSR RELEAS
      *- - - - - - - - - - - - - - - - - - - - - - - - - - - - - - -
     C           WR        BEGSR
      * Write/Read subroutine . . .
     C                     WRITEICRECORD
     C                     READ RQRECORD                 88
B001 C           *IN82     IFEQ *ON
   1 C                     EXSR RELEAS
E001 C                     ENDIF
     C                     CLEARICDATA
```

```
     C                     CLEARICERR
      *
     C                     ENDSR
      *- - - - - - - - - - - - - - - - - - - - - - - - - - - - - - - - -
      * Single transmission type of request . . .
     C           SINGLE    BEGSR
      *- - - - - - - - - - - - - - - - - - - - - - - - - - - - - - - - - -*
      * In this subroutine, only one transmission to the PC is
      *  required because all of the requested data will fit into
      *  one transmission record.  This example checks for the existance of
      *  something and returns only a message to the VB program . . .
      *
     C                     CALL 'Another Program'
     C                     PARM           RQDATA
     C                     PARM           RCODE   1
      * Return code of 0 = "(OK)". Return code of 1 = "(INVALID)" . . .
     C                     CLEARICERR
B001 C           RCODE     IFEQ '0'
   1 C                     MOVELMSG,3     ICERR
X001 C                     ELSE
   1 C                     MOVELMSG,4     ICERR
E001 C                     ENDIF
      *- - - - - - - - - - - - - - - - - - - - - - - - - - - - - - - - - -*
     C                     ENDSR
      *- - - - - - - - - - - - - - - - - - - - - - - - - - - - - - - - -
     C           MULTPL    BEGSR
      *- - - - - - - - - - - - - - - - - - - - - - - - - - - - - - - - - -*
      * This subroutine requires multiple transmissions to the PC.
      *   When the record going back to the PC is full, the Write/Read
      *   subroutine is executed, with a message of "(MORE)".  When all
      *   records have been sent, "(END)" is sent.
      *
     C           RQDATA    SETLLSomeDataBaseFile
     C                     READ ThatFile                20
B001 C           *IN20     DOWEQ*OFF
      *
      * ICF record is full - send & receive . . .
      *   (this example can hold 8 records)
B002 C           X         IFGE 8
      * Send "(MORE)" message to the VB program . . .
   2 C                     CLEARICERR
   2 C                     MOVELMSG,1     ICERR
      * Write to the VB program . . .
   2 C                     EXSR WR
   2 C                     CLEARX
```

```
E002 C                    ENDIF
     *
   1 C                    ADD  1         X       30
   1 C                    MOVELDBRecord  REC,X
   1 C                    READ ThatFileAgain           20
E001 C                    ENDDO
     *
     * Send remaining data and "(END)" message to the VB program.
     C                    CLEARICERR
     C                    MOVELMSG,2     ICERR
     *
     *- - - - - - - - - - - - - - - - - - - - - - - - - - - - - - - - - -*
     C                    ENDSR
     *- - - - - - - - - - - - - - - - - - - - - - - - - - - - - - - - - -*
     C          RELEAS    BEGSR
     *- - - - - - - - - - - - - - - - - - - - - - - - - - - - - - - - - -*
     * Request to detach received, release program device . . .
     C          'RQSDEV'  REL  APPCICF
     C                    MOVE *ON       *INLR
     C                    RETRN
     *- - - - - - - - - - - - - - - - - - - - - - - - - - - - - - - - - -*
     C                    ENDSR
     *- - - - - - - - - - - - - - - - - - - - - - - - - - - - - - - - - -*
     C          NVALID    BEGSR
     *- - - - - - - - - - - - - - - - - - - - - - - - - - - - - - - - - -*
     * This routine returns an "INVALID" error code. . .
     C                    CLEARICERR
     C                    MOVELMSG,4     ICERR
     *- - - - - - - - - - - - - - - - - - - - - - - - - - - - - - - - - -*
     C                    ENDSR
     *- - - - - - - - - - - - - - - - - - - - - - - - - - - - - - - - -
     C          EXCPTH    BEGSR
     *- - - - - - - - - - - - - - - - - - - - - - - - - - - - - - - - - -*
B001 C          MAJMIN    IFNE '0000'
   1 C                    MOVE *ON       *INLR
   1 C                    RETRN
E001 C                    ENDIF
     *- - - - - - - - - - - - - - - - - - - - - - - - - - - - - - - - - -*
     C                    ENDSR
     *- - - - - - - - - - - - - - - - - - - - - - - - - - - - - - - - -
     C          *INZSR    BEGSR
     *- - - - - - - - - - - - - - - - - - - - - - - - - - - - - - - - - -*
     *  Acquire ICF program device . . .
     C          'RQSDEV'  ACQ  APPCICF
     *- - - - - - - - - - - - - - - - - - - - - - - - - - - - - - - - - -*
```

```
     C                    ENDSR
      *- - - - - - - - - - - - - - - - - - - - - - - - - - - - - - - - - -
**
(MORE)
(END)
(OK)
(INVALID)
Available
Available
Available
Available
Available
Available
```

Things to note about this program:

- If you've ever written an RPG program to communicate with a peer system using Bisync (BSCEL or BSC), things are going to look familiar. The same techniques are used in AS/400 APPC programs.

- The program uses an ICF file to communicate with the VB program. This is very much like using a display file to communicate with a workstation. It's called a file, but you're really talking to a device. The device, in this case, is the PC, and the ICF file is like the Client Access/PCS router. You read and write to it.

- An ICF file has some automatic mechanisms that are presented shortly, but note the two File continuation (K) specs. The "INFDS FEEDBK" data structure is filled with reason codes when an ICF error occurs. You can look up the codes in the *Intrasystem Communications Programmer's Guide* to help in debugging problems. You don't have to code for error trapping, just provide the data structure and the K spec. The other K spec—"INFSR EXCPTH" attaches a subroutine, "EXCPTH," to an ICF error. Again, you don't have to execute the subroutine; it executes automatically.

- Next are a couple of arrays. "MSG" is a compile-time array of messages to send back to the VB program (note that there are 10 elements and only 4 are used), and "REC" is an execution-time array used to align multiple database records to the "ICDATA" field of the ICF file. (See the data structure "ICDATA" in the preceding code.)

- Next is the "FEEDBK" data structure mentioned previously.

- Refer to the *INZSR subroutine. The "ACQ" (acquire) op code checks the availability of the program device through the AS/400 communications support, and attaches the RPG program to the PC link.
- Okay, back up to the calcs. Notice that the indicator used on the "READ" statement is not the one used for the "DOWEQ" loop. That's because the indicator (82) will be returned by the ICF file when the VB program wants to end the link.
- Also notice that there are two record formats in the ICF file—one for the incoming requests (used with "READ"), and one for outgoing data (used with "WRITE").
- The "SELEC" structure gives examples for the two types of requests—single transmission and multiple transmission.
- Subroutine type 1 (single) simply fills the request and loads a message into the "ICERR" portion of the outgoing ICF record.
- Subroutine type 2 does pretty much the same thing as type 1, but over and over, executing the "WR" subroutine as needed, until the database records have all been sent. The message "(MORE)" is sent to tell the VB program that another transmission is coming. The "(END)" message is sent to indicate the end of the transmissions.
- Finally, when the VB program runs its procedure "Deallocate," indicator 82 comes on, and the subroutine "RELEAS" is executed. This subroutine releases the link to the VB program and ends the RPG program.

With this template as a starter, you can add all the processing needed to assemble meaningful sets of records from your own database that the VB program can then display or process.

The AS/400 is the essential element in the three-tier client/server model—the middle element called the *business server*. It's called the business server because it interacts with the AS/400 database in very precise ways, as defined by the application's *rules of business*. That is, in a given business concern, certain relationships among the files that make up a database and certain methods for conducting transactions over those files are established. They're established to ensure the integrity of the data and transactions.

Getting the RPG APPC Template on Your AS/400

You've got your choices on this one: you can do nothing and go straight to the actual TIME400 RPG program that follows and key it in, you can key in the template code as listed and use it to clone "TIME400" (probably the best way to become familiar with an ICF program), or you can upload the template and "TIME400" RPG source code from diskette.

If you choose to upload the template, there is a batch file that will do it for you, named "APPCRPG.BAT." You'll find it in the diskette's "Tools" folder.

The batch file uses the "rfrompcb.exe" program on the "I:\QIWSFL2" drive to upload the RPG source to QRPGSRC in VBLIB. This is accomplished using two other files—the Client Access/PCS transfer request, "APPCRPG.TFR," and a file description file, "APPCRPG.FDF."

The batch file tries to create a library on your 400 named "VBLIB," and a source file—"QRPGSRC." You must have proper authority to create a library and a source file.

If you don't want to use the AS/400 library "VBLIB," you can let the transfer request copy source records to "QRPGSRC" in VBLIB and move them into another AS/400 library, or you can edit the "APPCRPG.TFR" transfer request to point to another library.

This technique for distributing code to an AS/400 is the same method that IBM used in the "APIRTREX" sample application in the "QIWSTOOLS" folder. If you intend to distribute the AS/400 part of an application to other AS/400s, you may want to become familiar with this technique (and the Client Access/PCS commands "rfrompcb" and "rmtcmd").

The TIME400 RPG Program

The actual program that is the partner to the Visual Basic program will be named "TIME400."

With the RPG partner program template as a starting point, you can easily clone and modify "TIME400." (You can also key it in, or it can be uploaded from the accompanying diskette with batch file "TIME400.BAT" to "QRPGSRC" in library "VBLIB.")

In the TIME400 project, the RPG task is minimal. It is limited to receiving a request from the VB program, and servicing it with a single return transmission. The VB program then tells the RPG program to end by deallocating the link between the two. Very simple.

The changes to the template clone involve mostly stripping code out. You'll need only the single-transmission type of subroutine.

Creating the RPG Source Code for TIME400

Here's the modified "TIME400" RPG program as it exists on the accompanying diskette.

```
H
 *- - - - - - - - - - - - - - - - - - - - - - - - - - - - - - -
 *                                                              *
 *   Program - TIME400                                          *
 *             This program is the partner program to Visual    *
 *             Basic program TIME400.                           *
 *                                                              *
 *   Revisions                                                  *
 *     Date       Pgmr       Revision                           *
 *                                                              *
 *                                                              *
 *- - - - - - - - - - - - - - - - - - - - - - - - - - - - - - -
FTIME400 CF  E                    WORKSTN
F                                             KNUM        1
 *  Data structure to receive information about the ICF file . . .
F                                             KINFDS FEEDBK
 *  Error handling subroutine for ICF operations . . .
F                                             KINFSR EXCPTH
 *- - - - - - - - - - - - - - - - - - - - - - - - - - - - - - -
 *  Messages to the VB program . . .
E                    MSG     1  10 80
 *- - - - - - - - - - - - - - - - - - - - - - - - - - - - - - -
IICDATA      DS
I                                        1  120$BOTH
I                                        1   60$TIME
I                                        7  120$DATE
IFEEDBK      DS
I                                       38  45 FMTNM
I                                      401 404 MAJMIN
I                                      401 402 MAJCOD
I                                      403 404 MINCOD
 * Constant(s)
```

```
     I               'DATE&TIME'           C          @RQ1
      *- - - - - - - - - - - - - - - - - - - - - - - - - - - - - - -
      *  Indicators defined in the ICF file DDS:
      *    66  -  RCVFAIL
      *    82  -  RCVDETACH
      *- - - - - - - - - - - - - - - - - - - - - - - - - - - - - - -
      * Read from the Client Access/PCS router . . .
     C                     READ RQRECORD                 88
B001 C           *IN82     DOWEQ*OFF
      *
      * Incoming requests . . .
B002 C                     SELEC
      *
      * Requests where only one transmission is required . . .
   2 C           RQDATA    WHEQ @RQ1
   2 C                     EXSR SINGLE
      * Return an "Invalid" message when request can't be determined...
   2 C                     OTHER
   2 C                     EXSR NVALID
      *
E002 C                     ENDSL
      *
      * Get next request . . .
   1 C                     EXSR WR
E001 C                     ENDDO                          *in82
      * When ReceiveDetach is received, release ICF file and end
     C                     EXSR RELEAS
      *- - - - - - - - - - - - - - - - - - - - - - - - - - - - - - - -*
     C           WR        BEGSR
      *- - - - - - - - - - - - - - - - - - - - - - - - - - - - - - - -*
      * Write/Read subroutine . . .
     C                     WRITEICRECORD
     C                     READ RQRECORD                 88
B001 C           *IN82     IFEQ *ON
   1 C                     EXSR RELEAS
E001 C                     ENDIF
     C                     CLEARICDATA
     C                     CLEARICERR
      *- - - - - - - - - - - - - - - - - - - - - - - - - - - - - - - -*
     C                     ENDSR
      *- - - - - - - - - - - - - - - - - - - - - - - - - - - - - - - -*
     C           SINGLE    BEGSR
      *- - - - - - - - - - - - - - - - - - - - - - - - - - - - - - - -*
      * This routine fetches the AS/400 system date and time . . .
     C                     TIME           $BOTH
```

```
     * Return a message of "(OK)". . .
    C                    CLEARICERR
    C                    MOVELMSG,3     ICERR
     *- - - - - - - - - - - - - - - - - - - - - - - - - - - - - - - - -*
    C                    ENDSR
     *- - - - - - - - - - - - - - - - - - - - - - - - - - - - - - - -
    C          RELEAS    BEGSR
     *- - - - - - - - - - - - - - - - - - - - - - - - - - - - - - - - -*
     * Request to detach received, release program device . . .
    C          'RQSDEV'  REL  TIME400
    C                    MOVE *ON       *INLR
    C                    RETRN
     *- - - - - - - - - - - - - - - - - - - - - - - - - - - - - - - - -*
    C                    ENDSR
     *- - - - - - - - - - - - - - - - - - - - - - - - - - - - - - - -
    C          NVALID    BEGSR
     *- - - - - - - - - - - - - - - - - - - - - - - - - - - - - - - - -*
     * This routine returns an 'INVALID' error code. . .
    C                    CLEARICERR
    C                    MOVELMSG,4     ICERR
     *- - - - - - - - - - - - - - - - - - - - - - - - - - - - - - - - -*
    C                    ENDSR
     *- - - - - - - - - - - - - - - - - - - - - - - - - - - - - - - -
    C          EXCPTH    BEGSR
     *- - - - - - - - - - - - - - - - - - - - - - - - - - - - - - - - -*
B001 C          MAJMIN    IFNE '0000'
   1 C                    MOVE *ON       *INLR
   1 C                    RETRN
E001 C                    ENDIF
     *- - - - - - - - - - - - - - - - - - - - - - - - - - - - - - - - -*
    C                    ENDSR
     *- - - - - - - - - - - - - - - - - - - - - - - - - - - - - - - -
    C          *INZSR    BEGSR
     *- - - - - - - - - - - - - - - - - - - - - - - - - - - - - - - - -*
     *  Acquire ICF program device . . .
    C          'RQSDEV'  ACQ  TIME400
     *- - - - - - - - - - - - - - - - - - - - - - - - - - - - - - - - -*
    C                    ENDSR
     *- - - - - - - - - - - - - - - - - - - - - - - - - - - - - - - -
**
(MORE)
(END)
(OK)
(INVALID)
Available
```

```
Available
Available
Available
Available
Available
```

Admittedly, the program could be simplified considerably because of its simple task, but this format retains resemblance to the template. Some lines have been modified; other lines have been removed (like the whole "MULTPL" subroutine).

Sending Numeric Data through the Router

Take special notice of the manner in which numeric data is sent to the PC. There is no such thing as a "packed" numeric field on your PC. There are no EBCDIC-to-ASCII equivalents in the EHNAPPC API. Further, there's no telling how a value, as generated by a packed numeric's "over and under" representation, would be interpreted by communications programs. For these reasons, you must pass your numeric data as shown in this sample application (numeric data is assigned to the outgoing ICF data field with a data structure):

```
IICDATA      DS
I                                  1  120$BOTH
I                                  1   60$TIME
I                                  7  120$DATE
```

Had this numeric data been packed when it was delivered to the RPG program, it would have become "unpacked" in the process of being put into the data structure.

All right, there's only one more piece to the client/server relationship—the ICF file.

The ICF File

Intersystem Communication Function files have been around for a long time. They have been used for bisynchronous communications since before the days of the S/38. They have, however, been given the capabilities of Advanced

Program-to-Program Communications (APPC), and that is why they're used in this type of client/server application.

An ICF file is very much like a display file—it allows you to communicate with a device, but it also contains fields, like a database file.

Your RPG program fills requests by reading and writing to and from the ICF file.

The VB program sends a request to establish a conversation with the AS/400. Enclosed in the request is the name of a program that should be loaded on the 400 side to interact with the VB program. The 400 program (in this case an RPG program started by the named CL program) contains an ICF file. The ICF file responds to the request to establish a conversation, through communications support in OS/400, and completes contact with the Client Access/PCS router.

There are three elements involved when using an ICF file:

- The DDS specs that define the file (this defines the "container" for the data transmissions).
- The ADDICFDEVE CL command gives the ICF file the communications routing information needed to establish a link.
- The *acquire* operation within a high-level language (RPG op code "ACQ").

DDS Specs for an ICF File

As with the RPG program, a template of DDS specs for an ICF file is provided on diskette. You may upload it to "QDDSSRC" in "VBLIB" using the PC batch file "APPCICF.BAT," or you can key it in.

The ICF template looks like this:

```
A *- - - - - - - - - - - - - - - - - - - - - - - - - - - - - - -
A*                                                              *
A*  ICF File - APPCICF                                          *
A*             This ICF file is a template for using an ICF file *
A*             to communicate with a Visual Basic PC program.    *
A*                                                              *
A*   Revisions                                                  *
A*     Date       Pgmr       Revision                           *
A*                                                              *
A *- - - - - - - - - - - - - - - - - - - - - - - - - - - - - - -
A                                        INDARA
```

```
A                                      RCVFAIL(66)
A* This record matches the VB program's outgoing string "REQUEST"
A*  This is the incoming record to the RPG program.
A          R RQRECORD
A                                      RCVDETACH(82)
A            RQDATA        10A
A            RQTYPE         1A
A*
A* This record matches the VB program's incoming string "RECORD"
A*  This is the outgoing record to the RPG program
A          R ICRECORD
A            ICDATA       944A
A            ICERR         80A
```

In this template, the field lengths are purely arbitrary. They represent a small space for the incoming request and a request type, and a large compartment to contain data going back to the PC, which works well for the applications in this book. When coding your own applications, you'll have to modify these field lengths to fit. For instance, a data-entry application will probably have more data coming in to the RPG program than going out. In that case, the incoming record needs to be made larger and the outgoing record needs to be made smaller.

Things of note regarding the ICF specs:

- There are two record formats defined—one for data coming in to the RPG program, and one for data going out.

  The file uses a separate indicator area to keep indicators out of the data stream.

- Two APPC conditions, "RCVFAIL" and "RCVDETACH," are represented by indicators 66 and 82, respectively. When either condition is detected by the AS/400's communication support, the corresponding indicator comes on and the RPG program can respond.

There are a lot more sophisticated things that can be done with ICF files, but that is not within the scope of this book. For example, you can set up routines where a tighter bond is established between the 400 and the PC. That is, a closer monitoring of the conversation state can be achieved with such ICF operations as Receive-Confirm and Receive-End-Of-Group. During a large transfer of data, you may want to pause every so often and confirm reception of the data on the target system. See the *AS/400 ICF Programmer's Guide* for more information.

The ADDICFDEVE CL Command

The DDS for an ICF file describes the fields and indicators for that file. DDS does not, however, include the communications information needed to connect the RPG program to a program running on another computer. That information is called a *program device entry* for the ICF file and is placed there with the ADDICFDEVE CL command.

Once an ICF file is created, it can be connected to various remote systems by selecting different device entries attached to the file (on the RPG op code "ACQ"), or by using the OVRICFDEVE (override ICF device entry) command to temporarily override an existing entry.

A program device entry for an ICF file has these important parameters (presented in CL command form):

```
ADDICFDEVE    FILE(ApplicationLibrary/ICFFileName) +

PGMDEV(NameOfThisEntry) +

RMTLOCNAME(*REQUESTER) CMNTYPE(*APPC)
```

Take note of the parm "PGMDEV." This is the name for this particular entry for the ICF file. This entry name must match the name used in factor one of the RPG "ACQ" op code.

The parm "RMTLOCNAME(*REQUESTER)" tells the AS/400's communication support to route the link from the RPG program back to the remote system (the PC) that started the conversation.

The last parm—"CMNTYPE(*APPC)" specifies that the conversation between the two computers will be of type APPC.

The Acquire Operation

In order for the AS/400 to know with which location you want to communicate, you must select one of the ICF file's program device entries with an acquire operation. The acquire operation determines if the requested device is available, and, if so, connects to it.

In RPG, the "ACQ" op code is used to acquire an ICF file entry, like this example:

```
         *  Acquire ICF program device . . .

     C                          'RQSDEV'  ACQ  TIME400
```

Factor one is the name of the program device entry as used on the ADDICFDEVE command. Factor two is the name of the ICF file itself.

In the client/server projects presented in this book, with only one destination using only one ICF file, the *INZSR subroutine is used to issue the "ACQ" op code immediately after the RPG program is loaded.

This isn't the only way to generate the acquire operation. See the *AS/400 ICF Programmer's Guide* for more information.

You do not need to have a great knowledge of ICF files and APPC programming to make these things work for you.

Step by Step: Copying the ICF file DDS

1. The template for an ICF file (DDS source member APPCICF) and the "TIME400" source code are identical, so you only have to copy "APPCICF" to a new member named "TIME400."

The TIME400 project is almost complete. Here's what you've done so far:

- Created a VB project—"TIME400"—that uses the two APPC tools files, "APPC.GBL" and "APPC.BAS."
- Added a new code module to the VB project to hold code specific to "TIME400."
- Created the procedures "Initialize" and "Main," and keyed the code to make the VB program interact with the AS/400.
- Keyed or copied an RPG template for an APPC application named "APPCRPG" into the AS/400.
- Cloned and modified or keyed the actual RPG program ("TIME400") for this application.
- Keyed or copied the source specs for an ICF file template—"APPCICF."

- Copied the ICF file template into a new source member, also called "TIME400."

OK, that's it for source code. All that remains to putting this project into use is creating the AS/400 objects, starting with the ICF file.

Step by Step: Creating the AS/400 Objects

1. Add "VBLIB" to your library list.
2. Use the following AS/400 command to create the ICF file "TIME400:"

   ```
   CRTICFF FILE(VBLIB/TIME400) SRCFILE(VBLIB/QDDSSRC) SHARE(*YES)
   ```

   This step creates a basic ICF file—nothing fancy. Next, add the ICF program device (the communications information).

3. Use the following AS/400 command to add the program device entry for the newly created ICF file "TIME400:"

   ```
   ADDICFDEVE FILE(VBLIB/TIME400) PGMDEV(RQSDEV) +

   RMTLOCNAME(*REQUESTER) CMNTYPE(*APPC)
   ```

   This command adds an entry named "RQSDEV" to the ICF file. That entry converses with whichever device started the session (*requester), and the communication is held under the rules of APPC. Next, the RPG and CL programs.

4. Create the CL program in the same library as the ICF file.
5. Create the RPG program in the same library as the ICF file.

   That's it on the 400 side. The next step is to see if it all works.

Step by Step: The TIME400 Payoff

1. Make sure the Client Access/PCS router is started.
2. Bring up the VB Development Environment and the "TIME400" project.
3. Step through the program and see if it executes as you expect.

4. With the program paused between steps, look into the contents of variables like "REQUEST" before and after "AsciiToEbcdic" is run.

5. End the program, go to a DOS prompt, and change the PC's date to yesterday. (Key "date", press Enter, and fill in yesterday's date using the mm-dd-ccyy format.)

6. Run the program. Check the date. Did it change to match the 400?

7. Run the same test for the time.

You have created all the code to allow a PC program and an AS/400 program to connect, cooperate with each other, pass a request and a response, and end gracefully. In other words, a complete client/server application.

Of course, the actual programs that you develop will be much more involved and complex, reflecting the needs of your application. Nevertheless, the core of a c/s relationship remains the same as in this little application.

Your Own C/S Application

By now, you should have been getting ideas as to how you're going to develop your specific c/s applications. The tools have been laid out, inviting their use.

At this point, you would be well advised to develop your own small c/s application. Nothing as ambitious as an application, but one that uses your own AS/400 database records and your own specific RPG code to assemble them. The process, as was laid out in this chapter, is the same.

For instance, create your own customer inquiry application—similar to the IBM example. Create a front-end in VB that provides for input of a customer number and then displays customer information. The customer number is sent to the AS/400 and the returned information is placed into VB controls (like labels or list boxes) for display.

The application ends when the user clicks an "End" button, which you provide, that runs the "Deallocate" routine, and then ends the VB program.

A great deal of information has been presented on all this c/s stuff. It will all make more sense to you if you can apply it using your own files.

A Last Word About Design of a Client/Server System

As was stated previously, the designs of your client/server applications require the same straight-ahead approach you've used for your AS/400 applications. You have a task in mind, a solution presents itself (if not immediately, then in due course), and programming tools are used to accomplish it. Having Visual Basic and client/server among your tools doesn't mean that this design process is any less valid.

The fact that an RPG program acts as the business server puts control of the application in familiar territory. The RPG program can assume most of the complexity of, say, a database application; with the VB program playing a lesser role at the front-end.

Snap Fit IT Solutions

As the term *Information Systems*, or IS, fades away and is replaced with *Information Technology*, or IT, the process reflects the changing role of automation solution providers.

No longer is the answer to an application requirement as simple as writing a program; indeed, available software packages are being snap-fit into superior solutions. You can now bring the proper tool to bear in order to provide the best application. For example, for those special reports (like financial statements), you can write a VB program to bring the data in the reports down to a PC, print it using a good PC word processor or spreadsheet package, and produce a very high-quality look. In such a setup, there are at least three cooperative elements—the AS/400 programs that assemble the data, the PC word processing program that prints the data, and the VB program that brings the other two elements together. All this and the contemporary look and feel of Windows, to boot. Such a deal.

The next chapters deal with compiling your VB programs, how to include help text and icons in your VB applications, and creating distribution diskettes.

Summary

The TIME400 Example Program

The TIME400 project is presented as a first client/server application.

The client/server application establishes a conversation with the AS/400 and requests the date and time, as known to the 400, and sets the PC's clock to match.

The TIME400 project contains the two APPC tools created or copied previously—"APPC.GBL" and "APPC.BAS."

The application also requires two programs that run on the 400—"TIME400C," the CL program, and "TIME400," the RPG program.

The CL program is created and the RPG program is cloned (or copied).

The AS/400 equivalent of the Client Access/PCS router is a device file called an ICF (Intersystem Communication Function) file.

ICF files are like AS/400 display files. They are described in DDS and compiled.

A device entry must be made to an ICF file to give it the communications information needed to establish a communications link.

The AS/400 program that is using an ICF file must select a device entry and establish an APPC conversation with the "Acquire" operation. The RPG op code for the acquire operation is "ACQ."

You are urged to develop a similar, simple c/s application using your own AS/400 database.

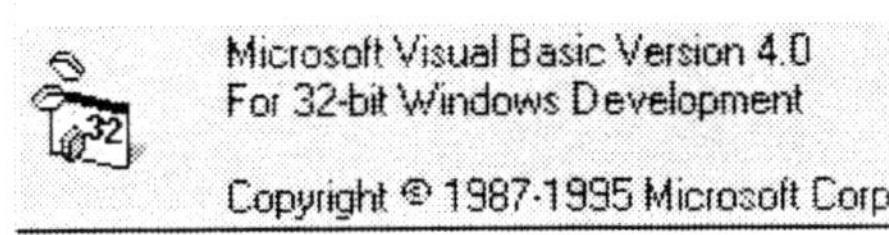

12

Adding a Help System to Your Application

This chapter presents one of the features available to Visual Basic that will greatly enhance the usability of your applications—a help system. You'll see how to use the help capabilities within Windows to produce a more useful and professional-looking application.

The chapter provides an overview and the basic implementation of a help system, together with a step-by-step tutorial for adding help text to the EditText project. For extensive information on all of the Windows capabilities for help systems, see the *Help Compiler Guide*. If adding a help system to your applications is not of interest to you, you may skip this chapter without risk of diminished understanding of other parts of this book.

Overview of a Help System

Creating a help system for Windows is much like creating a help system on the AS/400 using User Interface Manager (UIM).

An overview of the tasks required to create and use a Windows help system:

- Help text is created outside of the VB Development Environment by a text editor, and saved to a document file in *rich text format* (RTF).
- The document file is taken as source code by the *Help Compiler* which renders a compiled help file (extension name of ".HLP").
- A call to an external routine within the Windows API then displays the help text, just like it does for any other Windows application.

Help systems have these capabilities:

- Present help text in various fonts and colors, just like a document.
- Display graphics, like bitmaps and icons.
- Run macros (sound, video) or demo a help topic.
- Provide *hot spots* that jump to another topic or open a pop-up window for further clarification.
- Search by keyword.

In short, you can add all the slick things you've come to appreciate in Windows help systems to your applications. Why? Because, you are using the very same Windows API.

Creating a Help System for a VB Program

Creating a help system includes these tasks:

- Designing the content of the help system.
- Creating the input to the help compiler in an RTF.
- Creating a help project file (like a VB project file, except for help).

- Compiling the files.
- Adding the code to a VB application to invoke the help system.

Designing the Content of a Help System

Because a Windows help system is very capable and flexible, the design for it becomes a more complicated process. You can achieve a fairly worthwhile help system, however, without undue complexity.

A design for help systems that will probably fill 90 percent of your application requirements is presented as your starting point. If you seek additional capacity for your help system, see the *Help Compiler Guide* (Visual Basic version 3.0) or *Visual Basic Books Online.*

In order to conform to the Windows conventions for help systems, your help systems should include:

- A help menu.
- A contents screen.
- Text on individual help topics.

Optionally, for large help systems, you may also want to include:

- Keyword lists used to search for a topic.
- An index for locating a topic alphabetically.
- Graphics with optional hot spots.

(In this book, only the first three are accommodated.)

The design process is pretty straightforward:

- The features included in your help system become options on your help menu (like "Contents," "Search," or "About...").
- The major points of what you want to say in your help system become the *help* topics and are displayed on the "Contents" screen.
- The explanations of those topics become the *help text*. If your help text includes words that may be unfamiliar to the user, you can define them to a pop-up that brings up a glossary window.

- The example project EditText, created earlier, is used to illustrate how to create a help system. The system is modest in function and complexity.

The help system for EditText consists of these elements:

- A menu with only one item on it—"Help."
- A contents screen with four topics—"Overview," "Opening a File," "Editing a File," and "Saving a File."
- Help text for each topic.

The Help Menu

A help menu provides the user with access to your help system.

You recall that menus are what appear along the top of a window. You created a File menu already for the EditText project. (Of all the menus you may have in an application, the Help menu should be the rightmost on the menu bar.)

Step by Step: Creating a Help Menu

1. Bring the EditText project up in the 32-bit VB Development Environment (Win95) or 16-bit VB Development Environment (Win3.1).
2. Bring the first form "EditText.Frm frmMain" into the form design window.

3. Click on the "Menu Design" button in the toolbar, , and bring up the menu design dialog box:

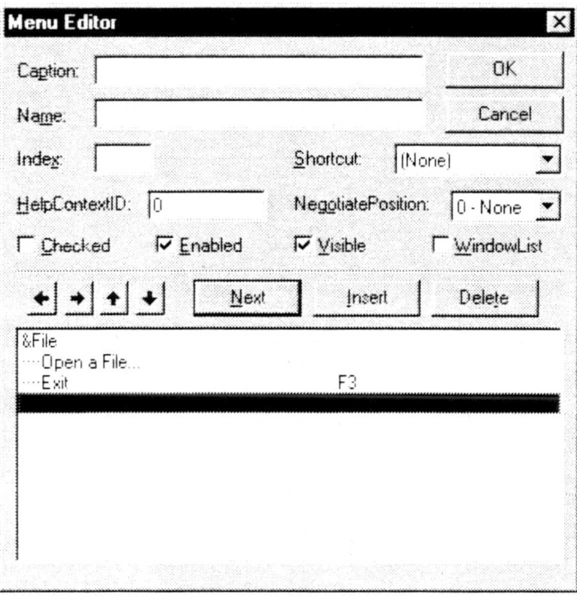

4. With the mouse, highlight the line immediately following "——Exit..." as shown.

5. Click on the "Caption:" box at the top. Fill in the caption box with "&Help" and the "Name:" box with "mnuHelp":

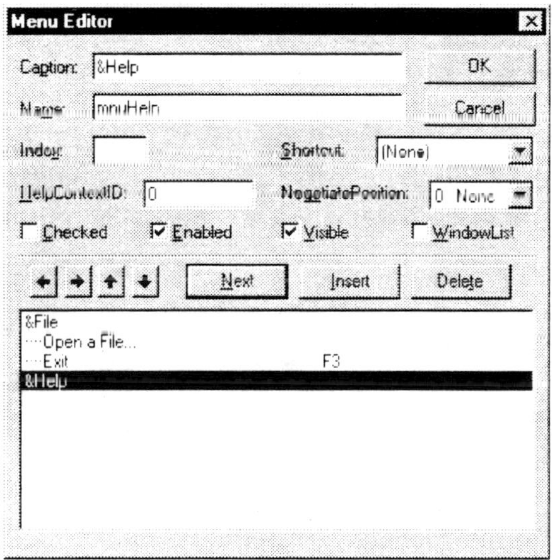

Recall that indenting items in this dialog box defines their placement on the menus. "&Help" is not indented at all, so it's defined as a menu, just like "&File." Also remember that an ampersand (&) preceding a letter of a menu caption allows the user to open the menu by holding the Alt key and pressing that letter.

6. Click on "Next." The highlighted bar moves down one line.
7. Click on the right arrow, ➜, to indent for an *item* on the Help menu.
8. Click on the "Caption:" box and fill it in with "Help". Fill the "Name:" box with "itmHelp".
9. Open the list of "Shortcut:" keys and select "F1."
10. Click on "OK." You should now have a menu bar with the menu on it like this:

11. Click on "Help" to open the menu. It should look like this:

12. Click on "Help F1" to bring the procedure "itmHelp_Click" into the code window. It is in this Sub procedure that code is inserted to invoke the Windows help API—but first the input to the help compiler is presented.
13. Save your project.

Creating Input to the Help Compiler—The RTF File

The input to the help compiler is a PC document file created by a word processing package.

Like UIM on the AS/400, the input to the help compiler is like a little language unto itself. Techniques available in an RTF document are used to specify the arrangements of your help system. For example, *context strings* are defined by attaching a hidden text field to the end of a word of help text. When the compiler sees that, it creates a *text hot spot* on that word that the user can click to cause an action. The hidden text field links the text hot spot to the action by name. (The term *hot spot* really refers to an area on a graphic, not text.)

An RTF file is a type of document that is produced by certain PC word processing packages. The package used to create the RTF (rich text format) document in these examples is Microsoft Word 6.0. You have to check the documentation for the word processing package you're using to see if it can create RTF documents.

The help compiler specifications that you key into an RTF file use a combination of the features of the document (like footnotes) and special characters and keywords that have meaning to the help compiler (like "#" and "Contents"). You associate the regular text that you key with the functions of Windows help by placing these special characters and keywords amid the text and footnotes.

Topics and Topic Files

The RTF document that you create as input to the help compiler is called a *topic file*. A *topic* is the main source of help text to the help compiler. A topic is subject-related help text with added control codes (RTF formatting codes) in a document.

A document, or topic file, can hold multiple topics. For most of your applications, a single document will hold all of the topics of your help system. You could, however, include common or universal help topics with your system from other topic files.

How Topics are Defined to the Help Compiler

Each topic in a topic file is separated by a hard page break. A topic, then, is the text and control codes between hard page breaks in an RTF document. The topic is then identified as such with a name, or *tag*. The tag is placed in the *footnote* area of the page.

Each footnote is associated with a word in the body of the topic with a *mark*. The mark is placed immediately to the left of the topic word and again to the left of the footnote. The footnote becomes the tag.

Step by Step: Creating the RTF File for a Help System

> ***Note:*** *Microsoft Word version 6.0a is the word processing package, or authoring tool, used in the following examples.*

1. Bring up a new document.
2. Using "Save As...," save the document *in RTF format* into the "C:\Program Files\Microsoft Visual Basic\Projects\EditText\" (Win95) or "C:\VB\PROJECTS\EditText\" (Win3.1) folder as "EditText.Rtf." This file will become part of your EditText project source files.
3. Click on the "Show/Hide" button, ¶, to show all paragraph and formatting marks in the document.
4. Select a common font (like Arial) and a large font size (like 18) for the title of your help system.
5. Key in "The Visual Basic Text File Editor" as the title.
6. Press Enter a couple of times to put in a couple of paragraph marks. Using a smaller font, key in "Select a topic from the following..."
7. Press Enter twice more and key in "OverviewOverview"—all one word. Press Enter.
8. Do the same for:

   "OpeningaFileOpening"

   "EditingaFileEditing"

   "SavingaFileSaving"

   Notice that there are no spaces between any of these words. This is not a requirement of the help compiler, and is only done here to facilitate selecting text. (Microsoft Word selects text by the word; but in this case you'll be selecting text by the character.)

9. After keying the last line, hold Ctrl and press Enter to insert a hard page break.

With the paragraph marks showing, your document should look something like this:

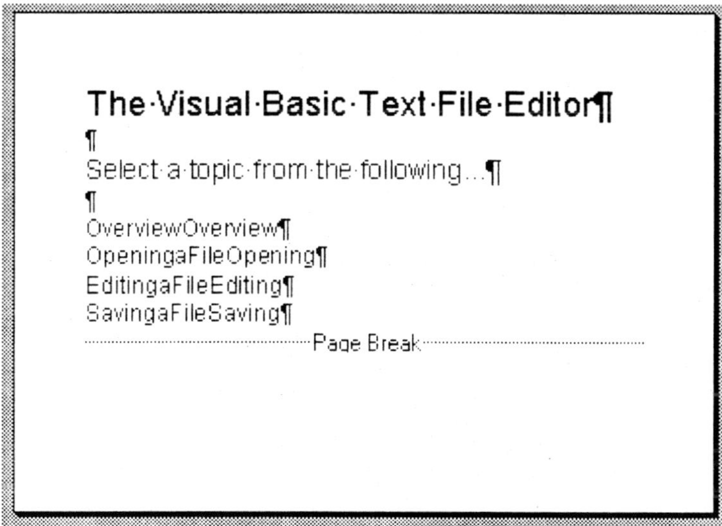

(In the example, the page size has been reduced.)

This page defines the "Contents" topic that almost all help systems have. The first topic of a help system is usually the one presented when the user clicks the "Contents" button (along the top of a help display).

This page needs to receive a tag name of "Contents." What you're going to do next is attach a footnote to the top line of text (the title) of this topic.

10. Place the cursor immediately to the left of the word "The" in the title, "The Visual Basic Text File Editor."

11. Open the Insert menu and click on "Footnote..." A dialog box opens:

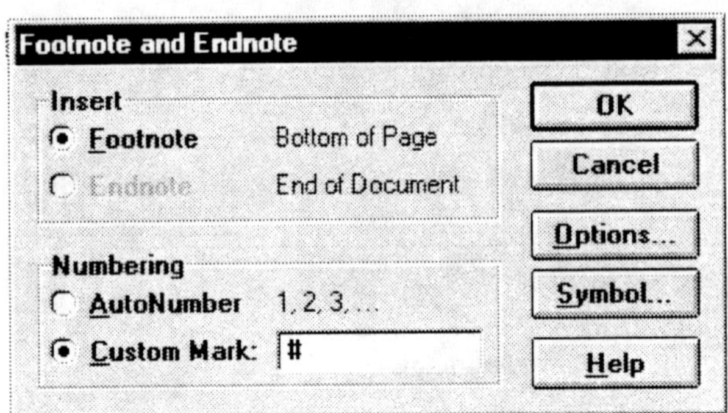

12. Click on the "Custom Mark:" box and key a pound sign ("#"), as shown.

> ***Note:*** *What you're doing here, within word processing terms, is called a custom footnote mark. You must use an authoring tool capable of creating custom footnote marks like this.*

13. Click on "OK." The footnote area opens, with the associating mark—"#"—already filled in.

14. Key in the word "Contents"—no quotes. Recall that the word "Contents" has special meaning to the help compiler.

All right. That's the "Contents" screen of the help system. Now the topics.

15. With the cursor, highlight the word "Overview" (just the first one):

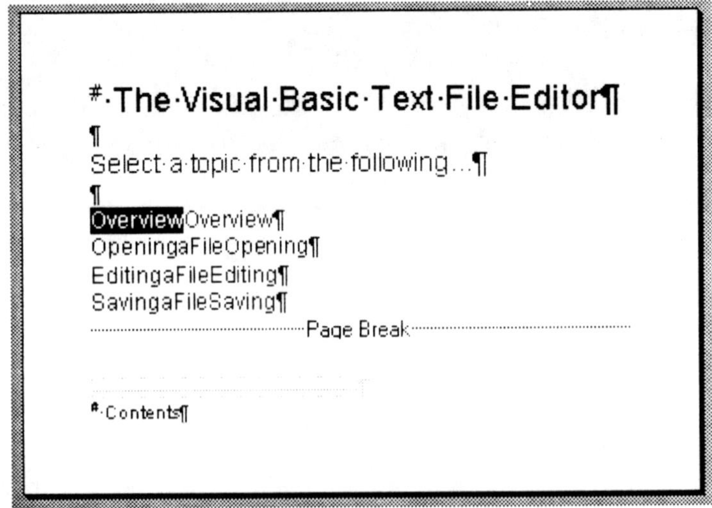

16. From the Format menu, select "Font..." to open a dialog box for the font.

17. In the "Underline:" list select "Double."

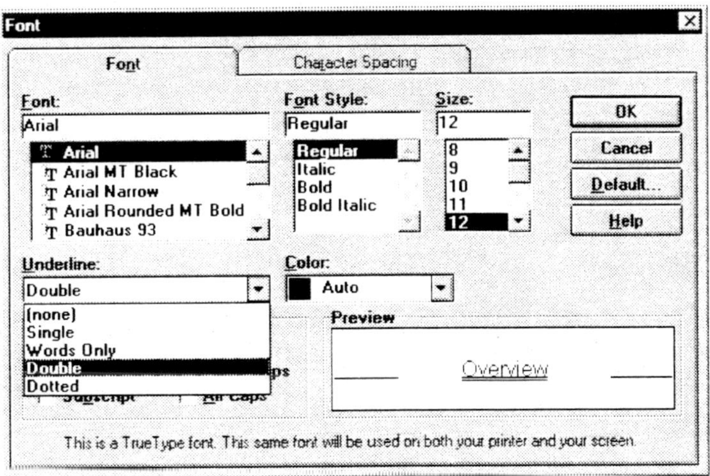

Double underlining also has special meaning to the help compiler. It signifies that clicking on the word "Overview" displays a topic. When the user clicks on the word "Overview," the topic identified in the word immediately following is displayed. That's why the word "Overview" is there twice. The second time, it's a reference to a tag.

18. With the cursor, highlight the second occurrence of "Overview." You're going to mark it as *hidden* text.

19. From the Format menu, select "Font..." as before. Find the frame "Effects" and click on "Hidden."

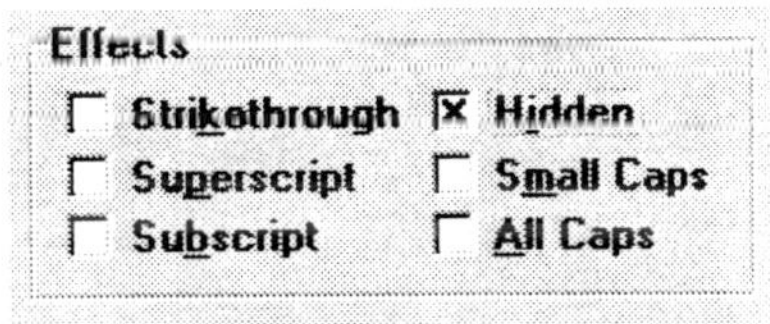

20. Click on "OK." Notice that the hidden text has dots under it.

21. Repeat these two steps for the other three topics, creating references to topics "Opening," "Editing," and "Saving." When finished, the topic page should look like this:

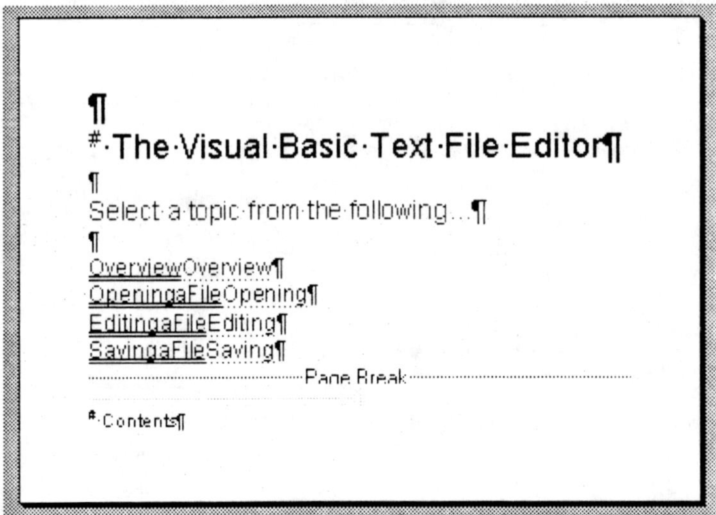

22. Insert blanks between words for the phrases "Opening a File," "Editing a File," and "Saving a File."

Step by Step: Adding Help Topics to a Help System

1. Press Page Down to go to the next page. This is where the text for "Overview" goes. Key the following:

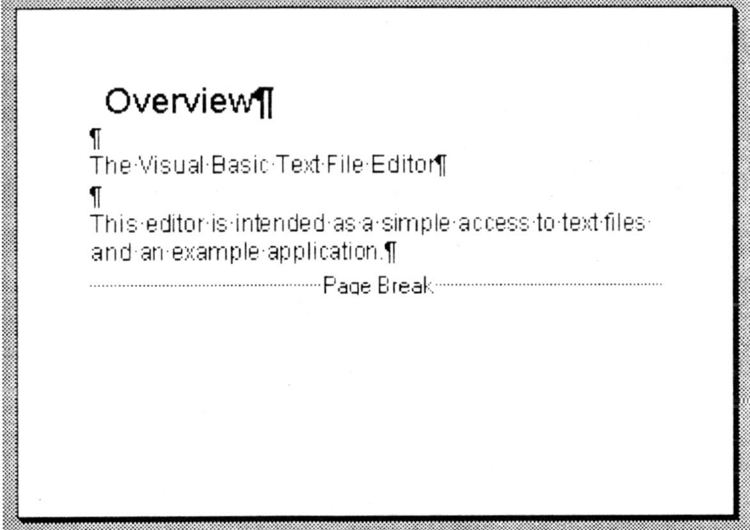
Overview¶
¶
The·Visual·Basic·Text·File·Editor¶
¶
This·editor·is·intended·as·a·simple·access·to·text·files·and·an·example·application.¶
Page Break

2. As before, place the cursor immediately to the left of the title of the topic. Select "Footnote..." from the Insert menu, click on the "Custom Mark:" box and key in a "#".

3. Key the tag name for this topic—"Overview". Press Page Down. Next topic.

4. Key in the text for the "Opening" topic and give it a tag name of "Opening":

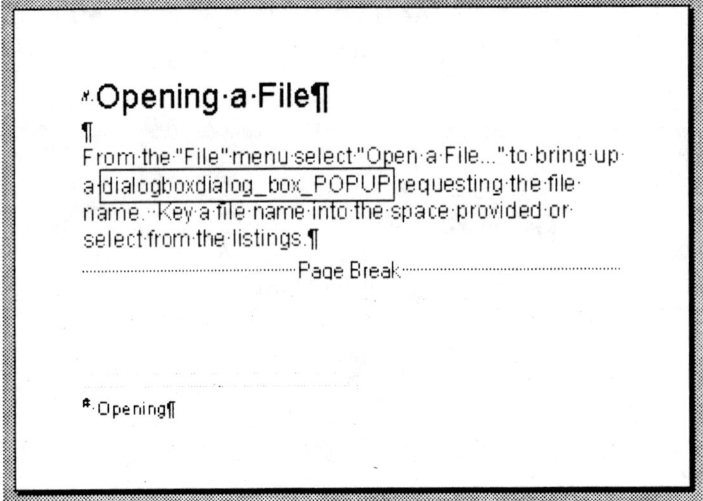

Note: The text inside the drawn-in box becomes a pop-up definition box shortly. It is keyed as "dialogboxdialog_box_POPUP"—no spaces. Spaces are added after highlighting is finished.

Next topic, next page.

5. Page down. Create the "Editing" topic like this:

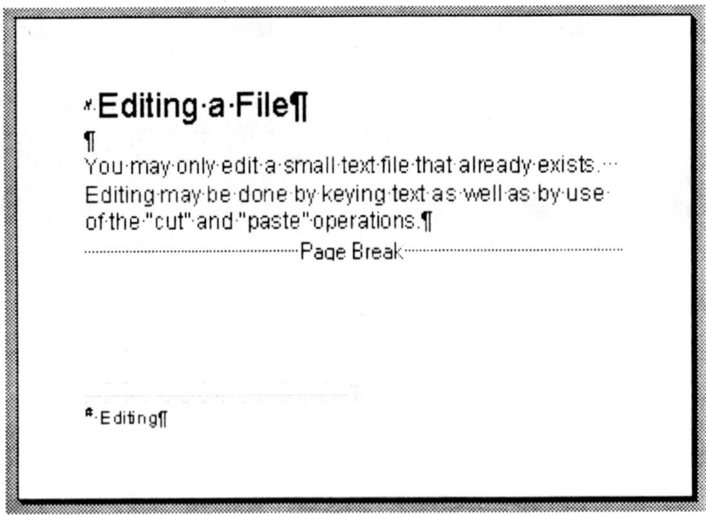

And the "Saving" topic:

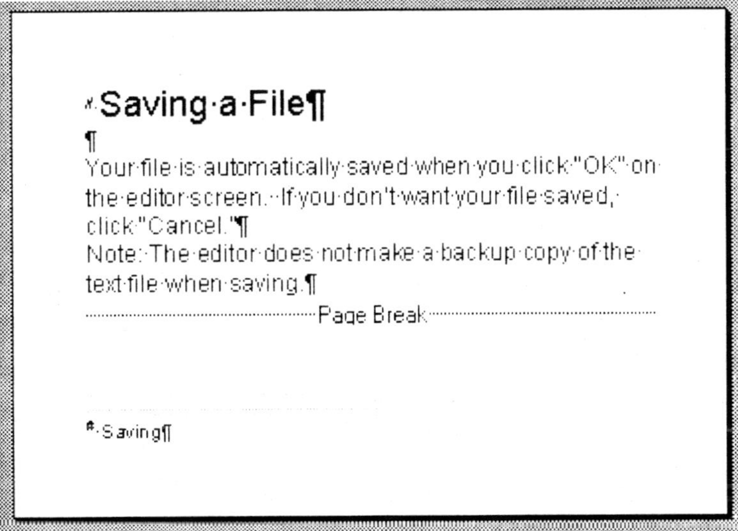

There's just one more topic—the text that will be in the *definition box* named "dialog_box_POPUP". A definition box is a window that pops up to explain a term in the help text. The user clicks on a word, shown in green, to open the box.

In the "Opening" topic, you keyed "dialogboxdialog_box_POPUP". Just as the items on the "Contents" screen became jumps to other topics by double-underlining them, a reference to a definition box is designated with a single underline.

6. Page down. New topic. Create the "dialog_box_POPUP" topic:

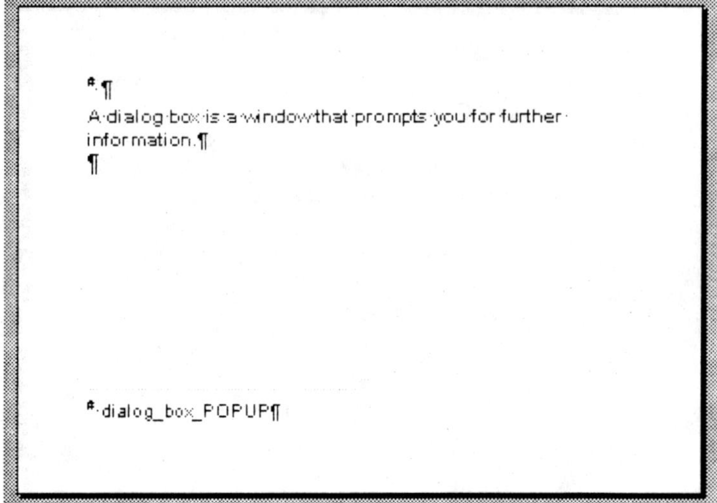

7. Go back up to the "Opening" topic page. Highlight "dialogbox" and *single*-underline it. A single underline specifies that a pop-up window appears when the user clicks the mouse button or presses Enter.

8. Insert a space between "dialog" and "box," and between "box" and "dialog_box_POPUP."

9. Highlight "dialog_box_POPUP." From the Format menu select "Font..." Click on "Hidden." Click on "OK."

10. Take the space out between "box" and "dialog_box_POPUP." All in all, you should have:

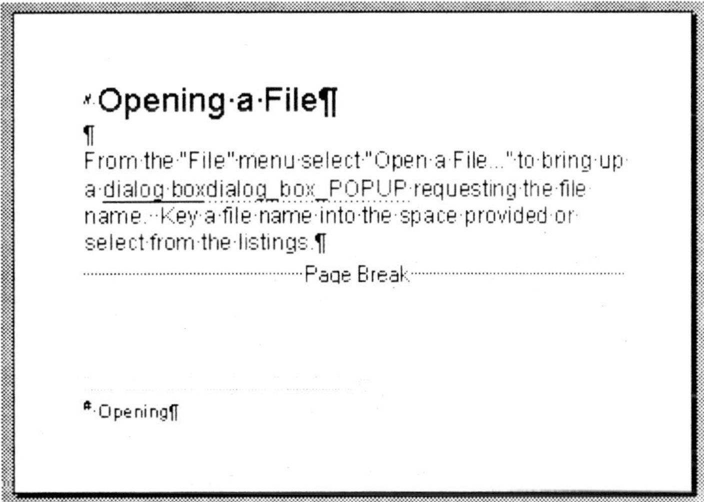

Okay, that's it for this simple help system. Bear in mind that more techniques are available if you choose.

11. Save the document. Make sure you save it in rich text format.

Once the RTF topic file has been created, it must be compiled into a ".HLP" file. The ".HLP" file is then ready to be input to the Windows help API.

Compiling a Help System

A program (or programs) came with your professional edition of Visual Basic to compile the help files. Depending on the version, the help compiler is named "HC.EXE" or "HC31.EXE."

Because you can have multiple topic files making up your help system, you need a means of specifying their names to the compiler. A *help project file* performs that function.

The Help Project File

Just like there is a project file for a VB program, there is a project file for a help system. It contains a list of the topic files that are input to the help compiler along with a number of configuration and specification parameters. Help project files have an extension name of ".HPJ."

You can specify many things in a help project file, but only three receive discussion here:

- Option—the options used during the compile process.
- Files—the topic files that will be input for the compiler.
- Windows—the dimensions of the initial help window.

Step by Step: Creating the Help Project File

1. Start the Windows Notepad.
2. Key in the following entries (note that the line beginning "main = " under the "Windows" section has been folded to fit the page):

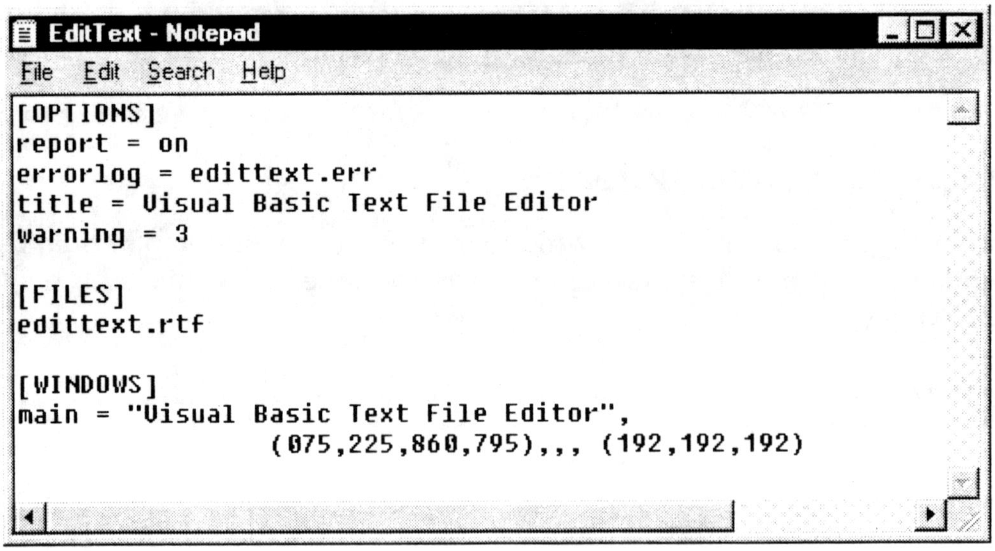

EditText - Notepad

File Edit Search Help

```
[OPTIONS]
report = on
errorlog = edittext.err
title = Visual Basic Text File Editor
warning = 3

[FILES]
edittext.rtf

[WINDOWS]
main = "Visual Basic Text File Editor",
                (075,225,860,795),,, (192,192,192)
```

3. Save the file in folder "C:\Program Files\Microsoft Visual Basic\Projects\EditText" (Win95) or directory "C:\VB\PROJECTS\EDITTEXT\" (Win3.1) as part of the overall project with a name of "EditText.Hpj."

   Here's what the entries mean:

- Options section:
  - *report = on*—Produces a compiler listing.
  - *errlog = edittext.err*—The file to receive the compiler error messages.
  - *title = Visual Basic Text File Editor*—The text for the help window title.
  - *warning = 3*—Causes all error messages to be logged.
- Files section:
  - *edittext.rtf*—The topic file(s) to be used for this help system.
- Windows section:
  - *main = Visual Bas...*—Specifies the size and position of the help window.

The stage is set. There is a rich text format file that defines the way the help system is to work, and a project file to instruct the compiler about the input. All that remains now is the help compiling process itself.

Step by Step: Compiling a Help System

A help compiler came with your professional edition of VB. It's called "HC31.EXE" in folder "C:\VB\HC" (VB 3.0) or "HC.EXE" in folders "C:\ProgramFiles\Microsoft Visual Basic\hc" and "C:\VB\HC" (VB 4.0). You engage the help compiler by calling it with a parameter of the help project file name.

> **Note:** *If you're using Microsoft Word version 6.0 or 6.0a, the help compiler ("HC31.EXE") will not work with some RTF files produced. You have to call Microsoft support for Visual Basic and download a PTF (called a corrective service pack or CSP). The CSP you need is*

"HC505.EXE." When run, program HC505 unfolds into two programs and a text file. The program "HC.EXE" replaces "HC31.EXE" as the help compiler.

1. Go to a DOS prompt (ironically, the Windows help compiler is a DOS program).
2. Key in "CD C:\VB\PROJECTS\EDITTEXT" (16 bit) or "CD C:\Progra~1\Micros~N\Projects\EditText" (where "N" is probably "1" or "2" depending on what Microsoft packages you have installed) to go to the project folder for EditText.
3. Key in "C:\VB\HC\HC.EXE EDITTEXT.HPJ" to call the help compiler. (This works with either the 16- or 32-bit version of VB 4.0, and with VB 3.0 CSP HC505. If you're using VB 3.0 without getting the CSP, replace "HC.EXE" with "HC31.EXE"):

```
C:\WINDOWS>cd\
C:\>cd c:\progra~1\micros~2\projects\edittext
C:\Program Files\Microsoft Visual Basic\PROJECTS\EDITTEXT>c:\vb\hc\hc.exe edittext.hpj
                                                                     (Windows 95
                                                                     "HC.EXE" syntax)
```

or

```
C:\VB\PROJECTS\EDITTEXT>c:\vb\hc\hc.exe  edittext.hpj                (Windows 3.1, VB 4.0
                                                                     "HC.EXE" syntax)
```

or

```
C:\VB\PROJECTS\EDITTEXT>c:\vb\hc\hc31.exe  edittext.hpj              (Windows 3.1 VB 3.0
                                                                     "HC31.EXE" syntax)
```

You should see the following messages run up the screen:

```
Microsoft (R) Help Compiler Version 3.10.505

Copyright (c) Microsoft Corp. 1990 - 1992. All rights reserved.

edittext.hpj

Compiling file edittext.rtf.
```

```
Resolving context strings.

Resolving keywords.
```

Note: In this example, use of both the newer help compiler "HC.EXE" and "HC31.EXE" is shown. See the preceding note about Word 6.0 RTF files.

Help Compiler Errors

If the help compiler can't compile your help file, you'll see error messages as to the nature of the problem. Messages are also logged into the file "EDITTEXT.ERR" in the folder specified in the help project file. In the example presented, the error file was built in the folder that was current at the time.

Displaying a Help File

Once successfully created, you may display the results of your efforts from almost any Win3.1 help screen. Remember, it's the Windows API that is used to display the help system, regardless of where it's invoked.

Step by Step: Test the Help File

1. Start the 16-bit VB Development Environment. Open the Help menu. Click on "Contents," which brings up the Contents screen for that help system.

2. Open the File menu within the help window. Click on "Open..." In the dialog box, specify the folder where your "EDITTEXT.HLP" help file resides and select the file. You should see:

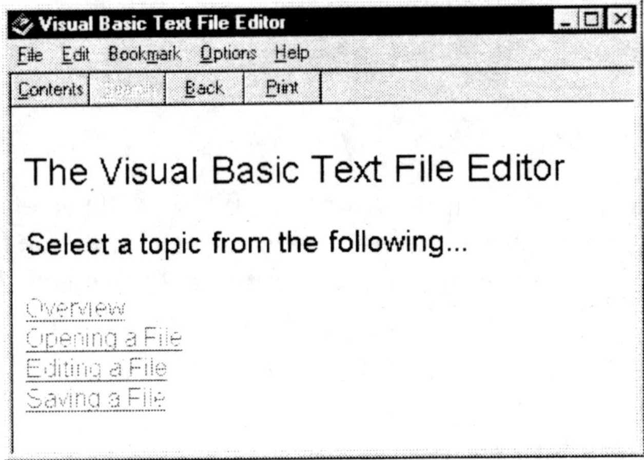

This is the"Contents screen for the help system. Whenever you click on the "Contents" button, this is what you get.

3. Click on "Overview." You go to the Overview topic. Click on the "Back" button. You return to the "Contents" screen.

4. Click on "Opening a File." In this topic display, there should be a green hypertext hot spot for the phrase "dialog box." Click it. This brings up the definition for the term "dialog box:"

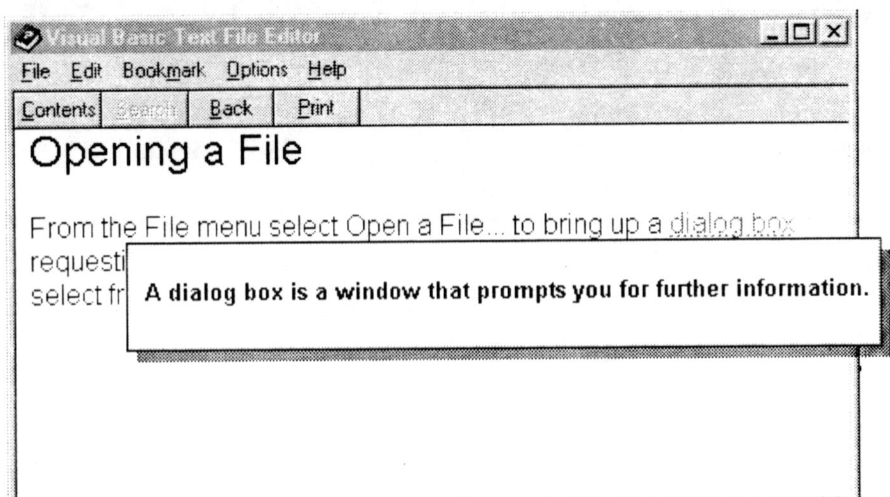

Again, it merits mentioning that a help system can do much more. In the final project presented in this book, The AS/400 Report Download Utility, other more advanced help techniques are employed.

Calling the Windows Help API from Your Program

In order to use a help system in one of your applications, you must call an external API—"WINHELP.EXE." This external API is called like the others presented previously. Here then, is the minimum code necessary to call Windows help.

Step by Step: Adding the Call to Windows Help to Your Program

1. Bring the project EditText into the VB Development Environment. Bring the declarations area for "EditText.Bas" into the code window.
2. Add the three statements within the drawn-in rectangle:

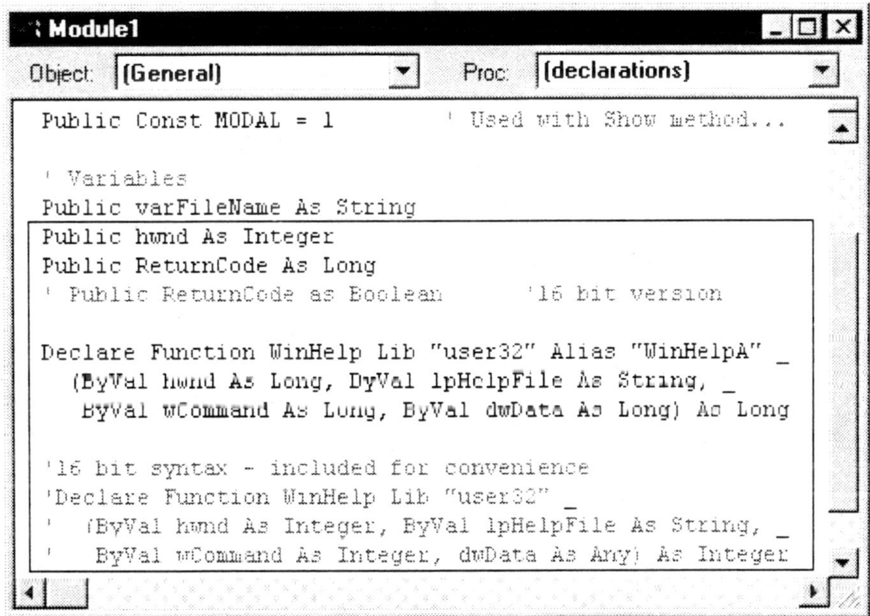

3. Close the code window. Bring the form "EditText.Frm frmMain" into the form design window. Click on "Help." The menu opens to show its only item:

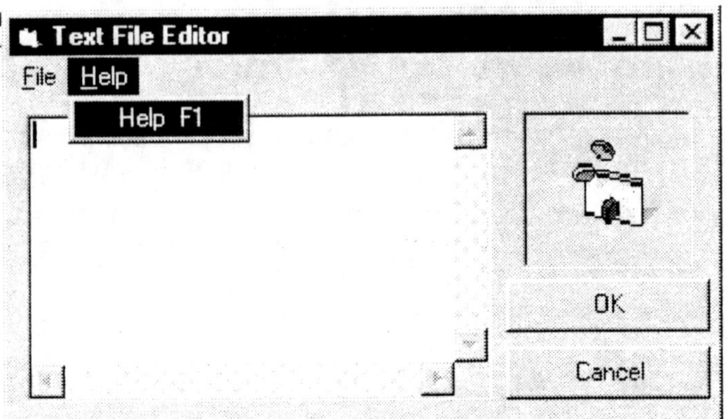

4. Click on "Help F1" to bring the click event into the code window for that event. Add this one statement (shown here as folded):

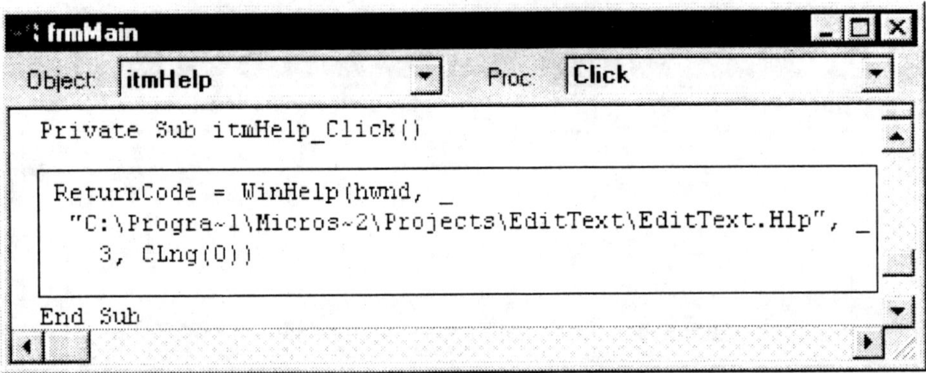

This code is executed when the user clicks on the "Help" item or presses F1. The function "WinHelp" is called, with the name of the ".HLP" file passed as an argument.

5. Save your project.

Normally, you wouldn't specify a project folder as a place for a help file. Generally, it would reside in the same folder as the finished project's ".EXE" file.

6. Now for the payoff. Click on the "Run" button. Open the File menu. Click on "Help F1." You should see your help system.

All right. There you have it. An application and source code to use as an example of a basic, yet useful, help system.

Please remember that this is the *minimum* code required to call WinHelp. Other more advanced help systems require more code.

Summary

A Help System

A Windows help system is much like an AS/400 help system.

Windows help text is created outside of the VB project by a text editor in a document saved in rich text format (RTF).

The text document becomes input to the help compiler, which renders a help file with an extension of ".HLP."

The help file is used by the Windows help API "WinHelp" to display the help system.

Help systems have these capabilities:

- Presenting help text in various fonts and colors, just like a document.
- Displaying graphics, like bitmaps and icons.
- Running macros that demonstrate a help topic.
- Providing hypertext and hot spots that jump to another topic or open another window for further clarification.
- Searching by keyword.

The Help Menu

A help menu usually provides access to the help system from within your VB program.

The RTF File

The RTF document file is prepared as input to the help compiler with a text editor capable of RTF formatting and custom footnote symbols.

The references to sections of the help system (tags) are placed in footnotes.

Special formatting (such as underlining) are instructions to the help compiler as to how you want your system to behave.

Each section of related text in a help system is called a topic and is separated in the RTF document with a hard page break.

The main topic of a help system is the first topic, called the "Contents."

Compiling the Help File

A help compiler comes with your professional edition of VB. It's called "HC31.EXE" in folder "C:\VB\HC" (VB 3.0) or "HC.EXE" in folders "C:\ProgramFiles\Microsoft Visual Basic\hc" and "C:\VB\HC" (Win95).

A help project file is required by the help compiler to tell it which topic files (RTF files) will be included with the help system. A help project file has an extension name of ".HPJ."

The help compiler is called from the DOS prompt:

```
C:\Help File Folder>c:\vb\hc\hc.exe HelpProjectFile.Hpj          (Windows 95
                                                                  "HC.EXE"syntax)
```

or

```
C:\Help File Folder>c:\vb\hc\hc.exe HelpProjectFile.Hpj          (Windows 3.1, VB 4.0
                                                                  "HC.EXE") syntax
```

or

```
C:\VB\PROJECTS\EDITTEXT>c:\vb\hc\hc31.exe HelpProjectFile.Hpj    (Windows 3.1 VB
                                                                  3.0 "HC31.EXE" syntax)
```

where "HelpProjectFile" is the name of your ".HPJ" file.

Calling a Help System

A help system can be opened from any other help system and is independent of its application.

A help system is called from within a VB program as an external routine within the WinHelp API. You must have a "Declare" statement and invoke the WinHelp function by referencing it in an expression.

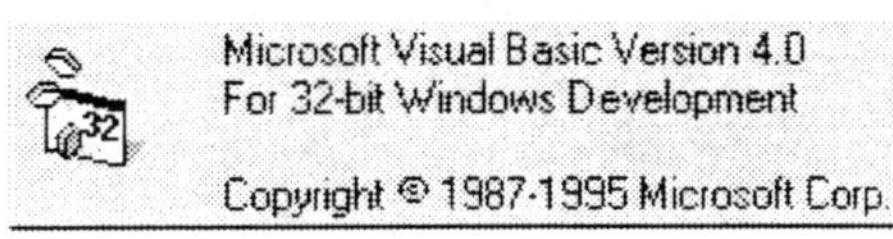

13

Compiling and Distributing Applications

This chapter deals with compiling your applications, adding icons, and distributing your programs to users.

The compile process is presented shortly, but first a diversion to add an icon to your EditText application.

Adding an Icon to an Application

All Windows apps worth their salt have an *icon*. An icon is a small graphic that is used by Windows to start and represent active programs. All programs on a Windows program group have an icon.

No effort is made within this book to present techniques of using the Image Editor (part of the Microsoft Software Development Kit or SDK) to create an icon. (VB 3.0 comes with a little icon editor that works well for Win3.1—see "ICONWRKS.MAK" in the "VB\SAMPLES\ICONWRKS" folder.) However, a discussion follows showing how an icon may be brought into your VB application as a resource.

Step by Step: Adding an Icon to an Application

1. Start the VB Development Environment and bring up the EditText project.

2. Select "EditText.Frm frmMain" in the Project box and click the right mouse button. Select "Properties" to open the properties box for the form.

3. Locate the "Icon" property.

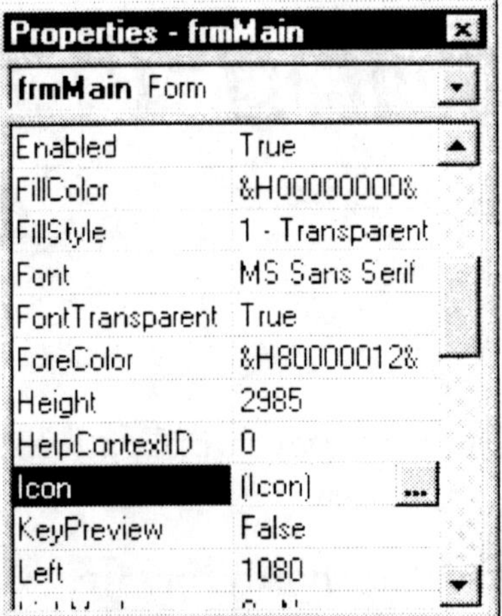

Use this property to specify an icon for any form that the user can minimize at run time.

For example, you can assign an unique icon to a form to indicate the form's function. Specify the icon by loading it using the Properties window at design time. The file you load must have the ".ICO" file name extension and format. If you don't specify an icon, the Visual Basic default icon for forms is used.

You can use the Visual Basic Icon Library (in the ICONS subdirectory) as a source for icons. When you create an executable file, you can assign an icon to the application by using the Icon property of any form in that application.

4. Click on the little three-dot button, ..., and open the file dialog box.

5. Specify an icon of your choice, or you may use the icon that is included on the companion diskette in the "A:\Projects\EditText" folder. This icon is named "EditText.Ico."

6. Save your project.

Compiling an Application

The process of compiling source code into a VB program is called *making an executable* or *".EXE"* file. Other than that, it's pretty much the same thing as on the AS/400. There is source code that acts as input to the compiling process; when it's finished, a new object is created—a program that can be executed on its own. (Well, almost on its own—remember the run-time DLLs for VB pseudo code?)

Compiling for a 16- or 32-bit Platform

You're well aware of the existence of two PC program platforms—16 bit and 32 bit. Although both versions of VB are nearly identical as far as your code is concerned, there are a few differences (WinAPI names, for example). With this, a problem arises—you must decide which platform to code to. But wait. Visual Basic provides a feature called *conditional compilation* that allows a single version of source code to be compiled into an executable that runs on either platform.

An example of conditional compilation code:

```
#If Win32 Then

       ' Call to Windows 95/NT API routines

#Else

       'Call to Windows 3.1 API routines

#End IF
```

Notice the "#" preceding the "If," "Else," and "End If" statements. These statements, called *compiler directives,* are used with built-in constants "Win32" and "Win16" (called *compiler constants*). See the *Visual Basic Programmer's Guide* for more information.

Step by Step: Compiling the EditText Project

1. Bring up VB and the EditText project.

2. Open the File menu and select "Make EXE File..." Specify the project folder—"EditText." That's all there is to it—the ".EXE" file is created.

   To complete the process, access to the executable needs to be provided by adding the program to a program group (Win3.1 users) or creating a Start menu link (Win95 users).

3. Add the program to a Windows program group. Win95 users may want to create a shortcut to the application or create a Start menu link (see your Windows documentation).

4. Now for the payoff. The application is compiled. It is replete with a help system and an icon on a program group. Run the program and check to see that all is as you expect. The program comes up, help works, F1 works, F3 works, etc.

   You may notice that, when you open a file, the current folder is shown—in this case, "EditText."

   > **Note:** *In most production systems, you would establish a new folder for the ".EXE" and ".HLP" files. That folder is where you would load the application files from a distribution diskette.*

Distributing Applications

Just as adding a help system to an application can greatly enhance its perceived worth, so can a professional installation program.

When you purchase a Windows software package, you normally install it using the Setup program from a "Run..." box. This lends a commercial look and a professional feel to the installation process. You can have the same type of setup program for your applications.

When one of your VB applications is installed, the user is already familiar with the setup process—having used it before—and your system garners credence by association.

The Setup Wizard

There is a tool shipped with VB that helps you create distribution diskettes for your VB applications. That tool is the *Setup Wizard.*

The Setup Wizard is a clever utility that renders VB *source* code for a program called "SETUP1." "SETUP1" has the instructions for a typical application installation, with specific references to elements of your application as put in during the cloning process. The program is created as source code, however, so you can augment the canned version when circumstances warrant.

To get you started with the application distribution process, though, things are kept as simple as possible.

Special Note Regarding Distributing Applications to Win3.1

> **Note**: *If you are using the Visual Basic Setup Toolkit version 3.0 to create installation diskettes that will be used under Windows 3.1, you must create those diskettes while running Windows 3.1.*
>
> *If you create installation diskettes while running Windows 95, those diskettes will contain Windows 95 system components. If those installation diskettes are used on a Windows 3.1 system, the Windows 3.1 files will be replaced with their Windows 95 equivalents, causing serious problems.*
>
> *If anyone using your program will be running Windows 3.1, create the setup diskettes while running Windows 3.1.*
>
> *(All references to the Setup Wizard that follow are for the 32-bit platform.)*

The end product of the Setup Wizard is diskettes. On each diskette are the objects that are required to run the application, plus the objects needed to install.

In a simple application—in this case "EditText"—these are the files that the Setup Wizard prepares for distribution:

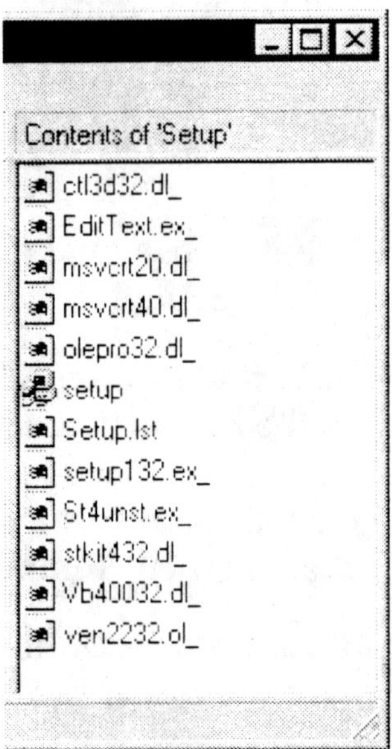

A lot of files for such a simple application, but much of the stuff is always there. Like the program to install the application ("setup132.exe") and the run-time support for VB (VB40032.DLL).

Here is a list of the objects and what they do for the EditText project:

EditText.ex_	Compressed version of the EditText program.
EditText.hl_	Compressed version of the help file.
setup.exe *	The program that starts it all—the only uncompressed executable on the diskette.
setup.lst *	A list of the objects to preinstall.
setup1.ex_ *	Compressed custom installation program.
st4unst.ex_	Compressed executable for uninstalling an application.
stkit432.dl_ *	Compressed setup routines library.

vb40032.dl_ *	The VB40032 Dynamic Link Library for run-time support for all VB programs.
Other DLLs *	Compressed run-time support DLLs.

(* Always there.)

Here's how to make a distribution set.

Step by Step: The Setup Wizard

1. Bring up VB and the EditText project. From the Tools menu, select "Custom Controls."
2. This particular project did not take advantage of any custom controls, so remove any check marks:

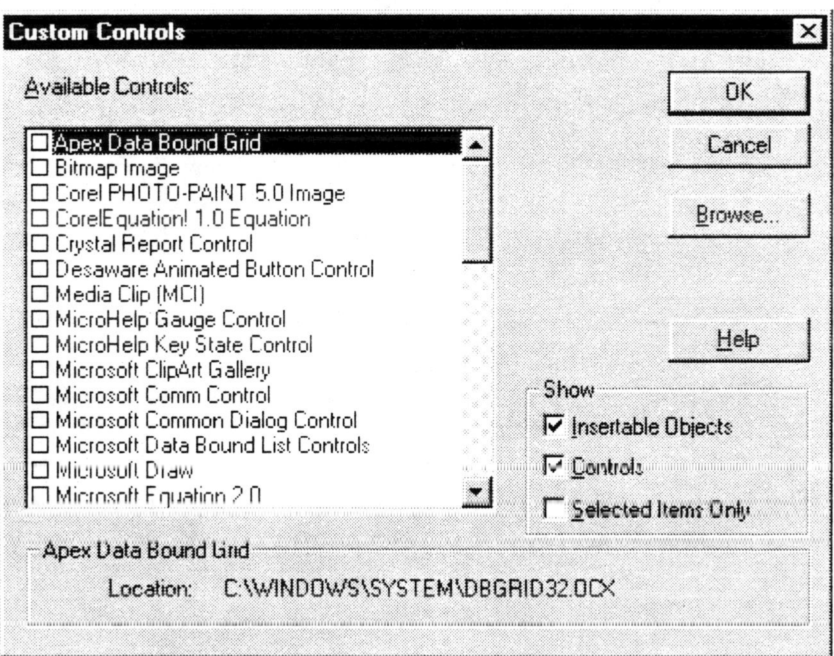

Unreferenced custom controls add extra baggage to your distribution files, so get rid of them for this process.

3. Select "References" from the Tools menu. Remove all check marks except "Visual Basic for Applications" and "Visual Basic objects and procedures." Again, this removes any extra baggage.

4. Save your project and exit VB.

5. Bring up VB and the EditText project again and recompile the executable.

   (Rumor has it that VB adds a good deal of clutter to the executable if it's created after activity in the VB Development Environment. It's suggested that, when you want to compile a program, you start VB and immediately run the compile.)

6. Close the VB Development Environment. The Setup Wizard will want to use VB and it can't if it's already in use.

7. You have your choice of creating distribution diskettes or distribution files in a folder on your C: drive. If you're going to create diskettes, have several *completely blank* diskettes ready. (In this example, files are placed in a folder where they may be "zipped" for more efficient distribution. An empty folder, "C:\Setup," has been created for this purpose.)

8. From the Visual Basic folder, double click on the "Application Setup Wizard" icon or bring it up with the "Start" button. This brings up the first dialog box of a seven-step wizard:

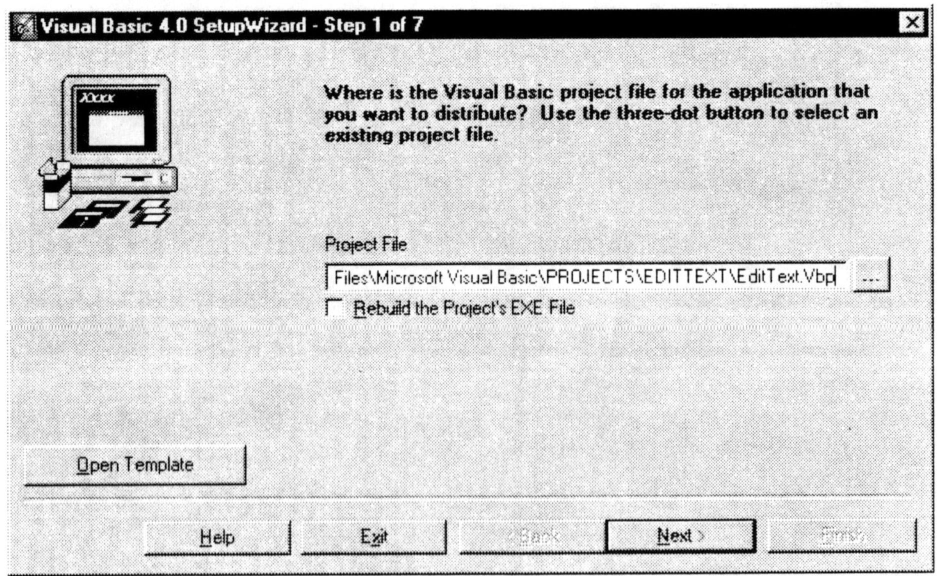

9. Click on the three-dot box. Find and open the project file "EditText.vbp," as shown. The Setup Wizard uses the entries in the project file to determine which objects need to be included with your program.

10. Click on the "Next>" button. Step 3 of 7 looks like this:

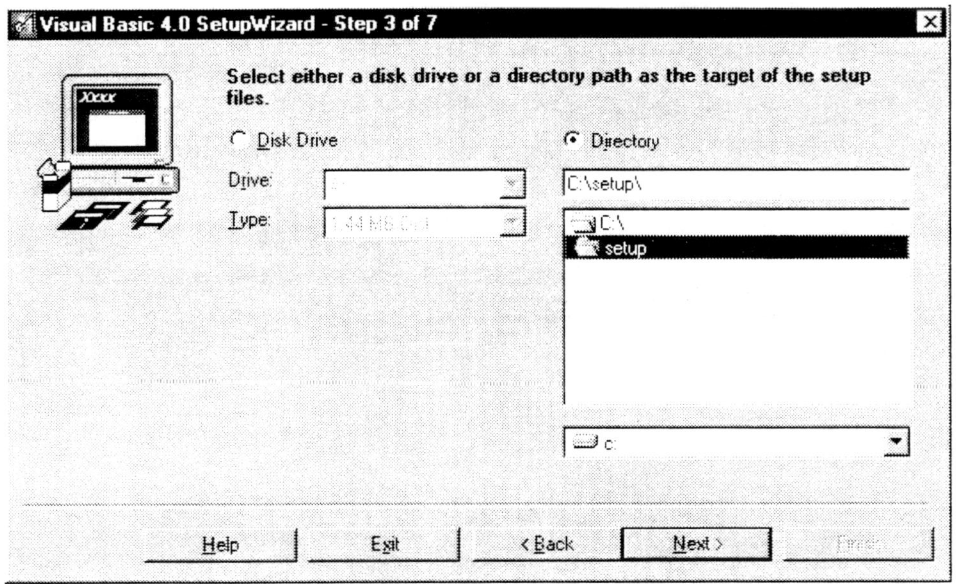

This is where you specify the destination media for the the distribution files. For this example, the hard drive folder "C:\SETUP" is used.

11. Click "Next>." The step 4 of 7 dialog box allows you to add OLE servers that your project may require. The Setup Wizard looks at the project file for the application to determine which objects should be included with the install package, but it can't tell if you're using certain features, so it asks you.

Obviously, this project requires no OLE Automation servers.

12. Click "Next>." The "deployment model" simply refers to where you want your program to run—as a stand-alone PC program, or as a shared OLE component. It only has meaning if the program is an OLE automation server —which it ain't.

Accept the default "Install in application directory" and click "Next>."

This is a summary of the files that will be included. You may remove files from the list if you know that the target system for the distribution already has them.

Choose the "Summary Info" button to see the storage size and number of files that have been selected. Choose the "File Details" button to see the file size, file date, version information, current location, and the install destination information for the selected file.

13. This application needs its help file "EditText.hlp." Click on "Add Files..." and add the "EditText.HLP" file. The box should look like this:

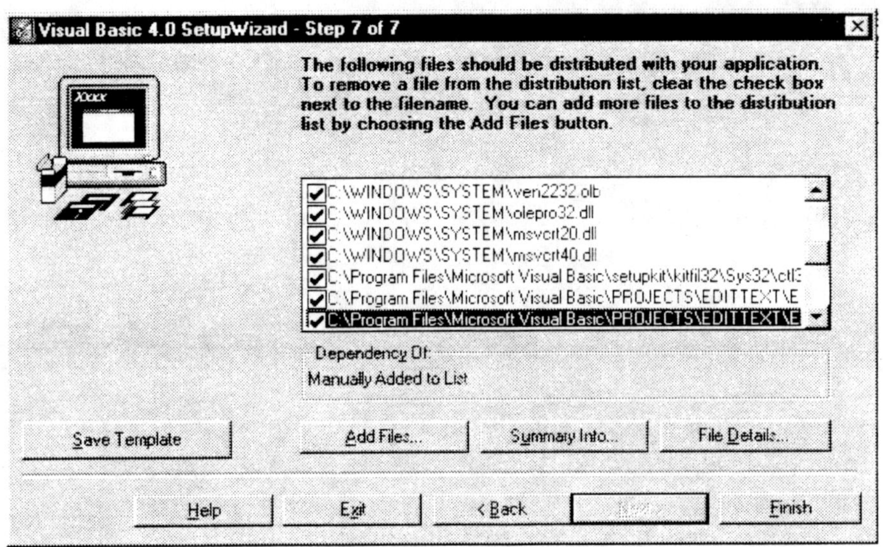

The help file will now be installed along with the executable file.

14. Get into a comfortable position to watch your screen and click "Next>."

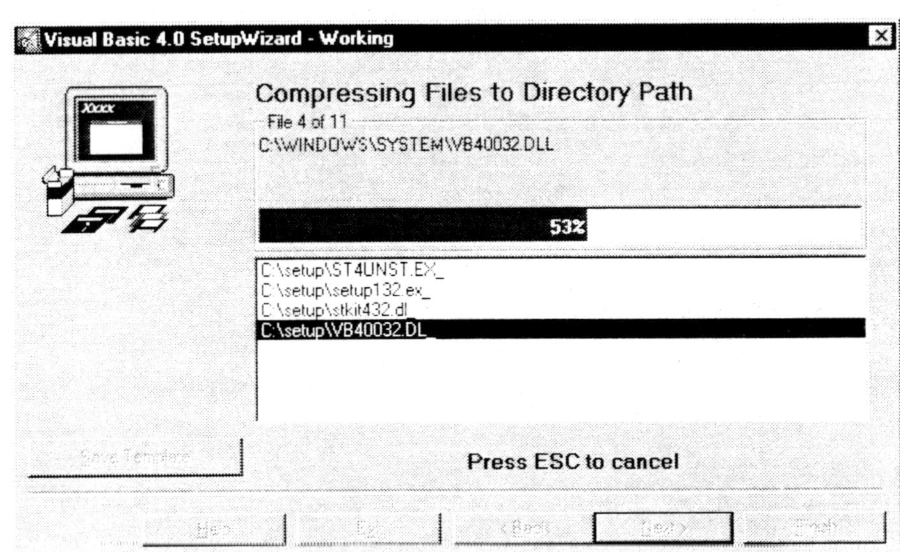

You see this screen as the Setup Wizard is doing several things:

- Compressing the files that are going to be copied.
- Giving the compressed files a name that has the last character of the extension changed to an underscore.
- Creating an executable installation file.
- And finally, determining the number of diskettes needed to copy it all.

15. As the files are copied, the Setup Wizard displays their names. When the task is complete, you get a nice little congratulatory message. Click on "Exit."

Now you know how to create distribution diskettes that you can take to another PC and, from a Windows "Run..." prompt, install the application.

16. Now for the payoff. Go to a "Run..." prompt. Specify "C:\SETUP\SETUP.EXE" if you used the same folder as the example, or "A:\SETUP" if you used diskettes.

17. Click on "OK" and follow the screens (they go by quickly with this little application). You should get a successful completion message.

Creating a Custom Version of the Setup Program

If you want to write a Setup program that has features not provided by the SetupWizard, such as using your own compression utility or providing the user with the option of installing different portions of an application, you can do so by writing your own Setup program using the *Visual Basic Setup Toolkit.* All of the tools required to use the Setup Toolkit are located in the "\SETUPKIT" subfolder of the main Visual Basic folder.

With the Setup Toolkit, you can:

- Compress your application files to fit the available disk space.
- Preinstall files that are required by your Setup program.
- Create a customized look and feel for your Setup program.
- Install your application files on the user's machine.
- Install files into the appropriate Windows directories ("\WINDOWS," "\WINDOWS\SYSTEM"), regardless of the actual directory names on the user's machine.
- Enable the installation of VB Remote OLE Automation servers on client and server sides.
- Remove Remote OLE Automation component (32-bit Enterprise Edition only).
- Use the VER.DLL functions in Windows to determine whether or not a file should be copied to the user's machine.
- Create Windows Program Manager groups and icons for your application with NT and Windows 3.1x, or create Start menu links with Windows 95.

The next step in the distribution process is to create a means of getting AS/400 programs installed.

Distributing an AS/400 Application

A client/server application of the type used in this book requires a partner program, an ICF file, and supporting objects, that run on the 400. Distributing that program to a 400 can be as slick as the Setup Wizard, using Client Access/PCS and a Setup program to drive it.

As the process employed in this book to distribute applications to an AS/400 has been discussed, the points aren't belabored here. However, a brief restatement of the process follows.

Step by Step: Creating Distribution Diskettes for AS/400 Programs

1. Go into Client Access/PCS and create a transfer request to download each AS/400 source code member for your application to your PC. Be sure to create the file description file for each (".FDF"). (The transfer request needn't be saved, or a common transfer request can be used for all source files, but be sure to create an ".FDF" file for each source member, even though they're all in the same format.)

2. Now go the other way. Create an upload transfer request, using the file description (".FDF" file) created in the last step as a reference for mapping fields. You don't have to run the transfer, just save the transfer request (".TFR") file.

3. Now you can use the Client Access/PCS API for running a transfer request as a command—"rfrompcb.exe"—to upload the file(s).

4. Create a batch file that uses the Client Access/PCS API "rmtcmd" to set the stage for the upload (like creating a library on the 400 and creating source file QRPGSRC).

5. The batch file then runs the upload, and calls more AS/400 commands to create the objects; and, perhaps, removes the source after successful compiles.

As was mentioned previously, this is the same method IBM uses in the sample application "APIRTREX" in the "QIWSTOOLS" folder to get AS/400 code onto your system. This is also the method used to copy files from the diskette that came with this book to your AS/400.

The "APPC.BAT" file that came on the accompanying diskette has these commands:

```
i:\qiwsfl2\rmtcmd crtlib vblib

i:\qiwsfl2\rmtcmd crtsrcpf file(vblib/qrpgsrc)

i:\qiwsfl2\rmtcmd crtsrcpf file(vblib/qddssrc)

i:\qiwsfl2\rmtcmd crtsrcpf file(vblib/qclsrc)
```

These statements use the Client Access/PCS API—"rmtcmd"—to invoke these AS/400 commands to set the stage for an upload of source code.

Other batch files—like "APPCRPG.BAT" in this example—upload the source with these statements:

```
call appc.bat

i:\qiwsfl2\rfrompcb appcrpg
```

In the first line, the "APPC.BAT" batch file is called to set the stage; the Client Access/PCS API "rfrompcb" then uploads the RPG source code to the AS/400, according to instructions found in the transfer request—"appcrpg.tfr"—the transfer name passed to the API.

The last piece of the batch file is to use the Client Access/PCS API—"rmtcmd"—this time with a little file of AS/400 commands called "cmds.rtr" (note the "/i" on the statement):

```
i:\qiwsfl2\rmtcmd /i cmds.rtr
```

and the commands file that is read:

```
addlible vblib

crtrpgpgm pgm(vblib/time400) srcfile(vblib/qrpgsrc)

dltf file(vblib/qrpgsrc)
```

This code renders a compiled object on the AS/400, compiled under whatever release of OS/400 is found there, ready to go. Naturally, the same steps can be performed for the other objects in a client/server project like ICF files and CL programs.

If your application will be installed on enough AS/400s to warrant it, you may want to create a custom Setup program, using the Setup Toolkit. The custom version runs the batch file you've created to install the AS/400 objects using the VB statement "SHELL."

To accomplish this, you have to edit the "SETUP.LST" file so as not to install things like "VB40016.DLL" or "VB40032.Dll."

Summary

Compiling an Application

A VB program is compiled from source code, just like RPG.

The compiler generates a new object—a ".EXE," or executable file that can run by itself (with the always present run-time DLLs).

Compilation may be conditional to accommodate both the 16- and 32-bit platforms.

Icons

An *icon* is a small graphic that is used by Windows to start and represent active programs. All programs on a Windows program group have an icon.

Icons can be attached to forms, and thereby made available to the ".EXE" file when the project is compiled.

Distributing Applications

Just as adding a help system to an application can greatly enhance its perceived worth, so can a professional installation program.

You can create an installation system (called a "SETUP") for your applications using the Setup Wizard, which comes with the professional and enterprise editions of VB.

The standard program "SETUP.EXE" preinstalls objects listed in the "SETUP.LST" file and calls "SETUP1.EXE" to start the remainder of the setup process.

Most of the objects are compressed for distribution using the Microsoft COMPRESS program in folder "SETUPKIT" or "KITFILES."

You can use the Setup Toolkit to customize the standard setup project if the version created by the Setup Wizard is not what you want. There are several things to note about the process, though (see the *Visual Basic Programmer's Guide*).

Distributing AS/400 Applications

You can distribute applications to an AS/400 using a PC with Client Access/PCS installed.

Client Access/PCS APIs "rfrompcb.exe" and "rmtcmd.exe" are used to upload and translate source code, and to compile programs and files from that source.

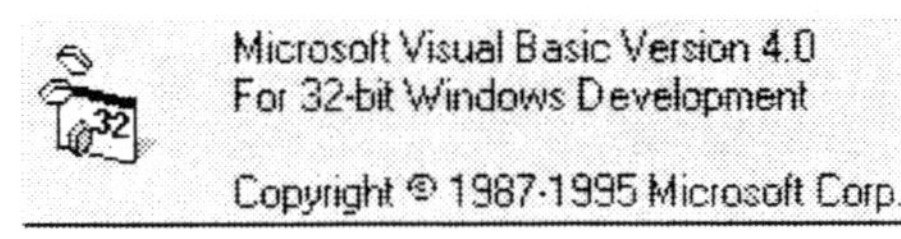

14

The AS/400 Report Download Utility

This chapter presents the AS/400 Report Download Utility. This is a fairly comprehensive and full-function client/server application that can be used by many shops.

In the utility, you may find some features of VB that haven't been presented. When an unfamiliar statement is encountered, it is explained, where possible, in AS/400 terms. As with all code and syntax presented in this book, only the most common usage is presented. You are urged to consult the *Visual Basic Programmer's Guide*, the *Visual Basic Language Reference*, and VB online help for complete details.

What the Utility Does

Aside from being an example of more advanced VB and client/server coding, the utility may be of use in your enterprise—or you may be able to make it so.

The utility does the following:

- Tests for the PCS router and attaches to the AS/400.
- Gets a list of AS/400 outques for selection or accepts a keyed-in outque name.
- Gets a list of AS/400 spool files from the outque for selection. Then the user may:
  - Preview the contents of an AS/400 spool file.
  - Download an AS/400 spool file to a PC text file.
  - Download an AS/400 spool file to an Excel spreadsheet and (optionally) run an Excel macro over the downloaded data.
  - Download an AS/400 spool file to a Word document and (optionally) run a Word macro over the downloaded data.

What Makes the Utility Different

The last two items in the preceding list—(optionally) run an Excel macro over the downloaded data and (optionally) run a Word macro over the downloaded data—are what make the utility most useful. These use a feature of PC office systems called DDE or *Dynamic Data Exchange*.

The utility downloads a spool file to a PC spreadsheet or document and then invokes Microsoft Excel or Word to perform processes on the data in the form of saved macro instructions. (Note that the software package used could be WordPerfect or Lotus, with modifications to the utility.)

This "run the macro" bit deserves a bit of thought. Suppose you have a precocious user in accounting that is constantly using her/his PC spreadsheet package to produce reports, financial statements, etc. The user is familiar with the PC package and is very good at using it. She/he may even be the one person that does everybody's spreadsheet macros.

This user would frequently like to take information from the AS/400, where, say, financial software resides, and move it into a PC spreadsheet where it can be processed further or spruced up for presentation purposes.

The problem is that it's such a nuisance:

- You have to get the data into a format on the 400 that is meaningful when passed—you can't just give the users listings of a bunch of file layouts and leave them to figure it out.
- You have to then use Client Access/PCS to get the data to the PC (create a transfer request and download the data, or run it interactively).
- Once on the PC, the file has to be imported to a package like Lotus or Excel.
- The file is then parsed into spreadsheet cells (parsing is the process of assigning text data to spreadsheet columns).
- And, finally, extra baggage like page headings, are stripped. (A spreadsheet macro can perform this step.)

It works, this stuff, but all this hasn't been put into production in many AS/400/PC installations because it's too complicated to perform on an ongoing basis. The AS/400 Report Download Utility accomplishes all these steps and is user driven. That power user in accounting is free of you, and you of him/her.

So, in place of all those steps to download data to a PC, you can do this:

- The power user generates his/her own query on the AS/400 to get the desired data collected and summarized to their satisfaction in the form of a report.

  or

  Any other existing AS/400 report is generated (the report is not printed, but kept in an outque).
- The user calls the Report Download Utility from her/his PC and displays a list of all the spool files in a given AS/400 outque, or displays a list of all AS/400 outques to which the user is authorized, and selects one.
- The user then selects a spool file entry for *Preview* to make sure it's the right one. The first 150 lines (about three pages or so) are displayed.

- The user then selects "Download to an Excel spreadsheet" and specifies an optional spreadsheet macro to be run once the data is loaded. This macro has been prepared to do the parsing, stripping, formatting, calculations and printing—or anything else the spreadsheet is capable of.
- Without leaving the download utility, the user selects the next file to be downloaded, or jumps back and forth to the spreadsheet.

So, the next thing the user sees is the finished output, perhaps coming off the laser printer, nicely formatted. The macro (which is usually the user's responsibility and, therefore, not yours) has been attached to the download process, which has been automated for the user. There are no Client Access/PCS transfer requests, FDF files, or intermediate steps—only the Client Access/PCS router is used. Next month, or the next time the user wants to download the same report, the macro is again called, thereby automating the entire process.

This Visual Basic client/server utility, then, is the "pivot man" in a larger process involving several different players—putting them all together in a cooperative processing environment. A role that VB is good at, and one that AS/400 professionals can live with.

A Simple Design for the Application

In many of your client/server applications, the PC plays the role of graphic display and enhanced user interface—i.e., a fancy workstation. Functions like editing are performed at the PC, but the edited data is handed over to the AS/400 to become part of its database. Data requested by the user, via the client workstation, is assembled by the 400 from various files in its database and served up (down?) to the PC in a concise format, representing a logical unit. The PC may interpret that data into a more meaningful display, or put it into a PC file for local processing (like to a spreadsheet). Nevertheless, the data assembly, and the logic for that assembly should reside on the AS/400.

This approach supports the three-tier client/server model. The VB program running on the PC represents the user interface, or client tier. The role for the client tier, under the model, is to collect and edit data while presenting the user with a consistent, easy-to-use interface.

The role of the back end (the AS/400 relational database) is that of a data repository or *warehouse* and a data server.

In the middle, acting as coordinator is the middle tier, called the *business server*. It's called the business server because it contains and enforces the particular *rules of business* for your concern. For example, suppose your line of business requires out-of-town customers to list their phone number(s) with you—say for reservations of some kind. That's a rule of business. It has nothing to do with computers. Indeed, the computer must be made to accommodate the rule—not the other way around.

To further the example, typically in your business, a customer has one or two phone numbers to give you, sometimes more.

So the rules are:

- If the customer is from out of town, there must always be a phone number.
- There may be one or many phone numbers per customer.

The business server is where processing takes place to determine if the rules are being followed by the user's operation of the interface. A request is received from the front end, the request is processed, and a response is sent back. The front end then either informs the user that the data was acceptable or redisplays the input screen.

In this book's approach to the three-tier model, the business server in the middle is a set of RPG and CL programs. So, with that in mind, the design may be approached with a more straight-ahead process of thought—let the 400 do what it's good at, and let the PC do what it's good at.

The AS/400 Report Download Utility design is simple. It is done in the same way that you would design on the AS/400:

- The progression of screens, and means of returning through them, is as you would design on the AS/400.
- An association is drawn between the program's functions and the separate screens and groupings of elements.
- If the user doesn't know what to specify, lists (like subfiles) are presented.
- Messages are displayed to the user informing her/him of requirements of the application's use, of the program's status, or of an error.

The AS/400 Download Utility is included with the book as a viable production utility and a source for examples of more complex VB applications. As such, the application is necessarily longer—making the threshold between it, and what you've been doing in VB so far, considerable.

Please don't approach this project as you have the others in this book. Instead, do this:

- After loading the utility on the PC and the AS/400, practice with it to understand the program's forms, events, and logic.
- Look the code over while bearing in mind that, just like in RPG, longer, complex routines are made up of short, simple ones.
- Bring the project into the VB Development Environment. Browse through the forms and controls while referring to the code associated with them.
- Run the program with the "Step Into" button and watch the code go round and round, looking into the contents of variables, setting breakpoints, etc.

Then, as you need to put something into one of your own applications that is similar to what you've seen, you'll know where to go get it.

Modifications to the Utility

All of the source code for the Download Utility is on the included diskette—both VB and AS/400. You may consider the utility as a starting point, and modify it to do other things. You could make it interface to other software packages like WordPerfect or Lotus, or extract routines from the utility and use them to start a new application of your own. Instead of downloading printer spool files, the utility could be made to download data base files.

You've seen how to place a picture into an image on a form (you placed a bitmap VB logo in project EditText). You could create your own bitmap picture in a utility like Paintbrush, and substitute it for the *Midrange Computing* logo on the utility's first form.

At this point, if you haven't already done so, please load the utility.

Installing the AS/400 Report Download Utility

There are two parts to a client/server application like this—the PC part and the AS/400 part—so the installation process, likewise, has two parts. The AS/400 part need only be done once per AS/400 as the programs are then available to all users; but the PC part has to be done, naturally, on each PC that uses it.

The PC code for this utility is written entirely for the 16-bit platform because of the extensive use of Client Access/PCS API routines—which are all 16-bit.

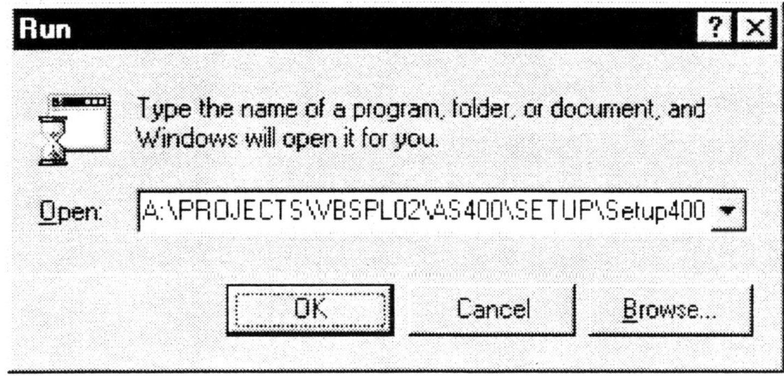

Step by Step: Installing the Report Download Utility—AS/400 Code

1. Insert the diskette that came with this book into drive A:.
2. Go to the Win95 "Start" button or the Win3.1 Program Manager, or File Manager, and select "Run..."
3. Click on "Browse..." Work your way through the folders on the diskette to get to the "A:\PROJECTS\VBSPL02\AS400\SETUP\" folder, and select the program "SETUP400.EXE."
4. Run the "SETUP400" program. This is an example of modifying the "SETUP1" VB source code to run a batch file. "Shell" is used to run the batch file. Note that the "SETUP400" program can't detect if the batch file ran successfully. The batch program is paused at the end for you to examine the screen messages for errors.

   What it does:

   - Creates a library named "VBSPL" on the AS/400. This is where the AS/400 portion of the utility will reside.

- Creates source files to receive the uploaded AS/400 source code.
- Uploads the various source files using the Client Access/PCS API "rfrompcb.exe."
- Compiles the AS/400 physical files, ICF file, RPG and CL programs for the application.

Note: *The setup utility creates/clears a library named "VBSPL" on the 400. Because of required hard-coded references to a specific library (the AS/400 CRTDUPOBJ command), you cannot run the utility from any other library without modifying the source code.*

Step by Step: Installing the Report Download Utility—PC Code

The installation program for the PC portion of the code is also a Windows "Setup" type.

1. Insert the diskette that came with this book into drive A:.
2. Go to a "Run..." box, as before. This time, select "SETUP" from the A: root folder. The rest is automatic.

   Again, this is a modified version of the Setup Wizard's clone project, "SETUP1," renamed to "SETUP" as it's compiled.

   What it does:

   - The "SETUP" program for the Report Download Utility started out the same as the "SETUP" program you made for EditText. The source code for project "SETUP1A" is in folder "C:\VB\SETUPKIT\SETUP1." It has been cloned and modified.

"SETUP" Project Source Code for the Download Utility

The source code for both the AS/400 and PC setup projects is on the accompanying diskette, as an example of creating your own setup programs (created with VB 3.0 for 16-bit DLLs):

- "Setup" project source code to install AS/400 part of client/server system is in:

```
\PROJECTS\VBSPL02\AS400\SETUP
```

- "Setup" project source code to install PC part of client/server system is in:

```
\PROJECTS\VBSPL02\PC\SETUP
```

Only the code in the declarations area and the Form_Load procedure has been altered. Each changed or added line has been identified in the code.

At this point please run the AS/400 Report Download Utility to see if you have any problems.

Requirements for Running the Download Utility

Of course, the principle requirement of running the utility is the Client Access/PCS router. If it is not running, you'll receive a message at startup.

The Extended DOS version of Client Access/PC Support must be loaded to your PC along with its attendant DLLs.

> **Note**: *There have been reported difficulties in running IBM Client Access API routines through NetSoft's router. It has also been reported that NetSoft's latest update to their router software overcomes the problem.*

You must install the PC portion of the Download Utility in folder "C:\VBSPL02." (Although the setup program prompts you for a destination folder name, it is ignored.)

You must have the following two Windows fonts installed on your PC:

- Courier New
- Terminal

These are nonproportional fonts that align properly when presented in subfile like lists (list boxes).

Depending on how your AS/400 security is set up, you may have to grant authority to users (or *PUBLIC) for the database files that come with the utility.

Those files are:

- VBSPL / PDDATA
- VBSPL / PQLIST
- VBSPL / PTLIST

In addition, any AS/400 outque that can be accessed by the utility should be specified as "Display any file - *YES". Otherwise, only the spool files belonging to the user profile that was used to start the router will be available.

Troubleshooting ICF Client/Server Programs

Should you experience problems while starting or running the utility, you may follow these tasks to determine the probable cause:

When the PC starts an ICF job through the router with the AS/400, an AS/400 job of type "CMNEVK" (Communications Evoke) is started in subsystem "QCMN" (if you have one, or "QBASE" if you don't). To see this job, start the utility and enter this AS/400 "Work Subsystem Job" command from another terminal or emulation session:

```
WRKSBSJOB  SBS(QCMN or QBASE) USER(User profile used to start the router)
```

This should display several jobs. Typically, there are one or two emulation sessions and a printer session. Below those entries is the router job.

Very often, when there's a problem, the AS/400 router job is sitting at a status of "MSGW"—"Message Wait." There will probably be a message at the QSYSOPR msgq. You may display the job's joblog, as well.

That message probably refers to an authority problem. A typical scenario: A generic user profile is used to sign on all routers, perhaps automatically, and that user profile has minimal authority. When the utility's CL command "CRTDUPOBJ" (Create Duplicate Object) is encountered it fails because the generic profile has no authority to the original object. The best solution—grant *Public authority to all the files in library "VBSPL."

If the utility loads properly, but no spool files appear for selection, the problem, again is authority. Remember, the user profile used to start the router is the profile used to start the AS/400 partner program, even if QSECOFR is signed on to one of the emulation sessions. If the router's profile is not authorized to an outque's spool file entries, no entries are returned. The solution—specify "Display any file - *YES" on the outque description.

The AS/400 Report Download Utility Source Code

The accompanying diskette includes all of the source code for the various elements of the Download Utility. See Appendix C for details about the companion diskette.

Installing the AS/400 portion of the Download Utility creates these source files in library VBSPL:

- QDDSSRC
- QRPGSRC
- QCLSRC

These source files contain all of the AS/400 code for the project.

The AS/400 objects are created (and the ICF file changed) as a result of the install, as well.

How It Works

First, start PC Support and Windows (only the PCS router is used by the utility; you don't need any WSF sessions). The install process creates a program group and icons. Once PC Support is started, you can launch the utility as you would any other Windows application by double clicking the icon:

After checking your PC for the Client Access/PCS router and the program PCSWIN, the utility checks for the presence of Microsoft Excel 4.0 or 5.0 and Microsoft Word. It only checks the standard installation folders for these applications. The following screen is then presented:

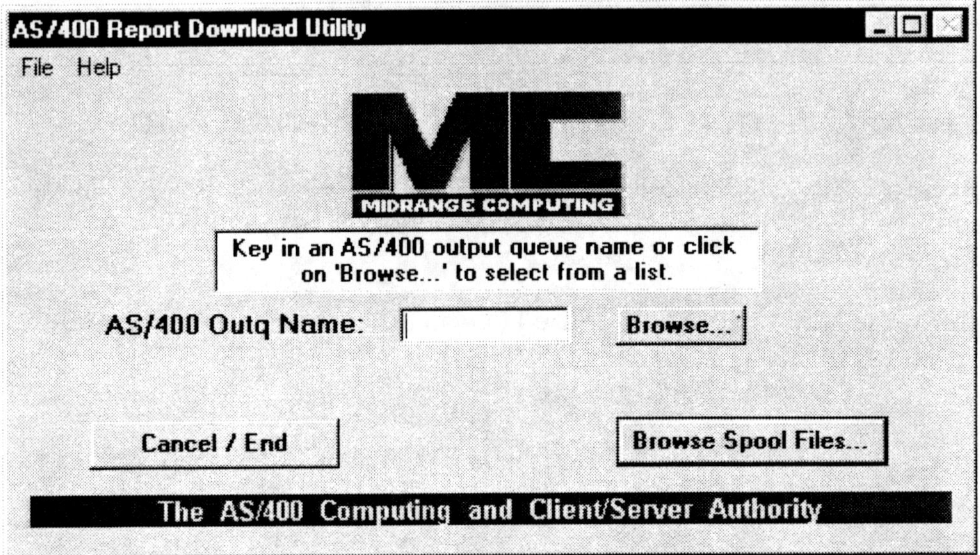

You may specify an outque or click "Browse..." to present a list of the outques on your AS/400 to which you're authorized:

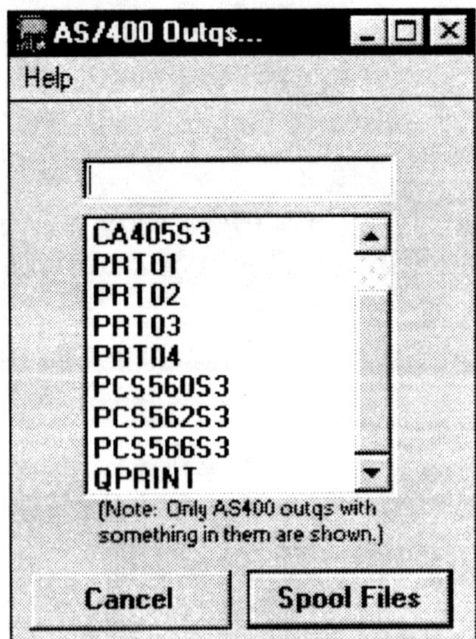

Once you specify an outque, a list of spool files is presented, like this example:

AS/400 Spool Files

Help

Spool File	User	User Data	Pages	Form	Seq#	Job	Date	Time
QPRINT	ISPCFP	OE_RPT	31	*STD	-	OERPT01	01/12/96	11:31:09
QSYSPRT	ISPCFP		11	GBAR	-	CICSDTV1	01/12/96	11:38:50
QPRINT	ISPCFP	REGISTR	1	WHITE	-	REGISTR	01/12/96	11:47:19
QPRINT	ISPCFP	OE_RPT	28	*STD	-	OERPT01	01/12/96	12:11:22
QPQUPRFIL	ISPCFP	MFEDIT	12	WHITE	-	QUERY	01/13/96	10:10:46

- Preview first few pages
- Load into a text file
- Load into MS Excel
- Load into Excel plus a macro
- Load into MS Word
- Load into Word plus a macro

You may preview the contents of the spool file (the first few pages only.) Note that blank lines are removed.

Continue

Return

Records

Notice the option buttons representing the different features available to process your downloaded report. (Excel and Word options are only available if those applications are found in their standard folders.)

If unsure as to which spool file to process, you may preview the first 150 lines or so (usually a few pages):

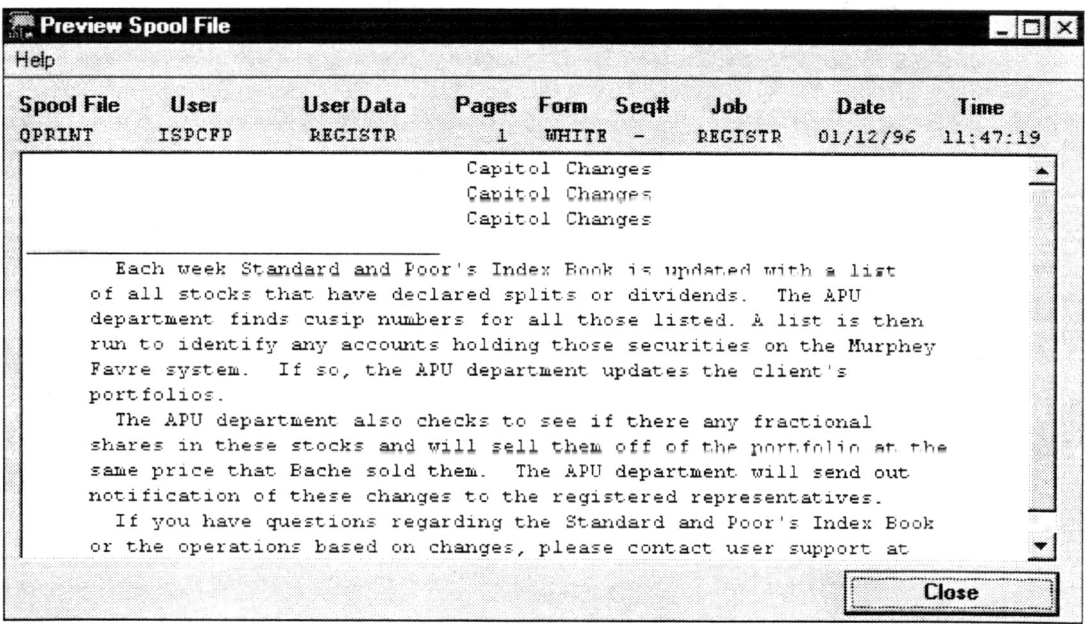

You can scroll through the preview display. Report widths to 132 or 198 columns display in correspondingly smaller fonts.

This example report was originally created on the AS/400 as a text document, as in Text Management or DisplayWrite. Note the effect of specifying bold print, say, for a heading ("Capital Changes" in the example). To create the effect, the bolded text is sent to the printer three times, without the benefit of a line feed. The utility picks up each iteration, however, as a new print line.

A dialog box comes up when you specify that you'll be loading a Word or Excel macro. Additionally, when you check the "Run macro" box, you are prompted for the macro name:

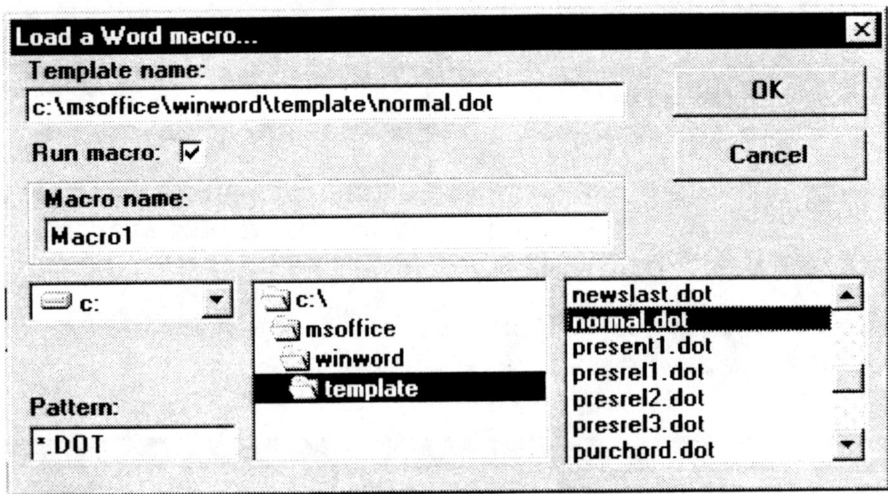

Word macros are kept in a template (".DOT" files), and Excel macros are kept in a macro sheet (".XLM" files.) The macro must be prerecorded and stored before it can be referred to here.

You may also specify that the downloaded report be sent to a PC text file, in which case you are presented with the following dialog box:

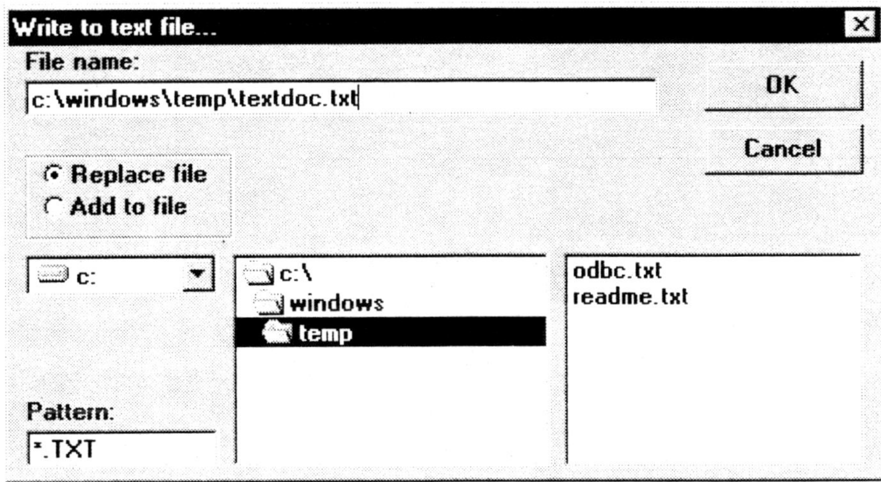

Note that you can either replace the PC file or add records to it. You could use this feature to accumulate several AS/400 reports into one file.

The utility also comes with a modest help system, accessed from the first form's menu:

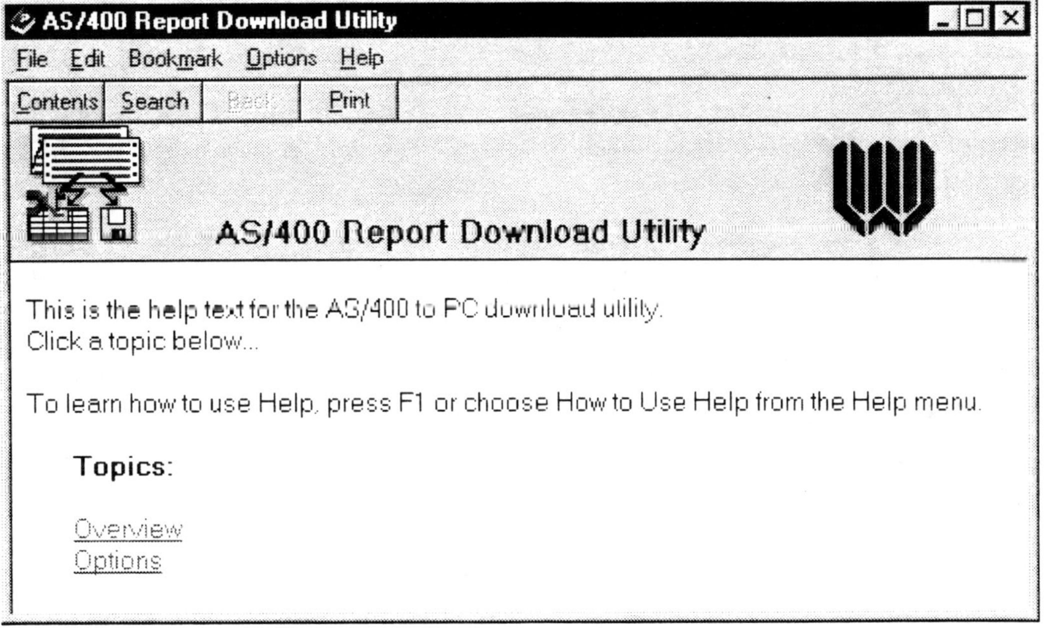

The help system explains all features of the utility to the user.

The AS/400 Report Download Utility is a fairly inclusive and full-function client/server application that ties together several elements of today's application solutions:

- The AS/400
- Windows
- Client Access/PC Support
- Microsoft Excel
- Microsoft Word

The utility uses a feature of PC office systems called Dynamic Data Exchange. DDE allows you to link objects within a Visual Basic program to other programs running in Windows. It also allows you to send commands to other programs. It is in this way that the function within Word or Excel is made available to the Visual Basic program.

AS/400 Report Download Utility Source Listings

The following listings represent source for all the elements of the Download Utility with the exception of the APPC tool "APPC.GBL," which was presented earlier. The routines in "APPC.BAS" have been, for the most part, moved to "VBSPL02.BAS."

The code is presented here, in alphabetical order, by file and then Sub/Function procedure.

> **Note**: *Some of the code has been lifted from the samples provided by IBM, and does not adhere to variable naming conventions presented in this book.*

The Visual Basic Program VBSPL02

The following subsections are listed by procedure name and explain what the program does.

Sub Deallocate ()

Releases the conversation with the AS/400.

Sub Form1Enter ()

Executes when "Enter" or "OK" button is pressed. Performs editing and shows SplfForm.

Sub GetDefSys (DefSys)

Gets the name of the default system in a multiple system environment.

Sub GetOutqs ()

Sends a request to the AS/400 for a list of outques to which the user is authorized. Outque file entries are put into a list box for selection.

Sub GetSpoolFiles ()

Sends a request to the AS/400 for a list of spool files for a requested outque. Spool file entries are put into a list box for selection.

Sub Initialize ()

Standard client/server ICF startup. Also determines if Microsoft Excel or Word is installed, and if so, which release.

Sub MakeUpFileName ()

Creates a new file name for temporary storage of a downloaded file headed for Excel or Word.

Sub ProcExcel ()

Writes downloaded records to a temporary file. Then establishes a DDE link to start Excel, passes the name of the temporary file for loading into the spreadsheet, (optionally) passes the name of an Excel macro sheet, and (optionally) specifies which macro to run.

Sub ProcHelp ()

Standard call to Windows help.

Sub ProcPreview ()

Displays the first 150 records of a selected spool file in a list box for verification of the selection.

Sub ProcTxt ()

Writes spool file records to a specified PC text file.

Sub ProcWord ()

Writes downloaded records to a temporary file. Then establishes a DDE link to start Word, passes the name of the temporary file for loading into the document, (optionally) passes the name of a Word macro template, and (optionally) specifies which macro to run.

AS/400 Source Code

Installing the AS/400 portion of the Download Utility creates these source files in library "VBSPL:"

- QDDSSRC
- QRPGSRC
- QCLSRC

These source files contain all the AS/400 code for the project. To help sort things out, a brief description of the AS/400 objects follows. All objects are created in library "VBSPL."

Physical Files

PQLIST—Holds a list of AS/400 outques.

PTLIST—Holds a list of AS/400 spool files.

PDDATA—Holds copied spool file records.

ICF File

VBSPLF —Standard ICF file for APPC connections. It contains fields for the transport of data and messages between the PC and AS/400.

CL Programs

VBSPLF1C—Sets the AS/400 environment for the utility (establishes the lib list and creates temporary files). Calls VBSPLF1R—the main AS/400 partner program.

CHEKOUTQ—Checks for the existence of a requested AS/400 outque.

GETOUTQS—Loads a file (PQLIST) with the names of the AS/400 outques.

GETSPLFS—Loads a file (PTLIST) with spool file entries for a specific outque.

GETSPLE—Loads a file (PDDATA) with records from a specific AS/400 spool file.

RPGProgram

VBSPLF1R—The main AS/400 partner program. It handles the APPC conversation with the PC and calls the other AS/400 programs. This is an example of a standard APPC application carried through an ICF file (VBSPLF1).

VB Code Listing for Download Utility

Form1 (VBSPL02.FRM)—Initial form; displays automatically when program loads

```
Option Explicit

Private Sub AboutItem Click()
  AboutForm.Show
End Sub

Private Sub CancelButton_Click()
  ' If conversation is active, deallocate it
```

```
  Call Deallocate
End Sub

Private Sub ExitItem_Click()
  ' If conversation is active, deallocate it
  Call Deallocate
End Sub

Private Sub Form_Load()
  Call Initialize          ' Like *INZSR
End Sub

Private Sub GeneralHelpItem_Click()
  Call ProcHelp
End Sub

Private Sub ListOutqsButton_Click()
  Call GetOutqs
End Sub

Private Sub ListOutqsItem_Click()
  Call GetOutqs
End Sub

Private Sub OKButton_Click()
  Call Form1Enter
  Form1.MessageText.Text = MESSAGE_1
End Sub

Private Sub OutqText_KeyPress(KeyAscii As Integer)
  If (KeyAscii = 13) Then
    Call Form1Enter
  End If
End Sub
```

OpenForm (OPENFORM.FRM)—Displays a list of outques

```
Option Explicit
Private Sub AboutItem_Click()
  AboutForm.Show MODAL
End Sub
Private Sub CancelButton_Click()
  OutqForm.Hide
  ' Setfocus makes a control active . . .
```

```
  Form1.OutqText.SetFocus
  Form1.MessageText.Text = MESSAGE_1
End Sub

Private Sub OKButton_Click()
  If Form1.OutqText.Text <> "" Then
    Form1.OutqText.Text = UCase(Form1.OutqText.Text)
    OutqForm.Hide
    Form1.Refresh
    Call Form1Enter
  Else
    MsgBox "An AS/400 outq name must be specified.", _
      48, "AS/400 Outq Selection..."
  End If

  Form1.MessageText.Text = MESSAGE_10

End Sub

Private Sub OptionsItem_Click()
  Call ProcHelp
End Sub
Private Sub OutqList_Click()
  OutqText.Text = OutqList.Text
  Form1.OutqText.Text = OutqList.Text
End Sub

Private Sub OutqList_DblClick()
  OutqText.Text = OutqList
  Form1.OutqText.Text = OutqList
  Form1.OutqText.Text = UCase(Form1.OutqText.Text)
  Call Form1Enter
End Sub
Private Sub OutqText_Change()
  Form1.OutqText.Text = OutqForm.OutqText.Text
End Sub
```

SplfForm (SPLFFORM.FRM)—Displays a list of spool files

```
Option Explicit

Private Sub ContentsItem_Click()
  Call ProcHelp
End Sub
```

```
Private Sub OptionButton_Click(Index As Integer)
  DownLoadType = Index
  Select Case DownLoadType
  Case 0
    SplfForm.MessageText = _
      "You may preview the contents of the spool file (the first few pages
         only.) Note that blank lines are removed."
  Case 1
    SplfForm.MessageText = _
      "Choose this option to load the spool file to a text file.  You will be
         prompted for the text file name."
  Case 2
    SplfForm.MessageText = _
      "You may load the spool file directly into an Excel spreadsheet."
  Case 3
    SplfForm.MessageText = _
      "You may load and (optionally) run an Excel macro sheet with the spool
         file. Select or key a macro sheet and (optionally) run a macro.  See
        'Help' for more information."
  Case 4
    SplfForm.MessageText = _
      "You may load the selected spool file into an MS Word document."
  Case 5
    SplfForm.MessageText = _
      "You may load the selected spool file into an MS Word document, load a
         Word macro to run over the document, and (optionally) run the macro.
         See 'Help' for more information."
  End Select
End Sub

Private Sub OptionButton_DblClick(Index As Integer)
  ' let the user double click a spool file to press enter...
  Call SplfOKButton_Click
End Sub

Private Sub SplfCancelButton_Click()
  ' reset . . .
  SplfForm.MessageText = ""
  RecordCount = 0
  SplfForm.RecordText = ""
  SplfForm.Hide
End Sub

Private Sub SplfList_DblClick()
```

```
  Call SplfOKButton_Click
End Sub

Private Sub SplfOKButton_Click()
  Dim RecordCount As Integer

  RecordCount = 0
  SplfForm.RecordText = ""

  Select Case DownLoadType
  Case 0
    SplfForm.MessageText = Message5
    ' call procedure to show first 150 spool file records
    Call ProcPreview
    SplfForm.MessageText = ""
  Case 1
    ' download to textfile . . .
    SaveForm.Show MODAL
  Case 2
    ' download to Excel . . .
    Call ProcExcel
  Case 3
    ' download to Excel plus macro . . .
    SplfForm.MessageText = Message11
    LoadForm.Show MODAL
  Case 4
    ' download to Word . . .
    Call ProcWord
  Case 5
    ' download to Word plus macro . . .
    SplfForm.MessageText = Message13
    WordForm.Show MODAL
  End Select
End Sub
```

ViewForm (VIEWFORM.FRM)—Preview of a spool file

```
Option Explicit

Private Sub ContentsItem_Click()
  Call ProcHelp
End Sub

Private Sub ViewList_Click()
```

```
  ViewForm.ViewList.ListIndex = -1
End Sub

Private Sub ViewOKButton_Click()
  ViewForm.Hide
End Sub
```

SplfForm (SPLFFORM.FRM)—Displays a list of spool files

```
Option Explicit

Private Sub AddReplaceOption_Click(Index As Integer)
  AddReplace = Index
End Sub

Private Sub CancelButton_Click()
  SaveForm.SaveText.Text = ""
  SaveForm.Hide
End Sub

Private Sub Dir1_Change()
  File1.Path = Dir1.Path
  SaveForm.SaveText.Text = Dir1.Path
End Sub

Private Sub Dir1_Click()
  File1.Path = Dir1.Path
  SaveForm.SaveText.Text = Dir1.Path
End Sub

Private Sub Drive1_Change()
  Dir1.Path = Drive1.Drive
End Sub

Private Sub File1_DblClick()
  If (Right$(SaveForm.Dir1.Path, 1) = "\") Then
    FileName = SaveForm.Dir1.Path & _
      SaveForm.File1.FileName
  Else
    FileName = SaveForm.Dir1.Path & _
      "\" & SaveForm.File1.FileName
  End If
  SaveForm.SaveText.Text = FileName
```

```
End Sub

Private Sub OKButton_Click()
  If SaveForm.SaveText.Text = "" Then
    MsgBox "No file name specified.", 48, _
      "Text File Selection..."
    SaveForm.SaveText.SetFocus
  Else
    FileName = SaveForm.SaveText.Text
    ' call procedure to load uploaded file to PC text file
    Call ProcTxt
    SaveForm.Hide
  End If
End Sub

Private Sub PatternText_KeyPress(KeyAscii As Integer)
  If (KeyAscii = 13) Then
    SaveForm.File1.Pattern = SaveForm.PatternText
  End If
End Sub

Private Sub SaveText_KeyPress(KeyAscii As Integer)
  If KeyAscii = 13 Then
    OKButton_Click
  End If
End Sub
```

LoadForm (LOADFORM.FRM)—Loads a spool file to Excel

```
Private Sub CancelButton_Click()
  LoadForm.Hide
End Sub

Private Sub Command2_Click()
  LoadForm.Hide
End Sub

Private Sub Dir1_Change()
  File1.Path = Dir1.Path
  LoadForm.MacroSheetText.Text = Dir1.Path
End Sub

Private Sub Dir1_Click()
```

```
  LoadForm.MacroSheetText.Text = Dir1.Path
End Sub

Private Sub Drive1_Change()
  Dir1.Path = Drive1.Drive
End Sub

Private Sub File1_Click()
  If (Right$(LoadForm.Dir1.Path, 1) = "\") Then
    MacroSheetName = LoadForm.Dir1.Path & LoadForm.File1.FileName
  Else
    MacroSheetName = LoadForm.Dir1.Path & "\" & LoadForm.File1.FileName
  End If
  MacroSheetText.Text = MacroSheetName
End Sub

Private Sub File1_DblClick()
  File1_Click
End Sub

Private Sub MacroCheckBox_Click()
  If MacroCheckBox.Value = 0 Then
    RunYN = ""
    MacroFrame.Visible = False
  Else
    RunYN = "Y"
    MacroFrame.Visible = True
  End If
End Sub

Private Sub NoMacroButton_Click()
  LoadForm.Hide
End Sub

Private Sub OKButton_Click()
  On Error GoTo FileError
  ' Put backslash into directory stream . . .
  If (Right$(Dir1.Path, 1) = "\") Then
    MacroSheetName = Dir1.Path & File1.FileName
  Else
    MacroSheetName = Dir1.Path & "\" & File1.FileName
  End If

  MacroSheetText.Text = MacroSheetName
  If MacroSheetName <> "" Then
```

```
    MacroYN = "Y"
  End If
  ' See if macro sheet exists . . .
  Open MacroSheetName For Input As #3
  Close #3
  ' Load file to Excel . . .
  Call ProcExcel
  LoadForm.Hide
  Exit Sub

FileError:
  Select Case Err.Number
    Case 70
      SplfForm.MessageText.Text = _
        "Your macro sheet is already loaded...  Continuing..."
      MacroYN = ""
      Resume Next
    Case 76
      MessageResponse = MsgBox _
        ("Macro sheet by that name not found...", 48, "Macro Load")
      Exit Sub
    Case Else
      MsgBox "File Error " & Str$(Err.Number), 48, "Macro Load"
      Exit Sub
    End Select

    Resume

End Sub

Private Sub PatternText_KeyPress(KeyAscii As Integer)
  If (KeyAscii = 13) Then
    LoadForm.File1.Pattern = LoadForm.PatternText.Text
  End If
End Sub
```

WordForm (WORDFORM.FRM)—Loads a spool file to Word

Option Explicit

```
Private Sub CancelButton_Click()
  WordForm.Hide
End Sub
```

```
Private Sub Dir1_Change()
  File1.Path = Dir1.Path
  MacroTemplateText.Text = Dir1.Path
End Sub

Private Sub Dir1_Click()
  MacroTemplateText.Text = Dir1.Path
End Sub

Private Sub Drive1_Change()
  Dir1.Path = Drive1.Drive
End Sub

Private Sub File1_Click()
  If (Right$(Dir1.Path, 1) = "\") Then
    MacroTemplateName = Dir1.Path & File1.FileName
  Else
    MacroTemplateName = Dir1.Path & "\" & File1.FileName
  End If
  MacroTemplateText.Text = MacroTemplateName
End Sub

Private Sub File1_DblClick()
  File1_Click
End Sub
Private Sub MacroCheckBox_Click()
  If MacroCheckBox.Value = 0 Then
    RunYNW = ""
    MacroFrame.Visible = False
  Else
    RunYNW = "Y"
    MacroFrame.Visible = True
  End If
End Sub

Private Sub OKButton_Click()
  On Error GoTo FileError

  If (Right$(Dir1.Path, 1) = "\") Then
    MacroTemplateName = Dir1.Path & File1.FileName
  Else
    MacroTemplateName = Dir1.Path & "\" & File1.FileName
  End If
```

```
  MacroTemplateText.Text = MacroTemplateName
  If MacroTemplateName <> "" Then
    MacroYNW = "Y"
  End If
  ' See if macro sheet exists . . .
  Open MacroTemplateName For Input As #3
  Close #3
  ' load spool file to Word document . . .
  Call ProcWord
  WordForm.Hide
  Exit Sub

FileError:
Select Case Err.Number
Case 70
  SplfForm.MessageText.Text = _
    "Your macro sheet is already loaded...  Continuing..."
  MacroYNW = ""
  Resume Next
Case 76
  MessageResponse = MsgBox _
    ("Macro template by that name not found...", 48, "Macro Load")
  Exit Sub
Case Else
  MsgBox "File Error " & Str$(Err.Number), 48, "Macro Load"
  Exit Sub
End Select

Resume
End Sub

Private Sub PatternText_KeyPress(KeyAscii As Integer)
  If (KeyAscii = 13) Then
    File1.Pattern = PatternText.Text
  End If
End Sub
```

modVBSPL02 (VBSPL02.BAS)—Standard code module

```
Option Explicit
'  Global Declarations . . .
Public hWnd As Integer
Public Request As String * 11          ' Message going to the 400
Public Header As String * 4            ' String to receive formatted header
```

```
Public Record As String * 1024          ' String to receive record from the AS/400
Public Message As String * 80           ' Message coming from the 400
'  Internal global fields . . .
Public ReturnCode As Integer            ' easier to declare once
Public OutqTemp As String * 10
Public SplfTemp As String * 116
Public Temp80 As String * 80
Public Temp132 As String * 132
Public Temp198 As String * 198
Public FileName
Public TempFileName
Public MacroSheetName
Public MacroYN
Public RunYN
Public MacroTemplateName
Public MacroYNW
Public RunYNW
Public MessageResponse
Public FileNameCounter As Integer
Public SpoolRecordLength As String * 3
Public ExcelVersion As String * 1
Public ExcelPath As String
Public WordPath As String
Public SpoolFile As String * 10
Public JobNumber As String * 6
Public JobName As String * 10
Public User As String * 10
Public SpoolNumber As String * 4
Public DownLoadType As Integer
Public AddReplace As Integer

'  Constants . . .
Public Const MODAL = 1
Public Const ARROW = 0
Public Const HOURGLASS = 11
Public Const MESSAGE_1 = "Key in an AS/400 output queue name or click on
        'Browse...' to select from a list."
Public Const MESSAGE_2 = "                        Retrieving a list of outqs.
        This will take a few seconds..."
Public Const MESSAGE_3 = "                     Retrieving a list of spool files.
      This will take a few seconds..."
Public Const MESSAGE_4 = "                          Checking AS/400 outq...                              "
Public Const MESSAGE_5 = "                      Retrieving spool file records...
      This will take a few seconds..."
Public Const MESSAGE_6 = "      Writing retrieved spool file records to file     "
```

```
Public Const MESSAGE_7 = "Load successful to file "
Public Const MESSAGE_8 = " Loading to Excel spreadsheet..."
Public Const MESSAGE_9 = " Available "
Public Const MESSAGE_10 = "Key in an AS/400 output queue name or click on a
        selection from the list..."
Public Const MESSAGE_11 = "You may load and (optionally) run an Excel macro
        sheet with the spool file. Select or key a macro sheet and (optionally)
        key a macro name.  See online Help for more information."
Public Const MESSAGE_12 = "You may preview the contents of the spool file (the
        first few pages only.)  Note that blank lines are removed."
Public Const MESSAGE_13 = "You may load and (optionally) run an MS Word macro
        over your spool file.  Select or key a template name and (optionally)
        key a macro name to (optionally) run.  See online Help for more information."

'   Help declarations.
'  Commands to pass WinHelp()
Public Const HELP_CONTEXT = &H1        ' Display topic identified by number in Data
Public Const HELP_QUIT = &H2           ' Terminate help
Public Const HELP_INDEX = &H3          ' Display index
Public Const HELP_HELPONHELP = &H4     ' Display help on using help
Public Const HELP_SETINDEX = &H5       ' Set an alternate Index for help file with more
                                        ' than one index
Public Const HELP_KEY = &H101          ' Display topic for keyword in Data
Public Const HELP_MULTIKEY = &H201     ' Lookup keyword in alternate table and display topic
' WinHelp API Declare . . .
Declare Function WinHelp Lib "User" (ByVal hWnd As Integer,_
        ByVal lpHelpFile As String, ByVal wCommand As Integer, _
        dwData As Any) As Integer

Type MULTIKEYHELP
    mkSize As Integer
    mkKeylist As String * 1
    szKeyphrase As String * 253
End Type

Function Allocate(ProgramName As String) As Integer
' This function allocates a conversation with the AS/400 program

' The conversation has the following characteristics:
'   Mapped conversation
'   1024 byte router buffer (minimum required)
'   Sync Level - none
'   No pip data
' If successful, the conversation ID is returned
```

```
    Dim PipData As String

    PipData = Chr$(0)    ' This routine sends no pip data
    ReturnCode = EHNAPPC_Allocate _
      (hWnd, 1024, EHNAPPC_MAPPED, EHNAPPC_SYNCLEVELNONE, SysName, ProgramName, 0, PipData,
      ConvID)
    If ReturnCode <> 0 Then      ' Allocate failed . . .
      MsgBox ("Allocate failed with return code " & Str$(ReturnCode))
      Call Deallocate
    End If

    Allocate = ReturnCode
End Function

Sub AsciiToEbcdic(StrName As String)
' This routine converts a String from ASCII to EBCDIC

Dim tlen As Integer
Dim Target As String

  Target = Space$(Len(StrName))        ' Initialize target string
  tlen = Len(Target)                   ' Set target string length
    ReturnCode = EHNDT_ASCIIToEBCDIC(hWnd, StrName, Target, Len(StrName), tlen)
    StrName = Left$(Target, tlen)      ' Move target to original string
End Sub

Sub Deallocate()
' This subroutine deallocates the active conversation
' specified in the ConvID Public variable

  On Error GoTo ExitErrorHandler
  If ConvID <> 0 Then
    ReturnCode = EHNAPPC_Deallocate(hWnd, ConvID, EHNAPPC_DEALLOCATESYNCLEVEL)
  End If

  ' Cleanup...
  Kill ExcelPath & "DLOAD???.TXT"
  Kill WordPath & "DLOAD???.TXT"

  End

ExitErrorHandler:

  Resume Next
```

```
End Sub

Sub EbcdicToAscii(StrName As String)
' This routine converts a String from EBCDIC to ASCII

Dim tlen As Integer
Dim Target As String

  Target = Space$(Len(StrName))       ' Initialize target string
  tlen = Len(Target)                  ' Set target string length
  ReturnCode = EHNDT_EBCDICToASCII(hWnd, StrName, Target, Len(StrName), tlen)
    StrName = Left$(Target, tlen)      ' Move target to original string
End Sub

Sub Form1Enter()

  Screen.MousePointer = HOURGLASS
  If Trim$(Form1.OutqText) > "" Then
    Form1.OutqText = UCase(Form1.OutqText)
    ' Check existance of outq on the 400...
    Form1.MessageText.Text = MESSAGE_4
    OutqTemp = Form1.OutqText
    Request = OutqTemp & "Q"
    ' Combined - send request to 400 and receive reply in field "Record". . .
    SendReceive (Request)
    Message = Mid$(Record, 945, 80)
    Screen.MousePointer = ARROW
    If Mid$(Message, 1, 4) = "(OK)" Then
      Form1.MessageText.Text = MESSAGE_3
      ' Outq found - request list of spool files from 400 . . .
      Call GetSpoolFiles
      ' Reset spool file list box . . .
      SplfForm.SplfList.ListIndex = 0
      Screen.MousePointer = ARROW
      SplfForm.Caption = "AS/400 Spool Files - " & Form1.OutqText
      SplfForm.MessageText = ""
      SplfForm.Show MODAL
    Else
      Form1.OutqText.SetFocus
      MsgBox "AS/400 outq name not found.", 48, "AS/400 Outq Selection..."
    End If
  Else
    Form1.OutqText.SetFocus
    MsgBox "An AS/400 outq name must be specified.", _
      48, "AS/400 Outq Selection..."
```

```
  End If

  Screen.MousePointer = ARROW
End Sub

Sub GetDefSys(DefSys$)
' This routine gets the default system into variable DefSys$
Dim DefSys As String

  DefSys = Space$(10)
  ReturnCode = EHNAPPC_GetDefaultSystem(hWnd, DefSys)
End Sub
Sub GetOutqs()

Dim X As Integer

  Screen.MousePointer = HOURGLASS
  Form1.MessageText.Text = MESSAGE_2
  ' initialize the list box and text box . . .
  OutqForm.OutqList.Clear
  OutqForm.OutqText = ""
  ' request going to the 400 - all authorized outq's . . .
  Request = "*ALL       Q"
  ' combined request send and response receive . . .
  SendReceive (Request)
  ' last 80 bytes transmitted is a message from the 400 . . .
  Message = Mid$(Record, 945, 80)

  ' get up to 90 outq names per transmission . .
  ' load names into listbox for user selection . . .
  Do
    For X = 1 To 90
      OutqTemp = Mid$(Record, ((X * 10) - 9), 10)
      If OutqTemp = "          " Then
        Exit For
      End If
      OutqForm.OutqList.AddItem OutqTemp
    Next X
    ' No more - exit . . .
    If Mid$(Message, 1, 5) = "(END)" Then
      Exit Do
    End If

    If Mid$(Message, 1, 9) = "(INVALID)" Then
      MsgBox "Access denied. Possible authority problem.", _
```

```
        48, "AS400 Report Download"
      Screen.MousePointer = ARROW
      Exit Sub
    End If

    SendReceive (Request)
    Message = Mid$(Record, 945, 80)
  ' Get another transmission - there's more . . .
  Loop

  Form1.MessageText.Text = MESSAGE_10
  Screen.MousePointer = ARROW
  OutqForm.Show MODAL
  Form1.MessageText.Text = MESSAGE_1
End Sub

Sub GetSpoolFiles()
  Dim X As Integer
  Dim SplfDisplay As String

  Screen.MousePointer = HOURGLASS
  ' Initialize list box . . .
  SplfForm.SplfList.Clear
  ' format request text to the 400 . . .
  Request = OutqTemp & "F"
  ' send request and receive reply . . .
  SendReceive (Request)
  ' substring "Record" from the 400 into listbox SplfList
  Do
    For X = 1 To 8
      SplfTemp = Mid$(Record, ((X * 116) - 115), 116)

      ' no more - exit do . . .
      If Mid$(SplfTemp, 2, 10) = "           " Then
        Exit For
      End If

      SplfDisplay = Mid$(SplfTemp, 2, 10) & " "                  'File name
      SplfDisplay = SplfDisplay & Mid$(SplfTemp, 13, 10) & " "   'User
      SplfDisplay = SplfDisplay & Mid$(SplfTemp, 24, 10) & " "   'User data
      SplfDisplay = SplfDisplay & Mid$(SplfTemp, 41, 6) & "    " 'Pages
      SplfDisplay = SplfDisplay & Mid$(SplfTemp, 55, 6)          'Form
      SplfDisplay = SplfDisplay & Mid$(SplfTemp, 74, 3) & "  "   'Seq. number
      SplfDisplay = SplfDisplay & Mid$(SplfTemp, 82, 10) & " "   'Job
      SplfDisplay = SplfDisplay & Mid$(SplfTemp, 100, 8) & " "   'Date
```

```
      SplfDisplay = SplfDisplay & Mid$(SplfTemp, 109, 8) & " "  'Time
      ' add the formatted string to the list box . . .
      SplfForm.SplfList.AddItem SplfDisplay
    Next X

    If Mid$(Message, 1, 5) = "(END)" Then
      Exit Do
    End If

    If Mid$(Message, 1, 9) = "(INVALID)" Then
      MsgBox "No spool files are available. Outq may be empty or possible
        authority problem.", 48, "AS400 Report Download"
      Screen.MousePointer = ARROW
      Exit Sub
    End If

    SendReceive (Request)
  Loop

  Screen.MousePointer = ARROW
End Sub

Sub Initialize()

Dim InitStep As String
Dim DefSysName As String

  On Error GoTo InitErrorHandler
  ConvID = 0                     ' Initialize conversation ID  (Public variable)
  DownLoadType = 0

  If EHNAPPC_IsRouterLoaded(hWnd) Then          ' Ensure Router is loaded
    Call GetDefSys(DefSysName)
    SysName = DefSysName
  Else                                          ' If Router not loaded
    MsgBox "Client Access/PCS router is not loaded.", _
      16, "AS/400 Spool File Download"
    Call ProcHelp
    End
  End If

  ' Allocate a conversation with the AS/400
  ReturnCode = Allocate("VBSPLF1C.VBSPL02")

  Form1.MessageText.Text = MESSAGE_1
```

```
SplfForm.MessageText.Text = MESSAGE_12
' Get directory for Excel . . .
'  (an attempt is made to open Excel's executable
'  in each of two directories - this can also be done through the
'  Windows API)
InitStep = "ExcelPath1"
Open "C:\MSOFFICE\EXCEL\EXCEL.EXE" For Input As #1
Close #1
If InitStep <> "" Then
  LoadForm.Dir1.Path = "C:\MSOFFICE\EXCEL"
  ExcelPath = "C:\MSOFFICE\EXCEL\"
Else
  InitStep = "ExcelPath2"
  Open "C:\EXCEL\EXCEL.EXE" For Input As #1
  Close #1
  If InitStep <> "" Then
    LoadForm.Dir1.Path = "C:\EXCEL"
    ExcelPath = "C:\EXCEL\"
  End If
End If

' Get version of Excel or disable options buttons if no Excel...
If ExcelPath <> "" Then
  InitStep = "ExcelVersion"
  Open ExcelPath & "EXCEL.EXE" For Input As #1
  If InitStep <> "" Then
    ' Length of file - Excel version 4
    If LOF(1) < 2767000 Then
      ExcelVersion = "4"
      SplfForm.OptionButton(2).Caption = "Load to Excel 4.0"
      SplfForm.OptionButton(3).Caption = "Load to Excel 4.0 plus macro"
    ' Length of file - Excel version 5
    ElseIf LOF(1) = 4185600 Then
      ExcelVersion = "5"
      SplfForm.OptionButton(2).Caption = "Load to Excel 5.0"
      SplfForm.OptionButton(3).Caption = "Load to Excel 5.0 plus macro"
    End If
  End If
  Close #1
Else
  SplfForm.OptionButton(2).Enabled = False
  SplfForm.OptionButton(3).Enabled = False
End If

' Get directory for MS Word . . .
```

```
   InitStep = "WordPath1"
   Open "C:\MSOFFICE\WINWORD\WINWORD.EXE" For Input As #1
   Close #1
   If InitStep <> "" Then
     WordForm.Dir1.Path = "C:\MSOFFICE\WINWORD"
     WordPath = "C:\MSOFFICE\WINWORD\"
     SplfForm.OptionButton(4).Caption = "Load to MS Word"
     SplfForm.OptionButton(5).Caption = "Load to MS Word plus macro"
   Else
     WordPath = ""
     SplfForm.OptionButton(4).Enabled = False
     SplfForm.OptionButton(5).Enabled = False
   End If

   Exit Sub

InitErrorHandler:
   Screen.MousePointer = ARROW
   Select Case Err.Number
   Case 53, 68, 76     ' file not found, device unavailable, invalid path . . .
     InitStep = ""
     Resume Next
   Case Else
     MsgBox "Initialize - Error " & Str$(Err.Number) & " - " & _
       Err.Description, 48, "AS400 Report Download"
     Call Deallocate
   End Select
   Resume

End Sub

Sub MakeUpFileName()

  FileNameCounter = FileNameCounter + 1
  TempFileName = "DLOAD" & Format$(FileNameCounter, "000") & ".TXT"
End Sub

Sub ProcExcel()
  ' this proc downloads a file and loads it into an Excel spreadsheet . . .
  On Error GoTo ErrorHandler
  Dim X As Integer
  Dim MacroExecute As String
  Dim DoneOnce As Integer

  Screen.MousePointer = HOURGLASS
```

```
Call MakeUpFileName
SplfForm.MessageText = "Writing records to temporary file " _
  & TempFileName & "..."

Open ExcelPath & TempFileName For Output As #2
' send request to 400 for the spool file
'   - a pointer to the spool file entry . . .
Request = Format$(SplfForm.SplfList.ListIndex, "0000000000") & "T"
SendReceive (Request)
' the length of the spool records is sent in the message area . . .
SpoolRecordLength = Mid$(Message, 78, 3)
' substring the spool file records according to the record size
'   and write them to a temporary PC text file . . .
Do
  If SpoolRecordLength = " 80" Then
    For X = 1 To 11
      Temp80 = Mid$(Record, ((X * 80) - 79), 80)
      If Trim$(Temp80) <> "" Then
        Print #2, Temp80
        RecordCount = RecordCount + 1
        SplfForm.RecordText = RecordCount
      End If
    Next X
  End If

  If SpoolRecordLength = "132" Then
    For X = 1 To 7
      Temp132 = Mid$(Record, ((X * 132) - 131), 132)
      If Trim$(Temp132) <> "" Then
        Print #2, Temp132
        RecordCount = RecordCount + 1
        SplfForm.RecordText = RecordCount
      End If
    Next X
  End If

  If SpoolRecordLength = "198" Then
    For X = 1 To 4
      Temp198 = Mid$(Record, ((X * 198) - 197), 198)
      If Trim$(Temp198) <> "" Then
        Print #2, Temp198
        RecordCount = RecordCount + 1
        SplfForm.RecordText = RecordCount
      End If
    Next X
```

```
    End If

    If Mid$(Message, 1, 5) = "(END)" Then
      Exit Do
    End If
    If Mid$(Message, 1, 9) = "(INVALID)" Then
      MsgBox "Access denied.  Possible authority problem.", _
         48, "AS400 Report Download"
      Screen.MousePointer = ARROW
      Exit Sub
    End If
    ' there's more - get another transmission . . .
    SendReceive (Request)
  Loop

  Close #2

  ' move the records from the temp PC file to Excel . . .
  SplfForm.MessageText = "Loading to Excel..."
  ' establish DDE link to Excel . . .
  If ExcelVersion = "4" Then
    SplfForm.LinkText.LinkTopic = "Excel|Sheet1"
  Else
    SplfForm.LinkText.LinkTopic = "Excel|System"
  End If
    SplfForm.LinkText.LinkItem = "R1C1"
  SplfForm.LinkText.LinkMode = 2
  ' load a macro sheet . . .
  If MacroSheetName <> "" And MacroYN <> "" Then
    SplfForm.LinkText.LinkExecute "[OPEN(""" & MacroSheetName & """)]"
  End If
  ' send instruction to Excel to open the text file . . .
  SplfForm.LinkText.LinkExecute "[OPEN(""" & ExcelPath & TempFileName & """)]"
  ' send instruction to Excel to run the specified macro . . .
  If RunYN <> "" Then
    MacroExecute = "[RUN(""" & LoadForm.File1.FileName & "!" & _
        LoadForm.MacroNameText & """" & ",FALSE)]"
    SplfForm.LinkText.LinkExecute MacroExecute
  End If
  ' drop link . . .
  SplfForm.LinkText.LinkMode = 0
  ' set flag so no attempt to start Excel is made, once opened . . .
  DoneOnce = 0
  ' reset . . .
  MacroYN = ""
```

```
  LoadForm.MacroCheckBox.Value = 0
  RunYN = ""
  LoadForm.MacroFrame.Visible = False
  Screen.MousePointer = ARROW
  SplfForm.MessageText = "Load to Excel complete under file name " _
    & TempFileName & ".  Click on Excel..."
  Exit Sub

ErrorHandler:
  Screen.MousePointer = ARROW
  Select Case Err.Number
  Case 70
    Call MakeUpFileName
  Case 282  ' link failure due to application not loaded - load it . . .
    If ExcelVersion = "4" Then
      If DoneOnce < 1 Then
        ReturnCode = Shell(ExcelPath & "EXCEL.EXE")
        DoneOnce = DoneOnce + 1
      Else
        MsgBox "Cannot start Excel 4.0 - Error " & _
          Str$(Err.Number), 48, "AS400 Report Download"
      End If
    Else
      If DoneOnce < 1 Then
        SplfForm.MessageText = "Starting Excel . ."
        ReturnCode = Shell(ExcelPath & "EXCEL.EXE ", 2)
        DoneOnce = DoneOnce + 1
      Else
        Screen.MousePointer = ARROW
        MsgBox "Waiting for Excel to finish loading...  (" & _
          Str$(Err.Number) & ")", 64, "AS400 Report Download"
        Screen.MousePointer = HOURGLASS
        Resume
      End If
    End If
  Case 285
    Resume Next
  Case 286
    If LoadForm.MacroNameText <> "" Then
      SplfForm.MessageText = _
        "Link error to Excel.  May be caused by the macro..."
    Else
      SplfForm.MessageText = "Link error to Excel.  (Error 286 - time out.)"
    End If
    SplfForm.LinkText.LinkMode = 0
```

```
    Exit Sub
  Case Else
    MsgBox "Error" & Str$(Err.Number), 48, "AS400 Report Download"
  End Select
  Resume
End Sub

Sub ProcHelp()
  ReturnCode = WinHelp(hWnd, "vbspl02.Hlp", HELP_INDEX, CLng(0))
End Sub

Sub ProcPreview()
  ' this proc uploads the beginning of a spool file for preview . . .
  Screen.MousePointer = HOURGLASS
  ViewForm.EntryLabel.Caption = SplfForm.SplfList
  ' format the request to the 400 - send RRN of the requested file . . .
  Request = Format$(SplfForm.SplfList.ListIndex, "0000000000") & "P"
  ' send request and get response . . .
  SendReceive (Request)
  ' the length of the spool file is went in the message area . . .
  SpoolRecordLength = Mid$(Message, 78, 3)

  If SpoolRecordLength = " 80" Then
    ViewForm.ViewList.FontName = "Courier New"
    ViewForm.ViewList.FontSize = 8.25
  Else
    ViewForm.ViewList.FontName = "Terminal"
    ViewForm.ViewList.FontSize = 4.5
  End If
  ' initialize the list box that will hold the spool file . . .
  ViewForm.ViewList.FontBold = False
  ViewForm.ViewList.Clear
  ' extract records from the transmission's data area . . .
  Do
    If SpoolRecordLength = " 80" Then
      For X = 1 To 11
        Temp80 = Mid$(Record, ((X * 80) - 79), 80)
        If Trim$(Temp80) <> "" Then
          ViewForm.ViewList.AddItem Temp80
          RecordCount = RecordCount + 1
          SplfForm.RecordText = RecordCount
        End If
      Next X
    End If
```

```
      If SpoolRecordLength = "132" Then
        For X = 1 To 7
          Temp132 = Mid$(Record, ((X * 132) - 131), 132)
          If Trim$(Temp132) <> "" Then
            ViewForm.ViewList.AddItem Temp132
            RecordCount = RecordCount + 1
            SplfForm.RecordText = RecordCount
          End If
        Next X
      End If

      If SpoolRecordLength = "198" Then
        For X = 1 To 4
          Temp198 = Mid$(Record, ((X * 198) - 197), 198)
          If Trim$(Temp198) <> "" Then
            ViewForm.ViewList.AddItem Temp132
            RecordCount = RecordCount + 1
            SplfForm.RecordText = RecordCount
          End If
        Next X
      End If
      ' no more records - exit . . .
      If Mid$(Message, 1, 5) = "(END)" Then
        Exit Do
      End If
      If Mid$(Message, 1, 9) = "(INVALID)" Then
        MsgBox _
          "No spool files available. Outq may be empty or possible authority problem.", _
          48, "AS400 Report Download"
        Screen.MousePointer = ARROW
        Exit Sub
      End If

      SendReceive (Request)
    Loop
    Screen.MousePointer = ARROW
    ViewForm.ViewList.ListIndex = -1
    ViewForm.Show MODAL
End Sub

Sub ProcTxt()
' this proc downloads a spool file to a PC text file . . .
  Screen.MousePointer = HOURGLASS
  SplfForm.MessageText = MESSAGE_6 & FileName
  On Error GoTo FileError
```

```
' open the PC file specified by the user for either "Add" or "Replace"
  If AddReplace = 1 Then
  Open FileName For Append As #1
Else
  Open FileName For Output As #1
End If
' format the request to the 400 and send/receive . . .
Request = Format$(SplfForm.SplfList.ListIndex, "0000000000") & "T"
SendReceive (Request)
' the spool file record length is sent in the message area . . .
SpoolRecordLength = Mid$(Message, 78, 3)
' substring the records out of the data transport transmitted . . .
Do
  ' the transmitted record can hold 11 80-byte records . . .
  If SpoolRecordLength = " 80" Then
    For X = 1 To 11
      Temp80 = Mid$(Record, ((X * 80) - 79), 80)
      If Trim$(Temp80) <> "" Then
        Print #1, Temp80
        RecordCount = RecordCount + 1
        SplfForm.RecordText = RecordCount
      End If
    Next X
  End If
'  the transmitted record can hold 7 132-byte records . . .
  If SpoolRecordLength = "132" Then
    For X = 1 To 7
      Temp132 = Mid$(Record, ((X * 132) - 131), 132)
      If Trim$(Temp132) <> "" Then
        Print #1, Temp132
        RecordCount = RecordCount + 1
        SplfForm.RecordText = RecordCount
      End If
    Next X
  End If
  '  the transmitted record can hold 4 198-byte records . . .)
  If SpoolRecordLength = "198" Then
    For X = 1 To 4
      Temp198 = Mid$(Record, ((X * 198) - 197), 198)
      If Trim$(Temp198) <> "" Then
        Print #1, Temp198
        RecordCount = RecordCount + 1
        SplfForm.RecordText = RecordCount
      End If
    Next X
```

```
    End If
    ' no more records - exit
    If Mid$(Message, 1, 5) = "(END)" Then
      Exit Do
    End If
    If Mid$(Message, 1, 9) = "(INVALID)" Then
      MsgBox "Access denied.  Possible authority problem.", 48, _
        "AS400 Report Download"
      Screen.MousePointer = ARROW
      Exit Sub
    End If
    ' get another transmission . . .
    SendReceive (Request)
  Loop
  Screen.MousePointer = ARROW
  Close #1
  SplfForm.MessageText = MESSAGE_7 & FileName
  Exit Sub
FileError:
  MsgBox "PC Level File Error" & Str$(Err.Number), _
    48, "AS400 Report Download"
End Sub

Sub ProcWord()
' this proc downloads a spool file to a MS Word document . . .
  On Error GoTo WordErrorHandler
  Dim MacroExecute As String
  Dim DoneOnce As Integer

  Screen.MousePointer = HOURGLASS
  Call MakeUpFileName
  SplfForm.MessageText = "Writing records to temporary file " _
    & TempFileName & "..."
  ' temporary PC file to write records to . . .
  Open WordPath & TempFileName For Output As #2
  ' send request to the 400 for spool file records . . .
  Request = Format$(SplfForm.SplfList.ListIndex, "0000000000") & "T"
  SendReceive (Request)
  ' the spool file record length is sent in the message area . . .
  SpoolRecordLength = Mid$(Message, 78, 3)

  Do
    If SpoolRecordLength = " 80" Then
      For X = 1 To 11
        Temp80 = Mid$(Record, ((X * 80) - 79), 80)
```

```
            If Temp80 <> "
" Then
              ' write records to the temp PC file . . .
              Print #2, Temp80
              RecordCount = RecordCount + 1
              SplfForm.RecordText = RecordCount
            End If
          Next X
        End If

        If SpoolRecordLength = "132" Then
          For X = 1 To 7
            Temp132 = Mid$(Record, ((X * 132) - 131), 132)
            If Temp132 <> "
" Then
              Print #2, Temp132
              RecordCount = RecordCount + 1
              SplfForm.RecordText = RecordCount
            End If
          Next X
        End If

        If SpoolRecordLength = "198" Then
          For X = 1 To 4
            Temp198 = Mid$(Record, ((X * 198) - 197), 198)
            If Temp198 <> "
" Then
              Print #2, Temp198
              RecordCount = RecordCount + 1
              SplfForm.RecordText = RecordCount
            End If
          Next X
        End If

        If Mid$(Message, 1, 5) = "(END)" Then
          Exit Do
        End If
        If Mid$(Message, 1, 9) = "(INVALID)" Then
          MsgBox "Access denied.  Possible authority problem.", 48, "AS400 Report Download"
          Screen.MousePointer = ARROW
          Exit Sub
        End If

        SendReceive (Request)
        Loop

        Close #2
```

```
    ' establish link to MS Word . . .
    SplfForm.MessageText = "Loading to MS Word..."
    SplfForm.LinkText.LinkTopic = "Winword|System"
    SplfForm.LinkText.LinkItem = ""
    SplfForm.LinkText.LinkMode = 2
    ' if macro is specfied, send instruction to Word to load the template
    If MacroTemplateName <> "" And MacroYNW <> "" Then
      SplfForm.LinkText.LinkExecute _
        "[FileOpen .Name = """ & MacroTemplateName & """]"
    End If
    ' Load the copied PC file into the Word document . . .
    SplfForm.LinkText.LinkExecute _
      "[FileOpen .Name = """ & WordPath & TempFileName & """]"
    ' send instruction to Word to run the macro if specified . . .
    If RunYNW <> "" Then
      MacroExecute = "[ToolsMacro .Name = """ & WordForm.MacroNameText.Text _
        & """, .Run, .Show = 0, .Description = """", .NewName = """"]"
      SplfForm.LinkText.LinkExecute MacroExecute
    End If
  ' drop link to Word . . .
  SplfForm.LinkText.LinkMode = 0
  ' reset . . .
  DoneOnce = 0
  MacroYNW = ""
  WordForm.MacroCheckBox.Value = 0
  RunYNW = ""
  WordForm.MacroFrame.Visible = False
  Screen.MousePointer = ARROW
  SplfForm.MessageText = "Load to Word complete under file name " &
 TempFileName & ".  Click on Word..."

  Exit Sub

WordErrorHandler:
  Screen.MousePointer = ARROW
  Select Case Err.Number
  Case 70
    Call MakeUpFileName
  Case 282    ' Word not started - start with "Shell" command . . .
    If DoneOnce < 1 Then
      SplfForm.MessageText = "Starting MS Word . ."
      ReturnCode = Shell(WordPath & "WINWORD.EXE")
      DoneOnce = DoneOnce + 1
    Else
      Screen.MousePointer = ARROW
```

```
      MsgBox "Waiting for Word to finish loading...  (" _
        & Str$(Err.Number) & ")", 64, "AS400 Report Download"
      Screen.MousePointer = HOURGLASS
      Resume
    End If
  Case 286
    SplfForm.MessageText = "Link error to MS Word. (Error 286 - time out.)"
    SplfForm.LinkText.LinkMode = 0
    Exit Sub
  Case Else
    MsgBox "Error - " & Str$(Err.Number) & _
      " - " & Err.Description, 48, "AS400 Report Download"
  End Select
  Resume
End Sub

Function RecvW(Rlen As Integer, buff As String) As Integer
' This function Receives data from the Router for the length specified
' and returns it in the string specified.
Dim IntBuff As String
Dim WhatRec As Integer
Dim rts As Integer
Dim ActLen As Integer

  IntBuff = Space$(Rlen)              ' Set up an intermediate
                                      '  buffer to receive data
  ReturnCode = EHNAPPC_ReceiveAndWait(hWnd, ConvID, _
    EHNAPPC_BUFFER, Rlen, IntBuff, WhatRec, rts, ActLen)
  If ReturnCode <> 0 Then
    MsgBox ("Receive failed with return code " & Str$(ReturnCode))
    Call Deallocate
  Else
    buff = Left$(IntBuff, ActLen)     ' Move received data to output string
    Rlen = ActLen                     ' Return actual length
  End If
  ' set value of function . . .
  RecvW = ReturnCode
End Function

Function Send(Sdata As String) As Integer
' This function sends the specified data to the AS/400
' It does not wait for a reply
' The data sent will be preceeded by the proper GDS header (11ID)

Dim GDSHdr As String * 4      ' GDS Header
```

```
Dim FData As String          ' Formatted Data (header & data)
Dim Slength As Integer       ' Work field for getting length into proper format
Dim Work As Integer          ' Work field for getting length into proper format
Dim rqs As Integer           ' Request received flag
Dim Dlen As String           ' Request length

  Slength = Len(Sdata) + 4   ' allow for header length
  Work = Slength / 256       ' get multiples of 256 for hex
  'multiples of 256 plus extra
  Dlen = Chr$(Work) & Chr$(Slength - (Work * 256))
  ' Format of GDS header is llID where ID=x'12FF'
  GDSHdr = Dlen & Chr$(&H12) & Chr$(&HFF)
  FData = GDSHdr & Sdata      ' Put together formatted data
  ReturnCode = EHNAPPC_SendData(hWnd, ConvID, Len(FData), FData, rqs)
  If ReturnCode <> 0 Then
    MsgBox ("Send failed with Return code " & Str$(ReturnCode))
    Call Deallocate
  End If
  Send = ReturnCode           ' Return return code
End Function

Sub SendReceive(Request As String)
' this proc sends the requests to the 400 and gets the response . . .
Dim GetSend As String

  Call AsciiToEbcdic(Request)                ' Convert data to EBCDIC
  If Send(Request) = 0 Then                  ' Send data to the AS/400
    If RecvW(4, Header) = 0 Then            ' Receive 4 byte header
      If RecvW(1024, Record) = 0 Then      ' Receive 1024 byte record
        Call EbcdicToAscii(Record)        ' Convert record to ASCII
        ReturnCode = RecvW(0, GetSend) ' Do one more receive to get change
                                        ' direction indicator(WhatReceived = Send)
      End If
    End If
  End If
  ' message area is last 80 bytes of transmission . . .
  Message = Mid$(Record, 945, 80)
End Sub
```

AS/400 Source Code

Physical Files

PDDATA:

```
A* WORK FILE FOR SPOOL FILE DOWNLOAD
A*                                            CFP
A*****************************************************
A           R PDDATA@                    TEXT('DOWNLOAD WORK FILE')
A             PDSKIP          3          TEXT('SKIP TO')
A             PDSPAC          1          TEXT('SPACE')
A             PDF001          1          TEXT('FILLER')
A             PDLINE        198          TEXT('PRINT LINE')
```

PQLIST

```
A* WORK FILE FOR SPOOL FILE TO PC DOWNLOAD - OUTQS
A*        3/21/94        -          CFP
A*****************************************************
A           R PQLIST@                    TEXT('WORK FILE')
A             PQF001          1          TEXT('FILLER')
A             PQOUTQ         10          TEXT('OUTPUT QUEUE NAME')
A             PQF002          3          TEXT('FILLER')
A             PQLIB          10          TEXT('LIBRARY')
A             PQF003          3          TEXT('FILLER')
A             PQFILS          5          TEXT('SPOOL FILES')
A             PQF004          3          TEXT('FILLER')
A             PQWRTR         10          TEXT('WRITER NAME')
A             PQF005          4          TEXT('FILLER')
A             PQSTAT          3          TEXT('STATUS')
A           K PQOUTQ
A           K PQLIB
```

PTLIST

```
A* WORK FILE FOR SPOOL FILE to PC DOWNLOAD
A*                              -          CFP
A*****************************************************
A           R PTLIST@                    TEXT('WORK FILE')
A             PTF001          1          TEXT('FILLER')
```

```
     A            PTSPLF         10          TEXT('SPOOL FILE NAME')
     A            PTF002          1          TEXT('FILLER')
     A            PTUSER         10          TEXT('USER')
     A            PTF003          1          TEXT('FILLER')
     A            PTDATA         10          TEXT('USER DATA')
     A            PTF004          2          TEXT('FILLER')
     A            PTSTAT          3          TEXT('STATUS')
     A            PTPAGE          8          TEXT('NUMBER OF PAGES')
     A            PTF005          3          TEXT('FILLER')
     A            PTCOPY          3          TEXT('COPIES')
     A            PTF006          2          TEXT('FILLER')
     A            PTFORM         10          TEXT('FORMS')
     A            PTF007          2          TEXT('FILLER')
     A            PTPRTY          1          TEXT('PRIORITY')
     A            PTF008          5          TEXT('FILLER')
     A            PTSPLN          4          TEXT('SPOOL FILE SEQ.#')
     A            PTF009          5          TEXT('FILLER')
     A            PTNAME         10          TEXT('JOB NAME')
     A            PTF010          1          TEXT('FILLER')
     A            PTNUMB          6          TEXT('JOB NUMBER')
     A            PTF011          1          TEXT('FILLER')
     A            PTDATE          8          TEXT('JOB DATE')
     A            PTF012          1          TEXT('FILLER')
     A            PTTIME          8          TEXT('JOB TIME')
     A            PTF013         17          TEXT('FILLER')
```

ICF File:

VBSPLF1

```
     A                                       INDARA
     A                                       RCVFAIL(66)
     A          R RQRECORD
     A                                       RCVDETACH(82)
     A            RQDATA        10A
     A            RQTYPE         1A
     A*
     A          R ICRECORD
     A            ICDATA       944A
     A            ICERR         80A
```

RPG Program

VBSPLF1R

```
     H
      *- - - - - - - - - - - - - - - - - - - - - - - - - - - - - - - - - - -*
      *                                                                    *
      *   Program - VBSPLF1R                                               *
      *             This program accepts requests from a visual basic *
      *             program for outq list, spool file list and spool   *
      *             file records for download to an Excel spreadsheet.*
      *                                                                    *
      *   Revisions                                                        *
      *     Date      Pgmr      Revision                                   *
      *               cfp       Created                                    *
      *                                                                    *
      *- - - - - - - - - - - - - - - - - - - - - - - - - - - - - - - - - - -*
     FPQLIST  IF  E           K        DISK                      UC
     FPTLIST  IF  E                    DISK                      UC
     FPDDATA  IF  E                    DISK                      UC
     FVBSPLF1 CF  E                    WORKSTN
     F                                              KNUM        1
      *  Data structure to receive information about the ICF file . . .
     F                                              KINFDS FEEDBK
      *  Error handling subroutine for ICF operations . . .
     F                                              KINFSR EXCPTH
      *- - - - - - - - - - - - - - - - - - - - - - - - - - - - - - - - - - -*
     E                    MSG     1  10 80
     E                    Q          90 10
     E                    P80        11 80
     E                    P132        7132
     E                    P198        4198
     E                    F           8116
     E                    #P          4  1
      *- - - - - - - - - - - - - - - - - - - - - - - - - - - - - - - - - - -*
     IICDATA      DS
     I                                        1 900 Q
     I                                        1 880 P80
     I                                        1 924 P132
     I                                        1 792 P198
     I                                        1 928 F
     I@PTREC     E DSPTLIST
     I                                       73  76 #P
     I            DS
```

```
     I                                          1   1 PDF001
     I                                          2 199 PDLINE
     I                                          1 199 #PDALL
     I                                         81 133 #TD132
     I                                        133 199 #TD198
     IFEEDBK      DS
     I                                         38  45 FMTNM
     I                                        401 404 MAJMIN
     I                                        401 402 MAJCOD
     I                                        403 404 MINCOD
      * Constant(s)
     I              '*ALL      '           C          @ALL
      *- - - - - - - - - - - - - - - - - - - - - - - - - - - - - - - - -*
      *  Indicators defined in the ICF file DDS:
      *    66  -  RCVFAIL
      *    82  -  RCVDETACH
      *- - - - - - - - - - - - - - - - - - - - - - - - - - - - - - - - -*
      * Read from the PCS router . . .
     C                     READ RQRECORD                 88
B001 C           *IN82     DOWEQ*OFF
      *
      * Requested data types . . .
B002 C                     SELEC
      * Outqs...
   2 C           RQTYPE    WHEQ 'Q'
   2 C                     EXSR QSUBR
      * Spool files...
   2 C           RQTYPE    WHEQ 'F'
   2 C                     EXSR FSUBR
      * Preview...
   2 C           RQTYPE    WHEQ 'P'
   2 C                     EXSR PSUBR
      * Load into text file . . .
   2 C           RQTYPE    WHEQ 'T'
   2 C                     EXSR TSUBR
      *
E002 C                     ENDSL
      *
   1 C                     EXSR WR
E001 C                     ENDDO                           *in82
      A
     C                     EXSR RELEAS
      *- - - - - - - - - - - - - - - - - - - - - - - - - - - - - - - - -*
     C           WR        BEGSR
      * Write/Read subroutine . . .
```

```
      C                    WRITEICRECORD
      C                    READ RQRECORD                 88
B001  C          *IN82     IFEQ *ON
   1  C                    EXSR RELEAS
E001  C                    ENDIF
      C                    CLEARICDATA
      C                    CLEARICERR
      *
      C                    ENDSR
      *- - - - - - - - - - - - - - - - - - - - - - - - - - - - - - - - - -*
      C          QSUBR     BEGSR
      *- - - - - - - - - - - - - - - - - - - - - - - - - - - - - - - - - -*
      *
B001  C          RQDATA    IFEQ @ALL
   1  C                    CALL 'GETOUTQS'
   1  C                    OPEN PQLIST
   1  C                    CLEARX
   1  C          *LOVAL    SETLLPQLIST@
   1  C                    READ PQLIST@                  20
B002  C          *IN20     DOWEQ*OFF
      * Only include outqs with something in them . . .
B003  C          PQFILS    IFNE '    0'
      * ICF record is full - send & receive . . .
B004  C          X         IFGE 90
   4  C                    CLEARICERR
   4  C                    MOVELMSG,1     ICERR
   4  C                    EXSR WR
   4  C                    CLEARX
E004  C                    ENDIF
      *
   3  C                    ADD  1         X       50
   3  C                    MOVE PQOUTQ    Q,X
E003  C                    ENDIF
      *
   2  C                    READ PQLIST@                  20
E002  C                    ENDDO
      *
   1  C                    CLEARICERR
   1  C                    MOVELMSG,2     ICERR
   1  C                    CLOSEPQLIST
      *
X001  C                    ELSE                             x - rqdata=*ALL
      * Check outq . . .
   1  C                    CALL 'CHEKOUTQ'
   1  C                    PARM           RQDATA
```

```
   1 C                       PARM           RCODE   1
      * Return code of 0 = OK.  return code of 1 = invalid...
   1 C                       CLEARICERR
B002 C             RCODE     IFEQ '0'
   2 C                       MOVELMSG,3     ICERR
X002 C                       ELSE
   2 C                       MOVELMSG,4     ICERR
E002 C                       ENDIF
E001 C                       ENDIF
      *- - - - - - - - - - - - - - - - - - - - - - - - - - - - - - - - - - -*
     C                       ENDSR
      *- - - - - - - - - - - - - - - - - - - - - - - - - - - - - - - - - - -*
     C             FSUBR     BEGSR
      *- - - - - - - - - - - - - - - - - - - - - - - - - - - - - - - - - - -*
      *
     C                       CALL 'GETSPLFS'
     C                       PARM           RQDATA
     C                       OPEN PTLIST
     C                       CLEARX
     C             1         SETLLPTLIST@
     C                       READ PTLIST@                    20
B001 C             *IN20     DOWEQ*OFF
      * ICF record is full - send & receive . . .
B002 C             X         IFGE 8
   2 C                       CLEARICERR
   2 C                       MOVELMSG,1     ICERR
   2 C                       EXSR WR
   2 C                       CLEARX
E002 C                       ENDIF
      *
   1 C                       ADD  1         X       50
   1 C                       MOVEL@PTREC    F,X
   1 C                       READ PTLIST@                    20
E001 C                       ENDDO
      *
     C                       CLEARICERR
     C                       MOVELMSG,2     ICERR
     C                       CLOSEPTLIST
      *
      *- - - - - - - - - - - - - - - - - - - - - - - - - - - - - - - - - - -*
     C                       ENDSR
      *- - - - - - - - - - - - - - - - - - - - - - - - - - - - - - - - - - -*
     C             PSUBR     BEGSR
      *- - - - - - - - - - - - - - - - - - - - - - - - - - - - - - - - - - -*
      *  Preview content of a specific spool file . . .
```

```
      *
      C                     MOVE RQDATA    #QDATA 100
      * Allow for VB indexing ( 0 - n instead of 1 - n...)
      C                     ADD  1         #QDATA
      C                     OPEN PTLIST
      C           #QDATA    CHAINPTLIST@              30
      C                     CLOSEPTLIST
 B001 C           *IN30     IFEQ *OFF
 B002 C           #P.1      IFEQ *BLANK
    2 C                     MOVE '0'       #P.1
 E002 C                     ENDIF
 B002 C           #P.2      IFEQ *BLANK
    2 C                     MOVE '0'       #P.2
 E002 C                     ENDIF
 B002 C           #P.3      IFEQ *BLANK
    2 C                     MOVE '0'       #P.3
 E002 C                     ENDIF
    1 C                     CALL 'GETSPLE'
    1 C                     PARM           PTSPLF
    1 C                     PARM           PTSPLN
    1 C                     PARM           PTNAME
    1 C                     PARM           PTUSER
    1 C                     PARM           PTNUMB
    1 C                     PARM           RCODE
 B002 C           RCODE     IFEQ '0'
    2 C                     CLEARX
    2 C                     CLEAR#COL1
    2 C                     CLEAR#COUNT
    2 C                     MOVE ' 80'     #LEN    3
    2 C                     Z-ADD11        #X      50
    2 C                     OPEN PDDATA
      * See what size - 80, 132 or 198 . . .
    2 C           1         SETLLPDDATA@
    2 C                     READ PDDATA@                20
 B003 C           *IN20     DOWEQ*OFF
 B004 C           PDF001    IFNE *BLANK
    4 C                     MOVE 'Y'       #COL1   1
 E004 C                     ENDIF
 B004 C           #TD132    IFNE *BLANKS
    4 C           #LEN      ANDNE'198'
    4 C                     MOVE '132'     #LEN
    4 C                     Z-ADD7         #X
 E004 C                     ENDIF
 B004 C           #TD198    IFNE *BLANKS
    4 C                     MOVE '198'     #LEN
```

```
   4 C                     Z-ADD4         #X
E004 C                     ENDIF
   3 C                     ADD  1         #COUNT  50
B004 C           #COUNT    IFGT 150
   4 C                     LEAVE
E004 C                     ENDIF
   3 C                     READ PDDATA@                20
E003 C                     ENDDO
   2 C                     CLEAR#COUNT
   2 C           1         SETLLPDDATA@
   2 C                     READ PDDATA@                20
B003 C           *IN20     DOWEQ*OFF
     * ICF record is full - send & receive . . .
B004 C           X         IFGE #X
   4 C                     CLEARICERR
   4 C                     MOVELMSG,1     ICERR
   4 C                     MOVE #LEN      ICERR
   4 C                     EXSR WR
   4 C                     CLEARX
E004 C                     ENDIF
     *
B004 C           #LEN      IFEQ ' 80'
B005 C           #COL1     IFEQ 'Y'
   5 C                     MOVEL#PDALL    #PD80
X005 C                     ELSE
   5 C                     MOVELPDLINE    #PD80
E005 C                     ENDIF
   4 C                     ADD  1         X
   4 C                     MOVE #PD80     P80,X
E004 C                     ENDIF
     *
B004 C           #LEN      IFEQ '132'
B005 C           #COL1     IFEQ 'Y'
   5 C                     MOVEL#PDALL    #PD132
X005 C                     ELSE
   5 C                     MOVELPDLINE    #PD132132
E005 C                     ENDIF
   4 C                     ADD  1         X
   4 C                     MOVE #PD132    P132,X
E004 C                     ENDIF
     *
B004 C           #LEN      IFEQ '198'
B005 C           #COL1     IFEQ 'Y'
   5 C                     MOVEL#PDALL    #PD198
X005 C                     ELSE
```

```
   5 C                        MOVELPDLINE    #PD198198
E005 C                        ENDIF
   4 C                        ADD  1         X
   4 C                        MOVE #PD198    P198,X
E004 C                        ENDIF
     *
   3 C                        ADD  1         #COUNT  50
B004 C              #COUNT    IFGT 150
   4 C                        LEAVE
E004 C                        ENDIF
     *
   3 C                        READ PDDATA@                 20
E003 C                        ENDDO
     *
   2 C                        CLEARICERR
   2 C                        MOVELMSG,2     ICERR
   2 C                        MOVE #LEN      ICERR
   2 C                        CLOSEPDDATA
X002 C                        ELSE
   2 C                        MOVE MSG,4     ICERR
E002 C                        ENDIF
E001 C                        ENDIF
     *- - - - - - - - - - - - - - - - - - - - - - - - - - - - - - - - - - -*
     C                        ENDSR
     *- - - - - - - - - - - - - - - - - - - - - - - - - - - - - - - - - - -*
     C              TSUBR     BEGSR
     *- - - - - - - - - - - - - - - - - - - - - - - - - - - - - - - - - - -*
     *  Load spool file to a text file . . .
     *
     C                        MOVE RQDATA    #QDATA
     * Allow for VB indexing ( 0 - n instead of 1 - n...)
     C                        ADD  1         #QDATA
     C                        OPEN PTLIST
     C              #QDATA    CHAINPTLIST@             30
     C                        CLOSEPTLIST
B001 C              *IN30     IFEQ *OFF
B002 C              #P,1      IFEQ *BLANK
   2 C                        MOVE '0'       #P,1
E002 C                        ENDIF
B002 C              #P,2      IFEQ *BLANK
   2 C                        MOVE '0'       #P,2
E002 C                        ENDIF
B002 C              #P,3      IFEQ *BLANK
   2 C                        MOVE '0'       #P,3
E002 C                        ENDIF
```

```
   1 C                     CALL 'GETSPLE'
   1 C                     PARM           PTSPLF
   1 C                     PARM           PTSPLN
   1 C                     PARM           PTNAME
   1 C                     PARM           PTUSER
   1 C                     PARM           PTNUMB
   1 C                     PARM           RCODE
B002 C           RCODE     IFEQ '0'
   2 C                     CLEARX
   2 C                     CLEAR#COL1
   2 C                     CLEAR#COUNT
   2 C                     MOVE ' 80'     #LEN    3
   2 C                     Z-ADD11        #X      50
   2 C                     OPEN PDDATA
     * See what size - 80, 132 or 198 . . .
   2 C           1         SETLLPDDATA@
   2 C                     READ PDDATA@                  20
B003 C           *IN20     DOWEQ*OFF
B004 C           PDF001    IFNE *BLANK
   4 C                     MOVE 'Y'       #COL1   1
E004 C                     ENDIF
B004 C           #TD132    IFNE *BLANKS
   4 C           #LEN      ANDNE'198'
   4 C                     MOVE '132'     #LEN
   4 C                     Z-ADD7         #X
E004 C                     ENDIF
B004 C           #TD198    IFNE *BLANKS
   4 C                     MOVE '198'     #LEN
   4 C                     Z-ADD4         #X
E004 C                     ENDIF
   3 C                     READ PDDATA@                  20
E003 C                     ENDDO
   2 C           1         SETLLPDDATA@
   2 C                     READ PDDATA@                  20
B003 C           *IN20     DOWEQ*OFF
     * ICF record is full - send & receive . . .
B004 C           X         IFGE #X
   4 C                     CLEARICERR
   4 C                     MOVELMSG,1     ICERR
   4 C                     MOVE #LEN      ICERR
   4 C                     EXSR WR
   4 C                     CLEARX
E004 C                     ENDIF
     *
B004 C           #LEN      IFEQ ' 80'
```

```
B005 C            #COL1      IFEQ 'Y'
   5 C                       MOVEL#PDALL     #PD80
X005 C                       ELSE
   5 C                       MOVELPDLINE     #PD80   80
E005 C                       ENDIF
   4 C                       ADD  1          X          50
   4 C                       MOVE #PD80      P80,X
E004 C                       ENDIF
      *
B004 C            #LEN       IFEQ '132'
B005 C            #COL1      IFEQ 'Y'
   5 C                       MOVEL#PDALL     #PD132
X005 C                       ELSE
   5 C                       MOVELPDLINE     #PD132132
E005 C                       ENDIF
   4 C                       ADD  1          X
   4 C                       MOVE #PD132     P132,X
E004 C                       ENDIF
      *
B004 C            #LEN       IFEQ '198'
B005 C            #COL1      IFEQ 'Y'
   5 C                       MOVEL#PDALL     #PD198
X005 C                       ELSE
   5 C                       MOVELPDLINE     #PD198198
E005 C                       ENDIF
   4 C                       ADD  1          X
   4 C                       MOVE #PD198     P198,X
E004 C                       ENDIF
      *
   3 C                       READ PDDATA@                   20
E003 C                       ENDDO
      *
   2 C                       CLEARICERR
   2 C                       MOVELMSG,2      ICERR
   2 C                       MOVE #LEN       ICERR
   2 C                       CLOSEPDDATA
X002 C                       ELSE
   2 C                       MOVE MSG,4      ICERR
E002 C                       ENDIF
E001 C                       ENDIF
      *- - - - - - - - - - - - - - - - - - - - - - - - - - - - - - -*
     C                       ENDSR
      *- - - - - - - - - - - - - - - - - - - - - - - - - - - - - - -*
     C           RELEAS      BEGSR
      *- - - - - - - - - - - - - - - - - - - - - - - - - - - - - - -*
```

```
      * Request to detach received, release program device . . .
     C           'RQSDEV'  REL  VBSPLF1
     C                     CLOSE*ALL
     C                     MOVE *ON       *INLR
     C                     RETRN
      *- - - - - - - - - - - - - - - - - - - - - - - - - - - - - - - -*
     C                     ENDSR
      *- - - - - - - - - - - - - - - - - - - - - - - - - - - - - - - -*
     C           EXCPTH    BEGSR
      *- - - - - - - - - - - - - - - - - - - - - - - - - - - - - - - -*
B001 C           MAJMIN    IFNE '0000'
   1 C                     MOVE *ON       *INLR
   1 C                     RETRN
E001 C                     ENDIF
      *- - - - - - - - - - - - - - - - - - - - - - - - - - - - - - - -*
     C                     ENDSR
      *- - - - - - - - - - - - - - - - - - - - - - - - - - - - - - - -*
     C           *INZSR    BEGSR
      *- - - - - - - - - - - - - - - - - - - - - - - - - - - - - - - -*
      *  Acquire ICF program device . . .
     C           'RQSDEV'  ACQ  VBSPLF1
      *- - - - - - - - - - - - - - - - - - - - - - - - - - - - - - - -*
     C                     ENDSR
      *- - - - - - - - - - - - - - - - - - - - - - - - - - - - - - - -*
**
(MORE)
(END)
(OK)
(INVALID)
Available
Available
Available
Available
Available
Available
```

CL Programs

VBSPLF1C

```
/*- - - - - - - - - - - - - - - - - - - - - - - - - - - - - - - - - - - -*/
/*   VBSPLF1C                                                            */
/*   This program is started by Visual Basic programs. It               */
/*     receives requests for outq & spool file services for             */
/*     downloading...                                                    */
/*                                                                       */
/*   Revisions                                                           */
/*     Date      Pgmr      Revision                                      */
/*               chris     program created                               */
/*                                                                       */
/*                                                                       */
/*- - - - - - - - - - - - - - - - - - - - - - - - - - - - - - - - - - - -*/
             PGM
             CHGJOB     DDMCNV(*DROP)
/*  Set lib list...                                                      */
             RMVLIBLE   LIB(VBSPL)
             MONMSG     MSGID(CPF0000)
             RMVLIBLE   LIB(QTEMP)
             MONMSG     MSGID(CPF0000)
             ADDLIBLE   LIB(VBSPL)
             MONMSG     MSGID(CPF0000)
             ADDLIBLE   LIB(QTEMP)
             MONMSG     MSGID(CPF0000)
/*  Create files for holding lists of outqs, spool files...              */
             CRTDUPOBJ  OBJ(PQLIST) FROMLIB(VBSPL) OBJTYPE(*FILE) +
                          TOLIB(QTEMP)
             CRTDUPOBJ  OBJ(PTLIST) FROMLIB(VBSPL) OBJTYPE(*FILE) +
                          TOLIB(QTEMP)
             CRTDUPOBJ  OBJ(PDDATA) FROMLIB(VBSPL) OBJTYPE(*FILE) +
                          TOLIB(QTEMP)
             OVRDBF     FILE(PQLIST) TOFILE(QTEMP/PQLIST)
             OVRDBF     FILE(PTLIST) TOFILE(QTEMP/PTLIST)
             OVRDBF     FILE(PDDATA) TOFILE(QTEMP/PDDATA)
/*  VBSPLF1R interacts with the VB program....                           */
             CALL       PGM(VBSPLF1R)
             DLTOVR     FILE(*ALL)
             MONMSG     MSGID(CPF0000)
             RCLRSC
             ENDPGM
```

CHEKOUTQ

```
/* - - - - - - - - - - - - - - - - - - - - - - - - - - - - - - - - - */
/* Program - CHEKOUTQ                                                */
/*          AS/400 to PC spool file download - check existance of */
/*          as AS/400 outq...                                        */
/*                                                                   */
/* - - - - - - - - - - - - - - - - - - - - - - - - - - - - - - - - - */
/*   Revisions                                                       */
/*     Date       Pgmr       Revision                                */
/*                cfp        Created.                                */
/* - - - - - - - - - - - - - - - - - - - - - - - - - - - - - - - - - */
            PGM        PARM(&OUTQNAME &RETURN)
            DCL        VAR(&OUTQNAME) TYPE(*CHAR) LEN(10)
            DCL        VAR(&RETURN) TYPE(*CHAR) LEN(1)
            CHGVAR     VAR(&RETURN) VALUE('0')
/*  Check object . . .                                                */
            CHKOBJ     OBJ(*LIBL/&OUTQNAME) OBJTYPE(*OUTQ)
            MONMSG     MSGID(CPF0001 CPF9810 CPF9801) EXEC(CHGVAR +
                         VAR(&RETURN) VALUE('1'))
 ENDIT:     ENDPGM
```

GETOUTQS

```
/* - - - - - - - - - - - - - - - - - - - - - - - - - - - - - - - - - */
/* Program - GETOUTQS                                                */
/*          AS/400 to PC spool file download - get list of outqs  */
/*                                                                   */
/*          This cl creates a file in qtemp containing the AS/400 */
/*          outq's - for outq/spool file selection (VB pgm.)       */
/*                                                                   */
/*                                                                   */
/* - - - - - - - - - - - - - - - - - - - - - - - - - - - - - - - - - */
/*   Revisions                                                       */
/*     Date       Pgmr       Revision                                */
/*                cfp        Created.                                */
/* - - - - - - - - - - - - - - - - - - - - - - - - - - - - - - - - - */
            PGM
/*  Create work file . . .                                           */
            CHKOBJ     OBJ(QTEMP/PQLIST) OBJTYPE(*FILE)
            MONMSG     MSGID(CPF9801) EXEC(CRTDUPOBJ OBJ(PQLIST) +
                         FROMLIB(VBSPL) OBJTYPE(*FILE) TOLIB(QTEMP))
            DLTF       FILE(QTEMP/PQTEMP)
            MONMSG     MSGID(CPF2105)
```

```
            CRTDUPOBJ  OBJ(PQLIST) FROMLIB(VBSPL) OBJTYPE(*FILE) +
                         TOLIB(QTEMP) NEWOBJ(PQTEMP)
            OVRPRTF    FILE(QPRTSPLQ) HOLD(*YES)
            WRKOUTQ    OUTQ(*ALL) OUTPUT(*PRINT)
            DLTOVR     FILE(QPRTSPLQ)
            CPYSPLF    FILE(QPRTSPLQ) TOFILE(QTEMP/PQTEMP) +
                         SPLNBR(*LAST) MBROPT(*ADD)
            MONMSG     MSGID(CPF3370)  /* TRUNCATED - NO ERROR */
            DLTSPLF    FILE(QPRTSPLQ) SPLNBR(*LAST)
            CPYF       FROMFILE(QTEMP/PQTEMP) TOFILE(QTEMP/PQLIST) +
                         MBROPT(*REPLACE) INCCHAR(*RCD 48 *EQ '  ')
            DLTF       FILE(QTEMP/PQTEMP)
            MONMSG     MSGID(CPF2105)
ENDIT:      ENDPGM
```

GETSPLE

```
/* - - - - - - - - - - - - - - - - - - - - - - - - - - - - - - - - */
/* Program - GETSPLE                                               */
/*          AS/400 to PC spool file download - get records for a   */
/*          specific spool file . . .                              */
/*                                                                 */
/* - - - - - - - - - - - - - - - - - - - - - - - - - - - - - - - - */
/*   Revisions                                                     */
/*     Date        Pgmr       Revision                             */
/*                 cfp        Created.                             */
/* - - - - - - - - - - - - - - - - - - - - - - - - - - - - - - - - */
            PGM        PARM(&SPLF &SPLNBR &JOBNAM &USER &JOBNBR +
                         &RCODE)
            DCL        VAR(&SPLF) TYPE(*CHAR) LEN(10)
            DCL        VAR(&SPLNBR) TYPE(*CHAR) LEN(4)
            DCL        VAR(&JOBNAM) TYPE(*CHAR) LEN(10)
            DCL        VAR(&USER) TYPE(*CHAR) LEN(10)
            DCL        VAR(&JOBNBR) TYPE(*CHAR) LEN(6)
            DCL        VAR(&RCODE) TYPE(*CHAR) LEN(1)
            CHGVAR     VAR(&RCODE) VALUE('0')
            CPYSPLF    FILE(&SPLF) TOFILE(QTEMP/PDDATA) +
                         JOB(&JOBNBR/&USER/&JOBNAM) +
                         SPLNBR(&SPLNBR) MBROPT(*REPLACE) +
                         CTLCHAR(*PRTCTL)
            MONMSG     MSGID(CPF0000) EXEC(CHGVAR VAR(&RCODE) +
                         VALUE('1'))
ENDIT:      ENDPGM
```

GETSPLFS

```
/* - - - - - - - - - - - - - - - - - - - - - - - - - - - - - - - - */
/* Program - GETSPLFS                                              */
/*           AS/400 to PC spool file download - get list of spool  */
/*           files.                                                */
/*                                                                 */
/*           This cl creates a file in qtemp containing the AS/400 */
/*           spool files for a passed-in outq name. (VB pgm.)      */
/*                                                                 */
/*                                                                 */
/* - - - - - - - - - - - - - - - - - - - - - - - - - - - - - - - - */
/*   Revisions                                                     */
/*     Date      Pgmr      Revision                                */
/*               cfp       Created.                                */
/* - - - - - - - - - - - - - - - - - - - - - - - - - - - - - - - - */
             PGM        PARM(&OUTQ)
             DCL        VAR(&OUTQ)  TYPE(*CHAR) LEN(10)
/*  Create work file(s) . . .                                       */
             CHKOBJ     OBJ(QTEMP/PTLIST) OBJTYPE(*FILE)
             MONMSG     MSGID(CPF9801) EXEC(CRTDUPOBJ OBJ(PTLIST) +
                          FROMLIB(VBSPL) OBJTYPE(*FILE) +
                          TOLIB(QTEMP))
             DLTF       FILE(QTEMP/PTTEMP)
             MONMSG     MSGID(CPF2105)
             CRTDUPOBJ  OBJ(PTLIST) FROMLIB(VBSPL) OBJTYPE(*FILE) +
                          TOLIB(QTEMP) NEWOBJ(PTTEMP)
             OVRPRTF    FILE(QPRTSPLQ) HOLD(*YES)
             WRKOUTQ    OUTQ(&OUTQ) OUTPUT(*PRINT)
             DLTOVR     FILE(QPRTSPLQ)
             CPYSPLF    FILE(QPRTSPLQ) TOFILE(QTEMP/PTTEMP) +
                          SPLNBR(*LAST) MBROPT(*ADD)
             MONMSG     MSGID(CPF3370)  /* TRUNCATED - NO ERROR */
             DLTSPLF    FILE(QPRTSPLQ) SPLNBR(*LAST)
             CPYF       FROMFILE(QTEMP/PTTEMP) TOFILE(QTEMP/PTLIST) +
                          MBROPT(*REPLACE) INCCHAR(*RCD 47 *EQ '   ')
             DLTF       FILE(QTEMP/PTTEMP)
             MONMSG     MSGID(CPF2105)
 ENDIT:      ENDPGM
```

Microsoft Visual Basic Version 4.0
For 32-bit Windows Development

15

Advanced Visual Basic Concepts

VB Release 4.0—Growing Up

Prior to release 4.0, (and even a bit still), Microsoft Visual Basic took considerable criticism from some PC programmers—mostly the Visual C++ folks. They said VB couldn't do many things that are essential to a viable OOP (object-oriented programming language). It lacked many features, and to them, it just wasn't organized correctly. You couldn't write a truly object-oriented application with VB. "But good for prototyping," they said.

To quiet the critics, and to establish VB as their standard back office code engine, Microsoft has greatly extended and shifted its architecture. Of course, VB 4.0 supports the 32-bit platform; but beyond that, it's acquired most of the capabilities of a true object-oriented development language.

The purpose of this chapter is to acquaint you with some of the terms and concepts you're likely to encounter as you progress with VB.

VB's Charm

Perhaps the most compelling characteristic of Visual Basic is its simplicity. That shouldn't be obscured by the advanced features now available. A new VB programmer can still write a functional program in one day. The language has become more capable, but not necessarily more complicated.

Objects

The concept of objects is familiar to AS/400 professionals. You know what objects are on the 400—like libraries, files, programs, data areas, and device descriptions. There are a set number of object types (call them *classes* for the moment), as determined by IBM. (Every once in a while a new class comes along—like "User Space.")

An object, as known to PC programmers, is more than that. It is just about anything you can conceive of as a unit. That is, a program is an object, but then so is a routine within that program. A spreadsheet is an object, and so is a range of cells, or even a single cell within the spreadsheet, if it is meaningful as a unit.

OK, so an object is something useful as a unit. How are they used?

Use of an object is made available to other objects by the object's ability to be referenced externally. The areas of the object that are accessible are said to be *exposed*. Here is an AS/400 analogy: Suppose you could write an RPG program where not only the program, but also a *subroutine* within the program, could be called. Or a data structure. That subroutine or data structure would then be exposed to other objects. Any objects within the program that are not available, then, are private to the program.

The concept extends to data, as well. The object that is a range of cells in a spreadsheet is only available if it's exposed.

Object-oriented Programming

In a nutshell, the central idea in object-oriented programming is to code your applications as a collection of objects, each with a specific purpose. A particular object is invoked when the function or data provided by an object is required. Data or arguments may be passed to the object, and the object provides data or processing, black-box style. The internal mechanisms of the object are unknown to other objects. Only the interface, or the means of communicating with the object, is known.

A truly object-oriented language, purists say, has to meet four criteria:

- Abstraction. The ability to create a pattern for an object, that is, a *class*.
- Encapsulation. The ability to put data (properties) and processing over the data (methods) together in a class. The class provides a public interface while hiding its internal implementation.
- Inheritance. The ability of a class to acquire properties and methods from a super class where common attributes are kept.
- Polymorphism. The ability to have distinct functionality, as defined across different classes, each with the same name. So an "Initialize" method can be invoked for objects of various classes, each performing its own appropriate processing.

Visual Basic 4.0 meets three of these four criteria. VB does not support inheritance. You can't create a super class and you can't inherit properties and methods from another class. You can, however, get a similar result through a technique called *containment*.

Common properties and methods can be kept in a class, and accessed from other classes by calling methods and procedures of the common class. The calling class is said to be a *wrapper* of the methods and procedures in the common class.

In the purist's world, VB is only an *object-based* language, meaning it's based on object-oriented design and features. In the real world, VB 4.0 is capable of creating an object-oriented, production-level application. It is, in that regard, an object-oriented language on a par with C++ or Delphi.

Class and Instance

In Windows, you are not restricted to the types of objects that came with the operating system. You can define your own. Suppose, for example, for an AS/400 application you need a special type of object—like a "date area." A date area, you decide, is like a data area, but for holding a date in system date format. Well, there's no such class of object available on the AS/400, so you can't. On the PC, in Windows, you can. You can create a new object type by creating a class and registering it with Windows. From then on, you can create objects of class "date area" (which might be a cell in a spreadsheet).

When the class is created, properties and methods are defined, just like they are for VB forms and controls. The methods and properties determine what the class does and what the interface is.

On the AS/400, there are many classes of objects—that is, allowable object types. But until you create an object of a certain class, only the class exists. In other words, just because you can have data areas on the 400 doesn't mean you do. You have to create objects of class "data area." Each one of those objects is said to be an *instance* of the data area class. Each instance of a class, once created, has the properties and methods defined by its class.

In VB, classes are defined by creating a new module type, the *class module*, in a VB program, and giving it properties and methods. See Chapter 7, "Introduction to Objects," in the *Visual Basic Programmer's Guide*.

Object Linking and Embedding

Object linking and embedding (OLE) is a technology that enables a programmer of Windows-based applications to create an application that can display data from many different applications. The user is then able to edit that data from within the application in which it was created. In some cases, the user can even edit the data from within the Visual Basic application.

You can create a VB program that can have an Excel spreadsheet embedded within one of the forms, for example. Or an embedded Microsoft Word document, also embedded within your program. But it's not just there as a display, it's actually an instance of Excel or Word. You could edit the spreadsheet or document right there, in your VB program, using the functions of Excel or Word.

OLE Automation

OLE Automation is a subset of the technologies supported by OLE. OLE Automation allows you to control objects from OLE servers using Visual Basic controls and code. OLE servers are applications that expose their objects to other applications—you can use any of those objects in your Visual Basic application.

You can use code to directly manipulate OLE Automation objects, using all of the object's properties and methods in your application. If it's an object that users can see on a form, also known as an insertable object (for instance, the Word Document object), and you want it to appear on a form, you can either add the object to the tool box, or use the OLE container control.

If the object has no visible interface (for instance, data access objects), or you don't want the object to appear on a form, you can add a reference to the object's type library and then declare instances of the object's class. You can also use the "GetObject" or "CreateObject" functions to create an instance of the class. For example, you can have a Microsoft Excel Worksheet calculate mortgage payments in a Visual Basic application, taking input from a text box and displaying output in a list box, without Microsoft Excel ever being visible. For details on using OLE Automation objects, see Chapter 9, "Programming Other Applications' Objects," in the *Visual Basic Programmer's Guide.*

Adding Insertable Objects to the Tool Box

If you find you are using another application's object repeatedly, consider placing that object in the Visual Basic tool box. For example, if you're developing many applications that use the Microsoft Word Document object, place that object in the Visual Basic tool box. Once the object is in your tool box, you can use OLE Automation and Visual Basic code to manipulate it like any other control.

OLE Container Control

Microsoft lists three main advantages to using the OLE container control to link or embed OLE Automation objects in forms:

- Users can insert any one of a variety of object types into an application's form at run time.
- Standard File and Help menus belonging to your Visual Basic application can be merged with the menus of the OLE servers, providing a consistent look and feel.
- Because OLE manages the starting and ending of OLE servers, fewer copies of the executables are required to be loaded into memory.

For information on using the OLE container control, see Chapter 8, "Using the OLE Container Control." For information on menu and toolbar negotiation, see the section, "Menu and Toolbar Negotiation," in Chapter 10, "Menus" in the *Visual Basic Programmer's Guide.*

Collection Objects

A *collection object* is an ordered set of items that can be referred to as a unit. The collection object provides a convenient way to refer to a related group of items as a single object. The items in a collection, known as members, need only be related by the fact that they are in the collection. It is not necessary that members of a collection be of the same data type.

For instance, suppose that your application requires you to create a number of instances of a class (like a bunch of Word document objects.) You can create a collection object, add members representing the object instances, and refer to them in code like this:

```
For Each element In group

        [statements]

        [Exit For]

        [statements]

Next [element]
```

In this manner, you could perform, say, an initialize or cleanup routine.

A collection can be created in the same way as other objects:

```
Dim X As New Collection
```

The New keyword creates a new instance of the collection object.

Once created, members can be added to the collection using the *Add method* and removed using the *Remove method*. Specific members can be returned from the collection using the *Item method*, while the entire collection can be iterated using the *For Each ... Next statement*, shown above.

The Windows API

Visual Basic is an *extensible* language. This means that VB can access external routines contained in Dynamic Link Libraries. You've already seen this when using the Client Access/PCS API.

The Windows API that comes built in to your Windows operating system contains perhaps a thousand routines, most of which you can use in your VB program. These are small, function-specific routines providing you with the means to control Windows. You've already done so just by using a VB program.

VB is closely tied to the API. In a sense, VB is a programmable shell for Windows. Through VB, common Windows control messages are sent to accomplish tasks like presenting forms, clicking buttons, and scrolling. Less common functions, like getting a look at system resources or looking up a value in a list box, are provided by the API.

Step by Step: Using the Windows API

Two examples of using the Windows API are presented. The first is a very simple API to retrieve system resource values and is created for the 16-bit platform. The second is a useful way to look up an entry in a list box, and is presented for 16- and 32-bit platforms.

Example 1

1. Bring up the 16-bit VB Development Environment or start a new project. This code will not necessarily be saved.

2. Start a new module and enter this "Declare" statement for the "GetFreeSpace" function:

The function has one argument—a flag variable of type integer. The function itself is of data type long.

3. Create a text box on "Form1" and key this call to the API in the form's load event:

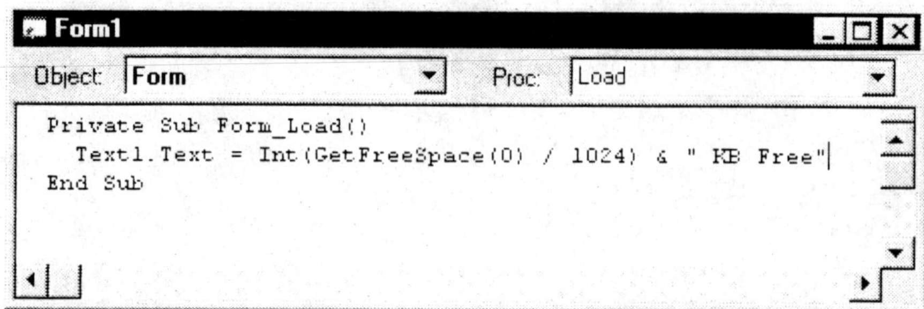

4. Run the program. Your actual mileage may vary, but you should see something like this:

Example 2

1. Bring up the 32-bit VB Development Environment. Create a new module and enter these constants and this "Declare:"

Module1

Object: (General) Proc: (declarations)

```
Option Explicit

Public Const LB_FINDSTRING = &H18F

Declare Function SendMessage Lib "user32" Alias _
  "SendMessageA" (ByVal hwnd As Long, ByVal wMsg As Long, _
   ByVal wParam As Long, ByVal lParam As String) As Long
```

Windows is a multitasking operating system, like the 400. And like the 400, the various concurrent actions within the system are controlled through messages. This API causes a message to be sent to a window (in this example, a list box) to which the window responds.

The symbolic constant "LB_FINDSTRING" is a hex representation of the message ID code—in this case, "List Box Find String." The "Alias" specifies that you want to use "SendMessageA"—the ASCII version of this API (there's also a Unicode version).

2. Draw a text box and a list box on "Form1." Clear the text property of the text box:

The idea is to look for an entry in the list box that matches the value keyed into the text box. This is much like you've seen many times in Windows help systems.

3. To illustrate the point, there must be some entries in the list box. Load some demo data into the list box in the form's "Load" event:

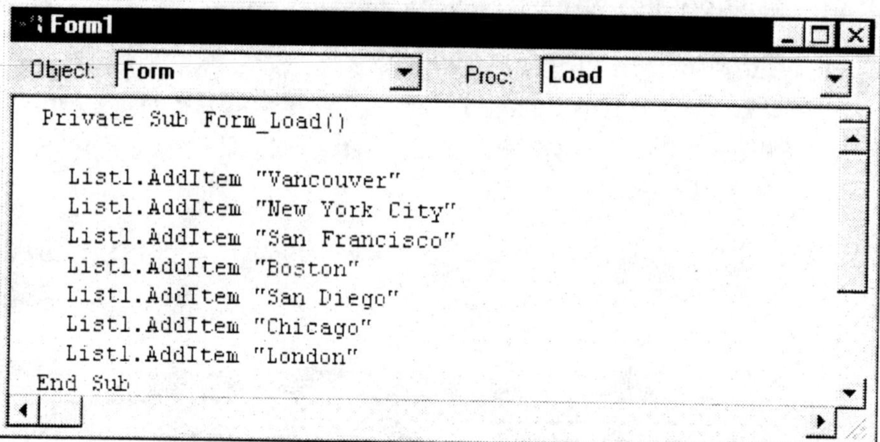

4. Key the call to the API function in the change event of the text box:

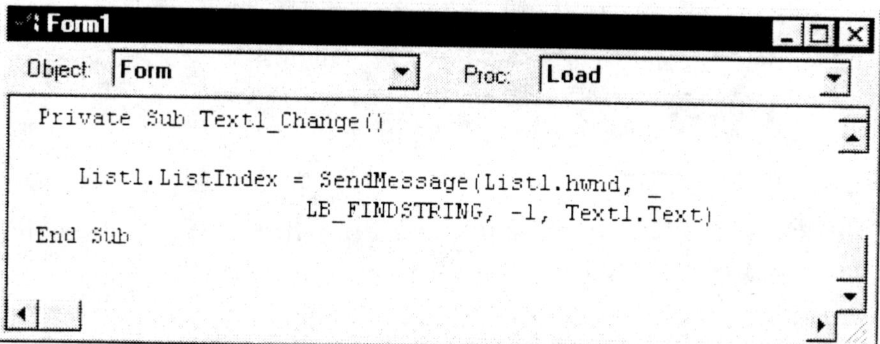

The API is being passed the *Windows handle* (identifier), the message ID, a message-dependent value (in this case -1), and the text to search for.

5. Run the program. The list box should respond to the value keyed in the text box.

This makes pretty short work of the lookup function. Much more convenient than if you were to handle this task yourself.

If a partial match (left to right) is found in the list box, its *index* (relative record number) is returned.

OK, there are all these Windows API routines available. How do you know what they are and how to use them?

The API Viewer

To help you with the myriad of API routines, Microsoft has included a utility called the *API Viewer*. There is a 16- and a 32-bit version in the corresponding VB group. The API Viewer is an online reference that allows you to browse through Declares, Constants, and user Data Types that are included in any text file or Microsoft Access (Jet) database that contains API information. You can copy these items into the clipboard, and then paste them into your VB code.

The VB Professional Edition, version 4.0, includes the WIN31API.TXT, WIN32API.TXT, and WINMMSYS.TXT API text files for the Windows 3.1 and the Win32 (32-bit version only) interfaces.

- WIN31API.TXT contains Constants, Declares, and Types for 16-bit versions of Windows API functions.
- WIN32API.TXT contains Constants, Declares, and Types for 32-bit versions of Windows API functions.

- WINMMSYS.TXT contains Constants, Declares, and Types for Windows 3.1 multimedia API functions.

Unfortunately, there is nothing within the API Viewer to help you determine which API function to use, or what its argument requirements are. No help, no hints. For this you must consult a reference text (see "Suggested Reading and References" in Chapter 16).

Step by Step: Using the API Text Viewer

This illustration of using the 16-bit API Text Viewer accomplishes the same lookup in a list box as in the last example. This example also illustrates how the 16-bit API syntax varies slightly from its corresponding 32-bit version. This is frequently the case.

1. Start the 16-bit API Text Viewer from the VB folder or program group.
2. From the File menu, select "Load Text File..." and load "C:\VB\WINAPI\WIN16API.TXT" (or you may create a "Jet" database over the text file and load that, if you wish). Available items appear in the "Available Items" list:

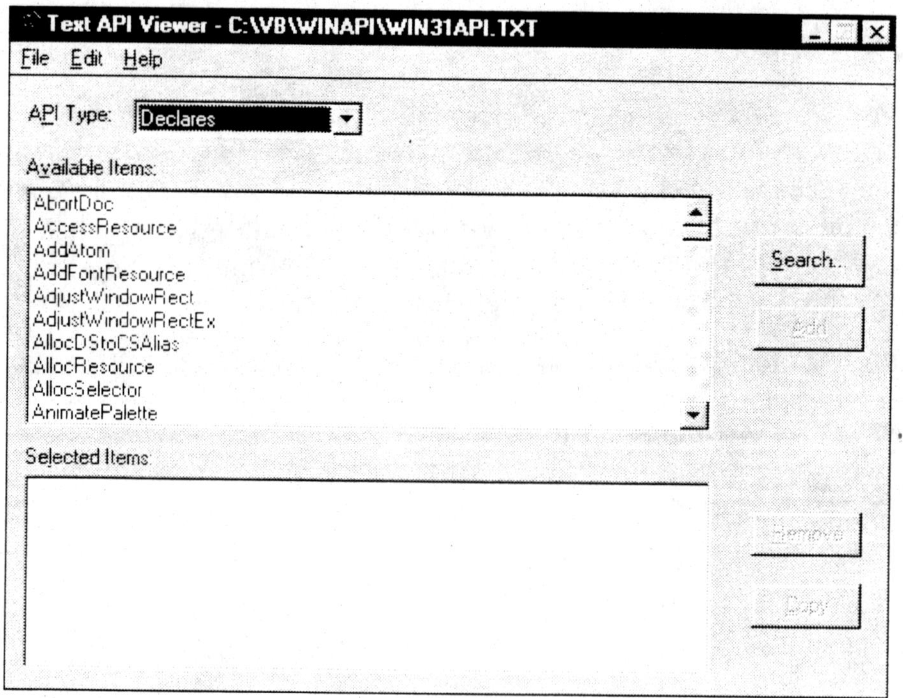

3. From the "API Type" combo box, select "Constants." Click on "Search" and locate "WM_USER." When "WM_USER" comes up, click "Add" to add the constant to the "Selected Items" box. "WM_USER" is a base constant value of 400 from which other constant values are derived. Locate and add "LB_FINDSTRING," as well.

4. Change the "Available Items" list to "Declares." Locate "SendMessage" and add it to the "Selected Items" list. Click "Copy" to place the constants and the declare in the clipboard.

5. Close the API Viewer and bring up 16-bit VB. Create a new module. Paste the API code into the module's declarations area.

   Notice that the last parm in the "Declare" statement is of type "Any." Change it to type "String" and add the ByVal keyword:

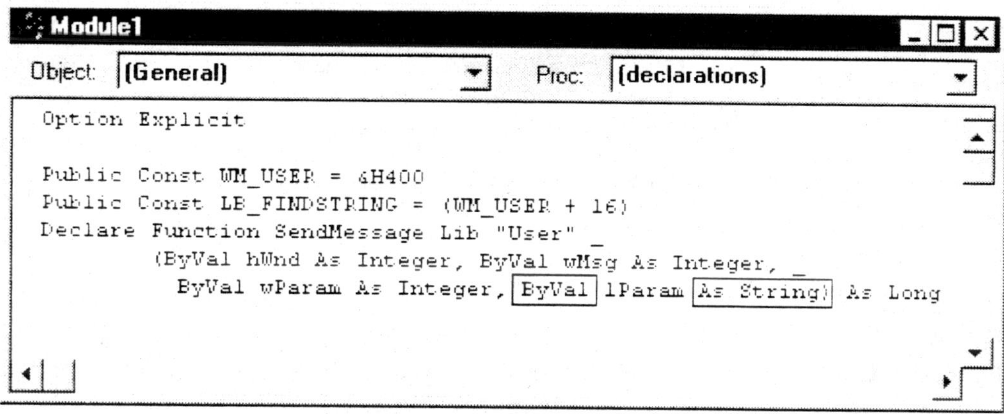

   This ensures that the parms passed will match type and the string is null terminated. Without this modification, the code is more likely to cause a General Protection Fault (GPF).

6. Place the same two controls on "Form1" as in the last example—a list box and a text box.

7. Add the following code into the form's "Load" event and the text box's "Change" event to complete the example:

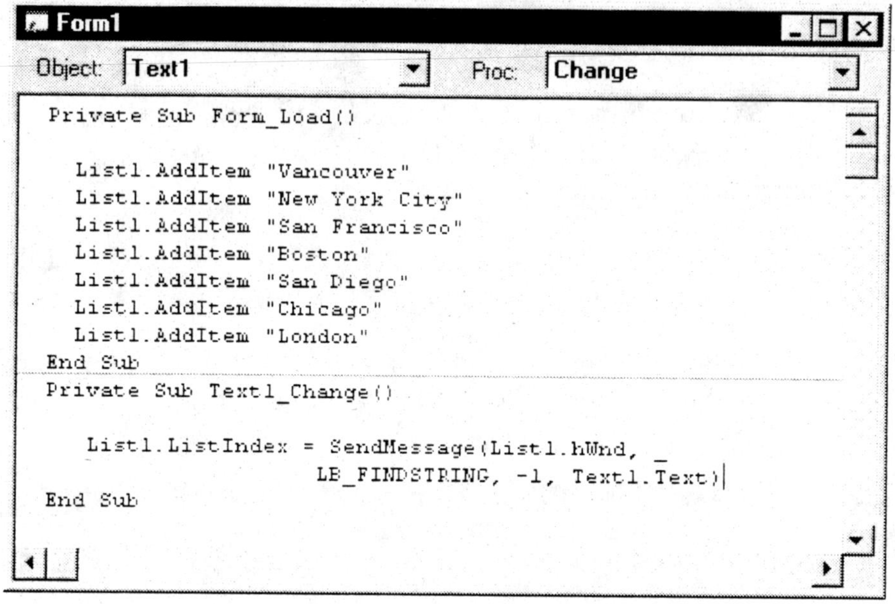

```
Form1
Object: Text1          Proc: Change

Private Sub Form_Load()

  List1.AddItem "Vancouver"
  List1.AddItem "New York City"
  List1.AddItem "San Francisco"
  List1.AddItem "Boston"
  List1.AddItem "San Diego"
  List1.AddItem "Chicago"
  List1.AddItem "London"
End Sub
Private Sub Text1_Change()

   List1.ListIndex = SendMessage(List1.hWnd, _
                    LB_FINDSTRING, -1, Text1.Text)
End Sub
```

8. Run the program. You should achieve the same result as before.

16- or 32-bit Platform

When you set out to develop an application in VB you have to decide which operating system to target. Your choice of operating system determines the type of Visual Basic application you can create and execute.

Each version accesses specific features of the target operating system. The following table shows which operating system versions support which type of VB application.

Operating System	Use to Create...	Can Execute Visual Basic...
Microsoft Windows/Windows for Workgroups versions 3.0 - 3.11	16-bit Applications	16-bit Applications
Microsoft Windows NT, NTAS, Windows 95	16- or 32-bit Applications	16- or 32-bit Applications

Frequently, gaining an understanding of a subject like VB is frustrated by being dealt a deluge of new terms and ideas. It is hoped that familiarity with the preceding concepts and techniques will provide a base from which you may make more sense of VB technical publications and manuals.

Microsoft Visual Basic Version 4.0
For 32-bit Windows Development

16

Where to Go from Here

The purpose of this book, you recall, is to get you going as a VB and c/s programmer. To this end, presentation of the VB language has been kept as AS/400- and RPG-like as possible.

Again and again you have been shown how VB and RPG are similar—but sometimes different is better. Now that you have a basic understanding of the VB language, you're ready to acquire accepted VB coding techniques, as established by long-time PC programmers. You're also ready to take advantage of some of the features of VB that PC programmers feel are superior to RPG.

This chapter presents some methods for acquiring solid coding techniques, some popularly held opinions about VB coding, and suggested reading.

Good VB Coding Techniques

Find Good Example Code

You didn't become an accomplished RPG programmer by reading one book. It takes more than that. But by studying other, more experienced programmers' code, and being open to new ways of doing things, you can develop your VB skills to match those of your other programming languages.

Seek out source code in VB programming magazines and books, and study the structures used. Observe how things like comments and naming conventions are used to produce clean, lucid code.

Collect tips. Just as you collect small AS/400 tips and techniques, so gather VB tricks.

Develop Shop Standards

Many roads lead to Rome. Find an accepted coding style that you feel holds the most potential for your shop and start developing standards—just as you have with AS/400 languages. Even with just a few VB programmers, it doesn't take long before various project files, in assorted coding styles, are present on all the programmers' PCs (and usually not backed up). So set standards early.

With VB 4.0 came the *Enterprise Edition*. The Enterprise Edition has capabilities and an add-in product designed for multiple-programmer shops. It contains additional capabilities like controlling source code among programmers and creating OLE server programs for PC/LAN-based systems.

More of Visual Basic

There is more of the VB language that is left uncovered by this book. However, you have a solid foundation upon which to continue learning VB. For example, once you know what a function is, you simply acquire knowledge of more and more of them. Once you know how to interact with a Windows API, it becomes a matter of finding and using the right one.

It was stated earlier that only the most commonly used VB syntax is presented in this book. You are urged to consult the VB online help for complete syntax details.

Scoping

To facilitate learning of the VB language basics, local scoping has been kept to a minimum in this book by use of global variables. Good VB coding technique requires that you become comfortable with scoping. (You're going to have to anyway when learning the AS/400's Integrated Language Environment programming.)

The Variant Data Type

Another feature of VB that has been avoided in this book is the variant data type. While argument against its use has been presented, it is nonetheless convenient, powerful, and commonly used by some experienced VB programmers.

What's Next

As visual programming gains acceptance, more and more languages are being outfitted with visual capability. Soon, you'll be programming with a visual language—whether it's VB or another, like Visual RPG.

Expect VB to become more "C+-like." Many of the enhancements to VB in release 4.0 are to that end. As an object-based language, VB 4.0 can take you well into the most important aspects of object-oriented programming.

It's expected that the next step will involve the increasing use of graphics and multimedia presentation within your client/server applications. It's also expected that Visual Basic will continue to evolve, keeping your investment of time and money worthwhile. Microsoft has shown a commitment to VB, and has established the VBA engine as the standard for back office solutions. It's not going to go away.

Suggested Reading and References

There are many sources for information on VB. There are dozens of books available dealing with areas of advanced VB. Some suggested information sources:

- Object-oriented VB Coding—*Doing Objects in Visual Basic 4.0*, by Deborah Kurata (Ziff-Davis Press, Emeryville, CA). Also, many articles in Visual Basic Programmer's Journal, written by Ms. Kurata (Fawcette Technical Publications, Palo Alto, CA).

- Windows Programming—Get Dan Appleman's *Visual Basic Programmer's Guide to the Windows API* (Ziff-Davis Press, Emeryville, CA). An excellent reference. Both Ms. Kurata and Mr. Appleman possess profound clarity of concept and presentation.

- VB Tips and Techniques—*The Official Guide to Visual Basic 4.0*, Visual Basic Programmer's Journal Editors (Que). Available through Fawcette Technical Publications—(800) 848-5523.

- Focused AS/400 Client/Server Information—Midrange Computing magazine, technical books, and videos. Some of the most informed and respected professionals in the AS/400 community produce material for MC. People like Richard Shaler, Kris Neely, Jim Hoopes, and Robin Klima. Pay particular attention to their opinions.

- Reference Information—CompuServe is the network of choice for many VB developers and educators. There are several forums where VB and Windows developers share information. There is also an AS/400 and a Client/Access forum.

- Development Kits—Through the Microsoft Developer's Network (MSDN), Microsoft offers a variety of development kits for their products. Advanced VB programmers may want to investigate the kits that are available—especially the SDK. This contains many tools, reference articles (called the Microsoft Knowledge Base), and code examples.

- *VB Books Online*—With your VB Professional CD package you received a subset of the Knowledge Base dealing with VB, together with a viewer called *Infoview*. Infoview allows you to query both the VB help system and the Knowledge Base as one. You may start this utility from the VB program group or folder.

Microsoft Visual Basic Version 4.0
For 32-bit Windows Development

Copyright © 1987-1995 Microsoft Corp.

A

AS/400 and VB Cross References

RPG Opcodes

RPG Opcode	VB Equivalent
ACQ	N/A
ADD	" + " operator used in an expression
ANDxx	And operator
BEGSR	Sub statement Function statement
CABxx	If...Then... Go To statement On...GoTo statement

RPG Opcode	VB Equivalent
CALL	CALL to a DLL Routine CALL to SubProcedure
CASxx	If...Then...GoSub...Return statements On...GoSub statement
CAT	" & " operator used in an expression-preferred " + " operator used in an expression
CHAIN (by index value)	Seek method Find First method
CHAIN (by relative record)	Get statement Input # statement
CHECK CHEKR	(none)
CLEAR	VariableName = "" (strings) VariableName = 0 (numerics) Clear method (list box, combo box)
CLOSE	Close statement or method Reset statement
COMIT	CommitTrans statement
COMP	If...Then statement StrComp function
DEBUG	Add Watch, Edit Watch Single Step, Procedure Step Breakpoints Stop statement
DEFN or a variable defined in columns 49-52 of calc specs	Dim statement Static statement Global statement
DELET	Delete method (table or Dynaset)

RPG Opcode	VB Equivalent
DIV	"/" operator used in an expression - returns a floating point "\" operator used in an expression - returns an integer
DO (number of times)	For...Next statement
DOWxx	Do While...Loop statement Do Until...Loop statement
DOUxx	Do...Loop While statement Do...Loop Until statement
DSPLY	MsgBox statement MsgBox function
ELSE	Else statement Else If statement
ENDDO	Loop statement (with "Do") Loop, Loop while, Loop until Next statement (with "For")
ENDIF	End If statement
ENDSL	End Select statement
ENDSR	End Sub statement End Function statement
EXCPT	(none)
EXFMT	Show method (forms)
EXSR	Call statement GoSub statement
GOTO	GoTo statement
Ifxx	If...Then statement
ITER	(none but tags may be attached to any statement and "Go To" used)

RPG Opcode	VB Equivalent
LEAVE	Exit Do statement Exit For statement Exit Sub statement Exit Function statement
LOKUP	(none)
MOVE	" = " operator used in an expression RSet statement Right$, Right functions RTrim, RTrim$ functions
MOVE alpha field to numeric field	CCur, CDbl, CInt, CLng, CSng functions Val function
MOVE numeric field to alpha field	CStr, CVar functions Format, Format$ functions Str, Str$ functions
MOVEA	(none)
MOVEL	" = " operator used in an expression LSet statement Left$, Left functions LTrim, LTrim$ functions
MULT	" * " operator used in an expression
MVR	Mod operator used in an expression
OCUR	Second dimension of VB arrays
OPEN	Open statement Open Table method
Orxx	Or operator
OTHER	Case Else (w/ Select Case statement)
PARM	Arguments are passed in parentheses ()

RPG Opcode	VB Equivalent
PLIST	Arguments are received in parentheses ()
READ (display files w/ WRITE)	(none)
READ (as with data base files)	Input # statement Input, Input$ functions MoveNext method (data controls)
READC (as with subfiles)	(none)
READE	FindFirst method (data controls) FindNext method (data controls)
READP	MovePrevious method (data controls)
REDPE	FindPrevious method (data controls)
REL	(none)
RESET	(none)
RETRN	(none)
ROLBK	Rollback statement
SCAN	InStr function
SELEC	Select Case statement On...GoSub statement On...GoTo statement
SETGT	FindLast method (data controls) MoveLast method (data controls)
SETLL	FindFirst method (data controls) MoveFirst method (data controls)
SETOF	N/A
SETON	N/A
SHTDN	N/A

RPG Opcode	VB Equivalent
SORTA	Sorted property (combo box, list box) Sort property (Dynaset)
SQRT	Sqr function
SUB	" – " operator used in an expression
SUBST	Mid, Mid$ function Mid, Mid$ statement
TAG	Label: (Any name followed by a colon)
TESTB	AND operator
TESTN	IsNumeric (variant data type only)
TESTZ	N/A
TIME	Date, Date$ functions Now function
UNLCK	Unlock
UPDAT	Update method
Whxx	Case (w/ Select Case statement)
WRITE (display files w/ READ)	Show method Add New method
WRITE (as with data base files)	Print # statement Write # statement
XFOOT	(none)
XLATE	Format, Format$ functions LCase, LCase$ functions UCase, UCase$ functions
Z-ADD	" = " operator used in an expression
Z-SUB	" = " operator used in an expression

RPG Special Words

RPG Special Word	VB Equivalent
*BLANK, *BLANKS	Space, Space$ functions
*INZSR	First form load event executes first
UDATE, *DATE	Date, Date$ function
UDAY, *DAY	Day function
UMONTH, *MONTH	Month function
UYEAR, *YEAR	Year function
*ZERO, *ZEROS	Literal "0"

Control Properties and Methods & AS/400 Subfile Equivalent

VB List and Combo Boxes Property / Method	AS/400 Subfile Equivalent
AddItem method - adds a list item	WRITE to record format subfile
Clear method - clear list	Subfile clear, Subfile initialize
Index property - pointer to a list item	RRN of subfile record
ListCount property - total item in the list	Total number of subfile records
ListIndex property - Index value of current list item	RRN of selected record (cursor position)
RemoveItem method - deletes a list item	DELET a Subfile record
Sorted property - sort alphabetically as items are added	N/A

VB Code - Substringing

VB Function or Statement	What It Does
Left/Left$, Right/Right$	Returns a substring from the left or the right of a larger string
LTrim/LTrim$, RTrim/RTrim$, Trim/Trim$	Returns a string with leading, trailing, or leading and trailing `blanks trimmed off
Mid/Mid$	Returns a substring from a larger string

VB Code - Data Conversion and Formatting

VB Function or Statement	What It Does
Asc	Returns an ASCII value for a character (opposite of Chr$)
CCur, CDbl, CInt, CLng, CSng, CStr, Cvar	Converts expressions into a specific data type
Chr/Chr$	Returns character for an ASCII value from 0 to 255 (opposite of Asc)
Format/Format$	Returns a formatted numeric or string variable according to instructions
InStr	Returns the position of the first occurrence of a scanned-for string within another string
LCase/LCase$	Returns lower case string
Len	Returns the length of a string
LSet statement	Left-aligns a string
RSet statement	Right-aligns a string

VB Function or Statement	What It Does
Space/Space$	Returns a string of a specified number of blanks
Str/Str$	Returns a string for a numeric variable (opposite of Val)
UCase/UCase$	Returns an uppercase string
Val	Returns the first numbers found in a string (opposite of Str$)

VB Code - Date and Time

VB Function or Statement	What It Does
Date/Date$ function	Returns the current system date
Date/Date$ statement	Sets the system date
Now function	Returns the current date and time
Time/Time$ function	Returns the current system time
Time/Time$ statements	Sets the system clock

Microsoft Visual Basic Version 4.0
For 32-bit Windows Development

B

Installing and Using the ODBC Driver

IBM APAR Information

Detailed information regarding installing and using the AS/400 ODBC driver is being made available here as a reprint of an IBM Documentation APAR on the subject.

The ODBC Driver

ODBC stands for Open Data Base Connectivity. It is a standard developed by Microsoft that allows Windows applications to access remote databases as if they were local. In this case, the remote database is the AS/400

Requirements to Run PCS ODBC

To use ODBC with the AS/400 you need the following:

- R230 or later of OS400 and PC Support/400.
- PTFs SF15199, SF15200, SF16065 and SF16285 (or supersedes). These are the ODBC Windows drivers that utilize the Remote SQL APIs included with PC Support/400 R230.
- PC applications that use MS ODBC Access engine may request statistics for the file being accessed. This information is only available on the AS/400 for files in SQL collections. In R230, applications with the Access engine are only supported for use with SQL collections with our ODBC driver. Errors may occur if you specify the physical or logical files in the triplets for the DSN that is used by Access engine.

Limitations of R230 ODBC Driver

PC applications using the Microsoft ODBC ACCESS engine may not be able to access or update data that is stored in an AS/400 physical or logical file. This limitation does not apply to data stored as part of an SQL collection. Access engine based PC applications may make use of certain ODBC function calls that request information concerning the file being linked to. With the R230 ODBC implementation, this data can only be provided if the file being linked to is part of a SQL collection. Errors will be received in the application when one of these function calls are used. For example, with Visual Basic or MS ACCESS 1.1, data can be read from a physical file. However, an attempt to insert new data or update existing data will fail.

There is a circumvention for the above problem. If a view is created on a physical file using Interactive SQL and if that view is used in the ODBC driver set up, then you are able to read or update a physical file.

These limitations DO NOT APPLY to R310 driver.

Step by Step: Installation of PCS ODBC Driver

1. From within Windows, select FILE/RUN from the Program Manager (or use the File Manager) and execute "I:\QIWSFL2\EHNSTP.EXE." This is the SETUP/INSTALL program for the ODBC drivers included in SF15426.

2. At the dialog box where "Install ODBC Drivers" and "Install ODBC Administration Utility" are found, verify that both boxes next to these statements have Xs in them, and then select "CONTINUE."

3. At the next dialog box, enter the path where you want to put the ODBC Administration Utility and select "CONTINUE."

4. Next, you are presented with a dialog box that has two Select Boxes in it. One says "Available Drivers," and the other "Installed Drivers." Simply click on the item in the Available Drivers box, click on the INSTALL button, and then click on "CONTINUE."

5. The next dialog box allows you to add "Data Sources." Click on the "AS/400 PC Support ODBC Driver" item in the "Installed Drivers" box, and click on the "ADD NEW NAME" button.

6. Now the "AS/400 ODBC DRIVER SETUP" dialog box is displayed.

   a) In the first two input fields, you can enter any text you wish (less than 18 characters, including spaces and no underscores). The "Data Source Name" field will be displayed in your application (e.g., MS-Access) when you wish to use your remote database.

   b) In the "System" field, simply enter the Local location Name (found in your PC Support CONFIG.PCS file) of the AS/400 to which you are connected (that also contains the desired database).

   c) In the "User ID" field, enter any valid common user ID (same as you use at the router sign-on).

   d) In the "Default Library" field, enter the LIBRARY/OWNER/FILE triplet. The slashes are mandatory. The "Library" is the library where your AS/400 database file is located, the "Owner" is the owner of the database file, and the "File" is the database file. You can also type multiple triplets separated by commas to access more than one file using the same driver.

   When you are finished filling in the fields, click on "CONTINUE." The Microsoft ODBC group will be created and a dialog box appears saying the install succeeded. Click on "OK" to quit.

Note: *Whenever a new PTF that relates to ODBC is applied to an AS/400, it is necessary that you run the "EHNSTP.EXE" program again from the "QIWSFL2" folder in the "I:" drive. This is required as applying the PTF doesn't automatically update the files on the PC.*

Step by Step: Connecting to an AS/400 Database from an Application Using the ODBC Driver

1. Start PC Support and sign on to the router. Start the VB Development Environment.

2. Open the Visual Basic sample project in the "QIWSFL2" folder called "Rqodbc.Mak."

3. Run the program. It opens up a window. Click the "Start Connection" button. It opens up another SQL sources window.

4. Select one of the data source names from the window and click "OK." After a few seconds, it displays the message "Connection established. Enter select statement here."

5. Clear that line and type your SQL statement. Then click "run query." Results of the query are displayed.

You can also test the connection from your application directly if you wish.

Some Common Questions About the ODBC

Q1: How do I find out who the owner of the database file is in SQL400?

A: On the AS/400, type STRSQL to enter interactive SQL and enter the following query: SELECT DBXOWN FROM QSYS/QADBXREF WHERE DBXFIL = 'file'. "file" is the database file you are looking at.

Another method is to use the AS/400 command:

```
DSPOBJD OBJ(lib/name) OBJTYPE(*ALL) DETAIL(*FULL)
```

Q2: Where is the documentation for ODBC?

A: The documentation is in the help file EHNODBC.HLP, which can be found on I:\QIWSFL2 or in your local Windows directory if you have already installed the PC Support/400 ODBC Drivers. To access this file, select FILE/RUN from the Program Manager, and enter "I:\QIWSFL2\WINHELP.EXE". When the help program comes up, select FILE/OPEN and open the EHNODBC.HLP file and path. For specifics on programming ODBC, refer to the *Microsoft ODBC 2.0 Programmer's Reference and SDK Guide,* MS Press, ISBN 1-55615-658-8, which can be obtained from Microsoft.

Q3: How do I add more databases to my list of Data Sources?

A: Run the Microsoft ODBC Administrator, found in the Microsoft ODBC windows group, and follow the instructions for Installation and Setup previously presented. You can add multiple database files adding several triplets separated by spaces.

Q4: I still can't connect to my driver or run a select. What's wrong?

A: A very common error is having two DLLs with the same name in your path. Many other ODBC drivers have a DLL named ODBC. Use the windows search feature under file manager to see if this is the case. PCS loads the following files:

- C:\WINDOWS\SYSTEM\ODBC.DLL
- C:\WINDOWS\SYSTEM\EHNODBC.DLL
- C:\PCS\EHNRQW.DLL

You may also want to try raising the size of the PCSWIN buffer in the STARTPCS.BAT file. PCSWIN /Z /B=48.

Q5: Msg7711 while trying to connect.

A: Most of the time, the above message pops up, when:

- You have not signed on to the router.
- A data source is not selected.
- Setting up the driver, the data source name is more than 18 characters including spaces and underscores.

Q6: 'Error in the SQL Cursor specified' when trying to access files in AS/400 using IBM's ODBC driver.

A: IBM's ODBC driver supports only to access files in an SQL collection. You may get the above error when you try to access native AS/400 files, which is not in a collection.

Q7: Can I run ODBC in OS2?

A: Yes, it is possible to use the PCS ODBC driver in OS2. You will need to run extended DOS PC Support under WIN-OS/2. Refer to Chapter 13 in the Red book "Using R230 DOS and OS2 PC Support/400 under OS2 2.1, Including Communications Manager/400, Communications Manager/2, and RUMBA/400 for OS2," number GG244070-00, or Appendix D of this book.

Q8: How do I use "Access engine" applications to access data in physical or logical files that do not belong to an SQL collection?

A: You need to create views for physical files that you want to access via your "Access engine" application. Those views should be in an SQL collection (different than the library that contains the PF or LF).

Q9: How do I create an SQL collection if I don't have SQL installed on my AS/400?

A: 1. Use Remote SQL API.

2. Use ODBC API that comes along with your application (not provided by IBM).

C

Contents of the Companion Diskette

The diskette that accompanies *AS/400 Client/Server Programming with Visual Basic 4.0* contains three packages:

- Examples of Visual Basic source code corresponding to the projects in the book.
- AS/400 client/server code templates, a constants file, and declare files.
- The AS/400 Report Download Utility.

Note: The AS/400 Report Download Utility, as shipped, is the latest version available. Because of restrictions in printing, source code listings within the book may not exactly match actual source code found on the diskette. The latest version of the utility may also be downloaded from the Midrange Computing BBS—file name "RDUPKG."

Summary of What's on the Accompanying Diskette

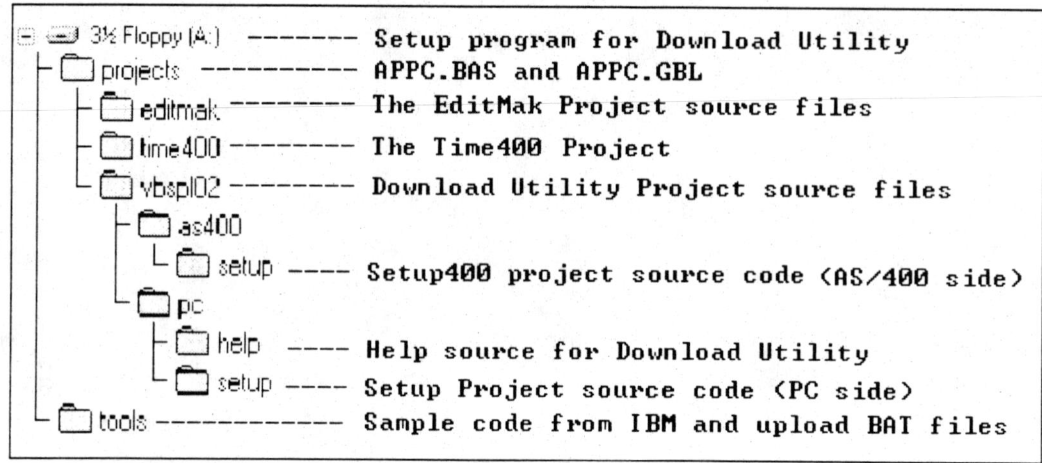

Projects in the Book

Source code for the example projects in the book are contained in the directories "EDITMAK"—for Chapters 3 through 7, 12, 13, "TIME400"—for Chapter 11, and "VBSPL02"—for Chapter 14. ("VBSPL02" and its subdirectories contain the source code, both VB and AS/400, for the AS/400 Report Download Utility—an included AS/400 client/server utility.)

AS/400 Client/Server Code Templates, Constants File, and Declare Files

The companion diskette also contains VB and AS/400 source code templates that can be used to create your own AS/400 client/server applications. They are primarily contained in directory "TOOLS." (See Chapters 10 and 11).

The AS/400 Report Download Utility

The AS/400 Report Download Utility is a production-type client/server application that is included with the book as an example of more advanced VB and AS/400 coding. The utility comes with two setup programs—"SETUP.EXE" in the root directory, and "SETUP400.EXE" in "A:\PROJECTS\VBSPL02\AS400\SETUP." These two programs install the PC part of the utility and the AS/400 part, respectively. See Chapter 14.

Reported Problems

Non-IBM routers. A problem has been reported where the IBM DLLs do not interact properly with certain non-IBM routers. The non-IBM router is recognized by the EHNAPPC.DLL routine "IsRouterLoaded," but send and receive operations fail. One such router vendor is NetSoft. It is also reported that NetSoft has a fix for the problem.

Execution on PCs that don't have IBM PC Support installed. The AS/400 Report Download Utility is an AS/400 client/server application that relies on elements of PC Support to run (IBM Dynamic Link Libraries EHNAPPC.DLL and PCSMOND.DLL). Without these PC files present, the utility will not execute.

> **Note:** *Refer to Chapter 14 for troubleshooting techniques for ICF client/server applications.*

Listings of the Companion Diskette Files

Root Directory

DDEML .DLL
README .TXT
SETUP .EXE
SETUPKIT.DLL
VBRUN300.DLL
VBRUN300.DL_
VBSPL02 .EXE
VBSPL02 .HLP

A:\PROJECTS

APPC.BAS
APPC.GBL

A:\PROJECTS\EDITMAK

EDITMAK .BAS
EDITMAK .ERR
EDITMAK .HLP
EDITMAK .HPJ
EDITMAK .MAK
EDITMAK .RTF
EDITMAK1.FRM

EDITMAK1.FRX
OPENFORM.FRM

A:\PROJECTS\TIME400
TIME400 .BAS
TIME400 .MAK

A:\PROJECTS\VBSPL02
ABOUTFOR.FRM
ABOUTFOR.FRX
DOWN5 .ICO
LOADFORM.FRM
LOADFORM.FRX
MCFOOT .BMP
MCSMALL1.BMP
OUTQFORM.FRM
OUTQFORM.FRX
SAVEFORM.FRM
SAVEFORM.FRX
SPLFFORM.FRM
SPLFFORM.FRX
VBSPL02 .BAS
VBSPL02 .BMP
VBSPL02 .FRM
VBSPL02 .FRX
VBSPL02 .MAK
VIEWFORM.FRM
VIEWFORM.FRX
WMLOGO3 .BMP
WORDFORM.FRM
WORDFORM.FRX

A:\PROJECTS\VBSPL02\AS400\SETUP
SETUP1 .FRM
SETUP1 .FRX
SETUP1 .MAK
SETUP400.EXE
SETUPKIT.DLL
VBSPL02 .VBZ

A:\PROJECTS\VBSPL02\AS400\SETUP\DISTDKT
VBCL1 .CL
VBCL1 .TFR
VBCL2 .CL
VBCL2 .TFR
VBCL3 .CL
VBCL3 .TFR
VBCL4 .CL
VBCL4 .TFR
VBCL5 .CL
VBCL5 .TFR
VBCMDS .RTR
VBDDS1 .DDS
VBDDS1 .TFR
VBDDS2 .DDS
VBDDS2 .TFR
VBDDS3 .DDS
VBDDS3 .TFR
VBDDS4 .DDS
VBDDS4 .TFR
VBRPG1 .RPG
VBRPG1 .TFR
VBSETDOS.BAT
VBSETUP .CMD
VBSRC .FDF
VBSRC .TTO

A:\PROJECTS\VBSPL02\PC\HELP
VBSPL02 .HPJ
VBSPL02 .RTF

A:\PROJECTS\VBSPL02\PC\SETUP
SETUP1 .FRM
SETUP1 .FRX
SETUP1 .MAK
SETUP1A .FRX
VBSPL02 .VBZ

A:\TOOLS
APIRTREX.ABS
APPC .BAS

APPC .BAT
APPC .GBL
APPCALL .BAT
APPCICF .BAT
APPCICF .DDS
APPCICF .FDF
APPCICF .TFR
APPCRPG .BAT
APPCRPG .FDF
APPCRPG .RPG
APPCRPG .TFR
CMDS .RTR
DBFILE .DDS
DBFILE .FDF
DBFILE .REC
DBREC .TFR
DDS .TFR
ICF .TFR
PCSMCPY .DLL
RPG .TFR
RQSAMP .FRM
RQSAMP .GBL
RQSAMP .MAK
RTRAPI .DDS
RTRCL .FDF
RTRCL .TFR
RTRREQ .ASM
RTRREQ .CL
RTRREQ .FDF
RTRREQ .MOD
RTRREQ .RPG
RTRSAMP .BAT
RTRSAMP .FRM
RTRSAMP .GBL
RTRSAMP .MAK
TIME400 .BAT
TIME400 .DDS
TIME400 .FDF
TIME400 .RPG
TIME400 .TFR
TIME400C.BAT
TIME400C.CL
TIME400C.FDF
TIME400C.TFR

TIME400D.BAT
TIME400D.DDS
TIME400D.FDF
TIME400D.TFR
WVBSAMP .ABS

Microsoft Visual Basic Version 4.0
For 32-bit Windows Development

D

Running VB Router Applications Under OS/2

Visual Basic for Win-OS/2 Users

Windows-based Visual Basic router applications can access the OS/2 communications manager version of the router through a virtual router layer running in a VDM or *Virtual DOS Machine*. This is the same configuration used when RUMBA is installed on an OS/2 machine. Assumes Windows, Client Access (V3R1 and up), or PC Support (V2R3); OS/2 for Windows, IBM Comm. Manager/2, and Corrective Service Pack for OS/2 are properly installed.

Step by Step: Configuring PCS for DOS

1. Select "Configure Client Access/400" from the Client Access/400 folder.
2. Select "General Options."

3. Select "OS/2 communications options for DOS."
4. Specify "Yes" to "Configure OS/2 communications for DOS."

   The configuration program modifies your CONFIG.SYS file,

   ```
   DEVICE=C:\PCSOS2\EHNPCVDD.SYS
   DEVICE=C:\PCSOS2\EHNPCPDD.SYS
   ```

   and your STARTPCS.CMD file,

   ```
   :SVDMRSERV
   VDMSERV /Z
   @IF ERRORLEVEL 20 GOTO EXIT
   :EVDMRSERV.
   ```

5. Create a batch file in directory PCS that contains:

   ```
   CALL C:\AUTOEXEC.BAT
   CALL C:\PCS\STARTPCS.BAT
   ```

6. Modify the contents of C:\PCS\STARTPCS.BAT by changing lines:

   ```
   E5250AH,
   STARTFLR,
   CFGFLR,
   PCSUPDT,
   LOADDQ  (if present)
   ```

   to remarks. The programs that need to run are:

   ```
   EIMPCS P=0 (may also be run as a device loaded by
   CONFIG.SYS,)
   PCSXI  %1,
   ```

```
STARTRTR   %1.

PCSWIN   /B=30.
```

Next, create a VDM icon on the OS/2 desktop.

7. Select the "TEMPLATES" folder from the desktop and drag the "PROGRAM" icon onto the desktop. Enter the name of your application under "Path and file name prompt" (e.g. "C:\VBSPL\VBSPL.EXE").

8. Select the "Session" tag. Select "WIN-OS/2" Window. Select "WIN-OS/2 settings..." Select the following DOS settings:

   DOS_AUTOEXEC—replace "C:\AUTOEXEC.BAT" in the Value box with the bat file you created earlier.

   DOS_HIGH—set to "ON."

   DOS_UMB—set to "ON."

   EMS_FRAME_LOCATION—set to "NONE."

   IDLE_SENSITIVITY—set to "100."

   INIT_DURING_IO—set to "ON."

9. Select the "Save" button and return to the settings notebook.

10. Select the "General" tab and enter the title you want to appear with your application icon.

11. Close the settings notebook.

Index

B

C

D

E

F

I

J

K

L

M

N

O

R

S

T

U

V

W

Z